COLE'S KITCHEN ARTS SERIES

STREAMLINED COOKING
for a Healthy Lifestyle

COLE
GROUP

Mary Carroll has been teaching the principles and techniques of healthy cooking for more than 15 years. She is the founder of Cuisine Naturelle, the West Coast's first natural-foods cooking school, and is a nationally known writer on low-fat cuisine for *Vegetarian Times* and a weekly syndicated newspaper column. As the staff chef for the Preventive Medicine Research Institute in San Francisco, she created the recipes used in a major study of the effects of diet on reversing heart disease. Mary has been a guest chef and lecturer throughout the country, and her recipes and unique approach have been featured in *USA Today,* Time-Life cookbooks, and many radio and television programs such as Lifetime cable TV's "Attitudes." Mary currently resides in the Minneapolis area, where she teaches healthy cooking classes and writes.

Front Cover   Healthy cuisine, such as this delightful combination of pasta, fresh herbs, and lean poultry, can be low-fat, nutritious, and tantalizing.

Title Page   The key to streamlined cooking lies in the use of fresh, healthy ingredients.

Back Cover

Upper   Virtually effortless to prepare, Spicy Salsa Chicken is light, savory, nutritious, and baked to perfection in minutes (see page 156).

Lower   A delicate filo crust, brushed with honey and applesauce, cradles thinly sliced apples to form Apple Tart, an elegant and nutritious ending to any meal (see page 219).

Special Thanks to: Staff and students of Cuisine Naturelle; Tony Moore; Cottonwood; Fillamento; Sue Fisher King; Vignette; Virginia Breier; Fioridella; Judy Goldsmith; Bernie Carrasco; Barbara Brown; Nancy Glenn; Ward Finer; Hal Freedman; Willi Rudowsky; Karen Kuhn in San Francisco; Elica's Paper Plate and Fauxcus, Glendale, California; Bea and Marty Glenn, Miami Beach, Florida; Dr. Dean Ornish; Jeffrey Long, Surface Studios, San Francisco, California.

Cole books are available for quantity purchases for sales promotions, premiums, fund-raising, or educational use. For more information contact the publisher.

Contributors

Nutritional Consultants
Michelle Hanson, Jane Rubey, M.P.H., R.D.

Nutritional Analysis
MasterCook II, Arion Software Inc.

Additional Photographers
Keith Ovregaard, front cover, title page; Michael Lamotte, back cover; Alan Copeland, pages 29, 34, 66, 98, 194; Beth Marsolais, author, at left; Marshall Gordon, page 207; Bob Montesclaros, page 155; Richard Tauber, pages 130, 159, 212, 219; Jackson Vereen, page 123

Food Stylists
Susan Devaty and Karen Hazarian

Photographic Stylists
Amy Glenn and Sara Slavin

Additional Stylists
Susan Broussard, Gina Farruggio, Kathleen Lewis, Eve Hinlien Shaw, Doug Warner

Photographer's Assistant
Bruce E. James

Photographic Design Consultant
Debbie Dicker

Cole's Kitchen Arts Series is published by Cole Group.

President and Publisher
Brete C. Harrison

VP and Director of Operations
Linda Hauck

VP of Publishing
Robert G. Manley

VP and Editorial Director
James Connolly

VP Marketing and Business Development
John A. Morris

Senior Editor
Annette Gooch

Editorial Assistants
Lynn Bell, Gina Poncavage, Ann Train

Production Coordinator
Dotti Hydue

© 1995 Cole Group, Inc.

All rights reserved under international and Pan-American copyright conventions. No portion of this book may be reproduced without written permission from the publisher. Cole Group and Cole's Kitchen Arts Series colophon are trademarks of Cole Publishing Group, Inc.

Cole Group, Inc.
1330 N. Dutton Ave., Suite 103
Santa Rosa, CA 95401
(800) 959-2717   (707) 526-2682
Fax (707) 526-2687

Printed in Hong Kong through Mandarin Offset.

G   F   E   D   C   B   A
1   0   9   8   7   6   5

ISBN 1-56426-067-4

Library of Congress Catalog Card Number 95-3769

Distributed to the book trade by Publishers Group West.

STREAMLINED COOKING
for a Healthy Lifestyle

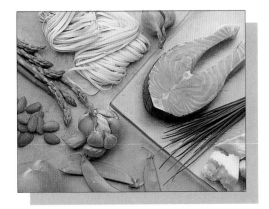

MARY CARROLL
Writer

MICHAEL LAMOTTE
KEITH OVREGAARD
Photographers

COLE
GROUP

C O N T E N T S

Meals based on a wide variety of appealing, satisfying, nutritious foods belong in a healthy lifestyle.

THE STREAMLINED APPROACH TO
HEALTHY COOKING

Contrary to popular belief, "healthy" cooking and
eating needn't mean a regime of bland, boring
meals that leave you feeling hungry and deprived.
By streamlining your approach to healthy cooking, you can
enjoy an immense variety of satisfying, tasty foods without
sacrificing good nutrition. This commonsense approach
emphasizes simple cooking techniques that contribute to good
nutrition and an abundance of delicious, wholesome foods—
the kind that belong in a healthy lifestyle.

COOK RIGHT TO EAT RIGHT

There's no doubt about it: Streamlined cooking is an important step in developing a healthy lifestyle. When you plan and prepare your own menus from fresh ingredients, you help ensure that you and your family are eating well-balanced meals and getting the nutrients needed for good health and well-being. Study after study suggests that good nutrition can help prevent the kinds of health problems that often begin with a poor diet. Moreover, an approach to cooking and eating that enhances your nutritional profile is very likely to help streamline your silhouette. What's more, healthy cooking doesn't require spending hours in the kitchen. Streamlined cooking can be fun, easy, and quick—even for busy people. In fact, the recipes in this book were selected not only for their nutritional value and delicious flavor, but also for their streamlined preparation methods.

There's no rule that says elegant food can't be simple to prepare. Despite what you may have heard, healthy cooking need not entail expensive cookware and ingredients or complex techniques. You can prepare most of the dishes in this book without spending one penny on new equipment, using simple techniques that are well within the ability of the beginning cook. You don't have to do without the foods you like to eat; you may need to make only minor changes in how you prepare your favorite foods. You may already be using many nutritious foods and healthful cooking techniques without being aware of it.

By using the healthful techniques in this book, you can prepare delicious cuisine that tastes good and is good for you. For example, you can learn to lower the fat in stir-fry dishes by using a small amount of flavorful Asian sesame oil combined with wine or other flavoring ingredients instead of a larger quantity of plain cooking oil. You can discover how to marinate skinless poultry and lean meats before cooking to keep them moist. You can develop the art of preparing delicious, healthy desserts that employ top-notch presentations.

You'll also find plenty of new ideas for innovative gourmet dishes, timesaving tips, and special notes on how dishes can be cooked ahead and frozen for quick meals. Included are complete menus and numerous hints for easy, elegant entertaining.

To ensure optimum flavor, the recipes focus on fresh ingredients—fruits and vegetables, whole grains and legumes, lean meats, poultry, fish, and low-fat dairy products. Many of the recipes use dry sherry or wine (instead of relying solely on oil or butter) for sautéing vegetables to create a "flavor seal" as the food cooks. Flavored vinegars, fresh herbs and spices, nonfat yogurt, monounsaturated oils, reduced-fat mayonnaise and cheeses, and other great-tasting, high-quality foods and seasonings replace their less healthy counterparts.

Wholesome, satisfying, delicious dishes, expertly prepared and served with pride, can become the hallmark of your cooking repertoire. By adopting a streamlined approach to cooking, you are embarking on an adventure to discover new flavors and different cuisines and, in the process, making a commitment to a lifestyle that can help you feel and look better.

ABOUT THIS BOOK

This book is designed to guide you in streamlining your cooking, beginning with the basics of good nutrition and healthy cooking techniques, which are introduced in this chapter. Succeeding chapters present, course by course, recipes and menus that will please your palate as well as help enhance your health and well-being. Besides being nutritious and delicious, the recipes are designed for busy lifestyles; many require less than one hour to prepare, and most take less time than that. Preparation times (how long the average cook takes to prepare the ingredients) are given for each recipe, along with the time needed for cooking, chilling, or marinating, as applicable.

For healthy cooking and eating to be enjoyable, the recipes should be exciting and varied. The recipes in this book span the globe, featuring dishes from Greece, such as Mediterranean Stuffed Eggplant (see page 95); China, Mu Shu Tofu (see page 103); and many other areas. This book also features classic favorites from the United States, such as Hearty Lima Bean Soup (see page 59), as well as upscale innovations such as Grilled Turkey Breast With Raspberry and Shallot Marinade (see page 151). For special occasions there are recipes such as Filo Pastries With Smoked Turkey and Mushrooms (see page 32) or Carob Cheesecake (see page 214) containing minimal amounts of butter, sugar, or other ingredients that are best used in moderation. These recipes are intended to be served in small portions.

Most of the recipes can easily be doubled or halved, depending on your menu needs. Almost all the dishes, except the salads and some of the desserts, freeze well. Throughout the book, special features offer nutritional information and tips on cooking techniques. As an added bonus, the last chapter offers recipes for people who want to reduce their intake of certain foods such as dairy products, or dietary elements such as fat, cholesterol, or sodium.

The information in this book follows current nutritional guidelines put forth by the United States Department of Agriculture (U.S.D.A.) and other nutritional authorities. Although the recommendations of different experts may vary slightly in certain respects, there is consensus about certain aspects of the average American diet. It typically does not contain enough of the following nutrients essential to good health: lean forms of protein, certain vitamins and minerals (such as vitamins A and C, calcium, and iron), complex carbohydrates, and fiber; it also contains too much saturated fat, salt, and refined sugar. Numerous studies, including reports by the U.S. Surgeon General's Office and other health experts, have identified improper diet (and a sedentary lifestyle) as a contributing factor in heart disease, certain types of cancer, and other health problems.

The recipes in this book emphasize sensible nutrition. They avoid excessive use of substances that are high in saturated fat, cholesterol, salt, and sugar, substituting healthier ingredients and relying on cooking techniques that support good nutrition. Nutritional data at the end of each recipe indicate the approximate amount of calcium, calories, carbohydrates, cholesterol, fat, fiber, protein, and sodium contained in one serving of the recipe. You can use this nutritional data, along with the following guidelines based on the U.S. Recommended Daily Allowances, to help plan and achieve your nutrient needs:

Calcium: 800–1,200 milligrams a day

Calories: approximately 1,500–2,500 calories a day

Carbohydrates: 300 grams a day

Cholesterol: less than 300 milligrams a day

Fat: less than 67 grams a day

Fiber: 25–35 grams a day

Protein: 44–56 grams a day

Sodium: 1,100–3,300 milligrams a day

Keep in mind that these are *general guidelines:* You may need more or less than the recommended amounts, depending on your age, gender, activity level, medical condition, and other personal factors.

A WORD OF CAUTION

This book does not attempt to lay out a weight-loss plan, nor does it promote some "miracle diet." Studies suggest that a long-term program of improving one's eating and exercise habits is far more effective in promoting good health than a "quick-fix" solution that focuses only on weight loss.

For most people, a healthy lifestyle includes a wide variety of nutritious foods, properly prepared for delicious, healthful dining—dishes that offer enough diversity to keep menus interesting, yet are easy to prepare. The streamlined approach to healthy cooking and eating is flexible enough to allow you to

plan meals that meet your personal requirements.

Because individual nutritional needs vary, you should always consult a qualified healthcare professional before making major dietary changes or embarking on any new nutritional or fitness program.

SIX STEPS TOWARD HEALTHIER COOKING

The initial steps you take toward streamlining your cooking practices will go a long way in determining your success at making lasting, positive changes in your lifestyle. The following suggestions, gathered from recommendations by health professionals, will help to smooth the transition to a healthy lifestyle:

1. *Learn the fundamentals of good nutrition.* Find out which foods your

Steaming and other healthy cooking techniques are vital for retaining the nutrients and flavor of fresh, whole foods.

A well-balanced meal such as Baked Salmon Provençale (see recipe on page 129) features a variety of nutritious foods and an appealing presentation.

body needs—and which foods it does not need—to stay in good working condition.

2. *Apply this basic knowledge to your specific health needs.* Perhaps your family has a history of heart disease, and you have heard that dietary cholesterol may be a contributing factor. To start developing an eating plan for yourself that addresses these kinds of concerns, you should learn which foods are high in saturated fats or other substances that may contribute to heart disease or other health problems. By becoming informed about which foods and nutrients are indispensable for good health and which are linked to disease and poor health, you are better prepared to make wise food choices.

3. *Become familiar with healthful cooking techniques.* How you cook is as important to good taste and nutrition as what you cook. Some cooking methods, such as stir-frying and steaming, enhance the flavor and retain the nutritional value of fresh ingredients. Other methods, such as prolonged boiling or

deep-frying, may destroy nutrients or are not appropriate for daily use in a streamlined approach to cooking.

4. *Choose varied, flavorful dishes that are relatively easy to prepare.* Having a wide assortment of tasty recipes to choose from adds to the enjoyment of healthy foods. These recipes also should fit your personal situation. Having a large collection of cookbooks on hand is of little practical value if the recipes in them are beyond your level of technical skills, require equipment you don't own, or take so long to prepare that you never have the time to try them.

5. *Plan your meals and menus ahead.* You are more likely to incorporate healthy foods and streamlined cooking techniques into your lifestyle if you plan and prepare meals in advance. An important part of streamlining your approach to cooking is learning how to shop, read labels, and store foods properly so that they retain maximum freshness and nutritional value. Also, organizing your kitchen efficiently can make cooking more enjoyable.

6. *Learn to enjoy healthy dining.* Once you learn the basics of light, healthy gourmet cooking, you will come to prefer the delightful taste of fresh fruits and vegetables to the taste of packaged, processed, and frozen foods. You will also relish the feeling of accomplishment that comes with knowing how to create beautiful, delicious meals that you know are good for you.

A STREAMLINED APPROACH TO NUTRITION

Adequate nutrition is essential to any healthy lifestyle. In the most recent nutritional recommendations prepared by the U.S.D.A., the six food groups currently recognized as essential for good health are symbolized by a pyramid. At the base of the pyramid are foods that should have the most prominent place in a healthy diet: the group that includes bread, cereal, rice, and pasta. Next come the fruit and vegetable groups, which, along with the first group, provide complex carbohydrates. Then come the two groups that are rich in protein: dairy products and meat, poultry, fish, eggs, legumes, and nuts. The tip of the pyramid comprises the group of foods that should be consumed in the smallest proportion: fats, oils, and sweets.

According to most authorities, carbohydrates should provide 55 percent or more of the total daily calories; proteins should contribute about 15 percent; and fats no more than 30 percent. The following overview of basic nutritional components can be useful in implementing these recommendations into your lifestyle.

CARBOHYDRATE—PRIME ENERGY SOURCE

Carbohydrates are the body's primary source of energy and also provide B-complex vitamins. Carbohydrates are

found in two very different forms: simple and complex.

Simple carbohydrates are found primarily in fresh fruit, fruit juices, refined starches such as bleached white flour, and refined sugars such as those in candy and other sweets. Fresh fruit is a necessary part of a healthy diet, since it provides essential vitamins and minerals, as well as carbohydrates. Refined sugars, on the other hand, are less beneficial for the body. You may feel a surge of energy after eating foods high in refined sugars, but these foods supply an ample amount of "empty" calories. Such foods fill you up (and out), but since they usually lack the nutrients the body needs to process the sugar they contain, they contribute little to total body health. In addition to containing little nutritional value, these foods typically leave you feeling dissatisfied when you eat them. Even if you are tempted to consume more to compensate for the lack of satisfaction, your

The most nutritious meals start with the freshest ingredients available.

body may feel tired as it struggles to restore the nutrients it lost in processing foods high in refined sugars.

Complex carbohydrates contain fiber, bran, germ, and other nutrients that are missing from refined sugars and refined starches. These foods take longer to break down than other foods and help keep your body warm and your metabolism balanced by generating fuel that maintains consistent energy levels. Excellent sources of complex carbohydrates include brown rice, barley, corn and cornmeal, wheat, millet, oats, whole wheat breads and pastas, and beans, lentils, and split peas. Complex carbohydrates also help stave off cravings for sugary foods and other foods that provide only "empty" calories.

Many nutritionists recommend consuming from half to three fourths your daily caloric intake in the form of complex carbohydrates. Besides being a good source of protein, they are low in fat and calories, and offer plenty of fiber, vitamins, and minerals. The average diet in the United States is low in complex carbohydrates and thereby fails to take advantage of the beneficial nutrients these foods can provide. Even in "restored" or "fortified" foods, such as certain breakfast foods with added vitamins and minerals, the fiber content cannot be replaced once it is removed. Fiber, bran, germ, and other components of whole grains and other foods high in complex carbohydrates promote proper digestion, enabling the body to burn the carbohydrate at an even rate, to supply energy as needed. When these important substances are refined out of complex carbohydrates, as occurs in the processing of wheat to make white flour, the body is deprived of these important aids to digestion.

If you have been following a lifelong diet of fatty meats, high-fat dairy products, canned or frozen vegetables, and sugary foods, switching to a diet high in complex carbohydrates might seem challenging at first. Make the transition gradually by incorporating legumes into soups or salads, switching to whole

grain bread, or trying entrées such as Pasta Shells With Peas and Chicken (see page 186), Polenta Pizza (see page 189), Barley-Stuffed Cabbage Rolls With Ginger Sauce (see page 92), and Bean Burgers (see page 101). For more information, see The Value of Complex Carbohydrates (page 190).

PROTEIN—THE BODY'S MAIN BUILDING BLOCK

All through life, protein functions as a building tool for the body to grow, nourish, and repair its cells. Protein carries oxygen to the cells and produces enzymes and hormones that regulate the metabolic process. It also helps fight infection and sustains the immune system by producing antibodies. There are several types of protein, and consuming a variety of protein types is essential to good health. Since the human body does not manufacture or store protein, it must be supplied daily through the food you eat. Meats, poultry, fish and shellfish, eggs, dairy products, legumes, and whole grains all contain significant amounts of protein.

Many people tend to rely for the majority of their protein on high-fat meats and dairy products. These foods are indeed rich in protein but also are higher in fat and cholesterol than complex carbohydrates. If you can obtain more of your protein from complex carbohydrates, you can reduce the amount of saturated fats and cholesterol and also reduce the total number of calories you take in—and without feeling hungry. For streamlined nutrition, animal protein is best obtained from lean sources, such as leaner cuts of red meats, poultry without the skin, fish, and low-fat or nonfat dairy products. Recipes such as Minnesota Chicken and Wild Rice Soup (see page 51), Baked Salmon Provençale (see page 129), and Turkey Chili Burritos (see page 150) are good sources of low-fat protein. For more information, see About Protein (page 166).

FAT—BLESSING OR BURDEN

Although fat is often maligned, it is an essential nutrient and has a purpose in the chemistry of the body. Fats aid in digestion, are a source of energy, and carry certain fat-soluble vitamins into the system. But some fats are better for you than others. The three types of fats—*saturated, polyunsaturated,* and *monounsaturated*—are identified by their chemical structure, according to the arrangement and number of their carbon and hydrogen molecules. From the standpoint of health, monounsaturated fats are the most beneficial because they help sustain levels of desirable high-density lipoprotein (HDL—"good" cholesterol) while helping to reduce levels of unhealthy low-density lipoprotein or very low-density lipoprotein (LDL or VLDL—"bad" cholesterol).

Saturated fats may contribute to dangerously elevated LDL cholesterol levels, which are associated with conditions such as clogged arteries. Most of the fat in the American diet is in the form of saturated fats—the most difficult kind for the human body to handle. This type of fat is usually, although not always, solid at room temperature, which makes it easier to identify. Saturated fats come from animal products, such as meat, lard, poultry, fish, and dairy sources, and from certain vegetable products, such as most margarines, hydrogenated shortenings, cocoa butter, and coconut and palm oils. Among animal sources, chicken, turkey, and fish are lowest in saturated fats. Saturated fats are also manufactured during hydrogenation, the process used to make margarine and vegetable shortenings. The process of hydrogenation can cause a polyunsaturated or monounsaturated fat such as vegetable oil to become saturated.

Polyunsaturated fats can help reduce levels of "bad" cholesterol (LDL), although an excess can also reduce the "good" type (HDL). These fats are most commonly found in veg-

You can enjoy eating well when you plan healthy menus, beginning with the basics: fresh fruits and vegetables, whole grains, and legumes.

Basics

MAKING WISE FOOD CHOICES

Use this chart as a quick, easy-to-use reference in making food choices for a streamlined approach to cooking and eating:

Foods to Emphasize

The following foods offer above-average nutrient levels and excellent flavor:

☐ Canola, olive, and sesame oil (in moderate quantities)

☐ Chicken (preferably with skin removed)

☐ Legumes, such as lentils, split peas, kidney beans, black beans, and navy beans

☐ Dark leafy greens, such as broccoli, spinach, chard, kale, and mustard

☐ Fresh and dried herbs and spices

☐ Fresh fish and low-cholesterol shellfish

☐ Fresh fruits, such as oranges, apples, pears, grapes, berries, peaches, grapefruit, and melon; fresh fruit juices

☐ Fresh vegetables, such as carrots, celery, cucumber, radishes, broccoli, sprouts, green onions, zucchini, tomatoes, green beans, peas, corn, potatoes

☐ Low-fat and part-skim cheeses, such as mozzarella, ricotta, and farmer cheese

☐ Nonfat and low-fat milk and yogurt

☐ Whole grains and grain products such as rice, millet, bulgur, couscous, oatmeal, cornmeal, whole grain flours, and whole grain breads and crackers

Foods to Avoid or Use With Caution

The following foods contribute few nutrients or are high in fats, refined sugars, or other substances that do not contribute to good health:

☐ Baked goods made primarily from refined sugar and saturated fats

☐ Butter and most margarines

☐ Cold cuts

☐ Deep-fried foods

☐ Fatty pork products, such as ham, bacon, or scrapple

☐ High-fat cheeses and other dairy products

☐ High-fat salad dressings

☐ Hydrogenated oils and fats, such as hydrogenated nut butters and solid shortening

☐ Mayonnaise (except small quantities of reduced-fat mayonnaise)

☐ Saturated fats, such as lard or coconut and palm oils

etable oils, such as corn, cottonseed, safflower, and soybean oils, but they also exist in tofu, walnuts, most fish, and a variety of other foods.

Monounsaturated fats are the most beneficial type because they sustain beneficial HDL cholesterol levels while helping reduce harmful LDL and VLDL levels. Good sources of monounsaturated fats include olive, canola, sesame, and peanut oils, as well as avocado, some nuts and seeds, and a number of other foods.

Fat contains 9 calories per gram, whereas carbohydrate or protein contains only 4 calories per gram. This means that you can eat twice as much carbohydrate or protein as fat for about the same amount of calories. Although many people in the U.S. are in the habit of consuming as much as 40 percent of their total calories in fat, medical and nutritional authorities urge that no more than 30 percent of the *total* number of calories you take in daily should be from fat, with no more than 10 percent derived from saturated fats.

Following a healthy lifestyle doesn't have to preclude occasionally enjoying foods that contain higher percentages of fat than those outlined above. Depending on your individual condition, it may be permissible from time to time to indulge in a fat-rich food. Just make sure that the other foods you eat are sufficiently low in fat to keep your daily average fat intake at 30 percent (or below) of the total calories consumed. In making wise food choices, as in everything else, common sense and reason are your best guides.

In light of these recommendations, a streamlined approach to cooking means emphasizing canola, olive, and other healthful vegetable oils instead of shortening, butter, lard, or bacon fat; eating a larger proportion of complex carbohydrates to fulfill your total caloric needs; and cutting back on high-fat dairy products and fatty meats. Recipes such as Stir-Fried Prawns in Black Bean Sauce (page 136) and Pita Quesadillas (page 29) are prime examples of how delicious and flavorful healthy cooking can be. For more information, see Tips on Dairy Products—Cutting Fat, Not Flavor (page 225) and Tips On Skimming Fat (page 228).

CHOLESTEROL—A LINK TO HEART DISEASE

Cholesterol is found in animal products and in the human body. It is manufactured by almost all body tissues and used for a variety of body processes. Although the body manufactures plenty of cholesterol for its needs, it is often unable to assimilate the kind contained in animal products. This "bad" cholesterol (LDL) is often stored along the arteries, which can result in clogged arteries (atherosclerosis). For overall good health, you should avoid or reduce your intake of fats that increase "bad" cholesterol or that lower "good" cholesterol. For more information, see About Cholesterol (page 161).

FIBER—DIGESTIVE AID AND DISEASE PREVENTER

Fiber is the component of food that cannot be broken down by enzymes in the human digestive tract. Virtually all fiber comes from plants, and most types of dietary fiber are complex carbohydrates; animal products contain very little, if any, fiber. Because fiber is largely indigestible, it aids in elimination as it passes through the digestive tract; fiber also promotes the sensation of feeling pleasantly satisfied after eating. In addition to its role in proper bowel function, fiber assists in fat and carbohydrate metabolism. Many studies show that fiber may also help to prevent cancer of the colon and other conditions such as diverticulitis.

Good sources of fiber are whole grains that have not had the bran removed; whole grain cereals, breads, and pastas; fresh fruits and vegetables; and legumes, seeds, and nuts. Sauerkraut Bread (see page 194) and Best Bran Muffins (see page 142) are rich in fiber. For more information, see The Benefits of Fiber (page 82).

SODIUM—IMPORTANT IN SMALL AMOUNTS

Although sodium helps maintain vital mineral balances in the system, many people take in an excess amount. Research has linked excess sodium to improper fluid balance (water retention), as well as to more serious problems such as hypertension and heart disease. For these and other reasons, many people are choosing to cut back on table salt and to use herbal salt substitutes and products such as low-sodium soy sauce and tamari.

If you have been using excess salt for years and decide to reduce your intake, your taste buds may take several months to adjust. Be patient with yourself if some foods seem to taste bland. For tips on reducing sodium, see Replacing Salt with Herbs and Spices (page 102).

VITAMINS—MAINTAINERS OF METABOLISM AND HEALTH

Vitamins are essential to almost all metabolic functions. They assist the catalytic action of enzymes, on which almost all body processes depend for chemical reactions and cell growth. Vitamins also help release energy to the system, build tissue, and regulate how the body utilizes nutrients.

Vitamins are classified by their solubility in water or fat. Fat-soluble vitamins, such as A, D, E, and K, are stored by the body; water-soluble vitamins, such as the C-complex and B-complex vitamins, are not. Because water-soluble nutrients can't be stored in the body, they must be restored daily for complete nutrition. Essential vitamins include A, B_1 (thiamin), B_2 (riboflavin), B_3 (niacin), B_6, B_{12}, biotin, C-complex, D, E, folic acid, and K. For more information on vitamins A and C, see The Four Most Overlooked Nutrients (page 110).

MINERALS—BUILDERS OF STRONG BONES AND TEETH

Minerals perform a variety of functions in the body: building strong bones and teeth, strengthening enzymes, and maintaining proper acid-alkaline balance. The most important minerals include calcium, fluoride, iodine, iron, phosphorus, potassium, sodium, and zinc.

The importance of calcium has been known for many years, but studies suggest that most people don't get enough. Calcium is essential to bone density and muscle function; it helps major muscles such as the heart contract and relax. Calcium-rich foods include leafy green vegetables such as broccoli, kale, and mustard greens, low-fat and nonfat milk products, whole grains, and beans. For more information on calcium and iron, see The Four Most Overlooked Nutrients (page 110).

Obtaining enough of both vitamins and minerals essential for health depends on selecting high-quality, nutrient-rich ingredients, as well as using cooking techniques that retain the maximum amount of vitamins and minerals in food (see page 17). Some nutritionists believe that changes in agricultural, distribution, and storage methods have adversely affected the vitamin and mineral content of our food. Although most experts agree that it is best to obtain nutrients directly from the food we eat, some people use vitamin and mineral supplements to help ensure that their nutritional intake is adequate.

WATER—A NECESSITY FOR GOOD HEALTH

Drinking sufficient amounts of pure water is an important health practice. Every day your body loses as much as 8 to 12 cups of water, and this fluid must be replaced regularly for good health. Eight glasses of water a day, if you're moderately active, or more if you're exercising strenuously, is the general recommendation. Climate and temperature, as well as your individual needs, are other factors in determining the

Enjoying a variety of appealing dishes, such as this Summer Melon Soup With Lime (see page 60), getting regular exercise, and maintaining a positive attitude all contribute to a healthy lifestyle.

quantity that is appropriate for you. However, many nutritionists suggest drinking only a small amount (a few ounces) of water or other fluids at mealtime to avoid interfering with proper digestion.

A STREAMLINED APPROACH TO WEIGHT CONTROL

A healthy lifestyle that emphasizes good nutrition and regular exercise offers many benefits: plenty of energy to meet the demands of life, a general sense of well-being, a positive outlook, and, for many people, an improved body image and ability to control their weight. How much you eat, as well as the kinds of foods you eat and how they are metabolized in the body are factors in weight control.

CALORIES

Calories, unlike vitamins, minerals, and other nutrients, are not a nutritional substance but merely a unit of measure that indicates the amount of energy the body requires to metabolize a certain food. Activity (exercise) speeds up the body's metabolism; one result of a lack of exercise is a lower metabolic rate. If

you eat more food than your body can expend through normal metabolic functions and activity, the excess is stored in the form of body fat.

To lose weight, you must take in less food or else expend more energy by increasing your level of activity; a streamlined approach to weight control emphasizes both tactics. You should select foods that provide the greatest nutritional benefits for the amount of calories the body must expend to metabolize them. From the perspective of managing your weight, the type of calories you consume is more important than the total number. It makes good sense to focus on complex carbohydrates, which are low in fat but high in other valuable nutrients, and to eat fewer high-fat foods.

An important but often neglected aspect of weight management is the variety of foods consumed. Many people react to a boring, repetitive "diet" by eating more of some particular food to compensate for the lack of variety. A more satisfactory approach to managing weight is to eat a broad range of healthy foods to help ensure the good nutrition essential to sensible weight control. Imaginative recipes—like the ones in this book—offer a wide range of nutritious foods.

NUTRIENT DENSITY

Nutrient-dense foods are high in nutrients and low in calories. They give the body long-lasting energy, are assimilated easily and efficiently, and add to the store of vitamins, minerals, and other life-enhancing substances. Fresh vegetables and fruits, low-fat or nonfat dairy products, cooked whole grains and legumes, whole grain breads and pastas, lean meats, fresh fish and shellfish, and chicken and turkey are all nutrient-dense foods.

Foods with low nutrient density may provide calories but little else in the way of nutrition. Most packaged snack foods, high-fat dairy products, desserts and sweets made primarily from refined flour or sugar, most commercially made creamy salad dressings, ice cream, and highly processed foods have low nutrient density.

Nutrient density appears to have a direct relation to weight control: Compared with foods that are low in nutrient density, nutrient-dense foods are more likely to be converted to energy than stored as fat (as long as the quantity consumed does not exceed the caloric needs of the body). For example, a large baked potato with a low-fat topping and a small bag of potato chips may contain the same number of calories, but the baked potato offers more protein, thiamin, riboflavin, niacin, vitamin C, and iron (not to mention less fat). Therefore, the baked potato is more nutrient-dense than the potato chips and thus is a healthier choice. For more information on selecting healthy foods, see Making Wise Food Choices (page 14).

ATTITUDE

Attitude plays an important part in a streamlined approach to a healthy lifestyle. Meals that satisfy the eye as well as the palate can go a long way to improve your attitude about eating foods that provide good nutrition. And the feeling of accomplishment that comes from creating an especially attractive, satisfying, nutritious meal can do a great deal for your self-confidence.

EXERCISE

Although this is not a book on physical fitness, no discussion of nutrition or weight control is complete without mentioning exercise. Besides burning calories and raising the metabolic level, exercise helps raise the level of "good" cholesterol (HDL) in the blood. It also develops lean muscle tissue and helps with appetite control by releasing glucose into the bloodstream. In addition to these physical benefits, regular exercise

offers psychological benefits—a general feeling of well-being, help in managing stress, and enhanced self-image—all of which are important to a healthy lifestyle.

A STREAMLINED APPROACH TO COOKING TECHNIQUES

Selecting nutritious foods is an important part of a healthy lifestyle, but how you prepare these foods is equally important to your health and your enjoyment of good food.

STEAMING, POACHING, AND BRAISING

When foods are steamed, they lose fewer nutrients than they do when boiled and, unless they are steamed too long, they retain more of their color. Steamed foods also cook more quickly than foods that are boiled. Try experimenting with different kinds of steamers for different foods. A folding stainless steel steamer is good for chopped vegetables. Stacking bamboo baskets are designed to hold larger vegetables and whole fish (see Steamed Fish With Ginger on page 122); you can also use a bamboo steamer for fish fillets. Simply place the fish on a heatproof plate inside the steamer before placing the steamer in the cooking pot. A stainless steel colander steamer that fits into a pot is excellent for artichokes and other large vegetables. Place a stainless steel or bamboo steamer in a deep pot above boiling water or stock, add vegetables, and cover. Steamed vegetables are ready when they appear bright in color and are tender when pierced with the tip of a knife.

Poaching is similar to steaming, except that the food sits directly in stock, wine, or fruit juice and absorbs the flavor of the liquid. Sweet poaching liquids, such as apple juice and dessert wine, are used for poaching desserts (see Compote of Winter Fruits in Red Wine

NOTE

DANGER ZONES

Certain occasions can present challenges when you're making the transition to a healthier lifestyle. To help stay on track, plan ahead for special social occasions, dining in restaurants, and traveling.

Social occasions You can enjoy yourself at weddings, holidays, and other social occasions while maintaining your commitment to a healthy lifestyle. To prevent impulse eating, try eating a light but nourishing meal or snack before you leave home; look for the fresh vegetable platter on the hors d'oeuvre table; and choose salads with the dressing on the side.

Restaurants Learn to recognize healthy menu items such as salads without heavy dressings, lean meats, poultry, broiled fish, baked potatoes without high-fat toppings (ask for plain yogurt), and low-fat desserts. Some restaurants offer special menus with low-fat, low-cholesterol selections.

Travel Plan ahead for travel: Call the airline a couple of days before flight time to request a special low-fat meal or vegetarian meal; take along nutrient-rich snack foods such as fresh fruits, fresh vegetable sticks, low-fat yogurt, or whole grain crackers; and pack a low-fat salad dressing in a carry-on bag.

Booking a hotel room with a kitchenette or even just a refrigerator and stocking it with nutritious foods can be convenient when you want a quick, healthy meal or snack but don't feel like going out.

TIPS

...ON HEALTHY EATING AND COOKING

Keeping your commitment to a healthy lifestyle is easier when you plan ahead for healthy eating and cooking:

☐ Keep an assortment of nutritious foods on hand. Take a look at Appetizers and Hors d'Oeuvres (see pages 24-45), where you will find a variety of finger foods and other healthful dishes for snacking.

☐ Drink alcoholic beverages in moderation. In addition to its high caloric content, alcohol tends to dull judgment and self-discipline, making it too easy to eat or drink too much. Instead of alcohol, try club soda with a twist of lime or lemon, flavored sparkling water, or even a nonalcoholic wine spritzer.

☐ Keep a food diary for a week or so to provide yourself with information about what you're actually eating—and when. If you're serious about reducing dietary fat, buy an inexpensive, pocket-sized guide to help you track the amount of fat and the percentage of calories derived from fat in the foods you eat. You may be amazed to learn the amount of fat hiding in some foods.

☐ Make it a practice to read the labels on food packaging. By taking the time to read labels, you can make wise choices about the foods you select.

☐ Organize your kitchen for efficiency *and* health. Go through the cupboards, shelves, pantry, and refrigerator. Get rid of any foods that don't contribute anything positive to your health. Unclutter the cabinets by boxing cookware, utensils, and equipment that you haven't used in years. Give the items you no longer need to someone who can use them or hold a garage sale.

☐ Shop efficiently. Make a shopping list and organize it into categories, such as produce, bulk foods and staples, meats, and dairy foods. One theory holds that you can shop in a supermarket without ever entering the middle aisles and still buy everything you need to eat well: The perimeter holds all the fresh foods and the middle contains mostly highly processed foods and impulse items.

☐ Make meals ahead. When you plan ahead, you can cook elegant, imaginative meals when it's convenient and serve them whenever you wish. Many of the recipes in this book include directions on preparing and refrigerating or freezing them until you want a quick meal. For more information, see Tips On Preparing Make-Ahead Meals (page 23).

☐ When it's time to eat, take time out to focus on your food. Eating hurriedly is unsatisfying at best and unhealthy at worst. When you develop the habit of rushing through meals, what you eat matters less and less. It takes time and effort to learn to enjoy eating: Pay attention to how you prepare a meal, take time to relax before and during the meal, and give yourself the time to savor and enjoy eating it.

on page 204 or Wine-Basted Pears on page 203). Savory liquids, such as stock and dry sherry, are preferred for fish and chicken (see Prawns With Peanut Sauce on page 134 or Coquilles Sauce Verte on page 120).

In braising, food is gently simmered in a liquid such as wine or stock. Start with a small amount of white wine, sherry, or defatted chicken stock (¼ cup per 2 cups of vegetables or meat to be braised), heat to the simmering point, and then add food to be cooked. Cover the pan and keep heat on medium-high, or high enough to maintain simmering. Braise until food is tender or it reaches the specifications in the recipe. Properly braised vegetables absorb flavor from the cooking liquid and retain their bright color and texture as well.

BAKING AND ROASTING

An oven temperature of 350° F is called for in most of the baked recipes in this book, with the exception of the pastries, which require a slightly higher temperature. Baking is a good way to avoid the less healthful cooking methods of frying and deep-frying. Chicken and fish, for instance, are easily baked instead of fried and, if covered with stock, juice, wine, light sauce, or salsa, will stay fresh and moist throughout the baking process. See Simple Baked Chicken With Orange and Cumin (page 146) and Mexican Baked Fish in Salsa Verde (page 121).

Roasting preserves the tenderness of meats and vegetables. Slow roasting is usually done in a 300° F oven, and regular roasting in a 375° F to 400° F oven. Roasted chicken and meats tend to emerge from the oven crisp on the outside and juicy inside. For poultry dishes in which the skin is removed to lower the fat content, the recipes in this book often suggest marinating or basting before roasting to retain the juicy flavor (see Grilled Chicken in Sweet Marinade on page 157).

BROILING AND GRILLING

A boon to the busy, health-conscious cook, broiling is easy and quick. The recipes featured in this book recommend broiling chicken and meat for the wonderfully rich flavors that develop during cooking. Broiled meats tend to retain their juices a little better than baked meats because they cook for less time and at a higher temperature. As with roasting, marinating or basting using low-fat liquids is often recommended.

Always broil meats on a rack to let the fats drip off while cooking. Meats broiled correctly are crisp on the outside, tender and juicy inside. Marinate fish fillets in lemon juice or teriyaki sauce before broiling: the extra liquid helps prevent them from drying out during the cooking process.

Grilling has become a popular way to prepare flavorful low-fat entrées. Chicken, fish, and lean meats can be marinated before grilling to help tenderize and enhance the flavor. Cook all fish and thinner cuts of meat and chicken right on the grill or in a stovetop grilling pan. Thicker sections of meat, whole chickens, potatoes, or winter squash usually need to be wrapped in aluminum foil and baked for 20 to 30 minutes before grilling in order to cook thoroughly. Grill small new potatoes, whole summer squash, and eggplants without peeling them; corn on the cob can be grilled wrapped in the husk. Other vegetables can be packaged in foil, sprinkled with water, lemon juice, or dry sherry, and steamed on the grill while the meat is cooking. Baste grilled foods with mustard, lemon juice, or marinades; try the sauce from Grilled Sweet-and-Sour Tuna Steaks (page 126).

SAUTÉING AND STIR-FRYING

Sauté derives from the French word for *leap* or *jump,* which is what properly sautéed food tends to do in an open skillet. A very small amount of oil keeps vegetables, chicken, lean meat, and fish from sticking to the pan as they cook and seals in the moisture, ensuring that the food retains flavor and color. Small

amounts of wine, sherry, stock, or water will serve the same purpose and will save calories and fat. In the process of cooking, the alcohol in wine or sherry evaporates, leaving the flavor without the unwanted calories.

Sautéing at medium temperatures develops a wonderfully sweet flavor in most foods, especially those in the onion and garlic family. As with stir-frying, medium-heat sautéing can be done with very small amounts of butter, oil, or a combination of oil and wine. Since less fat is used than in frying, sautéed food should be stirred frequently to avoid sticking. Heat the pan until it is too hot to touch, then add the oil, butter (if used), or liquid. Immediately add the food to be sautéed and stir quickly to coat the food thoroughly. Add a tablespoon or so of water if the food starts to dry out during cooking. This process, which combines steaming and sautéing, is similar to stir-frying. It seals in the nutrients and preserves color in food.

Favored by Asian cooks, stir-frying employs high heat and a rapid stirring

A few basic tools enable you to use the most efficient healthy cooking techniques and also make working in the kitchen more enjoyable. Invest in the essentials: a wok, a steamer or two, a few good knives, and a blender or food processor.

19

The well-prepared, health-conscious cook keeps a stock on hand of whole grains, dried legumes, condiments and seasonings, and fresh vegetables.

ing soups, stews, grains, and beans. Lighter pans are best for quick-cooking such as sautéing and stir-frying. Stainless steel or enamel-coated cast iron are good choices for long-lasting cookware.

You'll also want a roasting pan with a rack, one or more steamers, and perhaps a wok for stir-frying (see page 19). You may want a grill or a ridged grilling pan for use on top of the stove. A stainless steel pressure cooker is convenient for cooking beans and other foods in a hurry. Because many of the recipes call for fresh lemon juice, a citrus juicer and strainer are handy items to have. You may also want a few tart pans and ceramic soufflé dishes.

Plan to have three good knives on hand: a paring knife, a serrated knife, and a chopping knife, such as a 6- or 8-inch cook's knife. Keep them sharp with your own sharpener or have them sharpened professionally every six months or so. (A sharp knife actually causes fewer kitchen accidents than a dull one because it has less tendency to slip.) Keep knives on a magnetized knife rack or in a knife block, where they won't rub edges or become dull or nicked.

A perforated spoon is helpful for lifting foods out of marinating and cooking liquids. A broad wok spatula makes stir-frying with a wok easier.

process that cooks food quickly and prevents it from sticking and burning. Small amounts of flavorful oils, such as Asian (dark) sesame or other healthy vegetable oils, can be used, or a combination of sherry, white wine, and mirin (a sweet rice wine). Woks or deep, rounded skillets are recommended for stir-frying because they conduct heat more evenly than flat-bottom pans. For more information see Wok and Stir-Fry Techniques (page 159).

EQUIPMENT AND INGREDIENTS FOR HEALTHY COOKING

Streamlined cooking does not require a great deal of expensive equipment or a costly collection of rare ingredients. A few well-chosen pieces of equipment and a reasonable stock of fresh foods, basic staples, and other healthful ingredients are all you really need.

If you like the cookware and other equipment you use, you'll find cooking more enjoyable. Durable cookware is the best choice. Heavyweight pots and pans are best for slow-cooking and simmer-

WHOLE FOODS

Whole foods are an essential part of healthy cooking. The term *whole* refers to foods that are unrefined, unprocessed (or are only minimally processed), and preferably fresh rather than canned, frozen, or packaged with preservatives. Whole foods include fresh vegetables and fruits, whole grains and legumes, fresh seafood, poultry and lean meats, low-fat or nonfat dairy products, soy products such as tofu, and a variety of wholesome condiments, natural sweeteners, and seasonings. Most whole foods are available in supermarkets, but you may need to visit a specialty food shop or natural food store to find some of them.

Whole Grains

Providing abundant protein and other nutrients, whole grains and minimally processed grain products are a standard ingredient in many of the entrées, soups, salads, and desserts in this book. Many whole grains require longer cooking times than refined grains, but the added nutritional benefits they provide are well worth the effort.

Barley cooks fairly quickly and is a nutritious ingredient of many soups and stews (see Hearty Beef and Barley Soup, page 50).

Brown rice comes in two main varieties: Long-grain brown rice, which cooks up into fluffy, separate grains, is better for salads and pilafs (see Minnesota Vegetable and Wild Rice Pilaf With Cashew Gravy on page 88); the short-grain variety is more sticky and better for croquettes and stir-fried dishes. *Rice flour* is finely ground rice.

Bulgur is cracked wheat that is briefly steamed and then dried. This simple process transforms it into a fast-cooking grain. It is fluffy and tasty, and often used in salads or vegetarian entrées (see Minted Bulgur Salad, page 68).

Cornmeal is the finely ground corn kernel. *Polenta* is a coarsely ground variation that is popular in Italian cuisine (see Polenta and Curried Vegetables, page 90).

Couscous, popular in the Middle East, tastes like nutty pasta. It cooks in 15 or 20 minutes, and is often served with curried lamb or vegetables (see Couscous With Mushrooms and Curry, page 109). Packaged instant couscous is also available at many markets.

Millet has a fluffy consistency and a nutty taste, especially when dry-roasted before steaming.

Rolled oats, made by steaming and crushing whole oats, are ideal in creamy soups, cobbler toppings, and cookies.

Whole wheat flour is available in two forms: Whole wheat pastry flour, made from a special type of wheat grown in the summer or spring, is essential for light and flaky pie crusts, pastries, and muffins. Whole wheat bread flour is a darker, richer flour made from red winter wheat; it contains more gluten (bread protein) than pastry flour and is used in yeast breads and pasta. For recipes in this book, use whole wheat bread flour except where pastry flour is specified. If whole wheat flour is not available, use unbleached flour.

Legumes

Black beans are favored in southwestern cooking; they go well with chiles and cilantro. Cook them with onion and garlic for the richest flavor (see Martinique Casserole on page 90).

Kidney beans are excellent ingredients for chili and soups. They have a rich taste and lend a dark red color to tomato-based dishes (see Vegetarian Chili on page 230).

Lentils and *split peas* are quick-cooking and contribute a rich flavor to soups and stews. They give a thick texture to soup (see Swiss Lentil Soup on page 50).

Lima beans marinate well in salads because they hold their shape even after cooking. They are also good for soups, puréed spreads, and dips because of their buttery flavor (see Hearty Lima Bean Soup on page 59).

Natural Sweeteners

Although refined sugars provide energy, they provide almost no nutrients. Some nutritionists feel that, aside from contributing to tooth decay, sugar consumption may be relatively harmless. Others insist that refined sugars may be damaging more than our teeth. Some studies suggest that an excess of sugar can place stress on the pancreas, causing it to produce excess insulin, which also promotes fat storage.

Although not all researchers agree on the potential dangers of eating sugar, virtually all agree that the average American eats far too much of it: Refined sugars account for one fifth of the average daily caloric intake in the U.S. If you're trying to tame a sweet tooth, stay away from artificially sweetened foods, since they can promote a craving for sugar.

Many nutritionists recommend using natural sweeteners instead of refined sugars in baking and cooking. A number of the recipes in this book substitute the natural sweeteners described below for refined sugars. You won't miss the sugar in recipes such as Compote of Winter Fruits in Red Wine (see page 204) and Apple Strudel (see page 215).

Date sugar, made from finely ground dried dates, is a good substitute for brown sugar in pastries and pies. Because date sugar does not dissolve well in liquids, it should not be used in custards and soufflés but rather in crusts and cobbler toppings where its texture is an asset (see Tangy Lemon Custard Tart, page 220).

Honey is used instead of white sugar in many recipes in this book because of its flavor and aroma. Light-colored honeys, such as clover and wildflower, are the most versatile and readily available (see Carob Cheesecake, page 214).

Maple syrup is delicious in desserts that feature fresh fruit, such as Cranberry Turnovers With Maple Glaze, page 211. Store maple syrup in the refrigerator; otherwise it may ferment.

For more information, see Tips On Substituting Unrefined Sweeteners (page 208).

Healthy Condiments and Seasonings

A good selection of seasonings and condiments is important in healthy cooking. The following seasonings can add valuable nutrients and a variety of flavors:

Flavored vinegars (apple cider, raspberry, rice, balsamic, wine, and herbal vinegars) are delicious ways to broaden your seasoning repertoire. Apple cider is a good all-purpose vinegar; raspberry lends a sweet flavor and fragrance to foods; rice is recommended for Asian cooking; balsamic and wine vinegars add robust flavor; and delicate herbal vinegars are good additions to marinades and to salad dressings used over tender, fresh ingredients.

Herbal salt substitutes can greatly reduce your sodium intake while enhancing flavor. Use in the same amount as iodized salt when substituting in a recipe.

Low-sodium soy sauce and *tamari* offer other ways to decrease sodium intake. These Japanese soy products add rich flavor to stir-fries (see Broccoli, Mushroom, and Water Chestnut Stir-Fry With Noodles on page 100).

Mirin is a sweet rice wine that can enhance Asian-style sauces and sautés; *dry sherry* is also used in many Asian recipes. The alcohol evaporates during cooking, leaving a sweet, caramel flavor (see Szechwan Sautéed Tofu and Vegetables, page 98).

Miso is a paste made from fermented soybeans or a mixture of fermented soybeans and grains such as rice or barley. It is less salty than soy sauce, with a mild flavor that makes a wonderful base for soups and salad dressings (see Kombu Miso Soup on page 53).

Mustards, both stone-ground and Dijon, are good for hearty salad dressings (see Marinade for Bean Salads on page 83).

Vegetable oils—especially monounsaturated oils such as canola, sesame, and olive—are preferable to saturated fats such as lard or polyunsaturated fats such as cottonseed oil. Use canola or olive oil for sautéing and salad dressings. Asian (dark) sesame oil is preferred for stir-frying, and light sesame oil for Asian-style marinades or salad dressings. Olive oil, especially the first pressing, called extra virgin, is ideal for salads and Italian dishes (see Pasta With Walnut-Garlic Sauce on page 90).

Low-Fat Dairy Products and Protein Sources

Reducing consumption of high-fat protein foods, such as high-fat dairy products and fatty meats, is a step toward better health and reduced risk of heart disease. The following are good low-fat protein sources:

Low-fat cheeses (low-fat ricotta, mozzarella, farmer, and other cheeses) have a place in the healthy cook's kitchen. For tips on low-fat dairy substitutions, see Tips on Dairy Products—Cutting Fat, Not Flavor (page 225).

Nonfat or low-fat yogurt, a good substitute for sour cream, may be used in many salad dressings and creamy, low-fat sauces (see Green Goddess Dressing on page 83).

Tofu is a white, cheeselike substance made from soy milk. In Asian cooking it is often a prime protein source. Soft or silken tofus blend well into sauces and dressings; firm varieties are used in stir-fries (see Szechwan Sautéed Tofu and Vegetables, page 98). Similar in nature to tofu, *tempeh* is rich in vitamin B_{12} and a good source of protein. It has more texture than tofu, and is made from soybeans inoculated with a culture similar to yogurt culture or the yeast that is used in making beer (see Tempeh Olive Spread on page 42).

CHANGING YOUR DAILY MEAL PATTERNS

Scientific studies have shown the benefits of regular, moderately sized meals as opposed to the trend in the United States of no breakfast (or very little), rushed lunches, big dinners, and late-night snacks. Many people neglect to properly fuel their systems at peak energy hours—7:00 a.m. to 3:00 p.m.—and overload their bodies just as they are winding down for sleep. People who seem to gain weight easily often follow this daily meal pattern.

The body handles food best in moderate amounts and early in the day. Food metabolizes best when the body is at its peak activity level. The old adage, "Eat like a king for breakfast, a queen for lunch, and a pauper for dinner," is still true.

Breakfast

Breakfast is still the most important meal of the day, yet more people skip breakfast than any other meal. Most nutritional experts recommend a protein-based breakfast that includes a good source of complex carbohydrates.

Breakfast is a peak metabolic time, when the body is most prepared to utilize protein to rebuild cells and stabilize blood sugar levels, and to use carbohydrates to provide energy. Accompany

the protein with a source of vitamin C, such as fresh juice or fruit, and a whole-grain carbohydrate for energy. Variations in menus are limitless: Try low-fat cottage cheese with Orange-Date Muffins (see page 197) or Tempeh Olive Spread (see page 42) and a selection of fresh vegetable sticks for a quick breakfast. For special occasions, indulge in Eggs à la Suisse (see page 108) or French Buckwheat Crêpes With Mushrooms and Herbs (see page 88).

Lunch

A nutritious lunch should supply you with a substantial portion of your protein intake for the day and also give you an ample serving of vitamins, minerals, and fiber. Although many people eat out at lunch, with a bit of planning it's easy to prepare a homemade lunch that fits the streamlined approach.

Salads such as Tabbouleh (see page 66) and soups such as Hearty Beef and Barley Soup (page 50) make great lunch fare. Or you can warm up a previously prepared entrée such as Fresh Trout Florentine (see page 129) or Salmon and Julienned Vegetable Sauté (see page 128).

Dinner

Although the evening meal is traditionally the time for family gatherings or socializing, it is also the time when the metabolic processes of the body begin to slow down, so you should eat less. If you don't eat lightly at dinner, your body may become tired from working throughout the night to digest a heavy meal rather than resting as it should. When you enjoy a light but nutritious dinner, you will sleep better and wake up hungry. Many nutritionists recommend eating a combination of complex carbohydrates and a lean protein source for the dinner meal, as in Baked Salmon Provençale (see photo on page 10 and recipe on page 129).

Learn to be guided by your body's needs for food and rest. Eat when you need energy, not when your body is winding down. Eventually you will find your own balance in eating.

T IPS

...ON PREPARING MAKE-AHEAD MEALS

The secret of efficient healthy cooking is doing at least part of the preparation when you have the most time.

☐ When you come home from shopping, take the time to wash and prep vegetables. Wash lettuce, dry, and store in meal-sized portions for fast salads. Wash and trim beets and carrots; trim broccoli stems, asparagus, and bok choy; peel onions and trim green onions; and store all in lock-top plastic bags or containers.

☐ Wash, dry, and mince fresh parsley; store some in the refrigerator and some in the freezer. Juice lemons and freeze some juice in ice cube trays; drop frozen cubes into a bag—each cube equals about 2 tablespoons of juice—and store in the freezer.

☐ Choose several dishes that will form the basis for quick meals all week and assemble them up to the point when they should be cooked. Examples of easy make-ahead recipes are Roasted Chicken With Rosemary and Garlic (see page 148) and Easy Beef Fajitas (shown above; see recipe on page 166). Prepare a soup, such as Hearty Lima Bean Soup (see page 50), and a couple of lunch spreads, such as Tempeh Olive Spread (see page 42) and Cream Cheese and Garlic Dip (see page 26).

☐ Prepare a selection of whole grains or beans for meals during the week. Wash them well, then examine for debris. Place each type of grain or bean in a separate bowl and cover with water. Refrigerate if the temperature is warm. Soaking overnight reduces cooking time by one third. Cook grains or beans when you have an extra hour at home, and freeze or refrigerate.

☐ Organize prepared foods in the refrigerator according to the day you will be serving them: The appetizer and assembled entrée for the Friday dinner party get placed at the back of one shelf; lunch items occupy another.

☐ Start a soup stock (see page 51 for easy directions) while you prep other foods. Let the stock cool, then freeze in double lock-top plastic bags or in 2-cup containers. Good stocks form the basis for the best soups. You can also use them for poaching fish or chicken, steaming or stir-frying vegetables, and adding flavor to various sauces.

☐ Take note of what you can accomplish by planning ahead: You can have the basics for several easy meals. Lunches will be faster with spreads ready to make into sandwiches, and hearty salads will take only a minute to assemble. An impromptu poached fish dinner can be made by defrosting a few cubes of lemon juice, some ginger and parsley, and a fillet of fish. Entrées can be waiting in the refrigerator or freezer for the evenings when you might not feel like cooking from scratch. Even entertaining will be easier with an appetizer or entrée that's prepared ahead.

Elegant, nutritious appetizers frequently include fresh garden vegetables and whole grain breads and crackers.

APPETIZERS & HORS D'OEUVRES

The recipes in this chapter will serve triple duty in your menu planning: as appetizers, light meals, and healthy snacks. Pita Quesadillas and other appetizers with an international flair (see pages 29–31) as well as Mustard Chicken Wings and other crowd pleasers (see pages 32–35) are included alongside menus for a Holiday Hors d'Oeuvre Party (see page 44) and Super Bowl Grazing Party (see page 33). Tips on creating delicious, reduced-fat versions of your favorite dips (see page 43) provide a special bonus.

SAVORY APPETIZERS

Perfect for on-the-spot entertaining, these easy, yet elegant, appetizers pave the way for heartier main course fare. Many can be made ahead, frozen, and reheated just before serving. Rely on seasonally ripe produce for the best nutritional value and flavor, especially in recipes that call for fresh herbs or tomatoes.

STUFFED ARTICHOKE BOTTOMS

Artichokes are a delicious source of calcium, fiber, and vitamin C. In this recipe, the tang of marinated artichokes (usually packaged in jars) is highlighted by a creamy blue cheese filling. Make a trayful ahead of time, refrigerate after covering tightly with plastic wrap, and let sit at room temperature about 30 minutes before serving. For an exotic display, line a flat basket with banana leaves (available from most florists) and alternate Stuffed Artichoke Bottoms with Stuffed Snow Peas (see page 28).

        2 ounces reduced-fat cream
           cheese
        2 tablespoons crumbled blue
           cheese
        1 tablespoon reduced-fat
           mayonnaise
       12 marinated artichoke bottoms
           Paprika, for garnish

In a small bowl, mix together cheeses and mayonnaise. Spoon cheese mixture into artichoke bottoms and garnish with a dusting of paprika. Serve at room temperature.

Makes 1 dozen stuffed artichoke bottoms, 12 servings.

> *Preparation time:* 15 minutes
> *Per serving:* calcium 50 mg, calories 61, carbohydrates 10 g, cholesterol 5 mg, fat 2 g, fiber 5 g, protein 4 g, sodium 125 mg

MARINATED GOAT CHEESE

This savory appetizer originates in the antipasto platters of northern Italy. The fragrant wedges of marinated goat cheese can be served on a bed of lettuce and radicchio or can be spread on sourdough French bread or crisp rye crackers. The green olive oil used in this recipe is made from unripe olives; it can be found in most supermarkets.

       10 cloves garlic, thinly sliced
      1/3 cup extra virgin olive oil
      1/4 cup green olive oil
      1/4 cup imported Niçoise or Greek
           olives
           Pinch of freshly ground black
           pepper
        2 sprigs fresh thyme or
           1 teaspoon dried thyme
        2 sprigs fresh oregano or
           1 teaspoon dried oregano
        2 sprigs fresh tarragon or
           1 teaspoon dried tarragon
      1/2 pound goat cheese
           Lettuce leaves or rye crackers,
           for lining platter
           Olives, whole, peeled garlic
           cloves, or sprigs of fresh herbs,
           for garnish

1. In a heavy skillet over medium heat, sauté garlic slices in olive oils until slightly golden. Remove skillet from heat.

2. Add olives, pepper, thyme, oregano, and tarragon to oil.

3. Cut goat cheese into 1 inch pieces. Lay pieces in a flat-bottomed casserole. Pour oil mixture over cheese and cover with plastic wrap. Let marinate for 24 to 48 hours in the refrigerator before serving.

4. To serve, arrange cheese on lettuce. Garnish with olives, garlic, or herb sprigs.

Makes 16 servings.

> *Preparation time:* 15 minutes
> *Marinating time:* 24 to 48 hours
> *Per serving:* calcium 148 mg, calories 142, carbohydrates 2 g, cholesterol 15 mg, fat 13 g, fiber .2 g, protein 5 g, sodium 68 mg

CREAM CHEESE AND GARLIC DIP WITH PITA TOASTS

This creamy dip goes as well with a platter of crudités as with these crunchy pita toasts (see page 40). It can be made up to six weeks ahead of time and frozen, or will keep refrigerated for up to five days. Serve the dip in a hollowed-out red or green bell pepper for an elegant presentation.

        8 ounces reduced-fat cream
           cheese
        2 tablespoons reduced-fat
           mayonnaise
           Juice of 1/2 lemon
        3 large cloves garlic, pressed
      1/4 small onion, finely minced
        1 teaspoon dried dill
        1 teaspoon herbal salt substitute
           Hot-pepper sauce, to taste
        1 red bell pepper

Pita Toasts

        3 large rounds whole wheat pita
           bread
        1 teaspoon garlic powder

In a small bowl, mix together cream cheese, mayonnaise, lemon juice, garlic, onion, dill, and salt substitute. Add hot-pepper sauce to taste. Cut top off bell pepper and remove seeds. Spoon dip into hollowed-out bell pepper, cover with plastic wrap, and chill while you make the pita toasts.

Serves 12.

Pita Toasts Cut each round of pita bread into 4 equal wedges. Toast until crisp, then open each wedge and dust inside lightly with garlic powder. Then arrange on a platter with dip.

Makes 12 wedges.

> *Preparation time:* 10 minutes (dip); 10 minutes (Pita Toasts)
> *Chilling time:* 10 minutes
> *Per serving:* calcium 24 mg, calories 98, carbohydrates 11 g, cholesterol 15 mg, fat 5 g, fiber 1 g, protein 4 g, sodium 185 mg

FILO CHEESE PASTRIES

These savory pastries are filled with feta and low-fat ricotta cheeses, flavored with garlic and dill, and baked until lightly browned (see How to Prepare Filo, page 212). Made up to three days ahead of time, they can be frozen until ready to bake and serve.

Oil, for coating muffin tins
3/4 *cup low-fat ricotta cheese*
1/4 *cup low-fat cottage cheese*
1/2 *cup crumbled feta cheese*
1/4 *cup grated low-fat mozzarella cheese*
1 *egg*
2 *tablespoons dried dill*
1/4 *cup finely minced parsley*
1/2 *teaspoon pressed garlic*
8 *sheets filo dough*
4 *tablespoons plus 1 teaspoon unsalted butter, melted*

1. Preheat oven to 375° F. Lightly oil muffin tin. In blender or food processor, purée cheeses. Add egg and blend mixture well.

2. By hand, stir dill, parsley, and garlic into cheeses. Spoon mixture into a bowl and cover with plastic wrap. Refrigerate while proceeding with next steps.

3. Stack sheets of filo dough on a clean, dry surface. Brush each sheet with 1 teaspoon melted butter, and lay buttered sheets one on top of another. Cut piled sheets into 24 squares of 2 1/2 inches each.

4. Press squares into muffin tin cups, and spoon 1 tablespoon cheese filling into each. Fold edges of filo over filling and lightly brush top of each filo pastry with remaining butter.

5. Bake for 12 to 15 minutes, watching carefully so that pastries do not burn. Remove from tins, and let them cool slightly before serving.

Makes 2 dozen pastries, 24 servings.

Preparation time: 40 minutes
Baking time: 15 minutes
Per serving: calcium 59 mg, calories 64, carbohydrates 4 g, cholesterol 20 mg, fat 4 g, fiber .1 g, protein 3 g, sodium 89 mg

BASICS

HEALTHY SNACKING

Healthy menu plans can include snacks that have high nutritional value. The trick to making healthy snacks is organization—stocking up on nutritious, quick-to-prepare foods for busy times. For example, the Cream Cheese and Garlic Dip With Pita Toasts (shown above) can be prepared in 20 minutes. The flexibility of snacking fits the pace of contemporary life, providing a relaxing break during busy schedules.

Learn to choose foods for snacking that are high in nutrient density (see page 16) and to plan ahead to control impulse eating of junk foods.

Plan snacks to complement regular meals so that your total food intake provides required nutrients. If you know that you may miss lunch, for example, prepare snacks that will carry you through the day and provide adequate nutrients. A good way to avoid after-work overeating is to look for foods that are high in nutrients and low in empty calories. Some examples:

Fresh fruits and vegetables
Spread low-fat cottage cheese on apple slices; trim a handful of raw vegetable sticks and dip into Cream Cheese and Garlic Dip (see page 26); spread low-fat ricotta cheese on half a banana and sprinkle with raisins.

Toasted rye or wheat crackers
Cover with Salmon Spread (see page 38) and sprinkle with minced parsley or red onion.

Pita pizzas Top a split pita round with 1 or 2 tablespoons pizza sauce (see Basic Pizza Sauce, page 188) and top with sliced red or green bell pepper and grated low-fat mozzarella cheese. Broil until bubbly.

Hors d'oeuvres such as Stuffed Snow Peas and Stuffed Artichoke Bottoms (see page 26) are sure to be a hit at your next party. Combining tiny bay shrimp and reduced-fat cheeses, these tidbits are low in fat and cholesterol, high in fiber and flavor.

STUFFED SNOW PEAS

These delicate appetizers, very popular at parties, are made with a creamy blend of low-fat ricotta cheese, garlic, and dill. The low-fat cheese provides calcium, the shrimp is an excellent source of protein, and the fresh peas add fiber and vitamins. This is a very elegant and healthy appetizer, especially when combined on a platter with Stuffed Artichoke Bottoms (see page 26).

> 32 large snow peas
> 1 cup low-fat ricotta cheese
> 1 tablespoon dried dill
> 2 cloves garlic, pressed
> 3 tablespoons grated Parmesan cheese
> 32 cooked bay shrimp
> 32 sprigs (1 in. long) fresh dill

1. In a large stockpot bring 1 quart of water to a boil. Blanch snow peas by dropping in boiling water and cooking until they turn bright green (about 30 seconds), then rinsing in very cold water. Cut ends off snow peas, slit them open along one edge, and set aside.

2. In a small bowl mix together ricotta, dill, garlic, and Parmesan. Open slit side of each snow pea and fill cavity with ricotta mixture.

3. Garnish each stuffed snow pea with a bay shrimp and a tiny sprig of dill. Serve chilled or at room temperature.

Makes 32 snow peas, approximately 16 servings.

Preparation time: 45 minutes
Chilling time (optional): 30 minutes
Per serving: calcium 304 mg, calories 188, carbohydrates 26 g, cholesterol 44 mg, fat 3 g, fiber 8 g, protein 8 g, sodium 806 mg

INTERNATIONAL APPETIZERS

These international dishes are especially suited for entertaining. Transport guests to foreign ports by creating a theme buffet around the various countries represented by the hors d'oeuvres.

PITA QUESADILLAS

A favorite Mexican appetizer, these quesadillas (pronounced kay-suh-DEE-yuhs) are easy to make and use whole wheat pita bread for the base. Wear rubber gloves to peel and seed the fresh chiles (the chile oils can sting sensitive skin).

- ½ cup grated low-fat mozzarella or Monterey jack cheese
- 3 small jalapeño chiles, seeded and diced
- 2 tablespoons chopped cilantro
- ¼ teaspoon ground cumin
- 2 tablespoons pimiento, drained and diced
- 2 large whole wheat pita breads

1. In a small bowl combine grated cheese, diced chile, cilantro, cumin, and pimiento.

2. With a sharp knife slice open pita breads along edges, making 4 thin rounds of bread. Lay, cut side up, on a parchment-covered baking sheet and sprinkle with cheese mixture.

3. Broil until bubbly. Cut each pita into 4 wedges. Serve hot.

Makes 16 wedges, 8 servings.

Preparation time: 20 minutes
Broiling time: 5 minutes
Per serving: calcium 64 mg, calories 72, carbohydrates 11 g, cholesterol 4 mg, fat 2 g, fiber 2 g, protein 4 g, sodium 125 mg

ITALIAN ZUCCHINI PIZZAS

These "kid-sized" pizzas with a vegetable base are very easy to make and are great as snacks. The pizzas may be served as is or on thin crackers.

- 2 thick zucchini (see Note)
- 1 cup Chunky Tomato Sauce With Fresh Basil (see page 183)
- ½ cup thinly sliced large mushrooms
- ¼ cup grated Parmesan or Romano cheese

1. Preheat oven to 200° F. Cut zucchini into round slices about ⅛ inch thick. Place on a parchment-lined baking sheet and bake until soft and moist but not brown (about 20 minutes).

2. Place 1 teaspoon sauce in center of each round, and then top with 1 slice mushroom and ½ teaspoon grated cheese.

3. Broil pizzas until lightly browned and bubbly. Serve hot.

Makes 16 small pizzas, 8 servings.

Note Rounds of eggplant may be substituted for zucchini.

Preparation time: 15 minutes
Cooking time: 25 minutes
Per serving: calcium 40 mg, calories 40, carbohydrates 4 g, cholesterol 2 mg, fat 1 g, fiber 1 g, protein 2 g, sodium 75 mg

MARINATED MUSHROOM AND CHICK-PEA APPETIZER

This dish can be served along with other marinated vegetables. In Italian cookery, an antipasto can consist of any colorful vegetable, cooked or raw, and is usually presented before the pasta course. Serve your antipasto with crusty French bread.

- 2 cups button mushrooms, whole
- 2 cups chick-peas, cooked and drained
- 2 tablespoons capers
- 2 tablespoons minced parsley
- 2 tablespoons minced red onion
- 2 tablespoons white wine vinegar
- ⅓ cup olive oil
- 1 garlic clove, minced
- 1 teaspoon Dijon mustard
- ½ teaspoon honey
  Freshly ground black pepper, to taste
  Lettuce leaves or spinach leaves

1. Place mushrooms in one bowl and chick-peas and capers in another. Combine parsley, red onion, vinegar, and half of the oil; pour over chick-peas and capers. Mix remaining oil, garlic, mustard, honey, and pepper; pour over mushrooms.

2. Let both mixtures marinate for 6 to 8 hours.

3. Arrange a small serving of each on a leaf of lettuce or spinach. Mix remaining marinades together and spoon over chick-pea antipasto.

Serves 8.

Preparation time: 15 minutes
Marinating time: 6 to 8 hours
Per serving: calcium 38 mg, calories 158, carbohydrates 14 g, cholesterol 0 mg, fat 10 g, fiber .5 g, protein 4 g, sodium 45 mg

ARMENIAN MEATBALLS

This recipe gets its Armenian flavor from the cumin. The meatballs are easy to make ahead and will freeze well. This tasty hors d'oeuvre can be served in an elegant fondue pot set over a hot plate or candle warmer. Provide guests with fondue forks or toothpicks.

> 2 slices whole wheat bread
> 1 pound extra lean ground beef or lamb
> 1 clove garlic, minced
> 1 teaspoon ground cumin
> Freshly ground black pepper, to taste
> 1½ cups peeled and chopped plum tomatoes
> ¾ cup tomato sauce

1. Preheat oven to 350° F. Soften bread in tap water and then squeeze out excess liquid (to make the bread absorb more flavor than if used dry). In a large mixing bowl, mash together bread, beef, garlic, and cumin. Add black pepper, if desired.

2. Form into 1-inch-diameter meatballs and place in lightly oiled or nonstick skillet over medium heat.

3. Fry lightly on all sides until brown, pouring off any fat that develops. Transfer meatballs to an electric slow cooker or baking dish.

4. Blend tomatoes and tomato sauce and pour over meatballs. Bake for 1 hour (or cook in an electric slow cooker over high heat for 2 hours). Serve hot with the sauce.

Makes 2 dozen meatballs, 12 servings.

Preparation time: 45 minutes
Cooking time: 75 minutes
Per serving: calcium 13 mg, calories 116, carbohydrates 6 g, cholesterol 26 mg, fat 7 g, fiber 1 g, protein 8 g, sodium 157 mg

SUNOMONO

A delicious Japanese salad, often served in gourmet sushi bars, sunomono is traditionally a combination of grated or thinly sliced vegetables that have been marinated in a lemon-vinegar sauce. It is often served before tempura to freshen the palate. Serve in lettuce cups or in small, shallow bowls. This dish makes a light and refreshing first course for a stir-fry dinner.

> 1 cup shrimp meat
> 7 tablespoons rice vinegar
> 1 tablespoon lemon juice
> 1 tablespoon Asian sesame oil
> 5 tablespoons honey
> Pinch of salt or herbal salt substitute
> 1½ large cucumbers, peeled, seeded, and coarsely grated
> 2 green onions, minced
> ¼ cup finely shredded green cabbage

Mix all ingredients in a bowl and let marinate 2 hours before serving. Serve slightly chilled.

Serves 8.

Preparation time: 15 minutes
Marinating time: 2 hours
Per serving: calcium 50 mg, calories 107, carbohydrates 17 g, cholesterol 58 mg, fat 2 g, fiber 2 g, protein 8 g, sodium 91 mg

GINGERED MELON

Can you imagine a more refreshing appetizer? First simmered with ginger, then seasoned with pepper, these chilled melon slices make a particularly appealing partner to Asian-inspired hors d'oeuvres. Serve them at the peak of season when melons are ripest.

> 1 large or 2 small cantaloupe or honeydew melons, barely ripe
> 2 tablespoons minced crystallized ginger
> 2 tablespoons minced fresh ginger
> ½ cup rice wine
> Pinch sugar
> Pinch salt
> Half a cinnamon stick
> White pepper
> Lemon juice

1. Peel the melons; cut horizontally into six 1-inch-thick rings; remove seeds. Cut each melon ring into thirds.

2. In a small saucepan combine 1 tablespoon crystallized ginger, the fresh ginger, rice wine, sugar, salt, and cinnamon stick. Bring to a simmer. Add melon slices and simmer slowly for 1 to 2 minutes, depending on ripeness. (Less ripe melons will need to cook the longest.) Remove from heat and allow melons to cool in liquid.

3. Remove melons and strain liquid through a fine sieve. In a small saucepan over high heat, reduce liquid until syrupy. Pour over melons, then chill. To serve, season melons with a grinding of white pepper and a squeeze of lemon juice. Garnish with remaining crystallized ginger.

Makes 18 slices, 9 servings.

Preparation time: 20 minutes
Cooking time: 10 minutes
Per serving: calcium 16 mg, calories 48, carbohydrates 6 g, cholesterol 2 mg, fat 0 g, fiber 1 g, protein 1 g, sodium 6 mg

STUFFED CHILES

A favorite from the American Southwest, this recipe calls for fresh chiles; if they are unavailable in your area, use canned chiles or pimientos instead. Use a small paring knife to slit chiles and remove seeds and membrane. These chiles are great served with a mug of sangria and a platter of low-fat tortilla chips.

  12 *fresh Anaheim chiles (also known as California chiles)*
   1 *teaspoon oil, for baking dish*
  ¼ *cup dry sherry*
   1 *teaspoon olive oil*
  ½ *cup minced yellow onion*
  ½ *cup minced mushroom caps*
   1 *bunch spinach, stemmed and chopped*
  ½ *cup grated low-fat mozzarella cheese*
   1 *cup farmer cheese*
   2 *cups rye bread crumbs, coarsely ground*
  ½ *teaspoon ground cumin*
  ¼ *teaspoon cayenne pepper*
     Salt or herbal salt substitute, to taste

1. Preheat oven to 400° F. Leaving stems on chiles, slit lengthwise and remove seeds and white membrane (see Note). Set, cut side up, in lightly oiled baking dish.

2. In a medium skillet heat sherry and olive oil until mixture is simmering. Stir in onion and cook over medium-high heat. Keep stirring until onion begins to brown slightly. Add mushrooms and cover; lower heat and cook until mushrooms weep moisture. (Add small amount of water if necessary to prevent mushrooms from sticking.) Remove cover and add spinach. Cover again and cook until wilted (about 3 minutes).

3. Remove from heat and add cheeses, bread crumbs, cumin, cayenne, and salt; mix well. Stuff chiles with mushroom mixture.

4. Bake until chiles are softened and cheeses have melted (about 30 minutes). Serve hot.

Makes 12 chiles, 12 servings.

Note When you are cutting chiles, it is a good safety precaution to wear rubber gloves. The chiles' pungent oils can sting fingers and then be transferred to eyes. Gloves also protect fingers from the sharp blade of the paring knife.

Preparation time: 45 minutes
Cooking time: 45 minutes
Per serving: calcium 86 mg, calories: 145, carbohydrates 26 g, cholesterol 3 mg, fat 3 g, fiber 4 g, protein 6 g, sodium 205 mg

---

Mild Anaheim chiles are baked and stuffed with a savory sauté of diced mushroom, onion, spinach, and cheese. For a tasty prelude to a southwestern dinner, serve Stuffed Chiles with a mug of sangria.

PARTY PLEASERS

Here are several favorites for parties. They will become regulars in your entertaining repertoire because of their easy preparation.

STUFFED BROILED MUSHROOMS

Large white-capped mushrooms work best for this recipe.

- 12 large mushrooms
- 1 teaspoon olive oil
- 1 small onion, finely chopped
- 1 cup whole wheat bread crumbs, finely ground
- ¼ cup minced almonds
- 1 tablespoon dry sherry
- ¼ teaspoon marjoram
  Freshly ground black pepper, to taste (optional)

1. Preheat broiler. Remove stems from mushrooms by wiggling at base (stems should pop out). Chop stems finely and set aside.

2. Place caps with open side down on baking sheet and broil for 2 minutes or until caps become wrinkled and begin to weep moisture. Let cool. Keep broiler hot.

3. Heat oil in skillet and sauté onion until soft, then add the chopped mushroom stems. Cook until mushrooms begin to weep moisture (about 8 minutes). Add bread crumbs, almonds, sherry, marjoram, and cook 1 minute longer.

4. Stuff bread crumb filling into mushroom caps and place filled side up on baking sheet. Broil until light brown. Sprinkle with black pepper, if desired. Serve hot.

Makes 12 stuffed mushrooms, 12 servings.

> *Preparation time:* 20 minutes
> *Cooking time:* 15 minutes
> *Per serving:* calcium 18 mg, calories 64, carbohydrates 8 g, cholesterol 0 mg, fat 3 g, fiber 1 g, protein 2 g, sodium 80 mg

FILO PASTRIES WITH SMOKED TURKEY AND MUSHROOMS

See pages 212 and 219 for directions on preparing filo and forming it into shapes.

- 1 cup minced mushrooms
- 2 cloves garlic, minced
- ¼ cup minced onion
- ¼ cup dry sherry
- 1 teaspoon olive oil
- 3 tablespoons chopped parsley
- ½ cup crumbled feta cheese
- ¼ cup grated low-fat mozzarella cheese
- ¼ teaspoon dried oregano
- ¼ teaspoon dried thyme
- ¼ pound finely minced smoked turkey
- 15 sheets filo dough
- ⅓ cup unsalted butter, melted

1. In a large skillet over medium-high heat, sauté mushrooms, garlic, and onion in sherry and olive oil until soft. Add parsley, feta, mozzarella, oregano, thyme, and turkey. Remove from heat.

2. Preheat oven to 350° F. Lightly oil two 9- by 12-inch baking sheets.

3. Lay filo dough on a clean, dry surface. Cut each sheet in half width-wise to make 30 smaller sheets. Stack them evenly on top of each other, and cover with a piece of plastic wrap and a slightly dampened dish towel as you do the next step.

4. Butter 1 sheet and cut into 3 long strips. Lay the 3 strips on top of each other. Place about 2 tablespoons of filling in the lower right section near the edge. Fold bottom right corner of filo over filling to meet left edge, creating a small triangle. Continue folding pastry, as you would a flag, until you reach the top. You will end up with a triangle-shaped pastry.

5. Lightly butter top of filled triangle and place on prepared baking sheet. Repeat process until all the filling has been used.

6. Bake pastries until golden (20 minutes). Serve warm.

Makes 30 pastries, 30 servings.

> *Preparation time:* 35 minutes
> *Cooking time:* 35 minutes
> *Per serving:* calcium 30 mg, calories 72, carbohydrates 8 g, cholesterol 13 mg, fat 5 g, fiber .1 g, protein 4 g, sodium 130 mg

MUSTARD CHICKEN WINGS

These chicken wings are brushed with a sweet and spicy mixture of cayenne pepper, mustard, garlic, and date sugar (ground, dried dates), and are baked to a crunch.

- 12 chicken wings
  Freshly ground black pepper, to taste
- 1 tablespoon date sugar or honey
  Cayenne pepper, to taste
- 1 clove garlic, finely minced
- 2 teaspoons Dijon mustard
  Whole wheat bread crumbs, very finely ground
  Oil, for coating baking sheet

1. Preheat oven to 400° F. Remove as much skin as possible from wings. Sprinkle chicken with black pepper.

2. Combine date sugar, cayenne, garlic, and mustard. Brush mixture onto chicken, coating both sides lightly and evenly. Then dip chicken in bread crumbs.

3. Place on a lightly oiled baking sheet and bake until light brown (about 30 minutes). Serve hot.

Makes 12 chicken wings, 12 servings.

> *Preparation time:* 20 minutes
> *Baking time:* 30 minutes
> *Per serving:* calcium 6 mg, calories 54, carbohydrates 2 g, cholesterol 21 mg, fat 2 g, fiber 0 g, protein 8 g, sodium 41 mg

CHERRY TOMATOES STUFFED WITH RICOTTA

This recipe has become a popular one at outdoor parties and weddings. The stuffed tomatoes are beautiful to serve, and, in small quantity, are easy to make. When buying cherry tomatoes, look for fully ripened, red tomatoes if you are planning to make this recipe immediately, or green ones if you are planning to make it later. Tomatoes will ripen quickly at room temperature. After ripening, tomatoes should be kept at 50° F or lower.

You can prepare the filling and hollow out the cherry tomatoes ahead of time (and keep them wrapped in plastic in the refrigerator), but stuff them just before serving. Once filled with the cheese mixture, they lose their freshness within a few hours.

24 cherry tomatoes
1/3 cup low-fat ricotta cheese
2 tablespoons finely grated Parmesan cheese
2 tablespoons minced parsley
1 tablespoon minced garlic

1. With a sharp knife, cut off the stem and a "cap" from each cherry tomato and reserve. Using the small end of a melon baller, scoop out the pulp from the tomato. Save pulp for another use.

2. In a small bowl, combine cheeses, parsley, and garlic. Spoon some of the mixture, approximately 1 to 2 teaspoons, into each tomato. Place cap on top. Serve slightly chilled on a bed of greens.

Makes 24 stuffed tomatoes, 12 servings.

Preparation time: 30 minutes
Per serving: calcium 59 mg, calories 92, carbohydrates 18 g, cholesterol 3 mg, fat 2 g, fiber 4 g, protein 4 g, sodium 60 mg

SAVORY NUT BALLS

Made with a combination of ground nuts and seeds, these savory little appetizers can be made ahead and frozen. They are a great party hors d'oeuvre.

3/4 cup walnuts, finely ground
1/2 cup sunflower seeds, finely ground
1/2 cup cashews, finely ground
1/4 cup almonds, finely ground
1 small onion, coarsely grated
2 eggs, beaten
3/4 cup whole wheat bread crumbs, finely ground
1 cup cooked long-grain brown rice
1 tablespoon low-sodium soy sauce or tamari
1 teaspoon caraway seeds, ground
1/2 teaspoon poultry seasoning
2 tablespoons chopped fresh basil leaves or 1 tablespoon dried basil
1 cup alfalfa sprouts, chopped
Oil, for coating baking sheet
Stone-ground or Dijon mustard, for dipping

1. Preheat oven to 350° F. Mix together all ingredients except oil and mustard and form into 1-inch balls.

2. Place on a lightly oiled baking sheet and bake until light brown and crunchy (about 20 minutes). Serve warm with mustard.

Makes forty-eight 1-inch balls, 24 servings.

Preparation time: 35 minutes
Baking time: 20 minutes
Per serving: calcium 33 mg, calories 149, carbohydrates 11 g, cholesterol 27 mg, fat 10 g, fiber 2 g, protein 6 g, sodium 116 mg

MENU

SUPER BOWL GRAZING PARTY

Baked Artichoke Savories

Party Port and Cheddar Spread

Curried Stuffed Eggs

Hearty Beef and Barley Soup (see page 50)

Tossed Green Salad

Green Goddess Dressing (see page 83)

Apple-Apricot Pastries (see page 213)

Spiced Cider

The grazing party is ideal for a wintry Super Bowl Sunday. Various dishes are introduced at intervals throughout the game; by the end of the party, guests have eaten almost a full meal, but in stages. Start the pregame show with a platter of appetizers. At halftime, bring out the Hearty Beef and Barley Soup and a tossed green salad with Green Goddess Dressing. For postgame celebration (or condolences), pass around a plate of Apple-Apricot Pastries and mugs of hot cider spiked with cinnamon and vanilla. Menu serves twelve.

BAKED ARTICHOKE SAVORIES

Guests will devour these rich-tasting, melt-in-your-mouth pastries, so make plenty. Use marinated artichokes for the best flavor, and reduced-fat cheeses for the best nutritional value. This recipe can be made up to three weeks ahead of time and frozen until ready to bake and serve.

   2 *tablespoons chopped onion*
   1 *teaspoon pressed garlic*
 ⅓ *cup dry sherry*
   3 *egg whites*
   1 *whole egg*
 ¼ *cup whole wheat bread crumbs*
   3 *tablespoons minced parsley*
 ¼ *teaspoon dried dill*
 ⅛ *teaspoon cayenne pepper*
   1 *cup grated low-fat mozzarella cheese*
 ½ *cup low-fat ricotta cheese*
 10 *ounces marinated artichoke hearts, drained and chopped*

1. Preheat oven to 350° F. Lightly oil an 8-inch square baking pan.

2. In a heavy skillet over medium-high heat, sauté onion and garlic in sherry until soft but not browned. Lightly beat egg whites until soft peaks form. Spoon into a bowl and mix with whole egg, bread crumbs, parsley, dill, cayenne, cheeses, and artichokes. Add sautéed onion and garlic. Pour into oiled baking pan.

3. Bake until set (about 30 minutes). Let cool, then cut into about 24 squares. Serve warm or cold.

Makes 24 squares; serves 12.

> *Preparation time:* 20 minutes
> *Baking time:* 30 minutes
> *Per serving:* calcium 128 mg, calories 83, carbohydrates 6 g, cholesterol 26 mg, fat 3 g, fiber 2 g, protein 6 g, sodium 131 mg

PARTY PORT AND CHEDDAR SPREAD

This wine-flavored cheese spread can be served in a variety of ways: Spread it on celery or cucumber boats; roll it into a large ball and chill in wax paper until ready to serve; pack it into raw mushroom caps; or layer on rye crackers. The spread will keep for up to two weeks if refrigerated, and the wine flavor will deepen.

 ½ *pound low-fat Cheddar cheese, grated*
 ⅓ *cup port wine*
   1 *round loaf French bread*

1. Place cheese and port into a food processor or large bowl, and blend together until smooth.

2. Cut the top third off the round of French bread. Scoop out interior of bread and pack cheese into hollow loaf. Smooth top with a spatula.

3. Cover loaf with plastic wrap and refrigerate for 1 hour. Serve with crackers or chunks of French bread.

Serves 12.

> *Preparation time:* 15 minutes
> *Chilling time:* 1 hour
> *Per serving:* calcium 162 mg, calories 164, carbohydrates 21 g, cholesterol 4 mg, fat 3 g, fiber 1 g, protein 8 g, sodium 346 mg

CURRIED STUFFED EGGS

For a lighter version of deviled eggs, use less mayonnaise and other high-fat ingredients and more seasonings. The filling for this recipe is a mixture of chopped spinach and parsley seasoned with curry. The stuffed eggs can be made up to three hours ahead of time if tightly covered with plastic wrap and refrigerated. Garnish with paprika and minced chives for a colorful presentation.

   6 *hard-cooked eggs*
      Lettuce leaves, for lining platter
   1 *tablespoon curry powder*
 ⅓ *cup reduced-fat mayonnaise*
   1 *tablespoon minced parsley*
   1 *tablespoon minced spinach leaves*
 ½ *tablespoon Dijon mustard*
      Dill sprigs or chives, and paprika, for garnish

1. Peel eggs and halve lengthwise, remove yolks from whites, and place halved egg whites on bed of lettuce arranged on a platter. In a mixing bowl mash egg yolks with curry powder, mayonnaise, parsley, spinach, and mustard until smooth.

2. Spoon or pipe this filling into egg-white halves. Garnish with dill sprigs and paprika. Cover carefully with plastic wrap and chill for 15 minutes before serving.

Serves 12.

> *Preparation time:* 15 minutes
> *Chilling time:* 15 minutes
> *Per serving:* calcium 25 mg, calories 48, carbohydrates 2 g, cholesterol 109 mg, fat 3 g, fiber .2 g, protein 4 g, sodium 74 mg

A hearty yet healthy menu for Super Bowl Sunday features a variety of appetizers and a satisfying beef and barley soup.

SEAFOOD SPECIALTIES

Fish and shellfish can be a tasty addition to your hors d'oeuvre repertoire. Use the freshest fish available for best flavor.

CHILLED PRAWNS IN BEER

This slightly spicy prawn appetizer has become very popular in Cajun restaurants. The recipe calls for flat beer, which is simply beer that has been opened and allowed to stand at room temperature for several hours. Using one of the popular light beers will reduce calories.

   3 pounds jumbo prawns, well-rinsed
   4 cups flat beer
   1 small onion, minced
   1 teaspoon yellow mustard seed
   1 teaspoon anise seed
   2 teaspoons cayenne pepper, or to taste
   1 teaspoon curry powder
      Hot mustard, for dipping (optional)

1. In an uncovered pot boil all ingredients except hot mustard until prawns are bright pink (8 to 10 minutes), stirring occasionally.

2. Drain prawns and divide cooking liquid among small bowls. Serve prawns unpeeled—let guests peel prawns themselves and dip them into cooking liquid. Or peel prawns and serve on wooden toothpicks with a crock of hot mustard, if used.

Serves 12.

> *Preparation time:* 5 minutes
> *Cooking time:* 10 minutes
> *Per serving:* calcium 73 mg, calories 159, carbohydrates 5 g, cholesterol 173 mg, fat 2 g, fiber .5 g, protein 24 g, sodium 218 mg

CHINESE ABALONE BALLS

An exotic shellfish, abalone is ground and mixed with ginger, water chestnuts, eggs, and sesame oil, then formed into small balls and baked until crisp. Any firm white-fleshed fish can be substituted for abalone, but abalone tastes best in this recipe.

   1/2 pound raw abalone
   1/4 cup water chestnuts, peeled
   2 eggs, beaten
   2 tablespoons chopped green onion
   1 teaspoon low-sodium soy sauce or tamari
   1/2 teaspoon grated fresh ginger
   1 teaspoon sesame oil
      Finely ground whole wheat bread crumbs, as needed
      Oil, for coating baking sheet
      Soy sauce or tamari, for dipping

1. Preheat oven to 400° F. To make in food processor: Place abalone, water chestnuts, eggs, green onion, the 1 teaspoon soy sauce, ginger, and sesame oil into a food processor and blend into a coarsely ground mixture. To make by hand: Chop abalone and water chestnuts very finely and mix with eggs, green onion, the 1 teaspoon soy sauce, ginger, and sesame oil.

2. Form into 1-inch balls and roll in bread crumbs.

3. Lightly oil a baking sheet and bake the abalone balls for 12 to 15 minutes, until they turn crisp and light brown. Serve warm with soy sauce for dipping.

Serves 6.

> *Preparation time:* 25 minutes
> *Baking time:* 15 to 20 minutes
> *Per serving:* calcium 32 mg, calories 120, carbohydrates 11 g, cholesterol 103 mg, fat 4 g, fiber 1 g, protein 10 g, sodium 237 mg

WHITEFISH SEVICHE

In the Caribbean, seviche is made with freshly caught conch or abalone. This recipe uses fresh white-fleshed fish, such as haddock or cod. Always be sure to buy fish from a reliable market and buy only fresh fish. Traditionally the raw fish is marinated for several hours in a lemon or lime juice mixture, which gives it a delicate flavor.

   2 red onions, finely chopped
   4 to 5 cloves garlic, minced
   3 red bell peppers, seeded and chopped
   1/4 cup capers
   1/2 cup marinated artichoke hearts, thinly sliced
   2 pounds raw white-fleshed fish, cut into 1/2-inch pieces
   2 1/2 cups freshly squeezed lime juice
      Lettuce leaves, for accompaniment

1. Place all ingredients except lettuce leaves in a large bowl or shallow pan and toss well.

2. Cover bowl tightly with plastic wrap, place in the refrigerator, and let marinate for 4 to 8 hours or overnight. Serve slightly chilled on lettuce leaves.

Serves 12.

Note The marinade actually performs some of the cooking function usually done by heat. The citric acid in the lime juice breaks down the connective tissues of the fish and firms up protein in much the same way heat does.

> *Preparation time:* 15 minutes
> *Marinating time:* 4 to 8 hours
> *Per serving:* calcium 42 mg, calories 130, carbohydrates 8 g, cholesterol 45 mg, fat 5 g, fiber 1 g, protein 15 g, sodium 164 mg

PRAWNS WITH SNOW PEA BLANKETS

Use medium or jumbo prawns for this recipe. Save the marinating broth; it can be used to make a tasty dipping sauce for prawns (see Note).

    1 *pound medium prawns*
    2 *cups white table wine*
  ¹/₄ *cup Dijon mustard*
    1 *tablespoon chopped fresh tarragon or 1 teaspoon dried tarragon*
  ¹/₂ *teaspoon cayenne pepper*
    2 *tablespoons olive oil*
  32 *snow peas, for wrapping*

1. In a large saucepan boil prawns in wine at high heat until prawns turn pink (3 to 4 minutes). Drain, saving wine in a large bowl. Peel and remove veins from prawns with a sharp knife.

2. Add remaining ingredients, except snow peas, to wine and toss in prawns. Let marinate 4 to 8 hours or overnight.

3. Blanch snow peas briefly (about 30 seconds) in large pot of boiling water. Wrap a blanched snow pea around each marinated prawn, securing with a toothpick. Serve chilled.

Makes about 32 prawns, 16 servings.

Note The marinade can be thickened or reduced to a sauce by boiling it for 45 minutes at medium-high heat until one quarter the original volume.

Preparation time: 45 minutes
Cooking time: 5 minutes
Marinating time: 4 to 8 hours
Per serving: calcium 221 mg, calories 266, carbohydrates 34 g, cholesterol 43 mg, fat 4 g, fiber 14 g, protein 21 g, sodium 1,204 mg

Meaty prawns are poached; marinated overnight in a sauce of mustard, wine, and fresh tarragon; and wrapped with lightly blanched snow peas. The marinade is then reduced and served as a dipping sauce.

BLINI WITH SALMON SPREAD

Blini are the traditional yeasted pancakes used to break the Russian Orthodox Lenten fast. This recipe is made with whole wheat flour and egg whites instead of the white flour and yolks called for in typically rich blini recipes. Cook the thin pancakes on a griddle or in a crêpe pan, then stack until ready to serve with tangy Salmon Spread. Both recipes can be made the day before a party, wrapped well, and refrigerated. To reheat blini, wrap in a slightly dampened kitchen towel, place in a casserole, cover with aluminum foil, and warm in a 250° F oven for 15 minutes.

- 1 package active dry yeast
- ¼ cup warm water (98° F to 110° F)
- ½ tablespoon honey
- 1¼ cups whole wheat pastry flour
- ¾ cup sifted buckwheat flour
- 2 cups warm nonfat milk (98° F)
- ½ teaspoon herbal salt substitute
- 2 egg yolks
- 4 egg whites
- 1 cup evaporated nonfat milk
  Radishes, green onions, and cherry tomatoes, for garnish (optional)

Salmon Spread
- 1 cup finely chopped smoked salmon
- ¼ cup lemon juice
- 4 ounces reduced-fat cream cheese
- 4 ounces low-fat ricotta cheese
- ¼ cup minced red onion
  Freshly ground black pepper, to taste

1. In a small bowl combine yeast, the water, and honey, and stir well until yeast is dissolved. Let sit at room temperature until foam appears on top of the water (8 to 10 minutes).

2. Meanwhile, in a medium-sized mixing bowl, combine flours, nonfat milk, salt substitute, and egg yolks. Beat lightly with a whisk until well mixed. After yeast has foamed, add to flour mixture. Stir batter well, cover bowl with a clean dish towel, and let rise in a warm place, such as a gas oven with the pilot lit, for 1 hour.

3. Beat egg whites until stiff but not dry. Whip evaporated milk with electric beater until stiff peaks form. Add whipped milk to egg whites, and let mixture sit for 30 minutes while batter rises. After batter has risen, combine contents of two bowls.

4. To cook blini, lightly oil a crêpe pan or griddle. Pour ¼ cup batter onto pan. Cook on one side until pancake bubbles, then flip and cook on other side for 30 seconds. Place cooked pancakes on a paper towel. Continue until all batter is used.

5. Place crock of Salmon Spread on a platter, and arrange folded or rolled, warm blini around it. Garnish with radishes, green onions, and cherry tomatoes, if desired.

Makes 30 pancakes, 15 servings.

Salmon Spread Purée all ingredients in blender or food processor. Spoon into a crock, cover with plastic wrap, and refrigerate until serving time.

Makes about 2 cups, 15 servings.

Preparation time: 10 minutes (Blini); 10 minutes (Salmon Spread)
Rising time: 1 hour (Blini)
Cooking time: 50 minutes
Per serving: calcium 129 mg, calories 145, carbohydrates 17 g, cholesterol 41 mg, fat 4 g, fiber 2 g, protein 11 g, sodium 227 mg

---

SPICY CRABMEAT TACOS

Great for a quick meal, these healthy tacos are made with soft corn tortillas rather than the traditional deep-fried shells. Corn is a good source of fiber and vitamins, the crabmeat provides protein, and the vegetables contribute additional vitamins and minerals. Make the filling ahead and stuff into the warmed tortillas right before serving.

- ¼ cup minced red onion
- 1 teaspoon olive oil
- ½ teaspoon minced garlic
- 1 cup diced tomatoes
- 2 tablespoons minced cilantro
- 2 cups cooked crabmeat, shredded
- 6 corn tortillas
- 2 tablespoons lemon juice
- ¼ cup chopped green bell pepper
- ¼ cup peeled and chopped cucumber
- 1 cup shredded lettuce

1. Preheat oven to 350° F. In a large skillet over medium-high heat, sauté onion in oil until soft (about 3 minutes). Add garlic, tomatoes, cilantro, and crabmeat. Cook for 5 minutes.

2. Wrap corn tortillas in aluminum foil and place in oven until heated (about 5 minutes). In a large bowl mix together lemon juice, bell pepper, cucumber, and lettuce. Place equal amounts of lettuce mixture on tortillas, then top with crab mixture. Serve immediately.

Serves 6.

Preparation time: 15 minutes
Cooking time: 15 minutes
Per serving: calcium 104 mg, calories 115, carbohydrates 15 g, cholesterol 35 mg, fat 2 g, fiber 2 g, protein 10 g, sodium 202 mg

---

For a light meal, Spicy Crabmeat Tacos offer taste and charm, without the fat of the deep-fried version.

FEATURE

PREPARING HORS D'OEUVRES FOR ENTERTAINING

When planning your selection of appetizers for a party, consider the following:

Serving temperature Try to offer variety—a few hot hors d'oeuvres, a few at room temperature, and one or two chilled.

Shape Vary the shapes, arranging both round shapes and long, thin shapes on the same platter. For example, offer a scooped-out red bell pepper, filled with a low-fat cheese dip, accompanied by round melba toasts and raw vegetable sticks.

Color Serve an assortment of warm colors—red, orange, yellow (tomatoes, oranges, and squash)—and cool colors—green, purple, blue (lettuce, eggplant, blueberries)—for alluring hors d'oeuvre combinations. The contrasts are especially effective when combined on the same platter.

Texture Choose crunchy- and smooth-textured foods. For example, serve a creamy dip with a crisp spear of Belgian endive or a crunchy slice of bell pepper. Strive for good texture throughout the setting as well. Use woven baskets, polished brass or copper trays, rattan mats, or bright cotton cloths as backgrounds for the food.

Preparing Vegetables for a Crudités Platter

Many vegetables can be transformed into wonderful dip containers or stuffed for appetizers. Small pumpkins, eggplant, bell peppers, or large, ripe tomatoes can be hollowed out to hold dips for a crudités platter. Smaller vegetables can

be scooped out with a melon baller, stuffed with a cheese mixture or a vegetable pâté, and served as finger food.

To prepare a crudités platter, you can line the serving dish with lettuce that has been washed and checked for brown spots. Good vegetables for crudités platters include cherry tomatoes, celery and carrot sticks, broccoli and cauliflower florets, red or green bell pepper strips, whole banana peppers or small sweet chiles, green onions, whole snow peas or pea pods, diagonal slices of yellow summer squash, whole button mushrooms, endive spears, and asparagus tips. You may want to heat a small pot of water to boiling, and blanch the hard vegetables—broccoli, squash, peppers, carrots, and cauliflower.

When arranging the prepared vegetables on the platter, try to create interest by placing different colors and shapes together. For example, a long, green asparagus stalk might be placed next to a round, red cherry tomato for a colorful effect.

SENSATIONAL SPREADS AND DIPS

Spreads and dips are an excellent choice for an impromptu party. An elegant hors d'oeuvre table can be as easy as cutting up a few platters of fresh vegetables, laying out whole grain crackers, and opening containers of these homemade dips.

FRESH SALSA

Use this mild salsa as a dip for tortilla chips or as an accompaniment to chicken, fish, and vegetarian entrées. This recipe calls for fresh chiles and tomatillos. If they are not available, substitute canned chiles and red tomatoes.

- 3 small tomatillos, chopped
- 1 jalapeño chile, seeded and chopped
- 2 tablespoons minced garlic
- $^1/_2$ cup finely chopped white onion
- 2 tablespoons olive oil
- 1 tablespoon ground fresh rosemary
- 1$^1/_2$ cups cored and chopped plum tomatoes
- $^1/_3$ cup minced green bell pepper
- 2 tablespoons minced cilantro
- 3 tablespoons minced parsley
- $^1/_2$ teaspoon coriander powder
- $^1/_2$ teaspoon cayenne pepper, or to taste
- $^1/_2$ teaspoon chili powder
- $^3/_4$ teaspoon cumin
- $^1/_4$ teaspoon cinnamon
  Freshly ground black pepper, to taste
- 1 tablespoon lime juice

In a large mixing bowl combine all ingredients, cover, and let marinate in the refrigerator overnight. Serve chilled or at room temperature.

Makes 2$^1/_2$ cups, 10 servings.

Preparation time: 20 minutes
Marinating time: 24 hours
Per serving: calcium 38 mg, calories 48, carbohydrates 5 g, cholesterol 0 mg, fat 3 g, fiber 1 g, protein 1 g, sodium 41 mg

GOAT CHEESE AND SUN-DRIED TOMATO PÂTÉ

The full flavor of sun-dried tomatoes combines with goat cheese to make a delicious appetizer or picnic spread. For accompaniment, serve rounds of lightly toasted French bread. To reduce the fat in the spread, drain the olive oil from the jarred sun-dried tomatoes.

- 3 ounces jarred sun-dried tomatoes, drained and chopped
- 4 ounces goat cheese
- $^1/_8$ teaspoon dried thyme
- 8 large slices fresh French bread
- 2 teaspoons minced parsley

In a medium-sized bowl combine tomatoes, goat cheese, and thyme. Lightly toast French bread and spread with tomato mixture. Top with parsley and serve.

Serves 8.

Preparation time: 10 minutes
Per serving: calcium 156 mg, calories 156, carbohydrates 16 g, cholesterol 15 mg, fat 7 g, fiber .7 g, protein 7 g, sodium 231 mg

These tempting fruit kabobs are best made with fresh fruit in season and garnished with fresh mint leaves. The honey, nutmeg, and yogurt sauce is a sweet low-fat accompaniment.

FRUIT KABOBS WITH SOUR CREAM DIP

This light meal is an elegant variation on fresh fruit salad. Use a wide assortment of fruits, including one or two kinds of melons, pineapple, strawberries, bananas, and peaches. The sour cream dip, deliciously flavored with nutmeg and honey, can be made ahead and stored in a tightly covered container in the refrigerator for up to one week.

- 3/4 cup each cantaloupe cubes, pineapple chunks, sliced bananas, peach chunks, and whole strawberries
- 3/4 cup nonfat plain yogurt
- 1/4 cup sour cream
- 2 teaspoons freshly grated nutmeg
- 1 tablespoon maple syrup
- 1 tablespoon honey
  Fresh mint leaves, for garnish

1. Skewer chunks of fruit onto 12 bamboo or metal shish kabob skewers, alternating colors and types of fruit. Arrange on a platter or in a flat basket.

2. Mix together yogurt, sour cream, nutmeg, maple syrup, and honey, and pour into a small serving bowl. Garnish with mint leaves. Serve sauce with fruit kabobs.

Makes 1 dozen skewers, 4 servings.

Preparation time: 30 minutes
Per serving: calcium 121 mg, calories 175, carbohydrates 33 g, cholesterol 7 mg, fat 4 g, fiber 3 g, protein 4 g, sodium 45 mg

TEMPEH OLIVE SPREAD

Tempeh comes from Javanese cuisine, where it is served in tempura and stir-fry dishes, and is skewered on shish kabobs. It is abundant in B vitamins, low-fat protein, and calcium. Steaming the tempeh before using it neutralizes the yeasty flavor and softens it so that it absorbs spices. Tempeh looks like a thin block of textured cheese and is available in small packages in the frozen food sections of gourmet and natural food stores.

- 1 package (8 oz) tempeh
- 1 teaspoon olive oil
- 2 tablespoons low-sodium soy sauce or tamari
- 3 tablespoons reduced-fat mayonnaise
- 1 tablespoon minced green onion
- 1/4 cup minced celery
- 2 tablespoons minced parsley
- 1/4 cup pitted, chopped ripe olives
- 1/8 teaspoon cayenne pepper
- 1/8 teaspoon dried dill
  Assorted whole wheat crackers or rice cakes

1. Cut tempeh into 1-inch squares. In a shallow pan fitted with a steamer basket, steam tempeh for 15 minutes. Drain and set aside.

2. In a medium-sized skillet heat olive oil and lightly sauté steamed tempeh for 5 minutes, stirring frequently. Remove pan from heat and add soy sauce, mixing with tempeh. Spoon contents of pan into a medium-sized mixing bowl.

3. Mash together tempeh, mayonnaise, green onion, celery, parsley, and olives into a thick spread. Add cayenne and dill. Serve at room temperature on whole wheat crackers.

Makes 2 cups, 16 servings.

Preparation time: 20 minutes
Cooking time: 20 minutes
Per serving: calcium 25 mg, calories 39, carbohydrates 3 g, cholesterol 1 mg, fat 2 g, fiber .1 g, protein 3 g, sodium 97 mg

HUMMUS IN PITA WEDGES

A traditional dish in Middle Eastern cuisine, hummus is a healthy and very versatile hors d'oeuvre that combines sesame tahini and chick-peas to provide a good source of protein. Here, it is spread into whole wheat pita pockets and layered with chopped tomatoes, cucumbers, and lettuce. The pita sandwiches can be cut into wedges for snacks or appetizers or served with mugs of hot soup as a hearty lunch.

- 3 cups cooked, drained chick-peas
- 4 cloves garlic, minced
- 1 teaspoon low-sodium soy sauce or tamari
- 1/2 cup lemon juice
- 3/4 cup tahini
- 2 tablespoons minced parsley
- 2 tablespoons minced red onion
- 2 tablespoons minced celery
- 1 cup coarsely chopped tomatoes
- 1 cup peeled, seeded, and coarsely chopped cucumber
- 2 teaspoons apple cider vinegar
- 3 teaspoons olive oil
- 2 large rounds whole wheat pita bread
- 2 cups shredded lettuce

1. In a food processor or blender, purée chick-peas, garlic, soy sauce, lemon juice, and tahini until smooth. Set aside.

2. In a small bowl combine parsley, red onion, celery, tomatoes, cucumber, vinegar, and olive oil, and toss well. Let marinate at room temperature for 10 minutes.

3. Slice pita rounds in quarters. Open each quarter carefully and spread with hummus. Stuff with lettuce and marinated vegetables, including a small spoonful of the marinade. Serve immediately.

Serves 8.

Preparation time: 25 minutes
Marinating time: 10 minutes
Per serving: calcium 293 mg, calories 317, carbohydrates 36 g, cholesterol 0 mg, fat 16 g, fiber 3 g, protein 12 g, sodium 122 mg

BUFFALO CHICKEN WINGS WITH BLUE CHEESE DIP

This popular hors d'oeuvre has gained national fame in a short time. The original recipe calls for deep-fried chicken wings, but in this version they are baked. Serve hot with celery sticks and Blue Cheese Dip.

  2 tablespoons melted butter
  4 tablespoons hot-pepper sauce
  2 tablespoons rice vinegar
 32 chicken wings or drummettes
     Paprika, for dusting
     Lettuce leaves, for lining platter
     Celery sticks, for accompaniment

Blue Cheese Dip

  ½ cup soft tofu
  2 tablespoons rice vinegar
  ⅓ cup nonfat plain yogurt
  ¼ cup sour cream
  2 cloves garlic, pressed
  3 ounces blue cheese, crumbled

1. Preheat oven to 350° F. Mix together butter, hot-pepper sauce, and vinegar. Dip chicken into mixture, then place on a lightly oiled baking sheet. Dust with paprika.

2. Bake chicken until crisp and brown (about 30 minutes).

3. To serve, arrange chicken on a platter lined with lettuce leaves. Set a bowl of Blue Cheese Dip in the center and celery sticks on the side.

Makes 32 wings; 16 servings.

Blue Cheese Dip In a blender purée tofu, vinegar, yogurt, sour cream, and garlic until smooth. Stir in blue cheese. Spoon into a serving bowl, cover with plastic wrap, and chill until chicken is baked.

Makes about 1½ cups, 16 servings.

Preparation time: 15 minutes
Cooking time: 30 minutes
Per serving: calcium 60 mg, calories 250, carbohydrates 1 g, cholesterol 80 mg, fat 18 g, fiber .1 g, protein 19 g, sodium 161 mg

CURRY CHUTNEY DIP WITH HOMEMADE RUSKS

Serve this simple party dip with rusks, crackers, or vegetable sticks.

  ½ cup soft tofu
  ½ cup low-fat ricotta cheese
  ⅓ cup mango chutney, preferably without sugar
  1 tablespoon lemon juice
  2 teaspoons curry powder
  ¼ teaspoon cumin
  1 teaspoon Asian sesame oil

Homemade Rusks

  1 baguette whole grain French bread

Blend all ingredients and chill for 1½ hours.

Makes 1 cup, 8 servings.

Homemade Rusks Preheat oven to 200° F. Cut baguette into thick wedges and place on ungreased baking sheet. Bake at 200° F until very crisp (about 45 minutes).

Makes 20 rusks.

Preparation time: 10 minutes
Baking time: 45 minutes
Per serving: calcium 63 mg, calories 59, carbohydrates 7 g, cholesterol 5 mg, fat 3 g, fiber .5 g, protein 3 g, sodium 50 mg

NOTE

LIGHTENING YOUR FAVORITE DIPS

Transform a favorite party dip recipe by reducing the fat. The first recipe below is a traditional dip; the second is a low-calorie, reduced-fat version.

TRADITIONAL SOUR CREAM DIP

  ½ pint sour cream
  1 teaspoon prepared horseradish
  2 tablespoons minced chives
  2 teaspoons minced parsley
  1 tablespoon mayonnaise
  ¾ cup softened cream cheese
     Pinch salt

In a small bowl combine all ingredients; serve with crackers and raw vegetables.

Makes approximately 2 cups, 8 servings.

Preparation time: 10 minutes
Per serving: calcium 57 mg, calories 151, carbohydrates 2 g, cholesterol 37 mg, fat 15 g, fiber .1 g, protein 3 g, sodium 108 mg

LOW-FAT CREAM DIP

  1 cup nonfat plain yogurt
  ¾ cup blended low-fat ricotta cheese
  2 tablespoons reduced-fat mayonnaise
  1 teaspoon prepared horseradish
  2 tablespoons minced parsley

In a small bowl combine all ingredients; serve with crackers and raw vegetables.

Makes approximately 2 cups, 8 servings.

Preparation time: 10 minutes
Per serving: calcium 137 mg, calories 56, carbohydrates 4 g, cholesterol 10 mg, fat 2 g, fiber .1 g, protein 5 g, sodium 76 mg

Menu

HOLIDAY HORS D'OEUVRE PARTY

Greek Feta Filo Cigars

Cranberry Salsa and Neufchâtel Cheese Dip

Scooped-Out Green Bell Peppers With Whole Cherry Tomatoes

Whole Grain Crackers and Minibaguettes of French Bread

Chinese Abalone Balls (see page 36)

Armenian Meatballs (see page 30)

Filo Tart With Raspberries (see page 203)

Mulled Cider and Red Wine

Although holidays are typically a time of heavy eating and drinking, don't get caught in the high-calorie, high-fat humdrum of heavy sit-down dinners. For your holiday party, serve a platter of these hors d'oeuvres—your guests will appreciate the light touch of these international flavor treats. The menu theme is colorful: the reds of whole cherry tomatoes, tomato sauce, cranberry salsa, red wine, and raspberries; the greens of bell peppers and green onions.
Menu serves eight.

GREEK FETA FILO CIGARS

A rectangular, paper-thin pastry dough, filo dough is a great resource for instantly elegant appetizers (see How to Prepare Filo, page 212 and Shaping Filo Pastries, page 219).

> 1 cup low-fat feta cheese, crumbled
> 1/2 cup low-fat ricotta cheese
> 1 tablespoon grated Parmesan cheese
> 2 cloves garlic, minced
> 2 tablespoons minced fresh dill
> 2 eggs, lightly beaten
> 1/4 teaspoon freshly ground black pepper
> 10 sheets filo dough
> 2 tablespoons unsalted butter, melted

1. Preheat oven to 400° F. Mix cheeses, garlic, dill, eggs, and pepper until smooth. Reserve.

2. On a clean, dry surface, unroll the filo dough and stack in a pile. Using a pastry brush sprinkle the first sheet with 1/2 teaspoon of the butter. Repeat with second sheet and lay it on top of the first. Set aside. Repeat procedure with remaining filo dough and butter to create 5 sets of two-layered sheets.

3. Mark long side of each filo dough stack into fifths and cut into 5 equal strips, each 3 to 4 inches wide. Place a spoonful of the filling at the base of each double-layered strip and roll into a "cigar", tucking the edges in as you roll. Place cigars on a parchment-covered baking sheet. Repeat this process 4 times.

4. Bake cigars until brown (about 15 minutes). Serve hot.

Makes 25 small appetizers, approximately 8 servings.

> *Preparation time:* 30 to 45 minutes
> *Baking time:* 15 minutes
> *Per serving:* calcium 132 mg, calories 178, carbohydrates 14 g, cholesterol 79 mg, fat 10 g, fiber 0 g, protein 7 g, sodium 320 mg

CRANBERRY SALSA AND NEUFCHÂTEL CHEESE DIP

A colorful dip that is often served at holiday parties, this combines the piquant flavors of cranberries, orange peel, and red onion with Neufchâtel cream cheese. The dip has a lovely pink color. Serve it in halved red or green bell peppers surrounded by raw vegetable sticks or crackers.

> 1 cup cranberries, fresh or frozen and defrosted
> 2 teaspoons grated orange peel
> 1/2 cup frozen orange juice concentrate, thawed
> 3 tablespoons minced red onion
> 1 tablespoon minced cilantro
> 1/4 teaspoon cayenne pepper
> 1/2 cup reduced-fat cream cheese, such as Neufchâtel
> Bell peppers, halved, seeded, veined (optional)
> Assorted raw vegetable sticks or whole grain crackers, for accompaniment (optional)

1. Blend all ingredients except bell peppers and raw vegetables in food processor or in blender until very smooth.

2. Spoon into 2 or 3 bell peppers, if used, or a glass bowl and serve chilled with raw vegetable sticks.

Makes 2 1/2 cups, 8 servings.

> *Preparation time:* 10 minutes
> *Per serving:* calcium 17 mg, calories 54, carbohydrates 9 g, cholesterol 5 mg, fat 2 g, fiber .7 g, protein 1 g, sodium 43 mg

A festive array of healthy hors d'oeuvres celebrates the holiday season with international flair.

Good soups start with the basics: hearty stocks, flavorful fresh vegetables, lean meats, and a few well-chosen herbs and spices.

SOUPS

A nutritious soup can be a satisfying one-dish meal or a healthy accompaniment to a varied menu. Made from wholesome, economical homemade stocks and flavored with herbs and other healthful seasonings, the soups in this chapter are as delicious as they are good for you. Choose from a variety of soups for carefree entertaining— such as Bourride (see page 48) or hearty Chicken Gumbo Louisiana-Style (see page 48)—as well as simple mealtime favorites such as Pesto Summer Vegetable Soup (see page 57) or Hot and Sour Soup (see page 55).

SOUPS THAT MAKE A MEAL

Recipes in this section can be served as a light main course, and with the addition of bread and salad, make a dinner or lunch.

MEXICAN CHICKEN SOUP

Inspired by a fondness for cilantro (also called coriander), this soup is a happy marriage of chicken and Mexican seasonings.

    1   frying chicken (3 lb), skinned
        and cut up
    8   cups water
    3   carrots, coarsely chopped
    1   small russet or red potato,
        diced
    2   green bell peppers, julienned
    2   large onions, sliced
    1   large zucchini, sliced
    3/4 cup chopped cilantro, or to
        taste
        Herbal salt substitute and
        pepper, to taste
        Salsa, for accompaniment
        (optional)

1. In a large stockpot, place frying chicken, the water, carrots, and potato. Bring to a boil. Simmer for 45 minutes.

2. Pour stock through a colander into a big bowl; let cool, pick out and discard bones and gristle from chicken.

3. Return stock, chicken meat, and cooked vegetables to stockpot and add bell pepper, onion, zucchini, and cilantro. Cook over medium heat until vegetables are tender. Test for seasoning and add salt substitute and pepper, if needed. Serve hot, with salsa if desired.

Makes 12 cups, 8 servings.

Preparation time: 20 minutes
Cooking time: 60 minutes
Per serving: calcium 71 mg, calories 80, carbohydrates 10 g, cholesterol 23 mg, fat 2 g, fiber 2 g, protein 8 g, sodium 185 mg

CHICKEN GUMBO LOUISIANA-STYLE

This authentic-tasting version of Louisiana gumbo was invented by a woman in a little town north of Baton Rouge. Although the recipe is adapted for low-fat cooking, most of the original seasonings are kept intact, maintaining the stunning flavors prevalent in Creole cooking.

    1   large frying chicken (4 lb),
        skinned and cut up
    2   tablespoons whole wheat flour
        Herbal salt substitute and
        pepper, to taste
        Oil, for coating baking sheet
    1   large onion, chopped
    1   teaspoon olive oil
    5   green onions, chopped
    1   large clove garlic, mashed
    1/2 dried chile
    1   bay leaf
    1   sprig fresh thyme
    1/4 cup chopped parsley
    7   cups defatted Chicken Stock
        (see page 51)
    2   cups cooked brown rice
        Cayenne pepper, to taste

1. Preheat oven to 350° F. Coat chicken pieces with flour and sprinkle with salt substitute and pepper. Place on a lightly oiled baking sheet and bake, turning once, until well browned (about 20 minutes).

2. While chicken is baking, sauté onion in oil in a large heavy stockpot or Dutch oven. Cook until soft, then add green onion, garlic, chile, bay leaf, thyme, and parsley. Cook 5 minutes.

3. Add stock, rice, and baked chicken pieces. Simmer until chicken is tender (about 1 hour). Sprinkle with cayenne.

Makes 12 cups, 8 servings.

Preparation time: 35 minutes
Cooking time: 90 minutes
Per serving: calcium 136 mg, calories 198, carbohydrates 27 g, cholesterol 23 mg, fat 4 g, fiber 3 g, protein 14 g, sodium 403 mg

BOURRIDE

Bourride is a French fish soup that has a variety of exquisite seasonings. Serve Bourride when you happen upon some fresh fish and want to invite friends to dinner.

    2   teaspoons olive oil
    1/2 large onion, sliced
    1   medium carrot, sliced into
        rounds
    1   large leek, cleaned and sliced
        into rounds
    2   ripe tomatoes, cored and
        coarsely chopped
    6   cups defatted Fish Stock
        (see page 51) or water
    1/2 cup dry vermouth or dry white
        wine
    1   bay leaf
    1/4 teaspoon dried thyme
    1   clove garlic, halved
    1/4 teaspoon chopped orange peel
    2   pinches saffron
    1/4 teaspoon fennel seed
    1 1/2 pounds fresh, firm-fleshed fish
        Herbal salt substitute, to taste
    8   slices French bread

1. In a large stockpot over medium-high heat, heat oil; add onion and sauté until onion is very soft. Add carrot, leek, and tomatoes, and sauté 5 minutes, stirring frequently.

2. Add stock, vermouth, bay leaf, thyme, garlic, orange peel, saffron, and fennel seed. Bring to a boil. Simmer until vegetables are tender (about 10 minutes).

3. Wash fish and pat dry; remove all bones and cut fish into 3-inch chunks. Add fish to stockpot and cook just until fish flakes.

4. Season to taste with salt substitute and serve hot over sliced bread in large soup bowls.

Makes 12 cups, 8 servings.

Preparation time: 20 minutes
Cooking time: 20 minutes
Per serving: calcium 80 mg, calories 270, carbohydrates 21 g, cholesterol 49 mg, fat 7 g, fiber 2 g, protein 19 g, sodium 212 mg

SOUTHERN ITALIAN VEGETABLE SOUP

This soup has a hearty flavor and is thick enough to be served as a complete meal.

- 1 teaspoon olive oil
- 1 medium onion, sliced
- 1 medium carrot, sliced
- 2 medium red potatoes, diced
- 1 stalk celery with leaves, chopped
- 1 clove garlic, chopped
- 2 zucchini, sliced
- 1 cup chopped green cabbage
- 1 large tomato, cored and chopped
- 1/4 cup uncooked macaroni
- 4 cups defatted Chicken Stock (see page 51)
- 1 cup cooked navy beans (approximately 1/2 cup dried)
- 1 teaspoon dried basil
- 1/4 cup chopped parsley
  Herbal salt substitute and pepper, to taste

1. In a large stockpot, heat oil over medium heat. Add onion and slowly sauté until onion is soft and translucent. Add carrot and potatoes and cook 3 minutes.

2. Add celery, garlic, zucchini, cabbage, and tomato and cook 5 minutes more, stirring frequently. Add macaroni, stock, beans, basil, parsley, salt substitute, and pepper; bring to a boil.

3. Lower heat to simmer, cover, and continue cooking for 35 minutes. Taste for seasoning and serve hot.

Makes 8 cups, 6 servings.

Note You can use the listed fresh vegetables or substitute others.

Preparation time: 25 minutes
Cooking time: 45 minutes
Per serving: calcium 104 mg, calories 154, carbohydrates 26 g, cholesterol 0 mg, fat 2 g, fiber 3 g, protein 9 g, sodium 319 mg

Bourride is a hearty fish soup from southern France that is redolent of orange, fennel, and thyme. Serve it with crusty baguettes, a light green salad, and lemon- or lime-flavored sparkling water.

CANADIAN CHEESE SOUP

Perfect for cold weather, this rich soup combines minced fresh vegetables with a stock flavored with wine and cheese.

- ¼ cup minced onion
- 1 teaspoon unsalted butter or olive oil
- 2 tablespoons white wine
- ¼ cup minced celery
- ¼ cup minced carrot
- ¼ cup whole wheat flour
- 2 cups nonfat milk
- 1½ cups defatted Chicken Stock (see page 51)
- ½ cup grated farmer cheese Paprika and minced green onions, for garnish

1. In a heavy stockpot over medium-high heat, sauté onion in butter and wine until soft (about 3 minutes). Add celery and carrot and continue to cook for 5 minutes.

2. Stir in flour. Lower heat to medium and continue to cook, stirring frequently, for 2 more minutes. Pour in milk and stock, and bring soup to a boil.

3. Simmer soup, uncovered, on medium-high heat for 10 minutes. Right before serving, stir in cheese.

4. Ladle soup into prewarmed bowls and garnish with a dusting of paprika and a sprinkling of green onions.

Makes 6 cups, 6 servings.

Preparation time: 15 minutes
Cooking time: 20 minutes
Per serving: calcium 169 mg, calories 99, carbohydrates 10 g, cholesterol 10 mg, fat 3 g, fiber 1 g, protein 7 g, sodium 294 mg

HEARTY BEEF AND BARLEY SOUP

This thick soup has a rich aroma that will entice even the finicky eater. Chunks of lean stew meat are seared in olive oil and cooked slowly with vegetables and potassium-rich barley, seasoned with garlic, bay leaf, and basil. A meal in itself, this soup freezes well, so make a double batch and save half.

- ⅓ cup whole wheat flour
- 1 teaspoon herbal salt substitute
- 1 pound lean stew meat, cut into 1-inch chunks
- 2 tablespoons olive oil
- 1 cup chopped onion
- 1 tablespoon minced garlic
- ½ cup grated carrots
- ½ cup chopped celery
- 1 cup diced tomato
- 1 cup barley
- 5 cups defatted Chicken or Veal Stock (see page 51)
- 2 tablespoons basil
- 1 bay leaf
  Herbal salt substitute and pepper, to taste

1. In a shallow bowl combine flour and salt substitute. Dredge chunks of meat in flour mixture.

2. In a large stockpot over medium-high heat, quickly brown chunks of meat in hot oil. Add onions and garlic and cook until soft (3 to 5 minutes). Add carrots, celery, and tomato and continue cooking for 5 minutes.

3. Add barley, stock, and basil, and bring to a boil. Crush bay leaf and wrap in piece of cheesecloth or place into a tea ball. Add to soup. Lower heat to simmer and cook until barley is soft (20 to 25 minutes). Season to taste with salt substitute and pepper. Remove bay leaf before serving.

Makes 8 cups, 8 servings.

Preparation time: 15 minutes
Cooking time: 35 minutes
Per serving: calcium 70 mg, calories 346, carbohydrates 26 g, cholesterol 57 mg, fat 17 g, fiber 6 g, protein 23 g, sodium 371 mg

SWISS LENTIL SOUP

In this soup, the rich miso broth combines beautifully with the lentils, chopped tomatoes, and Swiss cheese. It has an aroma and dark flavor that work well in a European menu—perhaps with a caraway-studded rye bread, Balkan Cold Cucumber Salad (see page 68), and a frosty mug of German beer. Because the flavors need time to blend, let this soup sit overnight, if possible, before serving.

- 1½ cups chopped onions
- 1 teaspoon olive oil
- ⅓ cup dry white wine
- 1 cup julienned carrots
- 2 cups chopped tomatoes
- ½ teaspoon dried thyme
- ½ teaspoon dried marjoram
- 1 cup washed, uncooked lentils
- 3 cups defatted Chicken or Veal Stock (see page 51)
- 3 tablespoons miso, dissolved in ⅓ cup hot water
- ½ cup grated Swiss cheese Grated carrots and chopped green onions, for garnish

1. In a large stockpot over medium-high heat, sauté onions in oil and wine until soft but not browned. Add carrots, tomatoes, thyme, and marjoram, and continue to cook, stirring frequently, for 10 minutes.

2. Add lentils and cook for 2 more minutes. Add stock and bring to a boil. Lower heat to simmer and cook, covered, until lentils are soft (about 30 minutes).

3. Before serving, remove pot from heat and stir in miso. To serve, add about 2 tablespoons grated cheese to the bottom of each bowl and ladle soup on top. Garnish with grated carrots and chopped green onions.

Makes 6 cups, 6 servings.

Preparation time: 20 minutes
Cooking time: 45 minutes
Per serving: calcium 148 mg, calories 225, carbohydrates 28 g, cholesterol 9 mg, fat 5 g, fiber 12 g, protein 16 g, sodium 455 mg

MINNESOTA CHICKEN AND WILD RICE SOUP

Living in a state famous for blue lakes and blue skies, Minnesotans enjoy yearly harvests of vitamin-rich wild rice—the meaty, chewy seed of a grassy plant that grows in the northern lake country. This rich soup combines a hearty chicken stock studded with vegetables, chunks of chicken, and rice. Accompany each serving with French bread and a green salad for a delicious luncheon.

> $\frac{1}{2}$ cup chopped onion
> 2 teaspoons olive oil
> $\frac{1}{4}$ cup dry sherry
> $\frac{1}{2}$ cup chopped celery
> $\frac{1}{2}$ cup chopped carrot
> $\frac{1}{2}$ cup chopped spinach leaves
> 2 cups cooked and diced chicken
> 1 cup wild rice
> 5 cups defatted Chicken Stock (see sidebar, right)
> $\frac{1}{2}$ teaspoon dried thyme
> $\frac{1}{2}$ teaspoon dried marjoram
>   Pinch of ground ginger
> $\frac{1}{8}$ teaspoon cumin
>   Herbal salt substitute and pepper, to taste
> 2 tablespoons low-sodium soy sauce or tamari

1. In a large stockpot over medium-high heat, sauté onion in oil and sherry until soft but not browned. Add celery, carrots, and spinach, and continue cooking for 5 minutes, stirring frequently.

2. Add chicken, wild rice, stock, thyme, marjoram, ginger, and cumin, and bring to a boil. Lower heat, cover, and simmer until rice is tender (30 to 35 minutes). Before serving add salt substitute and pepper to taste, and soy sauce.

Makes 10 cups, 8 servings.

Preparation time: 15 minutes
Cooking time: 40 to 45 minutes
Per serving: calcium 38 mg, calories 250, carbohydrates 19 g, cholesterol 53 mg, fat 8 g, fiber 2 g, protein 24 g, sodium 404 mg

---

BASICS

HOMEMADE STOCKS

Regardless of the base—beef, veal, fish, vegetable, or chicken—do not boil the stock. Instead, simmer slowly. Boiling stock brings out acids and may also increase bitter tastes in vegetables and other bases.

BEEF OR VEAL STOCK

This hearty stock can be refrigerated, covered, for up to four days, and frozen for up to three months.

> 3 pounds beef or veal bones
> 1 teaspoon olive oil
>   Water, to cover
> 1 stalk celery
> 1 onion, quartered
> 1 bay leaf
> 1 carrot

In a stockpot brown the bones in 1 teaspoon olive oil. Then add remaining ingredients, simmer 3 hours, and strain.

Makes 4 cups.

FISH STOCK

Fish stock can be refrigerated, covered, for up to five days, and frozen for up to two months.

> 2 pounds fish tails, fish heads, shells from shrimp, or fish bones
>   Water, to cover
> 1 stalk celery
> 1 onion, quartered
> 1 bay leaf
> 1 carrot

In a large stockpot combine all ingredients; simmer 1½ hours and then strain.

Makes 4 to 6 cups.

VEGETARIAN STOCK

Vegetarian stock can be refrigerated, covered, for up to 10 days, or frozen for up to five months. The best vegetables to use are the ones with the richest flavors, such as tomatoes, mushrooms, onions, potatoes, and winter squash. Avoid using cucumbers, lettuce, spinach, bell peppers, and beet or carrot greens; they will give the stock an unpleasant flavor. For extra nutrition and stronger stock, replace the water with leftover liquid from steamed vegetables or cooked beans.

> 1 cup vegetable of choice
> 4 cups water
>   Herbal salt substitute and pepper, to taste

In a stockpot combine ingredients; simmer over low heat for 2 hours, then strain. Season with herbal salt substitute and pepper.

Makes 4 cups.

CHICKEN STOCK

This healthy chicken stock can be refrigerated, covered, for up to six days and frozen for up to two months (see Note).

> 2 pounds chicken bones, backs, and necks
>   Water, to cover
> 1 stalk celery
> 1 onion, quartered
> 1 bay leaf
> 1 carrot

In a large stockpot combine chicken bones, backs, and necks and the water. Add celery, onion, bay leaf, and carrot. Simmer over low heat 1½ hours. Strain.

Makes 4 to 6 cups.

Note To remove fat: Allow stock to chill for 2 hours. Fat will separate and rise to the top. Scoop fat off with spoon and discard. Remaining stock may be used in recipes calling for defatted chicken stock.

Artfully combining the pungency of capers with savory sautéed vegetables and chunks of white cod, this hearty fish soup makes an easy meal for a Sunday night supper.

FISH SOUP WITH CAPERS AND ONIONS

Sometimes called by its Russian name, *solyanka*, this soup uses a fresh or thawed, frozen whitefish, such as halibut, cod, or flounder, for the base. Serve with a dark rye bread.

> 2 cups minced onion
> 2 tablespoons unsalted butter or olive oil
> ²/₃ cup minced celery
> ²/₃ cup minced carrots
> 2 large tomatoes, seeded and cut into thin strips
> 1 cup dry white wine
> 1½ pounds whitefish, bones removed
> 1 cup peeled, seeded, and sliced cucumber
> 4 cups water
> 2 tablespoons capers, drained
> 2 tablespoons minced sour gherkin pickles
> 1 to 2 tablespoons lemon juice, to taste
> Herbal salt substitute and pepper, to taste
> Minced parsley, for garnish

1. In a large stockpot over medium-high heat, sauté onion in butter until soft but not browned. Add celery, carrots, tomatoes, and wine. Continue to cook for 5 minutes.

2. Add fish and cucumber. Cook for 3 to 4 minutes, then add the water. Bring to a boil. Lower heat and simmer until fish flakes (about 15 minutes). Add capers, pickles, lemon juice, and salt substitute and pepper to taste. Serve garnished with minced parsley.

Makes 11 cups, 8 servings.

Preparation time: 20 minutes
Cooking time: 30 minutes
Per serving: calcium 55 mg, calories 187, carbohydrates 6 g, cholesterol 59 mg, fat 8 g, fiber 2 g, protein 17 g, sodium 266 mg

BEAN AND BARLEY SOUP

A hearty addition to any meal, this thick bean soup should be made the day before for best flavor. Be sure to plan time to precook the dried beans (for a faster version, use canned, unsalted beans that are already cooked). Try making a double recipe and freezing half for later use.

$1/4$ cup dry sherry
2 teaspoons olive oil
1 cup sliced onion
2 cups sliced fresh mushrooms, such as domestic white, chanterelles, or shiitake
1 cup diced red potatoes
1 cup shredded carrot
1 teaspoon minced fresh basil
1 tablespoon minced garlic
2 cups cooked pinto beans (approximately $1^{1}/2$ cups dried)
1 cup barley
4 cups defatted Chicken Stock (see page 51)
2 tablespoons minced parsley
1 teaspoon herbal salt substitute
$1/8$ teaspoon cayenne pepper

1. In a heavy stockpot heat sherry and oil to simmering, then add onion. Stir well and cook over medium-high heat until soft but not too browned (5 to 8 minutes).

2. Add mushrooms, potato, carrot, basil, and garlic. Cook, stirring frequently, until mushrooms begin to weep moisture (about 8 minutes). Add beans and barley and cook for 2 more minutes.

3. Add stock, parsley, salt substitute, and cayenne. Bring to a boil, then lower heat to simmer. Cover pot and cook over medium heat until barley is tender (about 30 minutes). Serve hot.

Makes 8 cups, about 8 servings.

Preparation time: 20 minutes
Cooking time: 45 minutes
Per serving: calcium 71 mg, calories 210, carbohydrates 36 g, cholesterol 0 mg, fat 3 g, fiber 9 g, protein 10 g, sodium 240 mg

LIGHT AND EASY SOUPS

Perfect for a hot summer day, or as a simple make-ahead first course to an elegant dinner, these light and easy soups are a bonus when you have little time. Chilled soups are best served before the main meal, as their flavors are more delicate than those of hot soups. A light soup acts much like an appetizer—it stimulates the palate but does not overload the stomach.

LEEK AND MUSHROOM SOUP

In France, where this soup is a favorite, leeks are a popular vegetable. This soup relies on their light but distinctive flavor.

1 teaspoon olive oil
$1/4$ cup dry sherry
5 thick leeks, cleaned and sliced into rounds
2 cups thinly sliced fresh mushrooms
4 cups defatted Chicken Stock (see page 51)
2 teaspoons minced fresh chervil or parsley, or 1 teaspoon dried chervil or parsley
1 teaspoon dried basil

1. In a stockpot heat oil and sherry; add leeks and cook over medium-high heat until they are very soft and beginning to brown.

2. Add 1 cup of the mushrooms and cook over low heat until mushrooms weep moisture.

3. Add stock, chervil, and basil. Bring to a boil and cook 25 minutes over medium heat.

4. Add remaining mushrooms and simmer 5 minutes longer. Serve hot.

Makes 8 cups, 5 servings.

Preparation time: 15 minutes
Cooking time: 35 minutes
Per serving: calcium 97 mg, calories 138, carbohydrates 21 g, cholesterol 0 mg, fat 3 g, fiber 3 g, protein 7 g, sodium 325 mg

KOMBU MISO SOUP

A delicious vegetarian version of the popular miso (soy paste) soup that is served in restaurants, this soup uses a flavorful Japanese sea vegetable called *kombu*, which can be found in most Asian food stores. The recipe also calls for red and white miso.

For a graceful presentation, sliver green onion ends and float them on the surface of each bowl of soup. Top with black sesame seeds, which are also available at Asian markets and general supermarkets.

3 pieces kombu seaweed, dried (about 9 in. total)
6 cups water
$1/2$ cup red miso
$1/2$ cup white miso
4 ounces firm tofu, cut into $1/4$-inch cubes
1 green onion, minced
Low-sodium soy sauce or tamari, to taste (optional)

1. In a large stockpot, simmer kombu in the water for 30 minutes, then strain. Discard cooked kombu.

2. Heat kombu stock to boiling. Remove 1 cup of stock from stockpot and dissolve red and white misos into it, blending carefully with the back of a large spoon until all lumps are gone. Return mixture to stockpot.

3. Add tofu and green onion to stock. Turn off heat and let stand 3 minutes to heat tofu. Taste for seasoning and add soy sauce, if used.

Makes $7^{1}/2$ cups, 6 servings.

Preparation time: 5 minutes
Cooking time: 40 minutes
Per serving: calcium 176 mg, calories 151, carbohydrates 20 g, cholesterol 0 mg, fat 5 g, fiber 4 g, protein 10 g, sodium 1,802 mg

Rich-tasting Curried Acorn Squash Bisque is certainly harvest fare—a purée of baked acorn squash and red bell peppers, with sherry, ginger, pepper, and curry spices.

CURRIED ACORN SQUASH BISQUE

Serve this bisque with a light chicken or fish dish, crusty bread, and a fruit dessert.

    2 small acorn squash
    1 teaspoon olive oil
  1/2 cup minced onion
    2 cloves garlic, minced
    1 red bell pepper, seeded and finely diced
  1/3 cup dry sherry
2 1/2 cups defatted Chicken Stock (see page 51)
    1 cup freshly squeezed orange juice
  1/2 teaspoon ground cumin
  1/2 teaspoon ground coriander
    1 teaspoon grated fresh ginger
  1/4 teaspoon dry mustard
      Herbal salt substitute, to taste
  1/4 teaspoon cayenne pepper
  1/4 teaspoon white pepper
  1/4 cup nonfat plain yogurt

1. Preheat oven to 350° F. Split squash lengthwise, leaving in the seeds (to help the squash steam more quickly due to moisture content). Place halves, split side down, on an aluminum-foil-lined baking sheet. Bake until soft (about 40 minutes).

2. Scoop out squash seeds and discard. Scoop flesh from shells and mash well; set aside. Discard shells.

3. In a large stockpot, heat oil; add onion and sauté over medium heat until onion is soft.

4. Add garlic, bell pepper, and sherry; cook 5 minutes. Add reserved squash, stock, orange juice, cumin, coriander, ginger, dry mustard, salt substitute, cayenne, and white pepper.

5. Bring to a boil, lower heat, cover, and simmer for 35 minutes. Purée soup and stir in yogurt. Taste for seasoning and serve hot.

Makes 6 cups, 6 servings.

Preparation time: 20 minutes
Cooking time: 85 minutes
Per serving: calcium 87 mg, calories 130, carbohydrates 23 g, cholesterol 0 mg, fat 2 g, fiber .6 g, protein 4 g, sodium 195 mg

HOT AND SOUR SOUP

The trick with this soup is to attain a delicate balance between the savory stock, spicy pepper, sour vinegar, and mushroom flavors.

> 8 cups defatted Chicken Stock (see page 51)
> 1/2 cup dried black mushrooms, such as Japanese shiitake
> 1 teaspoon sesame oil
> 1 tablespoon sake
> 1/4 cup minced onion
> 8 ounces firm tofu, cubed
> 3 tablespoons arrowroot mixed with 1/2 cup cold water
> 3 1/2 tablespoons rice vinegar
> 1 beaten egg
> 3 teaspoons low-sodium soy sauce or tamari
> 1/4 teaspoon cayenne pepper
> 1/8 teaspoon freshly ground black pepper

1. In a large stockpot, heat stock. Add dried mushrooms and simmer for 15 minutes.

2. Strain out mushrooms, leaving stock simmering on the stove. Cut off and discard mushroom stems. Slice tops thinly and return to stockpot.

3. In a small skillet heat sesame oil and sake; add onion and sauté slowly until onion is very soft. Add onion and any pan liquor to stock in stockpot.

4. Stir in tofu, arrowroot mixture, vinegar, egg, soy sauce, cayenne, and black pepper; cook until egg forms into ribbons and soup thickens slightly from arrowroot (about 1 minute). Serve hot.

Makes 10 cups, 8 servings.

> *Preparation time:* 10 minutes
> *Cooking time:* 25 minutes
> *Per serving:* calcium 77 mg, calories 155, carbohydrates 17 g, cholesterol 27 mg, fat 5 g, fiber 3 g, protein 12 g, sodium 434 mg

SHOMINI ABOOR

This soup is served in the Middle East as a light meal or as a first course before lamb or beef. Try it with the Marinated Beef Kabobs on page 167.

> 4 cups defatted Chicken Stock (see page 51)
> 1 1/2 cups chopped spinach leaves
> 1/2 cup bulgur
> 1/2 cup dried lentils
> 1 clove garlic, mashed
>   Herbal salt substitute, to taste
> 2 cups peeled and chopped fresh tomatoes
> 2 tablespoons tomato paste
> 2 tablespoons dried basil

1. In a stockpot bring stock to a boil. Add spinach, bulgur, and lentils. Bring to a boil again; lower heat; cover; and simmer for 25 to 30 minutes.

2. Add garlic, salt substitute, tomatoes, and tomato paste; cook until lentils are soft (about 30 minutes). Add basil during last 5 minutes of cooking time.

3. Taste for seasoning and serve hot.

Makes 8 cups, 6 servings.

> *Preparation time:* 10 minutes
> *Cooking time:* 60 minutes
> *Per serving:* calcium 70 mg, calories 145, carbohydrates 24 g, cholesterol 0 mg, fat 2 g, fiber 9 g, protein 11 g, sodium 270 mg

FRENCH-STYLE CREAM OF BROCCOLI SOUP

The flavor of this light and simple soup depends on peak-of-the-season herbs and vegetables. It makes a pleasant first course or a light summer luncheon with a garden salad, crusty whole wheat bread, and a light fruit dessert such as Wine-Basted Pears (see page 203).

> 1 teaspoon olive oil
> 1/2 medium onion, finely chopped
> 1/2 cup firmly packed chopped celery leaves and stalk
> 2 large stalks of broccoli, chopped
> 1 cup defatted Chicken Stock (see page 51)
> 2 cups nonfat milk
> 2 teaspoons chopped fresh dill
> 1 teaspoon herbal salt substitute
> 1 teaspoon chopped fresh basil
> 1/2 teaspoon very finely minced fresh rosemary leaves
> 1/2 cup rolled oats

1. In a stockpot heat oil; add onion and sauté over medium heat until onion is soft and translucent.

2. Add celery, broccoli, and stock; cover and cook over low heat until broccoli is bright green (about 8 minutes).

3. Remove to blender; add milk, dill, salt substitute, basil, rosemary, and oats; purée. Return to stockpot and heat through. Taste for seasoning and serve hot.

Makes 6 cups, 6 servings.

> *Preparation time:* 20 minutes
> *Cooking time:* 15 minutes
> *Per serving:* calcium 136 mg, calories 80, carbohydrates 11 g, cholesterol 1 mg, fat 2 g, fiber 2 g, protein 6 g, sodium 234 mg

TIPS

...ON FREEZING SOUPS

Soups freeze better than almost any other kind of cooked food. You can use the freezer during several stages of soup making. Here are some tips:

☐ If you're planning to freeze a soup, undercook it just a little, so that the vegetables stay crisp and bright in color.

☐ Before freezing let the cooked soup come to room temperature, preferably in a cool spot.

☐ Pour soup into food-grade plastic containers or doubled sealable plastic bags; fill only three-fourths of the way (the soup will expand when frozen). It's best to package soup in 2-cup portions, so you won't have leftovers. Freeze solid. Do not refreeze any meat- or fish-based soups, since they can develop bacteria during the freezing process.

☐ Try freezing homemade stocks (see How to Make Soup Stocks, page 51) in ice cube trays: Pour hot soup into plastic or metal trays, freeze, then transfer the cubes to a heavyweight sealable plastic bag. This method is ideal for cooking small portions—four cubes, when defrosted, make approximately $\frac{1}{2}$ cup of stock.

☐ For an instant lunch: Sauté $\frac{1}{2}$ cup mixed vegetables, such as onion, carrot, celery, cabbage, and red bell pepper in 1 teaspoon olive oil. Add 4 frozen cubes of homemade stock, cover pot, and let cook on medium heat until stock is defrosted (about 5 minutes). Simply season to taste with fresh herbs, herbal salt substitute, and freshly ground pepper, and you have soup for a quick lunch.

GINGERED CAULIFLOWER SOUP

This light soup, reminiscent of Asian cooking, is thickened with rolled oats, which have a mild taste and create a wonderful creamy texture without the calories of cream. The jicama (pronounced HEE-ki-muh), a Mexican root vegetable, can be replaced by water chestnuts. As a nutritional bonus, the rolled oats provide a good source of fiber.

     1 teaspoon olive oil
    ¼ cup dry sherry
     1 medium onion, minced
     2 teaspoons grated fresh ginger
     2 cups chopped cauliflower
     4 cups defatted Chicken or
        Vegetarian Stock (see page 51)
     1 cup julienned jicama
    ¼ cup rolled oats
    ½ cup minced green onion,
        including greens
     1 teaspoon Asian sesame oil
        Herbal salt substitute and
        pepper, to taste

1. In a stockpot heat oil and sherry; add onion and ginger and sauté over medium heat until soft.

2. Add cauliflower and cook 3 minutes, stirring. Add stock, jicama, and oats; bring to a boil. Lower heat, cover, and simmer for 25 minutes.

3. Purée cauliflower mixture in blender. Return to pot and add green onion and sesame oil. Heat through. Add salt substitute and pepper and serve hot.

Makes 8 cups, 6 servings.

> *Preparation time:* 25 minutes
> *Cooking time:* 45 minutes
> *Per serving:* calcium 37 mg, calories 89, carbohydrates 9 g, cholesterol 0 mg, fat 3 g, fiber 3 g, protein 5 g, sodium 311 mg

GARLIC SOUP GILROY-STYLE

Gilroy, located east of Santa Cruz, California, is the "Garlic Capital" of the world. Each year the town conducts a garlic festival that fills the air with the aroma of roasting garlic. This Gilroy recipe simmers the hometown specialty to bring out its sweetness.

     1 teaspoon olive oil
     1 cup dry white wine
     1 medium onion, finely chopped
     5 bulbs of garlic, wrapped in
        cheesecloth and mashed
     4 cups defatted Chicken Stock
        (see page 51)
     2 bay leaves, crushed
    ½ teaspoon dried thyme
    ¼ teaspoon dried marjoram
     4 sprigs parsley, chopped
        Herbal salt substitute and
        pepper, to taste
    ½ cup nonfat milk

1. In a stockpot heat oil and wine; add onion and sauté over medium heat until onion is soft.

2. Add garlic wrapped in cheesecloth, stock, bay leaves, thyme, marjoram, and parsley. Bring to a boil; lower heat, cover, and simmer for 45 minutes. (Do not let soup boil rapidly or garlic will become bitter.)

3. Remove cheesecloth packet of garlic. Take soft, cooked garlic from cloth and force it through a sieve, leaving the papery skins behind; add mashed garlic to soup.

4. Add salt substitute, pepper, and milk; heat through and serve.

Makes 6 cups, 6 servings.

> *Preparation time:* 15 minutes
> *Cooking time:* 55 minutes
> *Per serving:* calcium 646 mg, calories 188, carbohydrates 25 g, cholesterol 0 mg, fat 4 g, fiber 5 g, protein 13 g, sodium 401 mg

PESTO SUMMER VEGETABLE SOUP

This French summer soup depends heavily on fresh, tasty produce, which is usually best when the harvest is at its peak.

  1 *teaspoon olive oil*
  ¹/₃ *cup sliced onion*
  ¹/₂ *cup diced red potato*
  ¹/₂ *cup sliced green beans*
  ¹/₂ *cup sliced zucchini*
  ¹/₄ *cup chopped celery leaves*
  ¹/₂ *cup peeled and chopped tomato*
  1 *cup cooked navy beans (approximately ¹/₂ cup dried)*
  ¹/₈ *teaspoon saffron*
  ¹/₂ *teaspoon freshly ground black pepper*
  4 *cups defatted Chicken or Vegetarian Stock (see page 51)*
  2 *tablespoons tomato paste*

Pesto

  2 *cloves garlic, minced*
  1 *cup chopped fresh basil leaves*
  ¹/₄ *cup walnuts, finely chopped*
  2 *tablespoons grated Parmesan cheese*

1. In a stockpot heat oil; add onion and sauté over medium heat until soft.

2. Add potato, green beans, zucchini, celery leaves, tomato, navy beans, saffron, pepper, and stock. Bring to a boil, cover, and simmer for 35 minutes, stirring occasionally. Stir in tomato paste and Pesto.

Makes 7 cups, 6 servings.

Pesto In a blender, combine garlic, basil, walnuts, and cheese, and purée.

Makes 1¹/₂ cups, 6 servings.

Preparation time: 25 minutes
Cooking time: 45 minutes
Per serving: calcium 323 mg, calories 166, carbohydrates 21 g, cholesterol 1 mg, fat 6 g, fiber 4 g, protein 11 g, sodium 297 mg

Alive with the flavors of midsummer, Pesto Summer Vegetable Soup is delicately seasoned with fresh basil and garlic. Serve with bread sticks.

SEASONAL SOUPS

Using fresh ingredients in soups is always a healthy idea. This is easy in summer, when produce is abundant. In winter, soups can be made with hearty cold-weather vegetables, beans, and grains.

SUMMER CURRIED PEA SOUP

Of East Indian origin, this soup is a brightly colored mixture of yellow and green, an ideal prelude to spicy entrées such as Indonesian Tempura (see page 134).

> 1 cup chopped onion
> 2 teaspoons Asian sesame oil
> 1/4 cup dry sherry
> 1 tablespoon minced garlic
> 1 tablespoon curry powder
> 1/2 cup chopped carrots
> 3 cups peas, fresh or frozen
> 2 tablespoons whole wheat flour
> 3 cups defatted Chicken Stock (see page 51)
> Herbal salt substitute and pepper, to taste
> Minced green onion and nonfat plain yogurt, for garnish

1. In a heavy stockpot over medium-high heat, sauté onion in oil and sherry until soft (8 to 10 minutes). Add garlic, curry powder, carrot, and peas, and continue to cook, stirring frequently, for 5 minutes.

2. Add flour and cook for 2 minutes, stirring constantly. Do not let flour brown. Add stock and bring to a boil.

3. Lower heat and simmer soup, uncovered, for 10 to 12 minutes. Purée half the soup at a time, and then return to pot. Heat through. Adjust seasonings if needed, and serve hot, garnished with green onions and nonfat yogurt.

Makes 6 cups, 6 servings.

> *Preparation time:* 25 minutes
> *Cooking time:* 30 minutes
> *Per serving:* calcium 40 mg, calories 131, carbohydrates 17 g, cholesterol 0 mg, fat 3 g, fiber 5 g, protein 7 g, sodium 200 mg

FRENCH SPRING GARDEN POTAGE

A delicate and simple soup, French Spring Garden Potage reflects the harvests of the spring garden—fresh herbs, tomatoes, green onions, and peas. For the best flavor, make the soup early in the day and let it sit for several hours before serving.

> 1 cup minced green onions, including green tops
> 1 teaspoon olive oil
> 1/2 cup diced carrots
> 1/2 cup diced turnips
> 1/2 cup string beans, sliced diagonally into 1/2-inch lengths
> 1/2 cup chopped tomatoes
> 1/2 cup shelled peas
> 3 tablespoons minced parsley
> 1 teaspoon chopped fresh mint
> 1 teaspoon light honey
> 1/4 teaspoon ground cloves
> 6 cups defatted Chicken or Vegetarian Stock (see page 51)
> Herbal salt substitute and pepper, to taste
> Nonfat plain yogurt, for garnish

1. In a heavy stockpot over medium-high heat, sauté green onions in olive oil until brightly colored and soft (4 to 5 minutes). Add carrots, turnips, beans, and tomatoes, and continue to cook for 8 minutes.

2. Add peas, parsley, mint, honey, cloves, and stock, and bring to a boil. Lower heat to simmer and cook for 15 more minutes. Taste for seasoning and add salt substitute and pepper to taste. Serve hot or chilled, garnished with a dollop of yogurt.

Makes 10 cups, 8 servings.

> *Preparation time:* 25 minutes
> *Cooking time:* 30 minutes
> *Per serving:* calcium 50 mg, calories 65, carbohydrates 7 g, cholesterol 0 mg, fat 2 g, fiber 2 g, protein 5 g, sodium 299 mg

UKRAINIAN SUMMER CUCUMBER AND LEMON BORSCHT

In the Ukraine, borscht is considered a great way to utilize abundant summer garden crops—even in this unusual beetless version. The yogurt provides calcium and, when combined with the cucumber, gives the soup a pleasant sweet-and-sour flavor. Try to use bottled water (tap water may flavor this uncooked soup too heavily). Serve the soup as an elegant first course before a fish entrée or a light veal dish such as Veal and Apple Scaloppine (see page 169).

> 4 cups peeled, seeded, and coarsely chopped cucumbers
> Juice of 2 small lemons
> 1 teaspoon herbal salt substitute or sea salt
> 1 tablespoon honey
> 1 cup nonfat plain yogurt
> 1 cup spring water or water that has been boiled and cooled
> 1 cup minced turkey ham
> 1 large tomato, chopped
> Herbal salt substitute and white pepper, to taste
> Fresh dill sprigs and nonfat plain yogurt, for garnish

1. Place cucumbers, lemon juice, salt substitute, honey, yogurt, and the water into a blender and purée until very smooth. Add minced turkey ham. Pour soup into a large bowl, cover with plastic wrap, and refrigerate overnight.

2. In the morning, purée tomato and add to soup. Taste for seasoning and add more salt substitute and pepper if needed. Serve soup in chilled bowls with a garnish of fresh dill and a dollop of yogurt.

Makes 6 cups, 6 servings.

> *Preparation time:* 20 minutes
> *Chilling time:* 8 to 24 hours
> *Per serving:* calcium 91 mg, calories 74, carbohydrates 9 g, cholesterol 14 mg, fat 1 g, fiber 1 g, protein 7 g, sodium 265 mg

MIDWESTERN CORN CHOWDER

Corn chowder is ideal for late summer or early fall parties in the backyard, especially in the Midwest corn belt. For a healthier version, nonfat milk and potato purée replace the rich cream base used in traditional recipes. This soup freezes beautifully, so make a double batch, especially when corn is at its peak.

3/4 cup chopped onion
1 teaspoon unsalted butter
1/4 cup dry sherry
1 cup chopped celery
2 cups diced red potatoes
1 bay leaf
2 cups defatted Chicken or Vegetarian Stock (see page 51)
2 cups chopped tomatoes
1 1/2 cups corn kernels
1 1/2 cups nonfat milk
1/2 cup chopped parsley
Freshly ground black pepper (optional)

1. In a large stockpot over medium-high heat, sauté onion in butter and sherry until soft but not browned. Add celery and potatoes and sauté for 2 minutes. Crush bay leaf and wrap in cheesecloth or place in a tea ball. Add stock and bay leaf to soup, and bring to a boil.

2. Lower heat to simmer and cook, covered, until potatoes are tender (20 minutes). Remove bay leaf and discard. Place 2 cups of the soup in a blender and purée. Return to pot. Add tomatoes, corn, and milk, and bring to a boil again. Lower heat and simmer for 5 minutes. Add parsley, taste for seasoning, and add pepper, if desired.

Makes 10 cups, 8 servings.

> *Preparation time:* 15 to 20 minutes
> *Cooking time:* 35 to 40 minutes
> *Per serving:* calcium 131 mg, calories 109, carbohydrates 18 g, cholesterol 2 mg, fat 2 g, fiber 3 g, protein 6 g, sodium 127 mg

HEARTY LIMA BEAN SOUP

This winter soup combines the salty flavor of turkey ham with sautéed carrots, baby lima beans, and green onions. Make the soup the day before serving and keep it overnight in the refrigerator—the flavors blend and deepen as the soup sits. Serve with toasted halves of pita bread and a tossed green salad.

1 1/2 cups chopped onion
1 cup thinly sliced carrots
4 tablespoons unsalted butter
1 tablespoon garlic powder
1 teaspoon herbal salt substitute
2 tablespoons lemon juice
2 cups diced turkey ham
1 package (10 oz) frozen baby lima beans
1 tablespoon dried marjoram
1/2 cup chopped parsley
4 cups water
Croutons, for garnish (optional)

1. In a heavy stockpot over medium-high heat, sauté onion and carrots in butter for 5 minutes. Add garlic powder, salt substitute, and lemon juice. Cook until onions are soft (about 5 minutes). Add turkey ham, lima beans, marjoram, parsley, and water.

2. Bring soup to a boil, then lower heat to simmer and cook for 20 minutes, covered, stirring occasionally. Serve hot, garnished with croutons, if desired.

Makes 8 cups, 8 servings.

> *Preparation time:* 30 minutes
> *Cooking time:* 30 minutes
> *Per serving:* calcium 110 mg, calories 250, carbohydrates 30 g, cholesterol 36 mg, fat 9 g, fiber 1 g, protein 16 g, sodium 381 mg

BASICS

SAUTÉING VEGETABLES FOR SOUPS

Sautéing can keep the vegetables for vegetable based soups from losing flavor. Always start with a very hot saucepan. Add a little oil or sherry and let it heat until very hot. Before sautéing, be sure that the vegetables are dry to prevent steam from forming when they are added to the oil. This is first a matter of safety for the cook; moisture that comes in contact with the hot oil splatters wildly. In addition, it is theorized that steam prevents the oil from sealing the food.

Add vegetables in the order given below, stirring until each is coated completely with oil or sherry. Cook until vegetables soften and brighten in color.

1. Onions, green onions, leeks, shallots, and other vegetables of the onion family

2. Carrots, beets, turnips, jicama, ginger, and other root vegetables

3. Cabbage, celery, bok choy, and other stalked vegetables

4. Peppers, squash, beans, peas, and other vine vegetables

5. Tomatoes

6. Mushrooms

7. Garlic

8. Fresh herbs

9. Dried herbs

Following this general order helps the soup develop a full, robust flavor.

Chilled Curried Zucchini Soup (see page 61) combines puréed zucchini, green onions, curry spices, and low-fat buttermilk for a refreshing summer treat. Here it is accompanied by a citrus salad tossed with a tangy vinaigrette dressing.

COOL AND REFRESHING SOUPS

The main ingredients in these soups are fresh fruits or vegetables; the soups are cooked slightly, seasoned subtly, and then refrigerated for several hours to blend the flavors. Use only the freshest, ripest fruits and vegetables, since the just-picked flavor is essential to the success of these soups.

SUMMER MELON SOUP WITH LIME

This soup makes a very refreshing dessert or first course.

> 2 cups peeled, seeded, and
>   chopped ripe cantaloupe
> 1 cup peeled, seeded, and
>   chopped ripe honeydew
> 2 cups peeled, seeded, and
>   chopped ripe casaba
> 1/3 cup freshly squeezed lime juice
> 1 teaspoon honey
> 1/4 cup nonfat plain yogurt
>   Fresh mint leaves, (optional)

In a food processor or blender, purée all ingredients except mint leaves. Chill thoroughly and serve garnished with mint, if desired, in small glass bowls.

Makes 6 cups, 6 servings.

> *Preparation time:* 20 minutes
> *Chilling time:* 60 minutes
> *Per serving:* calcium 51 mg, calories 60, carbohydrates 14 g, cholesterol 0 mg, fat .4 g, fiber 1 g, protein 2 g, sodium 23 mg

FRESH TOMATO SOUP WITH DILL

The best time to try this recipe is when tomatoes are at their summer ripest. Serve chilled or heated.

> 1 teaspoon olive oil
> 1/4 cup dry sherry
> 2 cups finely minced onion
> 1 tablespoon minced garlic
> 1/2 cup minced red bell pepper
> 5 large ripe beefsteak tomatoes,
>   peeled and coarsely chopped
> 2 cups defatted Chicken Stock
>   (see page 51)
> 2 tablespoons chopped fresh dill
>   Herbal salt substitute and
>   pepper, to taste

1. In a stockpot over low heat, warm oil and sherry. Add onion and sauté slowly, until onion is soft.

2. Add garlic and red pepper; cook 3 minutes, stirring. Add tomatoes and cook 5 minutes more.

3. Add stock and dill and bring to a boil. Lower heat, cover, and simmer for 45 minutes. Add salt substitute and pepper, and serve.

Makes 8 cups, 8 servings.

Preparation time: 25 minutes
Cooking time: 60 minutes
Per serving: calcium 42 mg, calories 54, carbohydrates 7 g, cholesterol 0 mg, fat 1 g, fiber 2 g, protein 3 g, sodium 175 mg

---

CHILLED CURRIED ZUCCHINI SOUP

This refreshing and delicate soup is ideal for a light summer lunch.

- 2 teaspoons olive oil
- 1 large onion, sliced
- 3 green onions, minced
- 3 to 4 medium-sized zucchini, sliced, plus grated zucchini, for garnish
- 1 tablespoon curry powder
- 1 tablespoon ground cumin
- 2 cups water
- 3 cups low-fat buttermilk
  Herbal salt substitute and pepper, to taste

1. In a large stockpot, heat oil; add onion and sauté over medium heat until onion is soft. Add green onion and zucchini and continue cooking over medium heat until zucchini is limp.

2. Add curry powder, cumin, and the water and cook for 5 minutes over medium heat.

3. Add buttermilk; transfer soup to blender and blend to a smooth purée. Add salt substitute and pepper; chill. Serve garnished with grated zucchini.

Makes 6 cups, 8 servings.

Preparation time: 15 minutes
Cooking time: 10 minutes
Chilling time: 60 minutes
Per serving: calcium 178 mg, calories 83, carbohydrates 12 g, cholesterol 3 mg, fat 3 g, fiber 3 g, protein 5 g, sodium 179 mg

MENU

MEXICAN GRILLING FIESTA

Guacamole-Shrimp Dip With Raw Vegetable Basket

Iced Sangria

Mushroom Kabobs

Green Gazpacho

Mexican Baked Fish in Salsa Verde (see page 121)

Mexican Bean Salad (see page 75)

Platter of Sliced Papaya, Mango, Melon, and Kiwifruit

Spicy Green Gazpacho and Baked Fish in Salsa Verde add the zing of fresh chiles to this outdoor south-of-the-border menu. Offer a selection of sparkling water or add fruit juice to red wine and chill for an icy sangria. Preheat the grill or barbecue about one hour before dinner, so that the coals will be ready when you are. Most of the menu can be prepared ahead and reheated at the last minute. Chill the fruit for dessert and then slice onto chilled platters and garnish with lime wedges. Menu serves from four to six.

GUACAMOLE-SHRIMP DIP WITH RAW VEGETABLE BASKET

Most guacamole dishes are made with oil, mayonnaise, and lots of avocados. This version blends avocado with low-fat cottage cheese, but tastes just as good. Use hard-skinned Hass avocados (black skin indicates ripeness), so the shells can be cut in half, scooped out, and stuffed. Believe it or not, an avocado pit stuffed into the center of a bowl of guacamole prevents guacamole from turning brown. It really works, but be prepared to explain to your friends why the pit is there.

- 2 ripe avocados, scooped out, with meat, shells, and pits reserved
- 2 tablespoons freshly squeezed lemon juice
- 1/2 cup low-fat cottage cheese
- 3 tablespoons salsa
- 1/4 cup cooked shrimp meat
- 3 cloves garlic, minced
- 1 tablespoon minced cilantro, plus chopped cilantro, for garnish (optional)
- 1 head curly endive or lettuce, separated into leaves
- 1 cup carrot sticks
- 1 cup whole cherry tomatoes
- 1 cup raw cauliflower florets

In a blender or food processor, place avocado meat, lemon juice, cheese, salsa, shrimp, garlic, and minced cilantro; purée. Spoon into scooped-out avocado shells. Bury a pit in the center of each shell. Line a platter with endive and on it arrange stuffed shells surrounded by carrot sticks, cherry tomatoes, and cauliflower florets. Garnish with chopped cilantro, if desired. Serve slightly chilled or at room temperature.

Serves 4 to 6.

Preparation time: 25 minutes
Per serving: calcium 89 mg, calories 179, carbohydrates 15 g, cholesterol 20 mg, fat 11 g, fiber 9 g, protein 8 g, sodium 151 mg

MUSHROOM KABOBS

Grilling, a popular outdoor summer activity, can easily be incorporated into your healthy meal planning. These vegetarian kabobs can be assembled and marinated the night before your meal or party.

Mushrooms absorb the flavor of olive oil well and grill easily. They are combined on bamboo skewers with cherry tomatoes, onion, bell pepper, and pineapple chunks for a colorful finger food.

- 2 cups whole button mushrooms
- 24 cherry tomatoes (see Note)
- 1 red onion, cut into 1-inch chunks
- 2 large red bell peppers, seeded and cut into 1-inch squares
- 1 cup pineapple chunks, unsweetened
- 2 teaspoons olive oil, for brushing

1. Prepare mesquite grill, if used. Presoak bamboo skewers in salted water (1 tablespoon salt per cup of water) for 15 minutes to prevent burning on grill. Arrange vegetables on bamboo skewers, alternating colors and shapes, until you have filled 12 skewers. Brush lightly with olive oil.

2. Grill kabobs briefly over hot coals or under a broiler, turning frequently until lightly browned and slightly crisp (about 15 minutes). Serve warm.

Makes 12 kabobs, serves 4 to 6.

Note You may want to add the cherry tomatoes near the end of grilling time to help keep their shape.

Preparation time: 20 minutes
Cooking time: 15 minutes
Per serving: calcium 47 mg, calories 200, carbohydrates 42 g, cholesterol 0 mg, fat 4 g, fiber 9 g, protein 7 g, sodium 67 mg

GREEN GAZPACHO

A traditional Spanish chilled vegetable soup, gazpacho is sometimes blended to a purée, sometimes left chunky. Gazpacho is usually a tomato-based soup, but here is a new version made with fresh green vegetables and a chicken stock flavored with snow peas.

- 6 cups snow peas
- 3 cups defatted Chicken Stock (see page 51)
- 1 small onion, finely minced
- 2 cloves garlic, pressed
- 1/2 cup chopped green bell pepper
- 1 small jalapeño chile, seeded and finely chopped
- 3/4 cup chopped celery stalk and leaves
- 2 teaspoons lemon juice, preferably fresh
- 1 teaspoon lime juice, preferably fresh
- 1/2 teaspoon dried tarragon
- 1/2 teaspoon ground cumin
- 1/8 teaspoon cayenne pepper, or to taste
  Herbal salt substitute, to taste
  Chopped fresh tomatillos, for garnish

1. In a stockpot place snow peas and stock; bring to a boil. Lower heat and simmer 35 minutes. Strain out snow peas and reserve (see Note).

2. Add onion, garlic, bell pepper, jalapeño, celery, lemon juice, lime juice, tarragon, and cumin; chill. Add cayenne and salt substitute and serve cold, garnished with chopped tomatillos.

Makes 5 cups, about 6 servings.

Note If desired, purée or chop the cooked snow peas and add to soup for a sweeter flavor.

Preparation time: 20 minutes
Cooking time: 45 minutes
Chilling time: 2 hours
Per serving: calcium 94 mg, calories 100, carbohydrates 15 g, cholesterol 0 mg, fat 1 g, fiber 5 g, protein 8 g, sodium 425 mg

A first course of grilled marinated Mushroom Kabobs is followed by Green Gazpacho and Mexican Baked Fish in Salsa Verde.

Create healthy, satisfying salads from a variety of garden-fresh greens, rich-tasting low-fat dressings, and eye-catching garnishes.

SALADS

Besides doing wonders for your nutritional profile, salads earn high marks for their fresh taste and exciting visual appeal. In this chapter you'll find not only an impressive assortment of fresh green salads, but also fruit, pasta, bean, and grain salad recipes. Recipes such as Taco Salad (see page 79), Spicy Chinese Potato Salad (see page 68), or Indonesian Peanut Slaw (see page 66) reflect the worldwide popularity of salads. A section on special tips for preparing healthy homemade salad dressings offers tasty, economical alternatives to the store-bought variety.

LIGHT AND EASY SALADS

In most European countries, preparing salads is not as complicated as in America. A salad bowl is filled with crisp butter lettuce and perhaps some curly endive, and then drizzled with vinegar, oil, salt, and pepper. This standard is served after the main course at every meal. The idea—which is exemplified by the following light, international salads—is to refresh and clear the palate, introduce some crispness of texture, and help stimulate the digestion with enzymes from green vegetables.

SPINACH AND PINE NUT SALAD

A variation on the spinach salad theme, this salad, when served with a Greek moussaka, makes a wonderful meal.

   2 bunches spinach, washed and stemmed
   1 red onion, sliced thinly
   ½ cup grated carrot
   2 tablespoons toasted pine nuts
   ¼ cup Greek olives, pitted
   1 cup crumbled feta cheese
   2 tablespoons olive oil
   1 tablespoon wine vinegar
   1 teaspoon lemon juice
   1 teaspoon Dijon mustard
   Herbal salt substitute and pepper, to taste

1. In a large salad bowl, mix spinach leaves, onion, carrot, nuts, olives, and feta cheese.

2. In another bowl, whisk together the oil, vinegar, lemon juice, mustard, salt substitute, and pepper. Pour over salad and toss. Serve immediately.

Serves 6.

Preparation time: 25 minutes
Per serving: calcium 128 mg, calories 145, carbohydrates 7 g, cholesterol 17 mg, fat 12 g, fiber 2 g, protein 7 g, sodium 387 mg

TABBOULEH

Tabbouleh (pronounced tab-BOO-lee) is a festive salad from Lebanon. Although it has many recipe variations, its standard ingredients usually include mint, parsley, olive oil, and lemon juice. In this low-fat version, colorful shredded vegetables are also added and olive oil is kept to a minimum. Tabbouleh keeps for up to five days if tightly covered and refrigerated.

   2 cups bulgur
   3 cups boiling water
   2 cups shredded red or green cabbage
   ½ large carrot, grated
   ½ cucumber, peeled and diced
   1 stalk celery, chopped
   ½ cup chopped fresh mint
   2 ripe tomatoes, chopped
   ¾ cup chopped green onions, including greens
   ¼ cup freshly squeezed lemon juice
   3½ tablespoons olive oil
   2 teaspoons herbal salt substitute
   1 cup chopped parsley
   1 small lemon, sliced, for garnish

1. In a bowl place bulgur and boiling water and cover with a plate. Let sit for 20 minutes.

2. Mix cooked bulgur with remaining ingredients except lemon slices and chill for 1 hour. Serve cold with slices of lemon.

Serves 6.

Preparation time: 20 minutes
Cooking time: 20 minutes
Chilling time: 1 hour
Per serving: calcium 258 mg, calories 297, carbohydrates 50 g, cholesterol 0 mg, fat 10 g, fiber 11 g, protein 10 g, sodium 79 mg

INDONESIAN PEANUT SLAW

Made with blended tofu, this is a delicious salad with a traditional Asian dressing.

   4 cups thinly sliced green cabbage (core removed)
   1 cup grated carrot
   1 cup chopped fresh pineapple
   2 tablespoons peanuts, chopped
   1 tablespoon currants
   1 teaspoon chopped cilantro
   1 cup soft tofu
   2 teaspoons light sesame oil
   3 tablespoons rice vinegar
   1 tablespoon frozen orange juice concentrate
   1 tablespoon honey
   ¼ teaspoon freshly ground black pepper
   2 tablespoons grated onion

1. In a large salad bowl, place cabbage, carrot, pineapple, peanuts, currants, and cilantro.

2. Mix tofu, oil, vinegar, juice concentrate, honey, pepper, and onion in a blender until smooth, then toss with cabbage mixture until well coated. Chill for 20 minutes, then serve.

Serves 4.

Preparation time: 25 minutes
Chilling time: 20 minutes
Per serving: calcium 115 mg, calories 175, carbohydrates 24 g, cholesterol 0 mg, fat 7 g, fiber 3 g, protein 7 g, sodium 55 mg

JAMAICAN PAPAYA SALAD

This salad features fresh papaya, watercress, and hearts of palm and is topped with chopped cilantro, lime juice, and avocado. A slightly sweet white wine, such as a Riesling, complements the salad.

  1   cup watercress
  2   cups peeled, seeded, and thinly sliced papaya
  1/4 cup thinly sliced avocado
  1   cup canned hearts of palm, drained and sliced
  1   cup thinly sliced tomato
  2   tablespoons lime juice
  2   tablespoons chopped cilantro
  1/4 teaspoon herbal salt substitute
  1/8 teaspoon ground coriander
  1/8 teaspoon allspice

1. Arrange watercress on 4 small salad plates. Layer slices of papaya, avocado, hearts of palm, and tomato on top.

2. Stir together lime juice, cilantro, salt substitute, coriander, and allspice. Drizzle over papaya salads. Cover with plastic wrap and chill 30 minutes before serving.

Serves 4.

Preparation time: 20 minutes
Chilling time: 30 minutes
Per serving: calcium 56 mg, calories 126, carbohydrates 27 g, cholesterol 0 mg, fat 3 g, fiber 4 g, protein 3 g, sodium 21 mg

You can almost hear the steel drums and the beat of the Caribbean in this savory Jamaican salad. As a bonus, the dish contains no cholesterol.

MINTED BULGUR SALAD

A lively variation on tabbouleh—the Middle Eastern salad made of fiber-rich cracked wheat, lemon juice, and parsley—this bulgur salad adds fresh mint, cucumber, and carrot, creating an excellent picnic or casual supper dish. It can be made the day before; cover tightly with plastic wrap and refrigerate after tossing the dressing with the vegetables and wheat. This salad is a good accompaniment to Grilled Lamb and Vegetable Medley (see page 171).

    1 cup bulgur
1½ cups boiling water
    2 cups shredded green cabbage
   ½ cup grated carrot
   ½ cup peeled and diced
       cucumber
   ⅓ cup diced celery
    1 cup chopped parsley
   ½ cup chopped fresh mint
    2 cups chopped tomatoes
   ¾ cup chopped green onions
   ¼ cup lemon juice
    2 tablespoons olive oil

1. Place bulgur in a medium-sized bowl. Pour the boiling water over bulgur and cover with plastic wrap. Let sit until all water has been absorbed (about 15 minutes).

2. In a large salad bowl, combine cabbage, carrot, cucumber, celery, and parsley. Add cooked bulgur.

3. Blend mint, tomatoes, green onions, lemon juice, and olive oil until smooth, then toss with salad. Let marinate for 30 minutes before serving.

Serves 4.

Preparation time: 30 minutes
Cooking time: 15 minutes
Marinating time: 30 minutes
Per serving: calcium 287 mg, calories 273, carbohydrates 47 g, cholesterol 0 mg, fat 8 g, fiber 11 g, protein 10 g, sodium 112 mg

---

SPICY CHINESE POTATO SALAD

Here is a potato salad that will certainly wake up your taste buds. It combines cooked chunks of red potatoes, red bell pepper, and celery with a spicy Chinese dressing of rice vinegar, sesame oil, and ginger. The dressing can be made up to five days ahead of time and refrigerated until needed. Plan enough time to chill the potatoes after cooking. Spicy Chinese Potato Salad is a good choice for a picnic potluck, or it can be served with a light beef entrée such as Stir-Fried Beef With Asparagus and Snow Peas (see page 165).

    3 cups diced red potatoes
   ¾ cup minced red bell pepper
   ½ cup minced celery
   ¼ cup finely chopped green
       onions
   ¼ cup rice wine vinegar
    2 tablespoons Asian sesame oil
    1 teaspoon grated ginger
    1 teaspoon honey
    1 tablespoon lemon juice
    1 tablespoon hoisin sauce
   ¼ teaspoon cayenne pepper or
       more, to taste

1. In a large saucepan over medium-high heat, cook potatoes until tender (about 20 minutes). Drain and chill for 20 minutes.

2. In a salad bowl combine red bell pepper, celery, green onions, vinegar, oil, ginger, honey, lemon juice, hoisin sauce, and cayenne. Add chilled potatoes and toss well. Cover with plastic wrap and set aside to marinate at room temperature for 20 minutes more. Serve at room temperature.

Serves 4.

Preparation time: 25 minutes
Cooking time: 20 minutes
Chilling time: 20 minutes
Marinating time: 20 minutes
Per serving: calcium 18 mg, calories 133, carbohydrates 16 g, cholesterol 1 mg, fat 8 g, fiber 2 g, protein 2 g, sodium 18 mg

---

BALKAN COLD CUCUMBER SALAD

Most often served on spinach leaves, Balkan Cold Cucumber Salad is an ideal first course to a fish or chicken dinner. It can also be made ahead, and will keep three to four days in the refrigerator. Paired with a slice or two of pumpernickel bread and Salmon Spread (see page 38), it makes a quick and healthy lunch.

    3 cups peeled, seeded, and thinly
       sliced cucumbers
    2 teaspoons sea salt
    3 hard-cooked eggs
    1 teaspoon Dijon mustard
   ½ cup nonfat plain yogurt
    1 teaspoon honey
    1 tablespoon apple cider vinegar
    1 bunch spinach, washed and
       stemmed
       Fresh dill sprigs for garnish

1. Trim cucumber slices into half-moon shapes. Place cucumbers in a large bowl with sea salt. Toss well. Let marinate at room temperature for 30 minutes. Rinse well to remove salt.

2. Slice eggs in half. Separate yolks and whites. Chop whites and set aside. Mash egg yolks with mustard, yogurt, honey, and vinegar.

3. Toss together cucumbers, egg whites, and egg-yolk mixture. Arrange spinach leaves on 4 salad plates. Spoon cucumber salad on top. Garnish with dill sprigs. Serve at room temperature.

Serves 4.

Preparation time: 25 minutes
Marinating time: 30 minutes
Per serving: calcium 96 mg, calories 89, carbohydrates 6 g, cholesterol 160 mg, fat 4 g, fiber .7 g, protein 7 g, sodium 94 mg

---

CURRIED PRAWN AND PASTA SALAD

Cooked prawns are tossed with rotelle (spiral) pasta and a curried reduced-fat mayonnaise dressing and garnished with chopped, toasted almonds. This seafood salad is best served chilled on a bed of lettuce leaves or spinach.

> 1   *pound medium prawns, peeled and deveined*
> ⅔ *cup white wine*
> 2   *cups rotelle*
> ¼ *teaspoon freshly ground black pepper*
> ½ *cup minced celery*
> ½ *cup reduced-fat mayonnaise*
> 1   *teaspoon lemon juice*
> 2   *teaspoons curry powder*
>   *Lettuce leaves, for lining platter or salad plates*
> 1   *tablespoon chopped, toasted almonds*

1. In a small saucepan over medium-high heat, place prawns and wine, and cook until prawns turn pink (about 2 minutes). Remove prawns and cut in half. Discard wine.

2. Cook pasta until al dente (about 8 minutes). Drain and refresh under cold water. In a large bowl mix pasta with cooked prawns, pepper, celery, mayonnaise, lemon juice, and curry powder. Chill 20 minutes. Arrange on a bed of lettuce and garnish with almonds.

Serves 4.

Preparation time: 20 minutes
Cooking time: 15 minutes
Chilling time: 20 minutes
Per serving: calcium 112 mg, calories 390, carbohydrates 46 g, cholesterol 185 mg, fat 6 g, fiber 2 g, protein 31 g, sodium 339 mg

When tossed with a low-fat curry dressing, the spirals of pasta form a bright yellow background for the pink prawns.

Grated beets, carrots, and turnips are sprinkled with a delicate dressing flavored with Dijon mustard.

SPICY TOMATO ASPIC

A family favorite in the South, this molded aspic is standard on many dinner tables in the summer when tomatoes are at their peak. Besides being a good source of vitamin C, juice from vine-ripened tomatoes is rich in minerals. Serve this salad with a chicken or beef entrée for a delicious luncheon. Allow plenty of chilling time—the salad must be refrigerated for at least two hours to completely set.

> 3 cups tomato juice or tomato-vegetable juice
> 2 teaspoons Worcestershire sauce
> 1 package unflavored gelatin
> ½ cup minced celery
> ½ cup corn kernels
> ½ cup reduced-fat mayonnaise
> Lettuce leaves, for lining platter

1. In a large pot, place tomato juice, Worcestershire sauce, gelatin, celery, corn, and mayonnaise. Whisk to blend mayonnaise into tomato juice. Bring to a boil and cook over medium heat for 3 minutes, whisking constantly.

2. Remove from heat and pour into a 5-cup decorative mold or bowl. Let chill for 2 hours or until set. Line a platter with lettuce leaves.

3. To unmold, dip mold or bowl into warm water to loosen aspic and invert it over platter.

Serves 6.

Preparation time: 20 minutes
Cooking time: 5 minutes
Chilling time: 2 hours
Per serving: calcium 40 mg, calories 102, carbohydrates 11 g, cholesterol 9 mg, fat 1 g, fiber 1 g, protein 14 g, sodium 597 mg

GRATED VEGETABLE SALAD WITH MUSTARD VINAIGRETTE

In this visually stimulating dish, a trio of grated raw vegetables—carrots, turnips, and beets—is arranged on a bed of greens. The vinaigrette balances the sweetness of the vegetables, combining Dijon mustard with lemon juice and garlic. You can make the salad and the dressing ahead of time, but be sure to toss the vegetables with lemon juice to prevent browning.

    1   large carrot
    1   small turnip
    1   Jerusalem artichoke
    1   large beet
    1   head lettuce
        Juice of $1/2$ small lemon
    2   teaspoons Dijon mustard
    1   teaspoon lime juice
    2   teaspoons minced garlic
    1   tablespoon apple cider vinegar
  $1/2$ teaspoon freshly ground black pepper
    2   teaspoons herbal salt substitute
 $2^1/2$ tablespoons olive oil

1. Grate carrot, turnip, Jerusalem artichoke, and beet, keeping them separated. Wash lettuce and arrange on 4 small salad plates. Spoon grated vegetables on top of lettuce. Sprinkle with fresh lemon juice.

2. Mix together mustard, lime juice, garlic, vinegar, pepper, salt substitute, and oil. Drizzle over grated vegetables. Serve extra dressing in a sauceboat or cruet.

Serves 4.

Preparation time: 25 minutes
Per serving: calcium 136 mg, calories 160, carbohydrates 19 g, cholesterol 0 mg, fat 10 g, fiber 5 g, protein 4 g, sodium 89 mg

TUNA, POTATO, AND GREEN BEAN SALAD NIÇOISE

The Mediterranean coast is the birthplace of many simple and healthy salads. This version of the traditional favorite from Nice combines chunks of low-fat, water-packed tuna, cooked marinated red potatoes, and blanched green beans. Strips of red bell pepper or a few Greek olives make a good garnish.

    2   cups diced red potatoes
  $1/3$ cup Greek olives, pitted
    3   tablespoons olive oil
 $1^1/2$ tablespoons apple cider vinegar
    1   teaspoon herbal salt substitute
  $1/4$ teaspoon freshly ground black pepper
    1   head lettuce
    4   ounces water-packed tuna, drained
    1   cup diagonally cut green beans
    1   cup sliced red bell pepper

1. In a large pot steam potatoes until tender. Place olives, olive oil, cider vinegar, salt substitute, and pepper in a blender and purée. Pour over potatoes and let marinate 40 minutes.

2. Wash and dry lettuce and arrange on a platter. Toss tuna, beans, and bell pepper with potatoes and marinade, then spoon over lettuce. Serve at room temperature.

Serves 4.

Preparation time: 20 minutes
Cooking time: 20 minutes
Marinating time: 40 minutes
Per serving: calcium 128 mg, calories 222, carbohydrates 16 g, cholesterol 18 mg, fat 14 g, fiber 5 g, protein 11 g, sodium 399 mg

CAESAR SALAD

This easy Caesar salad was adapted from the recipe of a San Francisco chef. Anchovies, traditional in Caesar salads, are optional here, but they do add a nice salty flavor to the dressing. Make the croutons ahead of time—they keep and are ideal for garnishing soups as well—and toss into the salad at the last minute.

    1   cup cubed French bread
  $1/4$ cup plus 1 teaspoon olive oil
    8   cups torn romaine lettuce leaves
    3   cloves minced garlic
    1   tablespoon Worcestershire sauce
    1   teaspoon dry mustard
  $1/4$ teaspoon herbal salt substitute
  $1/4$ teaspoon freshly ground black pepper
    1   tablespoon mashed anchovy fillets (optional)
    2   tablespoons grated Parmesan cheese
  $1/2$ teaspoon lemon juice
    1   egg

1. Toss cubed bread with the teaspoon of olive oil. Place cubes on a baking sheet and bake for 20 minutes at 250° F.

2. Place lettuce in a large salad bowl. In smaller bowl combine the $1/4$ cup oil, garlic, Worcestershire sauce, mustard, salt substitute, pepper, anchovies, if used, cheese, lemon juice, and egg. Toss with lettuce leaves. Add croutons and serve.

Serves 4.

Preparation time: 20 minutes
Baking time (croutons): 20 minutes
Per serving: calcium 94 mg, calories 186, carbohydrates 5 g, cholesterol 55 mg, fat 17 g, fiber 3 g, protein 5 g, sodium 113 mg

*For Avocado and Pine Nut Salad,
chicken and small chunks of
avocado marinate with grapefruit
in a ginger-tamari dressing.*

AVOCADO AND PINE NUT SALAD

The interesting contrast of flavors—the
piquant pink grapefruit sections and the
savory sesame oil-ginger dressing—will
make this dish a favorite in your entertaining repertoire.

- 1 head lettuce
- ½ cup diced avocado
- 1 large pink grapefruit, peeled
  and sectioned
- ¼ cup toasted pine nuts
- 1 cup cooked chicken breast, cut
  in large pieces
- ½ cup rice vinegar
- ⅓ cup honey
- 1 tablespoon low-sodium soy
  sauce or tamari
- 1 tablespoon grated ginger
- 1 tablespoon Asian sesame oil
- 1 teaspoon herbal salt substitute

1. Wash and dry lettuce, then tear into
bite-sized pieces. Place in a large salad
bowl. Add avocado, grapefruit sections,
pine nuts, and chicken.

2. Toss together vinegar, honey, soy
sauce, ginger, oil, and salt substitute.
Pour over salad and mix well. Serve
immediately.

Serves 6.

Preparation time: 25 minutes
Per serving: calcium 83 mg, calories
248, carbohydrates 26 g, cholesterol
25 mg, fat 13 g, fiber 4 g, protein 11 g,
sodium 117 mg

MARINATED SALADS

A cup of cooked beans, leftover spaghetti, sliced mushrooms, or sweet onions—by themselves they may be uninspiring, but paired with a lemon-herb marinade, they become a tasty salad. Marinating is a terrific way to add flavors to salads without adding fat.

MARINATED CHICK-PEA AND LIMA BEAN SALAD

A delicious solution to leftover cooked beans, this salad can be part of an antipasto platter (see Marinated Mushroom and Chick-Pea Appetizer, page 29) or can accompany a light fish or chicken entrée. Marinating the beans overnight improves the flavor dramatically. It can be prepared up to three days before serving, if stored in a tightly covered container in the refrigerator.

> 2 *cups cooked chick-peas*
> 2 *cups cooked jumbo lima beans (approximately ³/₄ cup dried)*
> 2 *stalks celery, minced*
> 1 *small onion, minced*
> 2 *tablespoons minced parsley*
> 2 *cloves garlic, minced, or more to taste*
> 3 *tablespoons olive oil*
> ¹/₃ *cup lemon juice*
> 3 *tablespoons red wine vinegar*
> ¹/₄ *cup capers, drained*
> 1 *tablespoon herbal salt substitute*
>   *Freshly ground black pepper, to taste*
>   *Lettuce leaves, for lining bowl*
>   *Red onion, thinly sliced, for garnish*

Mix all ingredients except lettuce and red onion and let marinate from 2 hours to overnight. Serve in a lettuce-lined bowl; garnish with red onion rings.

Serves 6.

> *Preparation time:* 20 minutes
> *Marinating time:* 2 to 24 hours
> *Per serving:* calcium 90 mg, calories 238, carbohydrates 32 g, cholesterol 0 mg, fat 9 g, fiber 5 g, protein 10 g, sodium 166 mg

GERMAN-STYLE POTATO SALAD WITH MINCED ONIONS

This potato salad gets its flavor from marinating warm potatoes in white wine. Serve with a light beef or chicken dish for an easy dinner. The salad will keep in a tightly covered container in the refrigerator for about four days. To avoid discoloring the potatoes, add radishes just before serving.

> 4 *cups diced, boiled red potatoes*
> ¹/₃ *cup dry white wine*
> ¹/₈ *teaspoon caraway seed, crushed*
> ¹/₄ *cup nonfat plain yogurt*
> 2 *teaspoons olive oil*
> 1 *teaspoon herbal salt substitute, or to taste*
> ¹/₂ *teaspoon freshly ground black pepper*
> 2 *teaspoons reduced-fat mayonnaise*
> 1 *teaspoon lemon juice*
> ¹/₂ *cup thinly sliced radishes*
> ¹/₂ *cup minced parsley*
> 1 *tablespoon chopped fresh dill or 1 teaspoon dried dill*
> ¹/₂ *cup chopped green onions or white onions*

1. Combine potatoes, white wine, and caraway seed and let marinate for 1 hour.

2. Add remaining ingredients and let marinate another 30 minutes before serving either chilled or at room temperature.

Serves 8.

> *Preparation time:* 20 minutes
> *Marinating time:* 90 minutes
> *Per serving:* calcium 91 mg, calories 67, carbohydrates 11 g, cholesterol 1 mg, fat 2 g, fiber 1 g, protein 2 g, sodium 71 mg

NOTE

SALAD SECRETS

Washing Use only the freshest greens for your salad. Inspect the edges and stalks of lettuce leaves, spinach, and other greens as you wash them, checking for wilted or browned spots. Spin the greens dry in a salad spinner or press dry on paper towels.

Storing Washed and dried greens can be kept for up to five days in the refrigerator without losing freshness. Just drain well after washing and store in a salad spinner or wrapped in slightly dampened paper towels in plastic bags.

Enhancing color and flavor Add color to your salads with reds and oranges—such as grated carrots (sprinkle with lemon juice to prevent browning), sliced or diced red bell pepper, cherry tomatoes, and sweet cherry peppers. Contrast flavors by mixing in a little curly endive for bitterness, grated Parmesan cheese for saltiness, and raisins for sweetening.

Choosing a salad dressing Select a dressing that contrasts with the rest of the meal, to balance the taste buds. If the meal is spicy, with sharp and pungent qualities, choose a creamy, mild-tasting dressing. If a low-key entrée or a rich but savory soup is planned, you may want to experiment with a vinaigrette.

Adding special touches Sprouts are fun in salads. Buy mung bean sprouts (an ingredient in many Chinese dishes), alfalfa sprouts, clover sprouts, and, for a zing, radish sprouts.

Shreds of carrot, green onion strips, and red cabbage compose this colorful slaw. The Asian-style dressing combines sesame oil, rice vinegar, and mustard. Serve with Lemon Chicken (see page 146) and roasted red potatoes for an easy picnic supper.

RED CABBAGE COLESLAW

Rich in nutrients, this salad is particularly colorful for a coleslaw. It will retain its texture and taste for two days if covered and stored in the refrigerator.

> 3 cups thinly sliced or shredded red cabbage
> 2 cups grated carrot
> 1/4 cup minced green onion
> 1/2 cup minced parsley
> 1/3 cup freshly squeezed lemon juice
> 1/4 cup rice vinegar
> 1 teaspoon Asian sesame oil
> 1 tablespoon frozen apple juice concentrate
> 2 tablespoons stone-ground mustard
> 1/2 cup nonfat plain yogurt
> 3 tablespoons olive oil
> 1 tablespoon celery seed
> 1 tablespoon poppy seed

1. In a salad bowl gently toss cabbage, carrot, green onion, and parsley.

2. Whisk remaining ingredients in another bowl and pour over cabbage mixture. Toss well and let stand 20 minutes before serving.

Serves 6.

> *Preparation time:* 25 minutes
> *Marinating time:* 20 minutes
> *Per serving:* calcium 196 mg, calories 157, carbohydrates 17 g, cholesterol 0 mg, fat 9 g, fiber 4 g, protein 4 g, sodium 134 mg

FRENCH BEAN SALAD

This delicate, yet filling, salad is lovely to look at. Steam the green beans until their bright color emerges and then immediately toss them with the marinade to keep the color bright. You can either leave the beans whole or slice them into bite-sized pieces, cutting diagonally. This salad will keep well for three to four days, if covered and refrigerated.

> 1 pound green beans, steamed lightly
> 1 cup cooked navy beans (approximately 1/2 cup dried)
> Juice of 1 lemon
> 2 ounces toasted, slivered almonds
> 1 tablespoon chopped parsley
> 1/4 cup diced red bell pepper
> 1/4 cup olive oil
> 1/3 cup rice vinegar
> 2 tablespoons Dijon mustard
> Lettuce leaves, for lining bowl (optional)

1. Combine all ingredients except lettuce and toss well to coat beans thoroughly.

2. Let marinate at room temperature for 45 minutes. Arrange in lettuce-lined bowl and serve.

Serves 6.

> *Preparation time:* 25 minutes
> *Marinating time:* 45 minutes
> *Per serving:* calcium 81 mg, calories 211, carbohydrates 18 g, cholesterol 0 mg, fat 14 g, fiber 4 g, protein 6 g, sodium 69 mg

SZECHWAN NOODLES

Asian flavors blended with the subtle texture of noodles create a spicy pasta salad. The udon noodles in this recipe can be found in most natural food or Asian stores. Szechwan Noodles tastes best when left to marinate for at least 45 minutes before serving, although it can be stored for up to 48 hours. Add the peanuts (a good source of protein) at the last minute so they hold their crunchy consistency.

12 ounces cooked udon noodles
2 tablespoons grated fresh ginger
5 ounces sliced water chestnuts
2 cups sliced mushrooms
2 tablespoons chopped peanuts
1/4 cup Asian sesame oil
5 cloves garlic, minced, or more to taste
6 green onions (including greens), minced
1 to 2 teaspoons cayenne pepper, or to taste
1/2 cup low-sodium soy sauce or tamari
1/2 teaspoon honey
Lettuce leaves, for lining bowl (optional)

1. Place pasta in a bowl. Mix together remaining ingredients except lettuce and toss with pasta.

2. Let marinate for 45 minutes before serving. Serve in a lettuce-lined bowl, if desired.

Serves 8.

Preparation time: 25 minutes
Marinating time: 45 minutes
Per serving: calcium 109 mg, calories 293, carbohydrates 49 g, cholesterol 0 mg, fat 9 g, fiber 4 g, protein 10 g, sodium 843 mg

MEXICAN BEAN SALAD

Here's an unusual and delicious salad, discovered while the author was finishing some leftover Mexican food. It should be topped with Fresh Salsa (see page 41) or bottled salsa, available in almost all supermarkets.

Legumes, which include such foods as lima and pinto beans, are a rich source of protein and essential minerals, such as potassium and phosphorous. They contain none of the saturated fat and cholesterol of an equal amount of meat.

Cook the beans the day before making the salad and chill them overnight. This bean salad will keep for three days in a covered container in the refrigerator. Serve this red and white salad on a bed of green spinach or lettuce for a colorful side dish to grilled fish. As a chilled dish, it can also provide a refresher when served with spicy Mexican food.

4 cups cooked lima beans (approximately 3 cups dried)
1 cup cooked pinto beans (approximately 2/3 cup dried)
2 cups Fresh Salsa (see page 41)
2 cups chopped lettuce
2 tomatoes, chopped
3 tablespoons chopped cilantro

1. Toss lima and pinto beans with salsa and marinate for 4 hours.

2. Place lettuce and tomato in salad bowl and spoon on beans; top with cilantro. Serve chilled.

Serves 6.

Preparation time: 10 minutes
Marinating time: 4 hours
Per serving: calcium 61 mg, calories 198, carbohydrates 37 g, cholesterol 0 mg, fat 1 g, fiber 12 g, protein 13 g, sodium 10 mg

SUMMER RICE SALAD

Adapted from a Los Angeles restaurant recipe, this inviting salad is perfect for lunch on a warm summer day. Be sure to seed the tomato so that it does not make the rice soggy.

2 cups cooked short-grain brown rice
1/4 cup minced green onion
1/4 cup seeded and minced green bell pepper
2 tablespoons minced parsley, plus minced parsley for garnish
1/2 cup peeled and diced jicama
1/4 cup minced celery
4 radishes, sliced
1/4 cup reduced-fat mayonnaise
1 teaspoon low-sodium soy sauce or tamari
1 tablespoon lemon juice
1/4 teaspoon cayenne pepper
1 tablespoon dry white wine
1 small tomato, seeded and cut into strips
Red bell pepper, seeded and cut into rings, for garnish

Combine all ingredients except garnishes and toss well. Chill before serving. Garnish with red pepper rings and minced parsley.

Serves 4.

Preparation time: 25 minutes
Chilling time: 30 minutes
Per serving: calcium 63 mg, calories 176, carbohydrates 36 g, cholesterol 6 mg, fat 1 g, fiber 2 g, protein 4 g, sodium 139 mg

MENU

MAKE-AHEAD DINNER FOR SIX

Jicama and Citrus Salad

Roast Lamb Breton-Style

Broiled Tomato Halves

Steamed Broccoli

Lemon-Strawberry Mousse

*Assortment of Sparkling Waters
With Lemon Slices*

---

*This menu has the advantage of many make-ahead elements: The salad can be prepared in the morning and chilled during the day; the broccoli can be washed and trimmed and the tomatoes can be halved the same morning; the lamb can be roasted and beans baked the night before; and the mousse can be whipped and spooned into individual dessert glasses hours before the guests arrive. Broil the tomatoes cut side up for 3 to 4 minutes just before serving. Leftover lamb can be made into stew or sliced for a marinated salad for lunch the next day.
All recipes serve six.*

JICAMA AND CITRUS SALAD

This colorful salad combines jicama with fresh citrus fruits.

> 2 *cups peeled and julienned jicama*
> 1 *red bell pepper, seeded and cut into thin strips*
> 1 *cup peeled orange sections*
> ½ *cup peeled grapefruit sections*
> 2 *tablespoons chopped fresh mint*
> 2 *tablespoons frozen orange juice concentrate*
> *Juice of 2 oranges*
> 1 *tablespoon lemon juice*
> ¼ *teaspoon minced garlic*
> *Watercress, for lining bowl*

Mix all ingredients and spoon over watercress in a decorative salad bowl. Cover with plastic wrap and chill for 30 minutes. Serve chilled.

Serves 6.

> *Preparation time:* 25 minutes
> *Chilling time:* 30 minutes
> *Per serving:* calcium 42 mg, calories 88, carbohydrates 21 g, cholesterol 0 mg, fat 0 g, fiber 3 g, protein 2 g, sodium 4 mg

ROAST LAMB BRETON-STYLE

In Brittany this main course is traditionally served in springtime.

> 1 *leg of lamb (about 3 lb)*
> *Herbal salt substitute and pepper, to taste*
> 4 *cloves garlic, sliced thinly*
> 2 *cups dried navy beans*
> 2 *cups chopped onion*
> 2 *bay leaves, crushed*
> 2 *cups chopped tomato*
> 1 *teaspoon butter*

1. Preheat oven to 325° F. Rub lamb with salt substitute and pepper. Pierce small holes in lamb and insert slices of garlic throughout. Place lamb in a roasting pan and cook until pink and juicy in the center and browned on the outside (about 2 hours).

2. While the lamb roasts, bring 5 cups of water to a boil and cook beans with remaining ingredients for 40 minutes, then add more water if needed, cover, and cook over medium heat until soft (about 1 hour longer). Remove bay leaves.

3. Transfer beans to baking dish. Add several spoonfuls of juice from roasting lamb to beans, place in the 325° F oven and bake for 15 minutes. To serve, slice roasted lamb and accompany with beans.

Serves 6.

> *Preparation time:* 10 minutes
> *Cooking time:* 2 hours
> *Per serving:* calcium 160 mg, calories 502, carbohydrates 35 g, cholesterol 94 mg, fat 24 g, fiber 9 g, protein 37 g, sodium 241 mg

LEMON-STRAWBERRY MOUSSE

This delightful, light dessert has a beautiful, bright pink color.

> ½ *cup puréed fresh strawberries*
> 3 *tablespoons arrowroot powder*
> ½ *cup freshly squeezed lemon juice*
> 3 *tablespoons honey*
> ¼ *teaspoon vanilla extract*
> 1 *egg yolk, lightly beaten*
> 6 *egg whites*
> *Lemon peel, for garnish*

1. In a saucepan over medium heat place strawberries, arrowroot, lemon juice, honey, vanilla, and egg yolk, stirring, until mixture thickens to a custard consistency (3 to 5 minutes). Immediately pour into a clean bowl and chill.

2. Whip egg whites until stiff peaks form. Gently fold into chilled custard and spoon mousse into 6 dessert dishes or wineglasses. Chill for 1 hour, then garnish with lemon peel and serve.

Serves 6.

> *Preparation time:* 20 minutes
> *Chilling time:* 1 hour
> *Per serving:* calcium 11 mg, calories 82, carbohydrates 15 g, cholesterol 35 mg, fat 1 g, fiber 1 g, protein 4 g, sodium 57 mg

This make-ahead menu features
*Roast Lamb Breton-Style, a light
citrus and jicama salad, and
lemon and strawberries whipped
into a creamy mousse.*

TIPS

...ON STREAMLINING SALAD DRESSINGS

Try these ideas for tasty, healthy salad dressings:

☐ In creamy dressings substitute nonfat plain yogurt or reduced-fat mayonnaise for sour cream, heavy cream, or regular mayonnaise. Or, use one-third the amount of oil specified in the recipe and beat it to a froth with a whisk or in a blender.

☐ Eliminate up to half the oil specified in the recipe and substitute a flavored vinegar. Simply heat to the boiling point 2 cups of apple cider vinegar. Remove from heat and add one of the following flavorings: two sprigs of fresh herbs, such as tarragon, thyme, or basil; 3 to 4 peeled cloves of garlic plus 1 teaspoon of cracked peppercorns; or ¼ cup raspberries or blueberries plus 1 teaspoon honey. Let the flavored vinegar marinate for 48 hours at room temperature, strain, and use.

☐ Purée fresh vegetables to add flavor and thickness to dressings. You can use celery, tomato, parsley, red bell pepper, chives, watercress, or green onion.

☐ Use soft tofu in place of sour cream, olive oil, or mayonnaise. Blend until smooth and chill slightly before serving.

☐ Try low-fat buttermilk and cottage cheese in dressings. A very simple, low-fat dressing can be made from blended buttermilk or cottage cheese, a little lemon juice or vinegar, garlic, chives, and parsley.

SALADS THAT ENLIVEN A MEAL

These salads are designed as side dishes that can also be a light meal for one or two persons. They are simple to prepare and satisfying.

SPINACH SALAD

A delicate curried dressing anoints this tasty salad, making it appropriate for special occasions. Serve in summer with a chilled soup and crusty bread.

>   8 cups washed and torn spinach leaves
>   1 small red onion, sliced into thin rings (see Note)
>   1 red Delicious apple, chopped or sliced, and sprinkled with 1 teaspoon lemon juice
>   2 tablespoons currants
>   1 teaspoon olive oil
>   1 clove garlic, minced
>   2 cups nonfat plain yogurt
>   1 tablespoon curry powder
>   1 tablespoon frozen apple juice concentrate
>   ½ teaspoon ground cardamom
>   ¼ teaspoon cayenne pepper
>   ½ teaspoon grated fresh ginger

1. Place spinach in a large salad bowl. Decorate with onion rings, apple, and currants.

2. Place all other ingredients in blender and purée. Pour over spinach salad and serve.

Serves 6.

Note To make red onion taste sweeter, place the rings in a bowl of ice water for 25 minutes before using to draw out bitter acids.

Preparation time: 20 minutes
Per serving: calcium 242 mg, calories 108, carbohydrates 19 g, cholesterol 1 mg, fat 2 g, fiber 4 g, protein 7 g, sodium 119 mg

CHILLED CURRIED CAULIFLOWER SALAD WITH RAISINS

Here's a great salad recipe with an East Indian flair. This version is made with raisins and strips of fresh bell pepper. As a cold curry recipe, it is a variation on the traditional hot Indian curry dishes. You will find that the hot peppers somehow have a cooling effect on the body. It's sweet and succulent—ideal for summer entertaining on your porch or patio.

>   4 cups broken cauliflower florets
>   1 cup julienned carrots
>   1 cup seeded and julienned red bell pepper
>   ½ cup apple juice
>   1 tablespoon Asian sesame oil
>   2 cloves garlic, minced
>   2 tablespoons curry powder
>   ½ teaspoon cinnamon
>   1½ teaspoons whole yellow mustard seed
>   2 teaspoons honey
>   ½ cup raisins
>   Lettuce leaves, for lining plates

1. Steam cauliflower, carrot, and bell pepper in apple juice until tender. Drain and toss with oil, garlic, curry powder, cinnamon, mustard seed, honey, and raisins.

2. Cover and chill for 2 hours or overnight. To serve, line plates with lettuce leaves and top with cauliflower mixture.

Serves 6.

Preparation time: 25 minutes
Chilling time: 2 hours to 24 hours
Per serving: calcium 54 mg, calories 127, carbohydrates 25 g, cholesterol 0 mg, fat 3 g, fiber 5 g, protein 3 g, sodium 36 mg

TACO SALAD

If you're a fan of Mexican food, especially the piquant flavor of tacos, you'll love this salad.

- 2 cups crumbled firm tofu
- 2 teaspoons ground cumin
- 2 tablespoons chopped cilantro
- 1/2 teaspoon chili powder
- 2 teaspoons herbal salt substitute
- 1/4 teaspoon freshly ground black pepper
- 2 teaspoons olive oil
- 6 corn tortillas
- 3 cups torn leaf lettuce, such as romaine or green leaf
- 3 large, ripe tomatoes, cored and coarsely chopped
- 1/2 cup minced red onion
- 1/2 cup seeded and diced cucumber
- 1/2 cup grated low-fat mozzarella cheese
- 1/2 cup Fresh Salsa (see page 41)

1. Preheat oven to 400° F. In a bowl mix tofu with cumin, cilantro, chili powder, salt substitute, and pepper.

2. In oil in a skillet over medium heat, brown tofu mixture lightly for 10 minutes. Let cool.

3. Cut tortillas into wedges; bake until crisp (about 15 minutes).

4. Place lettuce in a large salad bowl and spoon tofu mixture into the center of the leaves.

5. Arrange tomatoes, onion, and cucumber on top; sprinkle with cheese and salsa. Serve slightly chilled.

Serves 6.

Note You can also place the tofu mixture in a heatproof bowl, top with cheese, and broil until cheese melts just slightly. Then remove from oven and add to remaining ingredients.

Preparation time: 20 minutes
Cooking time: 20 minutes
Chilling time: 30 minutes
Per serving: calcium 321 mg, calories 228, carbohydrates 22 g, cholesterol 5 mg, fat 10 g, fiber 5 g, protein 17 g, sodium 165 mg

There's nothing as refreshing in the heat of summer as Spinach Salad, which features spinach leaves tossed with apples, currants, and red onion rings and dressed with a light curry sauce.

FRESH FRUIT SALADS

One welcome sight of approaching summer is the wide variety of fresh fruit appearing in the markets. Suddenly there are so many kinds of fruit; not just apples, bananas, and pears, but also peaches, plums, grapes, apricots, and berries. Following is a selection of easy recipes that make the most of fresh fruit flavors whether it's winter, spring, summer, or fall.

FIG AND YOGURT SALAD

This exotic sweet-tart combination is an excellent accompaniment for curries or Middle-Eastern foods. It can also be served like a chutney, with meats or chicken.

- 2 cups dried white figs (Calimyrna), stems removed, chopped
- 1/3 cup dry white wine or port wine
- 1 green apple, grated
- 1 small navel orange, peeled and chopped
- 1/4 cup diced celery
- 1/2 cup nonfat plain yogurt
- 1/8 teaspoon turmeric
- 1/8 teaspoon ground cardamom
- 1/4 teaspoon curry powder
  Lettuce leaves, for lining platter (optional)

Mix figs and wine and let stand for 2 hours at room temperature. Then combine with other ingredients and serve, chilled or lukewarm, on a bed of lettuce, if used.

Serves 4.

Preparation time: 15 minutes
Marinating time: 2 hours
Per serving: calcium 220 mg, calories 316, carbohydrates 76 g, cholesterol 1 mg, fat 1 g, fiber 11 g, protein 5 g, sodium 41 mg

GREEN APPLE SALAD

Here's a tart low-calorie version of the traditional Waldorf salad. It is a crunchy salad chilled in a tangy marinade and focused on fresh autumn produce. Prepare this dish within 2 hours of serving to keep it fresh and crunchy.

- 5 cups diced green apples (see Note)
- 1 cup halved seedless red grapes
- 1½ cups nonfat plain yogurt
- 2 teaspoons reduced-fat mayonnaise
- 1 teaspoon curry powder
- 1/2 cup currants
- 1/4 cup diced celery
- 1/4 teaspoon celery seed
- 1 tablespoon frozen apple juice concentrate
- 1 teaspoon lemon juice
  Herbal salt substitute and pepper, to taste
  Lettuce leaves, for lining bowl

Combine all ingredients and season to taste. Serve slightly chilled, on a bed of lettuce.

Serves 4.

Note To prevent apples from oxidizing (turning brown), you can place apple slices in a bowl of ice water mixed with lemon juice as you prepare them.

Preparation time: 20 minutes
Chilling time: 30 minutes
Per serving: calcium 207 mg, calories 200, carbohydrates 46 g, cholesterol 3 mg, fat 1 g, fiber 5 g, protein 7 g, sodium 91 mg

WATERCRESS AND GRAPEFRUIT ASPIC

Aspics are a beautiful way to present fresh fruits and vegetables: in a shimmering, lightly tinted gelatin. The delicate colors of watercress and pale fruits make this a perfect springtime salad that goes well with light fish dishes. You can prepare it up to a day in advance, but don't remove the mold until right before serving.

- 1 envelope unflavored gelatin
- 1/2 cup apple juice
- 1/4 cup freshly squeezed lemon juice
- 1 cup chilled grapefruit juice, preferably fresh
- 1/2 teaspoon oil, for mold
- 1 cup peeled grapefruit sections
- 1 cup shredded watercress, plus watercress for garnish
  Lettuce leaves, for lining platter

1. In a small saucepan combine gelatin and apple juice; simmer until gelatin dissolves. Add lemon and grapefruit juices and stir well.

2. Pour into a 9- by 12-inch glass baking dish and chill until gelatin begins to set.

3. Lightly oil dessert mold. Stir the grapefruit and watercress into the partially set gelatin and spoon into the prepared mold. Chill until completely set (about 1¼ hours).

4. To remove the mold, turn it on edge and tap gently, or run the bottom under hot water for a few seconds. Turn aspic onto lettuce-lined platter and garnish with additional watercress.

Serves 4.

Preparation time: 10 minutes
Chilling time: 75 minutes
Per serving: calcium 36 mg, calories 138, carbohydrates 15 g, cholesterol 0 mg, fat 1 g, fiber 1 g, protein 20 g, sodium 47 mg

MOLDED FRUIT SALAD

Another delicious aspic, this salad is molded in a grape juice mixture. Use purple grape juice for an informal, festive salad, or white grape juice for a more formal occasion.

    3 cups grape juice or
       nonalcoholic wine
    1 packet unflavored gelatin
  1½ cups halved seedless black or
       red grapes
    1 cup peeled and seeded
       tangerine sections (see Note)
    1 cup halved seedless green
       grapes
   ½ teaspoon oil, for mold
       Lettuce leaves, for lining
       platter (optional)

1. In a large saucepan, simmer grape juice with gelatin until it is dissolved. Pour mixture into a 9- by 12-inch glass baking dish and let partially congeal in refrigerator.

2. Mix black grapes, tangerine sections, and green grapes; mix into the partially congealed gelatin. Let chill until completely set (about 1¼ hours). (If desired, partially congealed gelatin can be transferred to a lightly oiled decorative mold or soufflé dish and chilled.)

3. To remove the mold, turn it on its edge and tap gently, or run the bottom under hot water for a few seconds. Turn Molded Fruit Salad onto a platter, lined with lettuce, if desired, and serve.

Serves 6.

Note If tangerines are unavailable, seeded orange sections may be used.

Preparation time: 15 minutes
Chilling time: 75 minutes
Per serving: calcium 33 mg, calories 185, carbohydrates 34 g, cholesterol 0 mg, fat 1 g, fiber 2 g, protein 14 g, sodium 33 mg

Almost a sculpture, this delicate Molded Fruit Salad can be made with white grape juice and slices of fresh tangerines and red and green grapes. Serve with iced mint tea.

NOTE

THE BENEFITS OF FIBER

What is fiber? Scientists have found it challenging to define this essential food component. In general, nutritionists agree that fiber is basically a complex carbohydrate, the fibrous component of plant foods that is not broken down by human digestion.

Dietary fiber comes in several varieties. Some of the common types are cellulose (abundant in oat bran), lignin (in grains), pectin (in fruit and vegetables), gums (in legumes), and mucilages (in seeds). Some fibers absorb water, some lower blood cholesterol, some increase fat excretion, and some maintain blood sugar levels. Consuming a good selection of these fibers daily is recommended, since they perform different functions in the body.

For those interested in weight control, fiber has been shown to increase the metabolism of fats. In addition, high-carbohydrate meals containing plenty of fiber satisfy the eater sooner than equal amounts of protein or fat.

Lower blood cholesterol and lower incidences of cardiovascular disease have been reported in populations where a large amount of fiber-rich pectin (from fresh fruit) and bran (from whole grains) is consumed.

People on high-fiber diets rarely are troubled by constipation. Fiber promotes healthy elimination and can absorb many times its weight in water, which aids regularity. Studies show that it also seems to increase elimination of fats, such as bile acids and sterols.

The typical diet in the United States, filled with refined and processed foods, contains little fiber. For example, white bread, made from bleached and refined wheat flour, contains only half the fiber of its unrefined, unprocessed cousin, whole wheat bread.

Studies suggest that fiber plays a role in preventing colon and rectal cancer, diverticulitis, gallstones, and varicose veins.

A high-fiber diet is composed of plenty of fresh fruits and vegetables, whole grains, and legumes. Look for recipes using these foods: whole grains, cornmeal or polenta, apples or bananas, potatoes, broccoli, carrots, kidney beans, lentils, and almonds. Try such fiber-rich recipes in this book as Sauerkraut Bread (see page 194) or Best Bran Muffins (page 142).

HEALTHY SALAD DRESSINGS

These healthy salad dressings will make your next salad a culinary work of art. Using a minimal amount of dressing and tossing your salad thoroughly will enhance the flavor and reduce the unnecessary fat.

LIME-MINT DRESSING

Light and refreshing, great with grapefruit and avocado.

6 tablespoons olive oil
2 tablespoons lime juice
1/2 teaspoon herbal salt substitute
1/8 teaspoon white pepper
1/2 teaspoon minced parsley
1/2 teaspoon minced fresh mint leaves
1/2 teaspoon chopped chives
1/2 teaspoon Dijon mustard

Combine all ingredients.

Makes about 1/2 cup, serves 12.

Preparation time: 15 minutes
Per serving: calcium 3 mg, calories 60, carbohydrates .3 g, cholesterol 0 mg, fat 7 g, fiber 0 g, protein 0 g, sodium 3 mg

TAHINI DRESSING

A fine party dip with raw vegetables.

1/2 cup tahini
1/3 cup reduced-fat mayonnaise
Juice from 1 lemon
1 teaspoon minced garlic
1/2 cup water
1/4 cup freshly squeezed orange juice
1 1/2 tablespoons apple cider vinegar
1 tablespoon low-sodium soy sauce or tamari
Pinch of cayenne pepper

Combine all ingredients.

Makes about 2 cups, serves 16.

Preparation time: 15 minutes
Per serving: calcium 82 mg, calories 55, carbohydrates 3 g, cholesterol 2 mg, fat 1 g, fiber .5 g, protein 2 g, sodium 57 mg

GREEN GODDESS DRESSING

Snappy and flavorful, this dressing is good on coleslaw.

- *½ cup reduced-fat mayonnaise*
- *¼ cup nonfat plain yogurt*
- *¼ cup chopped parsley*
- *1 teaspoon chopped chives*
- *2 tablespoons apple cider vinegar*
- *¼ teaspoon herbal salt substitute Dash of freshly ground black pepper*
- *½ teaspoon dried basil*

Blend all ingredients until smooth.

Makes about 1¼ cups, serves 6.

> *Preparation time:* 15 minutes
> *Per serving:* calcium 74 mg, calories 33, carbohydrates 5 g, cholesterol 9 mg, fat 1 g, fiber .3 g, protein 2 g, sodium 119 mg

PAPAYA SEED DRESSING

Try this one over greens or citrus.

- *1 teaspoon grated ginger*
- *1 tablespoon minced onion*
- *1 tablespoon papaya seeds, scooped from fresh papaya*
- *1 teaspoon dried tarragon*
- *1 teaspoon Dijon mustard*
- *1 teaspoon minced garlic*
- *¼ cup olive oil*
- *¼ cup water*
- *2 tablespoons lemon juice*
- *1 tablespoon lime juice*

Place all ingredients in a blender and purée.

Makes about ¾ cup, serves 6.

> *Preparation time:* 15 minutes
> *Per serving:* calcium 7 mg, calories 86, carbohydrates 1 g, cholesterol 0 mg, fat 9 g, fiber .2 g, protein 0 g, sodium 17 mg

MARINADE FOR BEAN SALADS

Marinate beans for at least 2 hours in this dressing.

- *1 teaspoon dry mustard*
- *2 tablespoons minced garlic*
- *¼ cup rice vinegar*
- *⅛ cup lemon juice*
- *¼ teaspoon herbal salt substitute Dash freshly ground black pepper*
- *¼ cup olive oil*

Combine all ingredients.

Makes about ¾ cup, serves 6.

> *Preparation time:* 15 minutes
> *Per serving:* calcium 8 mg, calories 87, carbohydrates 2 g, cholesterol 0 mg, fat 9 g, fiber .1 g, protein .3 g, sodium 1 mg

RUE DAUPHINE DRESSING

A heartier form of oil-and-vinegar.

- *½ cup reduced-fat mayonnaise*
- *¼ cup olive oil*
- *⅛ cup red wine vinegar*
- *1 tablespoon honey*
- *1 teaspoon celery seed*
- *1 teaspoon herbal salt substitute Dash of freshly ground black pepper*
- *2 tablespoons sesame seed*
- *¼ teaspoon dried basil*
- *¼ teaspoon dried tarragon*
- *¼ teaspoon dried oregano*

Combine all ingredients.

Makes about 1¼ cups, serves 8.

> *Preparation time:* 15 minutes
> *Per serving:* calcium 22 mg, calories 84, carbohydrates 4 g, cholesterol 6 mg, fat 8 g, fiber .1 g, protein .4 g, sodium 76 mg

COUNTRY PICNIC

Mushroom Pâté en Baguette

Cream of Sorrel Soup

Texas Blue Cheese Slaw

Poached Chicken Breasts With Lemon-and-Herb Mayonnaise (see page 148)

Baked Pear Gratin (see page 229)

California Chardonnay and Sparkling Waters

Invite friends for a day in the country. Find a shady spot by a quiet stream, open your picnic basket, and pull out this healthy and tasty picnic lunch. You might try stuffing the Mushroom Pâté into its hollowed baguette and wrapping it tightly in plastic the night before. The Cream of Sorrel Soup can be packed into a prewarmed thermos. The delicate Poached Chicken Breasts can be precooked and served either warm or cold. Finish with slightly decadent Baked Pear Gratin and a glass of California Chardonnay. Menu serves six.

MUSHROOM PÂTÉ EN BAGUETTE

Mushrooms and herbs are blended into a savory pâté, stuffed into a hollowed-out loaf of French bread, wrapped, and refrigerated. While the loaf chills, the pâté subtly flavors it. To serve, unwrap and slice into thin rounds, revealing a circle of bread surrounding each slice of pâté.

- ½ cup chopped onion
- 1 tablespoon olive oil
- ¼ cup sake or dry sherry
- ½ cup chopped green onions (including greens)
- 2 teaspoons minced garlic
- 1½ cups sliced mushrooms
- ½ cup minced celery
- ½ cup almonds or walnuts, minced
- ½ cup minced parsley
- 1 cup rye bread crumbs
- 1 teaspoon ground rosemary
- ½ teaspoon dried thyme
- 1 tablespoon low-sodium soy sauce or tamari
- 1 teaspoon herbal salt substitute
- ½ teaspoon dried basil
- ¼ teaspoon dried oregano
- 1 baguette French bread

1. In a large skillet over medium-high heat, sauté onion in the olive oil and sherry until soft but not browned. Add green onions, garlic, and mushrooms, and continue to cook for 5 minutes.

2. When mushrooms begin to exude moisture, add celery, walnuts, and parsley, and cook 3 minutes longer.

3. Spoon sautéed vegetables into a large bowl. Add rye bread crumbs, rosemary, thyme, soy sauce, salt substitute, basil, and oregano. Purée half of mixture in a blender and mix well with pâté remaining in bowl until a pastelike consistency is achieved.

4. Cut baguette in half and slice off each end. With your fingers, remove the soft center of the loaf, hollowing out both sections. Stuff pâté into the cavity, wrap in plastic wrap, and chill for 2 hours or more.

5. To serve, unwrap baguette and slice into rounds.

Serves 6.

Preparation time: 20 minutes
Cooking time: 15 minutes
Chilling time: 2 hours
Per serving: calcium 206 mg, calories 383, carbohydrates 58 g, cholesterol 0 mg, fat 12 g, fiber 6 g, protein 13 g, sodium 717 mg

CREAM OF SORREL SOUP

If sorrel is unavailable, substitute watercress or increase the spinach in this recipe. The soup cooks into a delicate, light green color and can be garnished with minced red bell pepper for an extremely attractive first course.

- ½ cup finely minced onion
- 1 teaspoon unsalted butter
- ¼ cup white wine
- ½ cup minced celery
- 1 cup chopped sorrel leaves
- 1 cup chopped spinach leaves
- 6 tablespoons whole wheat flour
- 3 cups defatted Chicken Stock (see page 51)
- ¼ cup half-and-half
- 1 cup nonfat milk
- 1 teaspoon lemon juice
- 1 teaspoon honey
  Herbal salt substitute and pepper, to taste

1. In a large stockpot over medium-high heat, sauté onion in butter and wine until soft but not browned (about 3 minutes). Add celery, sorrel, and spinach, and continue to cook for 5 minutes more.

2. Add flour and cook, stirring, for 2 minutes. Add chicken stock and bring to a boil.

3. In batches, purée soup in a blender until smooth. Return to pot and add half-and-half, milk, lemon juice, and honey. Heat through, but do not let soup boil. Season to taste with salt substitute and pepper. Serve soup hot or cold.

Serves 6.

Preparation time: 20 minutes
Cooking time: 15 minutes
Chilling time (optional): 2 hours
Per serving: calcium 236 mg, calories 122, carbohydrates 16 g, cholesterol 6 mg, fat 1 g, fiber 3 g, protein 3 g, sodium 262 mg

TEXAS BLUE CHEESE SLAW

Savoy cabbage is combined with nonfat yogurt, minced green onions, and chunks of blue cheese to make this hearty—and healthy—slaw. It keeps for 24 hours, so you can make it the night before a picnic.

- 4 cups finely shredded savoy cabbage
- ½ cup minced green onions
- ½ cup minced green bell pepper
- 2 tablespoons minced fresh dill
- 1 cup nonfat plain yogurt
- 2 tablespoons sour cream
- 3 tablespoons white wine vinegar
- 1 tablespoon honey
- 3 ounces blue cheese
  Herbal salt substitute and pepper, to taste

1. In a large bowl combine cabbage, onions, bell pepper, and dill.

2. Blend together yogurt, sour cream, vinegar, honey, and blue cheese. Toss dressing with cabbage mixture. Add salt substitute and pepper to taste.

Serves 6.

Preparation time: 20 minutes
Per serving: calcium 180 mg, calories 111, carbohydrates 11 g, cholesterol 13 mg, fat 5 g, fiber 2 g, protein 7 g, sodium 244 mg

All the dishes in this elegant and easily prepared Country Picnic can be made ahead, wrapped, and ready to go early in the day.

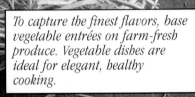

To capture the finest flavors, base vegetable entrées on farm-fresh produce. Vegetable dishes are ideal for elegant, healthy cooking.

VEGETABLE ENTRÉES & SIDE DISHES

Fresh vegetables are one of the mainstays of a healthy diet, providing essential nutrients and refreshing variety. With an emphasis on flavorful combinations of vegetables with whole grains, legumes, and soy products, recipes like Curried Vegetables With Raita and Chutney (see page 96), Tofu Teriyaki (see page 102), and Broccoli-Ricotta Soufflé (see page 105) will satisfy even people who usually prefer meat dishes. There are also special features highlighting the nutritional benefits of nutrient-rich tofu and ways to use herbs and spices as a substitute for salt.

HEARTY MAIN DISHES

For those evenings when you want a really satisfying meal, here is a collection of hearty entrées: casseroles and pot pies that are rich in nutrition but low in fat and sodium. Most can be made ahead and frozen for quick reheating. When entertaining, try French Buckwheat Crêpes With Mushrooms and Herbs (below). Pair with French Spring Garden Potage (see page 58) for an elegant menu. Pasta With Walnut-Garlic Sauce (see page 90) is a winner for informal parties or Christmas Eve dinners.

FRENCH BUCKWHEAT CRÊPES WITH MUSHROOMS AND HERBS

The aroma of sautéing mushrooms, seasonings, and wine is hard to resist. The applejack, a sweet apple brandy, melds well with the cheese and asparagus. A crêpe pan should be used for this recipe, but if you do not have one, a large heavy skillet will do. Crêpes are quick to make; if you are in a hurry, prepare the crêpes ahead of time. They keep for 10 days in the refrigerator or up to three months frozen (simply stack between sheets of waxed paper and cover tightly in plastic wrap). Make the filling ahead of time, too, and assemble the crêpes for last-minute baking.

  ½ cup buckwheat flour
  1 cup whole wheat pastry flour
  3 egg whites, lightly beaten
  1 whole egg
  1½ cups nonfat milk
  ½ teaspoon salt
  2 teaspoons olive oil
  4 cups sliced mushrooms
  ½ cup minced green onions
  1 cup asparagus tips
  1 teaspoon nutmeg
  ½ teaspoon dried thyme
  ¼ cup applejack, Calvados brandy, or white wine
  1 teaspoon oil, for coating baking dish
  ½ cup grated low-fat Monterey jack or mozzarella cheese

1. In a blender purée flours, egg whites, whole egg, milk, and salt until the consistency of heavy cream. In a crêpe pan or skillet over medium-high heat, heat ½ teaspoon oil until a drop of water sizzles on surface of pan. Ladle ¼ cup batter onto pan. Cook crêpe until lightly browned (30 to 60 seconds on each side). Set cooked crêpes on a plate, and continue until all batter is used.

2. Preheat broiler. In a skillet over medium-high heat, warm remaining oil and sauté mushrooms and green onions for 5 minutes, stirring frequently. Add asparagus, nutmeg, thyme, and applejack. Cook for 2 minutes, stirring frequently.

3. Lightly oil a baking dish. Spoon about 2 tablespoons filling into center of each crêpe. Roll and lay, seam side down, in baking dish. Stack them if you run out of room. Sprinkle grated cheese over top and broil until lightly browned and bubbling.

Serves 8.

> *Preparation time:* 25 minutes
> *Cooking time:* 40 minutes
> *Per serving:* calcium 134 mg, calories 180, carbohydrates 22 g, cholesterol 31 mg, fat 5 g, fiber 3 g, protein 10 g, sodium 345 mg

---

MINNESOTA VEGETABLE AND WILD RICE PILAF WITH CASHEW GRAVY

The Land of Lakes is also famous for its wild rice, and here is a favorite Minnesota recipe. Brown and wild rices are sautéed with onions, celery, and carrots, then mixed with pine nuts and herbs. A rich cashew gravy is poured over the rice for a satisfying side dish or whole-grain entrée. Serve it with Braised Pheasant (see page 150) for a tasty autumn meal.

  1 cup minced onion
  2 teaspoons olive oil
  ¼ cup dry sherry or white wine
  ½ cup minced celery
  ½ cup diced carrots
  1 teaspoon minced garlic
  ¼ cup pine nuts or chopped almonds
  2 cups wild rice
  1 cup long-grain brown rice
  3 cups Vegetable Stock (see page 51)
  ½ teaspoon thyme
  ¼ teaspoon sage
  1 teaspoon low-sodium soy sauce or tamari
  1 cup toasted whole cashews
  2 cups water
  2 teaspoons olive oil
  2 tablespoons whole wheat pastry flour
  2 teaspoons grated ginger
  2 teaspoons herbal salt substitute
  1 tablespoon minced parsley
  1 tablespoon miso

1. In a large saucepan or Dutch oven over medium-high heat, sauté onion in olive oil and sherry for 5 minutes, then add celery, carrots, and garlic. Cover and steam for 2 minutes. Add pine nuts, wild rice, and brown rice, and stir-fry for 1 minute.

2. Pour in stock. Raise heat to high and bring to a boil. Lower heat to medium and simmer, uncovered, for 15 minutes, then cover and steam until rices are soft but chewy (about 20 minutes). Add thyme, sage, and soy sauce.

3. While rice is cooking, purée cashews and the water in blender to a smooth gravy. In a saucepan over medium heat, heat olive oil and add flour. Stirring frequently, cook for 2 minutes. Add cashew gravy, ginger, salt substitute, and parsley. Cook until thick, whisking frequently.

4. Remove some of the cashew gravy to a small bowl, and mix with miso until smooth. Return to saucepan and take off heat. Serve over cooked rice.

Serves 8.

> *Preparation time:* 20 minutes
> *Cooking time:* 45 minutes
> *Per serving:* calcium 72 mg, calories 463, carbohydrates 68 g, cholesterol 1 mg, fat 16 g, fiber 6 g, protein 15 g, sodium 408 mg

TOFU POTPIE

This dish has all the appeal of a meat potpie.

- ³⁄₄ *cup rice flour*
- 1¹⁄₂ *teaspoons herbal salt substitute*
- 1 *teaspoon garlic powder*
- 1 *pound firm tofu*
- 2 *tablespoons olive oil*
- 1 *cup thinly sliced onions*
- ¹⁄₂ *cup thinly sliced carrots*
- 1 *cup shelled peas*
- 3 *tablespoons low-sodium soy sauce or tamari*
- 1¹⁄₂ *cups water*

1. In a small paper bag, place ¹⁄₂ cup of the rice flour, salt substitute, and garlic powder. Cut tofu into 1-inch cubes. Add to bag and shake to coat thoroughly with flour mixture.

2. In a large skillet over medium-high heat, heat 1 teaspoon of the olive oil. Sauté tofu until lightly browned. Place in a large casserole. Heat another 1 teaspoon of olive oil in pan and sauté onion until soft, then add carrots and cook for 3 minutes. Add peas and soy sauce. Cover and steam 2 minutes, then take off heat and place into casserole.

3. Preheat oven to 350° F. In a clean saucepan over medium heat, cook remaining flour until fragrant (about 3 minutes). Do not allow to brown. Add remaining olive oil and, whisking, pour in the water. Cook until mixture is as thick as gravy. Pour over tofu and vegetables.

4. Bake casserole until bubbling (about 10 minutes). Serve hot.

Serves 8.

> *Preparation time:* 20 minutes
> *Cooking time:* 25 minutes
> *Per serving:* calcium 72 mg, calories 463, carbohydrates 69 g, cholesterol 1 mg, fat 16 g, fiber 7 g, protein 15 g, sodium 404 mg

EGGPLANT CASSEROLE WITH TOFU

This casserole combines tofu and low-fat cheese to create a savory filling. The eggplant is sautéed lightly, then baked in a rich tomato-basil sauce for flavor.

- 1 *large eggplant*
- 2 *teaspoons olive oil, plus oil for coating pan*
- 1 *cup mashed firm tofu*
- ¹⁄₂ *cup grated Parmesan cheese*
- ¹⁄₄ *cup chopped parsley*
- ¹⁄₂ *cup whole wheat or rye bread crumbs*
- 1 *cup thinly sliced onion*
- 1 *teaspoon minced garlic*
- 1 *teaspoon minced fresh basil*
- ¹⁄₂ *cup thinly sliced green bell pepper*
- 1 *cup sliced mushrooms*
- ¹⁄₂ *cup grated low-fat mozzarella cheese*
- 1¹⁄₂ *cups low-fat spaghetti sauce*

1. Preheat broiler. Cut eggplant into slices about ¹⁄₂ inch thick. Lay on ungreased baking sheet and brush with 1 teaspoon olive oil. Broil until lightly browned (1 to 2 minutes). Turn slices over, brush with remaining oil, and broil. Set aside. Preheat oven to 375° F.

2. In a large bowl combine tofu, Parmesan, and parsley. Lightly oil a 9- by 12-inch baking pan and sprinkle with bread crumbs. Arrange sliced eggplant on top of crumbs.

3. Spoon tofu mixture over eggplant, then top with sliced onion, garlic, basil, bell pepper, and mushrooms. Sprinkle with any remaining bread crumbs and mozzarella. Top with spaghetti sauce.

4. Bake until well browned (45 to 55 minutes).

Serves 8.

> *Preparation time:* 20 minutes
> *Baking time:* 50 to 60 minutes
> *Per serving:* calcium 230 mg, calories 193, carbohydrates 21 g, cholesterol 8, fat 9 g, fiber 5 g, protein 11 g, sodium 451 mg

NOTE

NUTRITIONAL BENEFITS OF TOFU

Tofu is a soybean curd with a texture much like soft cheese. It is ivory in color and soft in texture and is used extensively as a protein source by Asian and Middle Eastern cultures. It is easy to make, inexpensive, and nutritious.

Like low-fat dairy products, such as cottage cheese or yogurt, tofu is an excellent source of calcium. Tofu is also a good source of iron, phosphorus, and potassium as well as B vitamins and vitamin E.

The process of making tofu is similar to that of making dairy cheese. Soaked soybeans are blended with water, then strained and heated, and a curdling agent is added. The agent causes the tofu to separate into solid curds and a clear liquid whey. The solid curds are poured into a tofu press, and after about 30 minutes, the tofu hardens into a block. The tofu is ready to eat.

Tofu keeps about 10 days, refrigerated and stored in a closed container in fresh water. The water should be replaced every two days.

Two different kinds of tofu are available (usually in the produce section of the supermarket): soft and firm (or nigari) tofu. Use soft tofu for blending into sauces, salad dressings, cream soups, and dessert toppings. Firm tofu is best for stir-fries since it holds its shape fairly well (see Szechwan Sautéed Tofu and Vegetables, page 98).

Tofu can also be frozen. After thawing, squeeze to remove excess water and crumble into small pieces. The resulting texture is similar to that of ground beef, and the tofu can be seasoned and added to chili, lasagne, and other traditionally meat-based dishes for a low-fat protein substitute.

PASTA WITH WALNUT-GARLIC SAUCE

A traditional favorite in southern France, this pasta dish is surprisingly simple and unusually delicious. The roasted garlic gives the sauce a sweet flavor that complements the walnuts. Decorate the top with minced fresh basil leaves and red bell pepper. It's a rich dish, so save it for a special occasion. Serve with a green salad with Lime-Mint Dressing (see page 82) and crusty French bread.

    2   large heads garlic
    1/3 cup olive oil
    1/3 cup walnuts
    1/4 cup boiling water
    1   teaspoon herbal salt substitute
    1/4 teaspoon cayenne pepper
    6   cups cooked linguine or egg
        noodles
    1   teaspoon chopped parsley
    2   tablespoons minced fresh basil,
        for garnish
    2   tablespoons minced red bell
        pepper

1. Preheat oven to 300° F. Slice tops of garlic heads to expose cloves. Brush lightly with 1 teaspoon olive oil. Place on ungreased baking sheet and roast for 20 minutes. Let cool slightly, then squeeze heads to extract roasted cloves without peel.

2. Place garlic into a blender or food processor. Add walnuts, remaining oil, the water, salt substitute, and cayenne. Blend until smooth.

3. Toss sauce with hot pasta, then add parsley. Garnish with basil and red bell pepper.

Serves 6.

Preparation time: 10 minutes
Roasting time: 20 minutes
Per serving: calcium 52 mg, calories 380, carbohydrates 44 g, cholesterol 53 mg, fat 18 g, fiber 2 g, protein 10 g, sodium 14 mg

---

MARTINIQUE CASSEROLE WITH RED PEPPERS AND BLACK BEANS

Besides being an excellent source of protein, the reduced-fat cheeses and black beans in this recipe are a tasty combination. They are paired with sautéed onions, red bell peppers, and yellow squash for a colorful and delicious casserole that freezes well. Be sure to examine the black beans before cooking—wash them well under running water, removing stones and broken beans.

    1   large acorn squash or
         1/2 large butternut squash
    1½   cups sliced onion
    1   teaspoon olive oil
    1/4 cup dry sherry
    4   julienned red bell peppers
    3   cloves garlic, minced
    2   teaspoons ground coriander
    2   teaspoons cumin
    1   teaspoon dry mustard
    1/2 cup nonfat plain yogurt
    1/2 cup sour cream or sour half-
         and-half, if available
    1/4 cup minced parsley
    1   cup cooked black beans
         (approximately 3/4 cup dried)
    1   cup cooked brown rice
    1/3 cup grated low-fat Monterey
         jack cheese
    2   tablespoons lemon juice
         Oil, for coating casserole pan
    1/4 cup thinly sliced red bell
         pepper, for garnish

1. Preheat oven to 350° F. Line a baking sheet with aluminum foil. Split squash in half and place, cut side down, on baking sheet, leaving in seeds (moisture from seeds helps speed cooking process). Bake squash for 20 minutes.

2. While squash is baking, in a large skillet over medium-high heat, sauté onion in olive oil and sherry until soft but not browned. Add red peppers and garlic to sauté and cook for 5 more minutes.

3. Mix sautéed vegetables with coriander, cumin, dry mustard, yogurt, sour cream, parsley, beans, brown rice, cheese, and lemon juice. When squash is baked, scoop out seeds and remove peel. Cube cooked squash and add to other ingredients.

4. Lightly oil a large casserole dish and spoon mixture into it. Garnish top with red pepper slices. Bake for 25 minutes.

Serves 8.

Preparation time: 30 minutes
Cooking time: 55 minutes
Per serving: calcium 159 mg, calories 174, carbohydrates 24 g, cholesterol 11 mg, fat 6 g, fiber 4 g, protein 7 g, sodium 168 mg

---

POLENTA AND CURRIED VEGETABLES

It is hard to find a family in Italy that does not appreciate slices of polenta—coarsely ground baked cornmeal often served with a rich tomato sauce and cheese. In this version the polenta is baked, then combined with sautéed vegetables in a slightly spicy curry sauce. Slice the polenta into wedges and arrange on a large platter, then spoon the brightly colored vegetable curry on top.

    1   teaspoon olive oil
    1   cup sliced onion
    1/2 cup julienned carrots
    1   teaspoon minced garlic
    3   tablespoons chopped parsley
    1/2 teaspoon cumin
    1   teaspoon ground coriander
    2   teaspoons curry powder
    1/4 cup apple juice
    1/2 teaspoon cayenne pepper, or to
         taste
    3/4 cup polenta
    1/2 cup cold water
    1/2 teaspoon herbal salt substitute
    2   cups boiling water
    1   cup grated low-fat Monterey
         jack cheese

1. In a large skillet over medium-high heat, heat oil and sauté onion for 5 minutes, stirring frequently. Add carrots, garlic, and parsley, and sauté 5 more minutes. Add cumin, coriander, curry, apple juice, and cayenne. Cover and reduce heat to low. Let vegetables continue to cook while you make polenta.

2. Preheat oven to 350° F. In a medium bowl, mix polenta, the cold water, and salt substitute into a paste. In medium saucepan place the boiling water and stir in polenta paste, whisking until smooth. Cook over medium heat, whisk-ing frequently, until thick (5 to 10 min-utes). Stir in cheese.

3. Spoon polenta into a lightly oiled 8-inch-diameter cake pan and bake 20 minutes.

4. To serve, slice polenta into wedges, then place on platter and top with cur-ried vegetables. Serve immediately.

Serves 6.

Preparation time: 25 minutes
Cooking time: 45 minutes
Per serving: calcium 193 mg, calories 162, carbohydrates 18 g, cholesterol 17 mg, fat 7 g, fiber 2 g, protein 7 g, sodium 215 mg

This polenta recipe is topped with a surprise—bright curried vegetables. Rich in protein, the dish will please health-conscious family members or dinner guests.

DOWN-HOME DINNERS

These family-style recipes are designed to please a crowd of hearty eaters. Most can be made ahead—a boon to the busy cook.

BARLEY-STUFFED CABBAGE ROLLS WITH GINGER SAUCE

This delicious recipe uses the salty flavor of hijiki, a common Japanese seaweed used for seasoning, to bring out the sweetness of the green cabbage. You can prepare these rolls ahead of time and refrigerate them for up to 24 hours before baking.

- 1 head green cabbage
- 3 tablespoons dried hijiki, rinsed well in running water
- 5 dried black Japanese mushrooms
- 1 cup boiling water
- 2 teaspoons Asian sesame oil
- 1 onion, sliced thinly
- 1/2 cup shredded carrot
- 1/2 cup shredded celery
- 1 cup cooked brown rice
  Low-sodium soy sauce or tamari, to taste
  Oil, for coating baking dish

Ginger Sauce

- 1 cup cashews
- 2 cups cold water
- 1 teaspoon Asian sesame oil
- 2 tablespoons fresh ginger, grated
- 2 tablespoons whole wheat flour
- 1/4 teaspoon white pepper
  Pinch cayenne pepper
- 1 teaspoon low-sodium soy sauce or tamari

1. Preheat oven to 350° F. With a sharp knife, core center of cabbage head, leaving head intact. Place cabbage in a large pot and fill with 3 to 4 inches of water. Steam until leaves are tender enough to peel off easily and fold without breaking (about 20 minutes). Drain cabbage and set aside. While cabbage is cooking, place hijiki and mushrooms in a small bowl with the boiling water and steep.

2. In a wok or skillet, heat 1 teaspoon of the sesame oil and sauté onion until soft but not browned. Add carrot and celery and cook, stirring, for several minutes more. Add rice and soy sauce, if needed. Remove from heat.

3. Drain hijiki and mushrooms. Slice stems off mushrooms and chop caps coarsely. Add caps and hijiki to rice mixture.

4. Separate leaves of cabbage. Lightly oil a 9- by 12-inch shallow baking dish.

5. Wrap reserved cabbage leaves around rice mixture by placing 1 to 2 tablespoons of filling on the bottom section of each leaf, folding sides in, and rolling up like a sleeping bag.

6. Place cabbage rolls, seam side down, in baking dish. Lightly brush with remaining 1 teaspoon sesame oil. Bake cabbage rolls for 45 minutes.

Serves 6.

Ginger Sauce

1. In a blender combine cashews with the water and purée. Strain through a sieve into a bowl.

2. In a saucepan heat sesame oil and sauté ginger for 1 minute, then add flour. Cook over low heat, stirring, for 2 minutes to eliminate floury taste. Slowly pour in cashew milk, stirring with a whisk as you pour. Mixture should thicken. Season with white pepper, cayenne, and soy sauce and serve with cabbage rolls.

> *Preparation time:* 40 minutes
> *Cooking time:* 75 minutes
> *Per serving:* calcium 121 mg, calories 268, carbohydrates 32 g, cholesterol 0 mg, fat 14 g, fiber 3 g, protein 8 g, sodium 234 mg

BLACK BEAN CHILI WITH CILANTRO

This southwestern chili has been influenced by South American cuisine. Black beans are savory and hold their shape while cooking.

- 1/4 cup dry sherry
- 1 tablespoon olive oil
- 2 cups chopped onion
- 1/2 cup chopped celery
- 1/2 cup chopped carrot
- 1/2 cup seeded and chopped red bell pepper
- 4 cups cooked black beans (approximately 3 1/2 cups dried)
- 2 cups Vegetarian Stock (see page 51) or water
- 2 tablespoons minced garlic
- 1 cup chopped tomatoes
- 2 teaspoons ground cumin
- 4 teaspoons chili powder, or to taste
- 1/2 teaspoon oregano
- 1/4 cup chopped cilantro
- 2 tablespoons honey
- 2 tablespoons tomato paste
  Grated onion, grated low-fat Monterey jack cheese, and nonfat plain yogurt, for garnish

1. In a large, heavy pot, heat sherry and oil and sauté onions until soft but not browned.

2. Add celery, carrot, and bell pepper and sauté 5 minutes, stirring frequently.

3. Add remaining ingredients except garnishes and bring to a boil. Lower heat and simmer for 45 minutes to 1 hour, covered. Chili should be thick with all water absorbed. Garnish with grated onion, cheese, and a dollop of yogurt.

Serves 8.

> *Preparation time:* 35 minutes
> *Cooking time:* 55 to 70 minutes
> *Per serving:* calcium 80 mg, calories 201, carbohydrates 33 g, cholesterol 0 mg, fat 3 g, fiber 10 g, protein 11 g, sodium 376 mg

TEX-MEX CHILI

This recipe combines the traditional Texas chili spices of cumin and hot peppers with the tangy cilantro of Mexican cuisine. Tex-Mex Chili can be easily made ahead and refrigerated for a week.

> 2 large onions, chopped
> ¼ cup Vegetarian Stock (see page 51) or white wine
> 3 cloves garlic, minced
> 1 bell pepper, chopped
> 2 teaspoons chili powder, or to taste
> 2 teaspoons ground oregano
> 1 teaspoon ground cumin
> 4 cups cooked kidney or pinto beans (approximately 3 cups dried)
> 2 cups water or vegetable stock
> 1 cup tomato sauce
> 2 tablespoons chopped cilantro plus chopped cilantro, for garnish
> Nonfat plain yogurt, for garnish

1. In a heavy Dutch oven or stockpot, sauté onion in vegetable stock until onion is soft, then add garlic, bell pepper, chili powder, oregano, cumin, 3 cups of the beans, and the water. Bring to a boil.

2. In a blender purée the remaining 1 cup beans with tomato sauce. Add this mixture to the chili with the 2 tablespoons cilantro.

3. Cook chili in stockpot over low to medium heat for 20 minutes, covered. Chili can also be slow-cooked in an electric slow cooker on low, for 6 to 8 hours. Stir occasionally. Serve hot, garnished with cilantro and yogurt.

Serves 8.

Note Chili improves in flavor if allowed to sit overnight in the refrigerator. It can also be frozen for up to two months.

> *Preparation time:* 20 minutes
> *Cooking time:* 35 minutes
> *Per serving:* calcium 82 mg, calories 144, carbohydrates 28 g, cholesterol 0 mg, fat 1 g, fiber 9 g, protein 8 g, sodium 358 mg

Velvety black beans are simmered with cumin, garlic, cilantro, and sherry to make a rich chili that rivals the best of the Southwest. Serve with corn-bread sticks and a small green salad.

BASICS

CASEROLE BUILDING

Vegetable casseroles are easy to make ahead. Here are a few easy tips to make your casseroles moist and flavorful. You will need the following:

Base such as sautéed vegetables, a cooked grain or bean, tofu

Liquid such as stock, nonfat milk, wine, water

Binder such as beaten egg, low-fat cheeses, bread crumbs

Flavoring such as herbs, spices, low-fat cheeses, onions, garlic

Casseroles are usually baked in a moderate (350° F) oven until they are set (about 40 minutes). You may want to cover the casserole with aluminum foil to allow the interior to cook faster, but remember to remove the foil during the last 15 minutes in order to lightly brown the top.

1. Start with an assortment of vegetables and sauté them in a very small amount of oil (less than 1 teaspoon), plus a little sherry or water. By sautéing the vegetables first, you'll get much more flavor in the casserole.

2. Then add the protein source, usually cooked grains (such as rice), beans (such as cooked pinto beans or chick-peas), or tofu. Mix everything together.

3. Now take the casserole dish and begin building. Fill the dish with the above mixture to about three fourths of the way to the top. Pour in wine or stock, about ¼ cup, just to keep everything from drying out as the casserole cooks.

4. To bind the casserole, add beaten egg, small amounts of grated low-fat cheeses, or bread crumbs. Pour binder over the casserole or sprinkle on top. As the casserole bakes, these ingredients will help to solidify the mixture.

STUFFED SWEET RED BELL PEPPERS

Try this recipe when sweet red bell peppers are in season. Choose well-shaped peppers that, when stuffed, can stand up in a dish. The light filling and sauce can be made ahead, and even frozen. Prepare the peppers right before baking, however, because they will lose their color and flavor if allowed to sit too long.

4 *medium-sized red bell peppers*
1 *teaspoon sesame oil*
1 *onion, chopped finely*
2 *cups sliced mushrooms*
1 *teaspoon minced garlic*
1 *cup corn (frozen or fresh)*
2 *eggs, beaten*
1 *cup low-fat ricotta cheese*
2 *tablespoons grated Parmesan cheese*

1. Preheat oven to 350° F. Heat a saucepan of water to boiling. Cut tops off bell peppers. Remove ribs and seeds. Chop tops and reserve. Immerse scooped-out bell peppers in boiling water for 2 minutes to soften, then rinse under cold water. Set aside to stuff later.

2. In a skillet heat oil and sauté onion until soft, then add mushrooms and garlic and cook until mushrooms begin to weep moisture.

3. Add chopped pepper tops and corn to skillet. Sauté, stirring frequently, for 3 minutes, then add eggs and ricotta and Parmesan cheeses and turn off heat.

4. Place peppers in a deep baking dish and stuff with sautéed filling. Cover with foil and bake until bubbling, lightly browned, and soft (about 45 minutes). Serve hot.

Serves 4.

Preparation time: 35 minutes
Cooking time: 60 minutes
Per serving: calcium 243 mg, calories 332, carbohydrates 43 g, cholesterol 127 mg, fat 12 g, fiber 2 g, protein 17 g, sodium 310 mg

EGGPLANT AND CHICK-PEA MOUSSAKA

Greek cooks traditionally salt eggplant before baking, to allow the fibers to soften and therefore better absorb the flavors of the sauce. The salt can be rinsed off before cooking. This savory dish will freeze well and keeps for seven days covered tightly with plastic wrap in the refrigerator.

1 *large eggplant, sliced very thinly*
  Salt
1 *tablespoon olive oil*
1 *large onion, sliced*
2 *cloves garlic, minced*
2 *large ripe tomatoes, chopped*
3 *tablespoons chopped fresh basil*
1 *to 2 teaspoons dried oregano*
½ *cup white wine*
  Oil, for coating pan
1 *cup cooked chick-peas*
2 *eggs, beaten lightly*
2 *tablespoons grated Parmesan cheese*

1. Preheat oven to 300° F. Place eggplant slices on a large baking tray (use two trays if needed) and lightly sprinkle with salt. Bake until easily pierced with a fork (10 to 15 minutes).

2. While eggplant is baking, heat olive oil in a skillet and sauté onion until soft, then add garlic, tomatoes, basil, oregano, and wine. Continue to sauté until tomatoes soften (about 10 minutes).

3. Rinse eggplant, if desired, and place in a lightly oiled 9- by 12-inch baking dish. Raise temperature of oven to 350° F.

4. Spread chick-peas over eggplant; top with beaten eggs. Spoon tomato sauté over eggs. Sprinkle with cheese and bake for 45 minutes. Serve hot.

Serves 6.

Preparation time: 35 minutes
Cooking time: 75 minutes
Per serving: calcium 76 mg, calories 154, carbohydrates 16 g, cholesterol 72 mg, fat 6 g, fiber 3 g, protein 7 g, sodium 153 mg

MEDITERRANEAN STUFFED EGGPLANT

Eggplant and zucchini are ideal for stuffing and baking. You can then serve them as entrées or side dishes. This Mediterranean-style stuffed eggplant carries the flavors of tomato, garlic, olive oil, and peppers. Steam, bake, or blanch the eggplant before using so that the texture is as soft as the filling.

 2 *medium-sized eggplants*
 2 *teaspoons olive oil, plus oil for coating pan*
 ¼ *cup dry sherry*
 ½ *cup chopped onion*
 3 *to 4 cloves garlic, minced*
 1 *cup coarsely chopped plum tomatoes*
 1 *green onion (including greens), chopped*
 ½ *cup seeded and chopped bell pepper*
 ¼ *cup black olives, chopped*
 1 *teaspoon minced fresh basil*
 ½ *teaspoon oregano*
  Herbal salt substitute and freshly ground black pepper, to taste
 ½ *to ¾ cup whole wheat bread crumbs, plus finely ground whole wheat bread crumbs, for topping*
 ⅓ *cup grated Parmesan cheese Chopped fresh basil or parsley, for garnish*

1. Preheat oven to 350° F. Slice eggplants in half lengthwise. Place eggplants, cut side down, on an aluminum-foil-lined baking sheet. Brush outside of eggplants with olive oil. Bake until a knife inserted into skin pierces easily (about 20 minutes), then remove from oven and let cool.

2. With a sharp-edged spoon, scoop out the insides of the eggplants into a bowl. Place the eggplant shells in a lightly oiled baking dish, wedging them together so they stay upright.

3. In a skillet heat sherry and sauté onion until soft but not browned. Add garlic, tomatoes, green onion, bell pepper, olives, basil, oregano, and salt substitute and pepper and sauté for 5 minutes, stirring frequently.

4. Remove from heat and stir in bread crumbs and Parmesan cheese, adding enough bread crumbs to form a thick filling.

5. Stuff filling into eggplant shells and top with finely ground bread crumbs. Season, if desired, with salt substitute and pepper.

6. Bake stuffed eggplants until browned and bubbling (about 25 minutes). Serve hot, garnished with basil.

Serves 4.

Preparation time: 35 minutes
Cooking time: 55 minutes
Per serving: calcium 181 mg, calories 256, carbohydrates 38 g, cholesterol 5 mg, fat 7 g, fiber 9 g, protein 9 g, sodium 432 mg

Eggplant is softened by baking, then spread with tomatoes, onions, chick-peas, cheese, and pungent spices, and baked again. Serve Eggplant and Chick-Pea Moussaka (see page 94) crisp and hot; it makes hearty fare for chilly weather.

CURRIED VEGETABLES WITH RAITA AND CHUTNEY

Here is a medium-hot curried vegetable dish, accompanied by a cooling Cucumber Raita (pronounced RIGHT-ah) and a sweet chutney. The curried vegetables and chutney freeze well, but serve the raita within 24 hours of making it, for best flavor.

    2   tablespoons turmeric
    1   tablespoon cumin seed,
        ground
    2   teaspoons freshly ground black
        pepper
    1   teaspoon cayenne pepper
    2   tablespoons coriander seed,
        ground
    1   tablespoon caraway seed,
        ground
    2   tablespoons cinnamon
    1   tablespoon grated fresh ginger
    2   tablespoons ground
        cardamom
    1   teaspoon olive oil
  1/2   cup dry sherry
    2   cups sliced onions
    4   cups peeled and cubed
        eggplant
    1   cup sliced carrot rounds
    1   small russet or red potato,
        diced
    2   cups thinly sliced mushrooms
    1   tablespoon minced garlic
    2   cups apple juice
  1/4   cup freshly squeezed lemon
        juice

Cucumber Raita

    2   teaspoons whole cumin seed
    1   teaspoon herbal salt substitute
    1   large cucumber, peeled,
        seeded, and coarsely grated
  1/2   small apple, coarsely grated
  1/8   teaspoon cayenne pepper
  1 1/2 cups nonfat plain yogurt

Ginger-Apple Chutney

    3   cooking apples, chopped
    3   ripe pears, cored and chopped
    1   clove garlic, minced
    2   tablespoons grated fresh ginger
  1/2   cup orange juice

  1/2   cup apple juice
    1   teaspoon cinnamon
    1   teaspoon ground cloves
    1   teaspoon herbal salt substitute
  1/4   cup apple cider vinegar
  1/4   cup honey
        Dash of cayenne pepper

1. In a large skillet place turmeric, cumin seed, black pepper, cayenne, coriander seed, caraway seed, cinnamon, ginger, and cardamom. Roast over low heat, stirring frequently, until an aroma emerges from the mixture (about 5 minutes).

2. Add oil, sherry, and onions, and cook over medium heat until onions are soft but not browned (8 to 10 minutes).

3. Add eggplant, carrot, potato, mushrooms, garlic, apple juice, and lemon juice. Bring to a boil, then lower heat to simmer and cook 15 to 20 minutes. Serve hot.

Serves 6.

Cucumber Raita

1. In an ungreased skillet roast cumin and salt substitute over low heat until aroma emerges (about 5 minutes).

2. Grind cumin and salt substitute in a blender or spice mill. In a bowl combine with remaining ingredients and chill until serving time.

Makes 3 cups.

Ginger-Apple Chutney

1. In a saucepan bring all ingredients to a boil, and cook over medium-high heat for 30 minutes.

2. Mash with a potato masher, or purée lightly in blender. Serve warm or cold.

Makes 3 cups.

Preparation time: 55 minutes *Cooking time:* 55 minutes *Per serving:* calcium 278 mg, calories 377, carbohydrates 82 g, cholesterol 1 mg, fat 3 g, fiber 12 g, protein 8 g, sodium 271 mg

BAKED TOFU

Try these tofu cutlets in sandwiches or as a light entrée.

    1   pound firm tofu, drained
    3   tablespoons whole wheat flour
    1   tablespoon minced garlic
    1   tablespoon onion powder
  1/4   teaspoon ground oregano
    1   teaspoon poultry seasoning
    1   teaspoon low-sodium soy sauce
        or tamari
    1   teaspoon Asian sesame oil
        Oil, for coating pan

1. Preheat oven to 350° F. Slice tofu into eight equal-sized slabs. Place them on a paper-towel-lined baking sheet; cover with another single layer of paper towels and weight tofu with a phone book or a large cutting board for 30 minutes.

2. In a bowl mix together flour, garlic, onion powder, oregano, and poultry seasoning. In another bowl combine soy sauce and sesame oil.

3. Lightly oil a 9- by 12-inch baking sheet.

4. Coat tofu pieces with soy sauce mixture, then with flour mixture, covering all surfaces. Place on the baking sheet and cook, turning once, until both sides are lightly browned (15 to 25 minutes). Serve hot.

Serves 4.

Preparation time: 45 minutes *Baking time:* 15 to 25 minutes *Per serving:* calcium 249 mg, calories 215, carbohydrates 11 g, cholesterol 0 mg, fat 12 g, fiber 4 g, protein 19 g, sodium 58 mg

BAKED MACARONI PRIMAVERA

Primavera is a much-loved Italian springtime dish of pasta and vegetables in a light cream sauce. This version combines whole wheat macaroni with a medley of fresh vegetables sautéed in sherry and olive oil, and is tossed with a light béchamel made from nonfat milk and a little Parmesan cheese.

  8 *ounces dried whole wheat, spinach, or artichoke macaroni*
     Oil, for coating baking dish
  ¼ *cup dry sherry*
  1 *teaspoon olive oil*
  ⅓ *cup chopped green onion (including greens)*
  1 *teaspoon minced garlic*
  1 *red bell pepper, seeded and chopped*
  ¼ *teaspoon ground cumin*
  ½ *teaspoon dried oregano*
  1 *tablespoon chopped fresh basil*
  ½ *cup asparagus, cut diagonally into 2-inch lengths*
  1 *cup halved cherry tomatoes*
  ½ *cup trimmed snow peas*

Primavera Sauce

  2 *teaspoons butter or margarine*
  2 *teaspoons whole wheat flour*
  1 *cup nonfat milk*
  ⅓ *cup grated Parmesan cheese*
  ¼ *teaspoon white pepper*

1. Preheat oven to 400° F. In a large pot heat water to boil. Add pasta and, uncovered, cook until al dente (cooked but not mushy). Drain and rinse pasta under cold water. Place in a large bowl and set aside.

2. Lightly oil a large baking dish. In a skillet heat sherry and olive oil and sauté green onion, garlic, and bell pepper until pepper is soft but not mushy. Add cumin, oregano, basil, asparagus, cherry tomatoes, and snow peas, and sauté 2 minutes, stirring frequently.

3. Remove from heat and toss with pasta and Primavera Sauce. Spoon into baking dish. Bake until lightly browned and bubbling (about 25 minutes).

Serves 6.

Primavera Sauce In a saucepan heat butter and stir in flour. Cook 2 minutes, stirring, to eliminate floury taste, then slowly add milk, stirring with a whisk. If milk is added slowly enough, the sauce should thicken to a heavy cream consistency. Add cheese and pepper.

Preparation time: 45 minutes
Cooking time: 45 minutes
Per serving: calcium 147 mg, calories 226, carbohydrates 36 g, cholesterol 8 mg, fat 5 g, fiber 1 g, protein 10 g, sodium 154 mg

The bright colors of fresh vegetables join wheat macaroni in a light cheese sauce. Baked Macaroni Primavera is an elegant springtime dish served with tossed green salad and a fruit dessert.

WOK-COOKED ENTRÉES

Main dishes prepared in a wok are perfect for the busy cook—they are fast to make, and the ingredients can be chopped, sliced, and diced up to four hours before cooking. (If you don't have a wok, use a large, deep skillet.) Wok cooking is always done rapidly, over medium-high or high heat. This fast cooking method preserves the color, texture, and flavor of the ingredients, as well as the nutrient value.

SZECHWAN SAUTÉED TOFU AND VEGETABLES

The Szechwan and Hunan provinces of China are famous for their hot chiles. This recipe combines lightly sautéed tofu squares with an assortment of vegetables. Cooking the ingredients quickly in the wok maintains their bright color and texture.

- *2/3 cup sliced green onions*
- *1 tablespoon grated ginger*
- *1/4 teaspoon honey*
- *2 teaspoons Asian sesame oil*
- *1/3 cup low-sodium soy sauce or tamari*
- *1/4 teaspoon dried chile flakes*
- *1 pound firm tofu*
- *1/2 cup sliced Chinese cabbage*
- *1/2 cup sliced mushrooms*
- *1/4 cup sake or dry sherry*
- *2 tablespoons arrowroot powder*
- *1/3 cup cold water*
- *1/4 cup whole wheat pastry flour*
- *2 eggs*
- *2 teaspoons olive oil*

1. In a large bowl combine green onions, ginger, honey, sesame oil, soy sauce, and dried chile flakes. Slice tofu into 2-inch squares and add to mixture. Carefully toss to mix thoroughly and set aside to marinate for 20 minutes.

2. In another large bowl combine cabbage, mushrooms, and sake. Toss well and set aside to marinate for 15 minutes.

3. In a small bowl mix together arrowroot and 3 tablespoons of the cold water. Set aside.

4. In a fourth bowl mix together flour, eggs, and the remaining water. Remove tofu from its marinade and dip slices into flour batter. In a flat-bottomed skillet, over medium-high heat, heat olive oil and sauté tofu on both sides until lightly browned. Remove tofu and set on a platter.

5. In a wok over medium-high heat, stir-fry contents of both bowls of marinade for 5 minutes, then add arrowroot mixture and cook until mixture thickens (about 2 minutes). Add tofu, cover, and steam 1 minute. Serve immediately.

Serves 8.

Preparation time: 20 minutes
Marinating time: 20 minutes
Cooking time: 10 minutes
Per serving: calcium 139 mg, calories 163, carbohydrates 10 g, cholesterol 53 mg, fat 9 g, fiber 2 g, protein 12 g, sodium 352 mg

TOFU AND BELL PEPPERS IN SWEET-AND-SOUR SAUCE

Crunchy, brightly colored bell peppers complement the white cubes of protein-rich tofu in this entrée. The sweet-and-sour sauce is slightly spicy. The vegetables and tofu can be marinated ahead of time in sesame oil for added flavor. Cook the dish the night before and reheat for lunch the next day—it gets better as it sits and the flavors blend.

- *1 cup thinly sliced red bell pepper*
- *1/2 cup thinly sliced green bell pepper*
- *1/3 cup thinly sliced yellow bell pepper*
- *2 teaspoons Asian sesame oil*
- *1 tablespoon arrowroot powder*
- *1/2 cup rice vinegar*
- *1/2 cup pineapple juice*
- *1/2 cup lemon juice*
- *1/3 cup honey*
- *1/2 teaspoon herbal salt substitute*
- *1/2 teaspoon grated ginger*
- *1 pound firm tofu*
- *2 tablespoons low-sodium soy sauce or tamari*
- *1/4 teaspoon cayenne pepper, or to taste*

1. In a wok over medium-high heat, sauté bell peppers in the sesame oil until shiny (about 5 minutes).

2. In a large bowl combine arrowroot, vinegar, pineapple juice, lemon juice, honey, salt substitute, and ginger. Pour over peppers and cook, stirring, until mixture thickens slightly.

3. Cut tofu into thin slices. Add to wok, cover, and steam 3 minutes. Add soy sauce and cayenne. Toss well and serve.

Serves 6.

Preparation time: 10 minutes
Cooking time: 10 minutes
Per serving: calcium 170 mg, calories 217, carbohydrates 29 g, cholesterol 0 mg, fat 8 g, fiber 3 g, protein 13 g, sodium 174 mg

Stir-fry squares of fresh tofu and bell pepper strips, then toss with a honey-sweetened sauce of pineapple, lemon, and ginger to make this dish (see page 98).

Sliced shiitake mushrooms absorb the flavor of the sesame oil and soy sauce and add a meaty texture to this healthy vegetarian stir-fry.

BROCCOLI, MUSHROOM, AND WATER CHESTNUT STIR-FRY WITH NOODLES

A colorful yet simple combination, this recipe is easy to make after a busy day at the office. Precut the broccoli stalks, slice the mushrooms and water chestnuts, and cook the noodles the night before; store in plastic bags. Cooking takes only 10 minutes. Be sure not to overcook the broccoli; its crispness and bright green color are essential to the success of this dish.

> 2 teaspoons minced garlic
> 2 teaspoons Asian sesame oil
> 1 cup sliced shiitake or domestic mushrooms
> 4 cups broccoli florets
> 1/2 cup sliced water chestnuts
> 4 cups cooked linguine or rice noodles
> 2 tablespoons low-sodium soy sauce or tamari
> 1/4 cup minced green onions

1. In a wok or large skillet over medium-high heat, sauté garlic in sesame oil for 1 minute. Add mushrooms and cook until they exude moisture.

2. Add broccoli and water chestnuts and stir-fry for about 3 minutes. Add noodles, soy sauce, and green onions. Toss together well. Cover and steam for 2 minutes, then serve.

Serves 6.

> *Preparation time:* 10 minutes
> *Cooking time:* 7 to 10 minutes
> *Per serving:* calcium 57 mg, calories 226, carbohydrates 44 g, cholesterol 0 mg, fat 3 g, fiber 6 g, protein 9 g, sodium 183 mg

BURGERS AND CROQUETTES

Here are some delightful recipes for vegetable burgers and croquettes that fit easily into lunch and light supper menus.

TOFU SLOPPY JOES ON WHEAT ROLLS WITH OVEN-BAKED FRENCH FRIES

An excellent substitute for ground beef, this crumbled tofu mixture is reminiscent of the sloppy joes that are a favorite with children. Serve with Oven-Baked French Fries and coleslaw.

- 1 teaspoon olive oil
- 2 tablespoons dry sherry
- 1 onion, finely chopped
- 1/2 cup minced green bell pepper
- 2 cloves garlic, minced
- 1/3 cup whole wheat bread crumbs
- 2 cups firm tofu, drained and crumbled
- 1 teaspoon low-sodium soy sauce or tamari
  Herbal salt substitute and freshly ground black pepper, to taste
- 2 cups tomato sauce
- 1 teaspoon cayenne pepper, or to taste
- 1/2 teaspoon ground cumin
- 6 whole wheat hamburger buns

Oven-Baked French Fries

- 4 russet potatoes or 8 red potatoes
- 1/2 teaspoon oil, for coating baking sheet

1. In a skillet heat oil and sherry; sauté onion over medium heat until soft but not browned.

2. Add bell pepper and garlic and cook until pepper is soft.

3. Add bread crumbs, tofu, soy sauce, and salt substitute and pepper; mix well, cooking 3 minutes more to blend flavors.

4. Remove from heat and add tomato sauce, cayenne, and cumin. Lightly toast insides of hamburger buns, and fill with sloppy joe mixture.

Serves 6.

Oven-Baked French Fries

1. Preheat oven to 250° F. Slice potatoes into French fry strips and place on lightly oiled baking sheet.

2. Bake for 20 minutes and turn over when bottoms of fries begin to brown. Cook until lightly browned on all sides.

Preparation time: 45 minutes
Cooking time: 45 minutes
Per serving: calcium 234 mg, calories 355, carbohydrates 51 g, cholesterol 0 mg, fat 10 g, fiber 5 g, protein 18 g, sodium 910 mg

PECAN BURGERS

Years ago an enterprising young cook made these fantastic vegetarian burgers and sold them on the streets of a small mill town on the East Coast. The original recipe follows and is sure to appeal to any hamburger lover.

- 1 cup ground pecans (pecan meal)
- 1/2 cup wheat germ
- 1/2 cup wheat bran or oat bran
- 1/2 onion, grated
- 1/2 large carrot, grated
- 1 tablespoon Asian sesame oil
- 1 teaspoon low-sodium soy sauce or tamari
  Oil, for coating skillet

1. In a large bowl mix all ingredients and form into 6 patties.

2. In a lightly oiled skillet, fry lightly on both sides until browned.

Makes 6 burgers, 6 servings.

Preparation time: 15 minutes
Cooking time: 25 minutes
Per serving (not including bun): calcium 21 mg, calories 186, carbohydrates 12 g, cholesterol 0 mg, fat 16 g, fiber 5 mg, protein 4 g, sodium 76 mg

BEAN BURGERS

These hearty burgers are great after a football game or for a tailgate party.

- 1/4 cup finely minced onion
- 1/3 cup diced celery
- 1 tablespoon minced garlic
- 1 teaspoon olive oil, plus oil for coating baking sheet
- 2 cups cooked and mashed chick-peas
- 1/2 cup Chunky Tomato Sauce With Fresh Basil (see page 183)
- 1/4 cup cooked and mashed red or russet potatoes
- 1 1/2 cups whole wheat bread crumbs or crushed whole wheat cracker crumbs
- 1/4 teaspoon thyme
- 1 teaspoon minced fresh basil
  Pinch ground rosemary
  Freshly ground black pepper, to taste
  Herbal salt substitute, to taste

1. In a medium-sized heavy skillet, sauté onion, celery, and garlic in oil until soft but not browned (5 to 8 minutes). Add chick-peas and tomato sauce and cook 3 minutes over medium heat, stirring often. Remove from heat.

2. Preheat oven to 400° F. Lightly oil a 9- by 12-inch baking sheet.

3. In a large bowl mix together the sautéed vegetables, potato, bread crumbs, thyme, basil, rosemary, pepper, and salt substitute. Form into 4 patties.

4. Place on baking sheet and bake until browned and firm (about 15 minutes per side). Serve hot.

Makes 4 burgers, 4 servings.

Preparation time: 20 minutes
Cooking time: 40 minutes
Per serving (not including bun): calcium 86 mg, calories 330, carbohydrates 55 g, cholesterol 0 mg, fat 7 g, fiber 3 g, protein 13 g, sodium 335 mg

NOTE

REPLACING SALT WITH HERBS AND SPICES

Excess sodium has been linked to high blood pressure, heart disease, and kidney disease. To cut down on salt, try flavoring foods with herbs and spices, sauce reductions, and wines.

When cooking with herbs, remember that the longer herbs sit after they have been added to other foods, the more their flavor develops. Certain herbs actually fare better under brief cooking conditions. For example, dill and basil lose their flavor when subjected to prolonged cooking, and sage, rosemary, and thyme can become unpleasantly pungent and bitter.

Spices are often sweeter and more flavorful after they are dry-roasted. Roast spices over medium heat in an ungreased skillet until you smell a nutlike aroma. Instead of salting lean meats and chicken before grilling, rub them with fresh garlic or ginger.

Here's a list of dried and fresh herbs, spices, and flavorings that bring out the best of different foods:

Beans (dried): bay leaf, chili powder, coriander, cumin, mustard

Beans (fresh green): dill, dried lemon peel, summer savory

Potatoes: chives, oregano, paprika, parsley, rosemary, tarragon

Rice and other grains: curry powder, marjoram, saffron, parsley, thyme

Salad dressings (such as vinaigrettes): fresh or dried basil, tarragon, cumin, thyme, oregano, celery seed, chervil, fresh dill, parsley

Soup stock: bay leaf, fresh or dried basil, marjoram, fresh parsley, thyme

Tomatoes (fresh): fresh or dried basil, celery seed, fresh dill, garlic, tarragon

Tomatoes (cooked): chervil, garlic, marjoram, oregano, fresh parsley, sage

EASY FOR ENTERTAINING

Ever wonder what to serve to health-conscious friends who are trying to cut back on meat? Now you can choose one of the following vegetarian recipes from around the world and serve it with pride.

TOFU TERIYAKI

Here's a great combination—sweet-and-sour vegetables and tofu—that you can prepare ahead of time, and keep in a tightly covered container in the refrigerator for up to four days before serving.

- 1 tablespoon Asian sesame oil
- 1 pound firm tofu, drained and cut into 1-inch cubes
- 2 cups chopped vegetables (onion, red bell pepper, squash, and broccoli, or whatever you have available)
- 2 tablespoons rice vinegar
- 1/2 cup low-sodium soy sauce or tamari
- 3 tablespoons honey
- 1/3 cup dry sherry or mirin (Japanese sweet rice wine)

1. In a skillet or wok heat 2 teaspoons oil and lightly sauté tofu until browned. It may fall apart a little, which is fine. When browned, remove tofu to a platter and set it aside.

2. Add a little more sesame oil to skillet, if needed, and sauté vegetables until tender.

3. In a small saucepan heat rice vinegar, soy sauce, honey, and sherry until boiling. Reduce heat and simmer sauce for 5 minutes.

4. Add tofu to vegetable sauté and pour sauce over all. Heat through and serve hot.

Serves 4.

Preparation time: 20 minutes
Cooking time: 15 minutes
Per serving: calcium 260 mg, calories 299, carbohydrates 25 g, cholesterol 0 mg, fat 14 g, fiber 4 g, protein 20 g, sodium 1,062 mg

---

SPINACH AND CHEESE SOUFFLÉ ROLL

This scrumptious entrée is rolled and sliced like a jelly roll. The French call it a roulade.

- 1/3 cup finely minced onion
- 1 teaspoon olive oil
- 3 cups washed and chopped spinach leaves
- 1/3 cup finely minced parsley
- 1/4 cup grated low-fat mozzarella cheese
- 6 eggs, separated
  Olive oil, for coating parchment
- 2 cups low-fat ricotta cheese
- 2 tablespoons grated Parmesan cheese

1. Preheat oven to 400° F. In a medium skillet over medium-high heat, sauté onion in olive oil until onion is very soft. Add spinach and parsley and cover. Cook over low heat for 2 minutes. Drain if needed.

2. Transfer to a bowl. Stir mozzarella and egg yolks into spinach mixture.

3. Cut a piece of parchment paper to fit into a 9- by 12-inch shallow baking dish; lightly oil the parchment.

4. In a separate bowl beat egg whites until soft peaks form and fold them into spinach mixture. Spoon into the parchment-lined baking dish. Cover with another piece of lightly oiled parchment. Bake for 25 minutes.

5. In a small bowl mix ricotta and Parmesan cheeses. When soufflé is baked, flip it out of the baking dish onto a counter. Peel off the top sheet of parchment and spread the cheese mixture over soufflé.

6. Roll soufflé and cheese mixture as you would a jelly roll, peeling off the second sheet of parchment as you go. Cut into thick slices and serve.

Serves 6.

Preparation time: 20 minutes
Cooking time: 35 minutes
Per serving: calcium 386 mg, calories 239, carbohydrates 8 g, cholesterol 242 mg, fat 15 g, fiber 1 g, protein 19 g, sodium 291 mg

---

MU SHU TOFU

A favorite Chinese dish is mu shu pork, a stir-fried mixture wrapped in small pancakes and dipped into a rich sauce. This vegetarian version uses a savory stir-fry of carrots, onions, and tofu and a spicy peanut sauce for dipping. The pancakes are easy to make, but you can cook just the stir-fry and serve it with the peanut sauce for a delicious dinner. The sauce keeps two weeks in the refrigerator and is good over chicken or fish, too.

> 1 teaspoon Asian sesame oil
> 1 cup grated carrot
> 2 cups tofu, cut into small chunks
> 2 green onions, cut into diagonal slices
> 2 tablespoons grated fresh ginger
> 2 tablespoons dry sherry
> 1/2 teaspoon honey
> 2 tablespoons Vegetarian Stock (see page 51) or water

Pancakes

> 2 cups whole wheat pastry flour
> 3/4 cup boiling water (approximately)
> 2 teaspoons Asian sesame oil

Peanut Sauce

> 2 tablespoons chunky peanut butter
> 1/4 teaspoon cayenne pepper
> 1 1/2 tablespoons honey
> 2 tablespoons low-sodium soy sauce or tamari
> 2 teaspoons rice vinegar
> 1 tablespoon minced green onion
> 1 1/2 teaspoons ground coriander
> 2 teaspoons Asian sesame oil

1. Prepare Pancakes. In a wok or skillet, heat sesame oil and sauté carrots and tofu for 3 minutes, stirring constantly. Add remaining ingredients and increase heat until the mixture begins to bubble.

2. Cook uncovered until most of the liquid has evaporated. While vegetables are cooking, prepare Peanut Sauce.

3. To assemble, each person places a few spoonfuls of filling on top of a pancake, adds sauce, and rolls pancake into a cylinder.

Serves 6.

Pancakes

1. In a large bowl mix flour and boiling water with a wooden spoon and turn onto a lightly floured surface. Knead together until an elastic dough forms that is soft, pliable, and not sticky.

2. On a floured surface roll out dough to about 1/4-inch thickness; cut into 2 1/2-inch rounds. Roll out each round to 5-inch-diameter pancake.

3. Lightly brush one side of each pancake with sesame oil. Place pairs of pancakes back-to-back, with oil in between them. (Oil keeps one side of pancake soft during cooking and later in wrapping and filling stages.)

4. Heat an ungreased skillet and cook each ungreased side of the pair of pancakes over low heat until slightly brown. Remove from skillet, peel apart and stack under a dampened dish towel until ready to use.

Makes 12 to 15 pancakes.

Peanut Sauce In a small bowl stir together all ingredients. Serve with pancakes and filling.

Makes 1/2 cup.

Preparation time: 45 minutes
Cooking time: 20 minutes
Per serving: calcium 129 mg, calories 332, carbohydrates 48 g, cholesterol 0 mg, fat 10 g, fiber 4 g, protein 13 g, sodium 215 mg

---

STEP BY STEP

HOW TO MAKE CRÊPES

1. *Heat 6-inch crêpe pan over medium-high heat until hot. Brush with 1/4 teaspoon oil. Pour 4 tablespoons of batter into center of pan. Gently tilt pan so batter coats entire surface. Cook crêpe 60 seconds or until it begins to bubble.*

2. *Turn crêpe with metal spatula (when bottom is browned). Lightly brown other side (about 30 seconds). Transfer crêpe to a plate and fill.*

RATATOUILLE CRÊPES

These whole wheat crêpes are thin, briefly cooked pancakes rolled around a slightly spicy filling of tomatoes, eggplant, and bell peppers. Crêpes (unfilled) can be made ahead and frozen.

- 2 cups chopped eggplant (peeled or unpeeled)
- 1 onion, sliced thinly
- 1 clove garlic, minced
- 2 red bell peppers, seeded and chopped coarsely
- 2 medium zucchini, sliced into rounds
- 3 large tomatoes, cored and chopped coarsely
- 1 tablespoon chopped fresh basil
- 2 tablespoons olive oil, or as needed
- 1/2 cup grated low-fat Monterey jack cheese

Crêpe Batter

- 3/4 cup whole wheat pastry flour
- 1 1/4 cups nonfat milk
- 2 eggs, beaten

1. Prepare Crêpe Batter. Combine eggplant, onion, garlic, bell peppers, zucchini, tomatoes, and basil in a stockpot or Dutch oven and cook over medium heat until soft (about 25 minutes).

2. While ratatouille is cooking, heat 1 teaspoon of the olive oil in a crêpe pan or small skillet and ladle into it 2 to 3 tablespoons of batter. Tilt pan to allow batter to evenly coat surface of pan. Cook crêpe over medium-high heat and flip it when it begins to bubble and brown. Cook 30 seconds on other side, then flip onto a plate. Use more olive oil, as needed (up to 2 tablespoons), to oil the crêpe pan.

3. To assemble crêpes, spoon 1/2 cup of ratatouille vegetable mixture into the center of each crêpe; roll and place seam side down in a baking dish. Sprinkle crêpes with cheese and broil until cheese melts. Serve hot.

Serves 6.

Crêpe Batter In a blender combine flour, milk, and eggs at high speed for 30 seconds.

Makes 12 to 15 crêpes.

> *Preparation time:* 25 minutes
> *Cooking time:* 30 minutes
> *Per serving:* calcium 170 mg, calories 213, carbohydrates 23 g, cholesterol 80 mg, fat 10 g, fiber 3 g, protein 10 g, sodium 197 mg

BROCCOLI-RICOTTA SOUFFLÉ

Adapted from a recipe by James Beard, this easy dish demystifies soufflé making. These are sturdy soufflés, especially if cooked in ramekins, or individual soufflé dishes. Try to cook the dish just before serving so it stays light.

- 1 teaspoon olive oil, plus olive oil for coating baking dish
- 1/2 cup minced onion
- 1 cup cooked broccoli stems and florets, chopped finely
- 2 cups low-fat ricotta cheese
- 1/3 cup grated low-fat mozzarella cheese
- 1/2 cup grated Parmesan cheese
- 4 eggs, separated

1. Preheat oven to 375° F. Lightly oil 6 ramekins or one 1½-quart soufflé dish with small amount of oil.

2. Heat oil in a skillet and sauté onion until soft but not browned. Remove from heat and stir in broccoli, cheeses, and egg yolks.

3. Beat egg whites until soft peaks form; fold into broccoli mixture. Spoon carefully into prepared soufflé dish or ramekins.

4. Place on baking sheet (to make carrying easier) and bake until lightly browned and puffy (25 to 40 minutes). Serve immediately.

Serves 6.

Preparation time: 20 minutes
Cooking time: 35 to 45 minutes
Per serving: calcium 390 mg, calories 231, carbohydrates 6 g, cholesterol 176 mg, fat 15 g, fiber 1 g, protein 19 g, sodium 355 mg

Bring Paris to the kitchen with this trio of French dishes: a tangy, herb-scented French Bean Salad (see page 74), served chilled; a spinach soufflé (see page 102) rolled around a cheese filling; and savory Ratatouille Crêpes.

These refined Vegetarian Sushi Rolls are stuffed with bright strips of vegetables and served with a tongue-tingling Wasabi-Ginger Dipping Sauce. They are delicious with Szechwan Noodles (see page 75) and Kombu Miso Soup (see page 53).

VEGETARIAN SUSHI ROLLS

You can fill sushi rolls with a variety of foods, from traditional Japanese ingredients to California-style crab and avocado. When cooking the rice, add extra water to make it sticky.

   3 *cups cooked brown or white rice*
   ¼ *cup rice vinegar*
  1½ *tablespoons dry sherry*
   3 *tablespoons honey*
   2 *teaspoons salt or herbal salt substitute*
   6 *sheets of toasted nori*
   1 *firm cucumber, peeled, seeded and cut into long strips*
   2 *carrots, peeled and cut into thin strips*
   2 *red bell peppers, seeded and cut into thin strips*

Wasabi-Ginger Dipping Sauce

   ¼ *cup prepared wasabi (mix 2 tablespoons powdered wasabi with 2 tablespoons cold water to form a paste)*
   3 *tablespoons low-sodium soy sauce or tamari*
   2 *tablespoons grated ginger*

1. In a large bowl place cooked rice. In a saucepan over high heat, cook vinegar, sherry, honey, and salt for 5 minutes, stirring occasionally. Pour over rice to make sticky and stir.

2. Lay out the six sheets of nori and spread an equal amount of sushi rice mixture over each, extending rice almost to edges. Lay a strip of each vegetable along the length of the rice.

3. Roll sushi tightly to form a cylinder, then slice into six rounds.

Serves 6.

Wasabi-Ginger Dipping Sauce

Mix ingredients together and serve as dipping sauce with sushi.

Preparation time: 45 minutes
Per serving: calcium 199 mg, calories 241, carbohydrates 54 g, cholesterol 0 mg, fat 1 g, fiber 3 g, protein 6 g, sodium 1,198 mg

EASY MINI-MEALS

For the occasions when you just don't have time to cook a large meal, here are some mini-meals that are great for brunch or light suppers. Try Eggs à la Suisse (see page 108), a new version of eggs Benedict, for a springtime Sunday.

BROCCOLI MOUSSE WITH HORSERADISH SAUCE

This recipe is an eye-catcher: The bright green of the broccoli contrasts with the slightly pink beet and yogurt sauce. It originated in the Caribbean, where bright colors are common to many dishes. Serve on a bed of greens or shredded cabbage as a light salad entrée, or slice into wedges for an elegant side dish for a fish entrée, such as Baked Fish in Lettuce Packets (see page 133).

> 3 cups chopped broccoli
> 4 teaspoons lime juice
> 1½ cups defatted Chicken Stock (see page 51)
> 1 envelope unflavored gelatin
> ⅓ cup minced green onions
> 1 egg white, beaten
> ¼ cup reduced-fat mayonnaise
> 1½ tablespoons dried dill
> Oil, for coating soufflé dish
> 1 cup nonfat plain yogurt
> ¼ cup minced cooked fresh beets or minced canned beets
> ¼ cup prepared horseradish
> Lettuce leaves, for lining salad plates

1. In a small saucepan steam broccoli until tender. Drain and purée in blender with lime juice.

2. Heat stock to boiling. Dissolve gelatin in hot stock. Let cool. Mix with broccoli.

3. Add green onions, egg white, mayonnaise, and dill to broccoli mixture. Lightly oil a 1½-quart soufflé dish and pour mixture into it, then chill in refrigerator for 3 hours.

4. While mousse is chilling, mix yogurt, beets, and horseradish, and chill for 1 hour. Stir well again and set aside until serving time. To serve, spoon equal amounts of broccoli mousse onto 6 salad plates lined with lettuce leaves. Garnish each with a dollop of horseradish sauce.

Serves 6.

Preparation time: 30 minutes
Chilling time: 3 hours
Per serving: calcium 134 mg, calories 75, carbohydrates 11 g, cholesterol 5 mg, fat 1 g, fiber 2 g, protein 7 g, sodium 339 mg

Almost a work of art, Broccoli Mousse With Horseradish Sauce is a healthy gourmet addition to any entertaining menu.

Rather than using a heavy cream-based sauce, as in eggs Benedict, this poached egg dish is served Swiss style, with a low-fat cheese mixture spread on the English muffins.

EGGS À LA SUISSE

This special-occasion brunch item features lightly poached eggs nestled on English muffin halves spread with reduced-fat cream cheese, then sprinkled with green onions, Parmesan cheese, and nutmeg. Serve with mimosas made from champagne or nonalcoholic sparkling wine and fresh orange juice, and accompany with Carrot-Ginger Breakfast Muffins (see page 197).

    2 *cups water*
    8 *large eggs*
    4 *whole wheat English muffins, split in half*
    4 *ounces reduced-fat cream cheese*
  ¹/₂ *cup minced green onions*
    1 *teaspoon freshly grated nutmeg*
  ¹/₄ *cup grated Parmesan cheese*

1. In a large skillet over medium-high heat, bring the water to a boil. Lower heat to keep water at an even simmer. Break each egg one at a time into a small bowl and gently slide egg into the simmering water. Repeat until all eggs are in water. Poach for 3 minutes.

2. While eggs are poaching, toast English muffins and spread each half with cream cheese. Place a poached egg on each half. Sprinkle each half with green onions, nutmeg, and Parmesan. Serve immediately.

Serves 4.

Preparation time: 10 minutes
Cooking time: 8 to 10 minutes
Per serving: calcium 251 mg, calories 387, carbohydrates 30 g, cholesterol 451 mg, fat 19 g, fiber .5 g, protein 22 g, sodium 602 mg

MUSHROOM TART

A light pastry crust is filled with wine-cooked mushrooms, onions, carrots, and broccoli mixed with cheeses and tofu, and baked until lightly browned and firm. This dish is equally good served hot out of the oven as an entrée or cold for a brown-bag lunch the next day.

- 1/4 cup minced onion
- 1 teaspoon minced garlic
- 1 teaspoon butter or olive oil
- 1/4 cup dry white wine
- 2 cups sliced mushrooms
- 1/4 cup grated carrots
- 1/4 cup minced broccoli
- 1 teaspoon dried thyme
- 1/2 teaspoon dried marjoram
- 1/2 pound soft tofu
- 3/4 cup nonfat plain yogurt
- 3 tablespoons minced parsley
- 1/4 cup grated low-fat Swiss cheese
- 1/4 cup grated low-fat Cheddar or mozzarella cheese
- 1 nine-inch pie shell

1. Preheat oven to 350° F. In a large skillet over medium high-heat, sauté onion and garlic in butter and wine until soft (2 to 3 minutes). Add mushrooms and cook until they exude moisture.

2. Add carrots, broccoli, thyme, and marjoram, and cook 5 minutes more. Remove pan from heat and set aside.

3. With your hands, gently squeeze block of tofu to remove excess water, then purée in blender or food processor with yogurt until smooth. Stir into vegetable mixture.

4. Stir parsley and cheeses into vegetable mixture and spoon into pie shell. Bake until firm in the center and lightly brown (about 40 minutes). Let cool slightly before slicing. Serve hot or cold.

Serves 8.

Preparation time: 30 minutes
Cooking time: 60 minutes
Per serving: calcium 175 mg, calories 171, carbohydrates 15 g, cholesterol 4 mg, fat 9 g, fiber .1 g, protein 8 g, sodium 228 mg

COUSCOUS WITH MUSHROOMS AND CURRY

Platters of couscous are often a staple in Middle Eastern households; the accompaniment varies from lamb to chicken to vegetables. Couscous, available in the gourmet section of supermarkets, is a lightly steamed wheat that tastes a little like orzo pasta—slightly nutty and sweet. In this recipe sautéed mushrooms, carrots, and onions are combined with turmeric, coriander, and a touch of cinnamon to create a spicy assortment of flavors. This is a good dish to make ahead.

- 1/2 cup sliced onion
- 2 teaspoons minced garlic
- 1 teaspoon olive oil
- 1 cup sliced mushrooms
- 1/2 cup grated carrots
- 1 teaspoon curry powder
- 1/4 teaspoon turmeric
- 1/2 teaspoon ground coriander
- 2 teaspoons cinnamon
- 1/2 cup raisins
- 3 cups defatted Chicken Stock (see page 51)
- 2 tablespoons low-sodium soy sauce or tamari
- 1/2 cup chopped parsley
- 2 cups uncooked couscous

1. In a large skillet over medium-high heat, sauté onions and garlic in oil for 2 minutes, stirring frequently. Add mushrooms and carrots and cook for 5 minutes.

2. Add curry powder, turmeric, coriander, cinnamon, and raisins, and cook for 3 minutes more. Add stock and bring to a boil.

3. Stir in soy sauce, parsley, and couscous. Cover pan and remove from heat. Let it sit for 15 minutes. Fluff couscous with a fork. Serve hot.

Serves 4.

Preparation time: 20 minutes
Cooking time: 25 minutes
Per serving: calcium 183 mg, calories 486, carbohydrates 96 g, cholesterol 0 mg, fat 3 g, fiber 8 g, protein 19 g, sodium 475 mg

WHOLE GRAIN SIDE DISHES

Besides contributing fiber and complex carbohydrates to your diet, whole grains are a rich source of B-complex vitamins. Add a grain dish to your next chicken or fish menu for more balanced nutrition or enjoy it as a small meal in itself.

GREEN RICE

Green Rice gets its color from minced or chopped parsley, spinach, green onions, and basil. It is a healthy version of Chinese fried rice—only a teaspoon of oil goes into this dish. Try this colorful accompaniment to fish or chicken with Mediterranean Chicken (see page 149) or Fresh Trout Florentine (see page 129).

- 1/2 cup minced green onion
- 2 tablespoons minced garlic
- 1 teaspoon olive oil
- 1/4 cup dry sherry or white wine
- 1/2 cup chopped parsley
- 1/3 cup minced spinach leaves
- 2 tablespoons minced fresh basil
- 3 cups cooked long-grain brown rice
- 2 tablespoons pine nuts
- 2 tablespoons minced red bell pepper
- 1/4 cup grated Parmesan cheese

1. In a large skillet over medium-high heat, sauté green onion and garlic in olive oil and sherry for 5 minutes, stirring frequently. Add parsley, spinach, and basil and cook for 3 more minutes.

2. Add rice and pine nuts and heat through, stirring constantly, for about 5 minutes. Remove from heat and stir in bell pepper and Parmesan cheese. Serve hot.

Serves 4.

Preparation time: 20 minutes
Cooking time: 15 minutes
Per serving: calcium 220 mg, calories 273, carbohydrates 42 g, cholesterol 4 mg, fat 7 g, fiber 2 g, protein 9 g, sodium 137 mg

FEATURE

THE FOUR MOST OVERLOOKED NUTRIENTS

Iron, calcium, vitamin A, and vitamin C are all essential to maintaining good health, yet they are often lacking in the diets of many people in the United States. Fast food, skipped meals, and packaged instead of fresh vegetables deprive many people of adequate amounts of these nutrients.

Vitamin A

Many people grew up hearing, "Eat your carrots: They're good for your eyes." Well, it was good advice. Carrots, as well as other dark yellow, red, and leafy green vegetables, such as broccoli, collards, and spinach, contain large amounts of vitamin A. This vitamin is essential for a number of visual functions, including the formation of the photosensitive visual purple in the human retina, which helps prevent night blindness. Vitamin A also helps increase resistance to disease and infections and promotes bone and tooth development.

A diet rich in fresh fruits and vegetables provides you with more than enough vitamin A. One half cup of carrots alone contains 8,140 International Units of vitamin A, almost double the daily requirement of 4,000 to 5,000. Look for vitamin A in such foods as sweet potatoes, carrots, broccoli, spinach, chard, tomatoes, squash, apricots, cantaloupe, peaches, beef, liver, eggs, and cheeses. Some nutritionists believe that getting vitamin A from foods is a safer resource than supplements, since vitamin A is a fat-soluble vitamin and can build up in the body, possibly causing toxic levels in the process.

Iron

Iron is an essential part of hemoglobin, the part of the blood that transports oxygen. But only small amounts of iron are available in most foods. Women require about 18 milligrams of iron per day; men need less, about 10 milligrams per day. Absorption of iron is enhanced by eating foods rich in vitamin C or by using cast-iron cookware. Some iron-rich foods include prunes; dried peaches, apricots, and raisins; liver; beans and rice; clams and oysters; and spinach and beet greens. One-half cup prune juice provides 5.2 milligrams of iron, one-half cup dried peaches almost 5 milligrams.

Calcium

Calcium, a major ingredient of the skeletal structure—the bones and teeth—also retards bleeding and aids in muscle contraction and in nerve impulse transmission. The body can store excess dietary calcium in the bones: If your diet is chronically low in calcium, however, too much calcium is removed from the bones and osteoporosis may result.

The daily requirement of calcium is around 1,000 milligrams per day—the equivalent of 3 cups of kale or three glasses of milk. Milk and dairy products are good sources of calcium, but it can also be found in leafy greens, tofu, and certain fish and shellfish.

Vitamin C

Vitamin C forms the substances of the cell that hold it together, such as collagen. It aids in strengthening blood vessels and is essential in the healing process.

It is a delicate vitamin that is easily destroyed by heat, light, or exposure to air. The daily vitamin C requirement is about 60 milligrams per day, or the equivalent of one-half cup fresh orange juice. Other good sources of vitamin C are green and red bell peppers, broccoli, lemons, strawberries, and tomatoes. Storing fresh fruits and vegetables in the refrigerator helps to preserve their vitamin C content.

MUSHROOM MILLET BAKE

Millet is a nutritious grain that grows in northern climates. It has a pearly white color and a nutty flavor similar to some pastas. In this simple recipe it is combined with mushrooms sautéed in a sherry sauce and freshly grated low-fat Cheddar cheese, then baked until lightly browned. It makes a good side dish with Braised Pheasant (see page 150) or Roast Breast of Duck With Sherry (see page 152).

Oil, for coating pan
1/2 cup minced green onion
1 teaspoon butter or olive oil
1/3 cup dry sherry
1 cup thinly sliced mushrooms
1/4 cup minced celery
1 teaspoon minced garlic
2 cups cooked millet
3 tablespoons grated low-fat Cheddar cheese

1. Preheat oven to 350° F. Lightly oil an 8-inch-square baking pan or casserole dish.

2. In a large skillet over medium-high heat, sauté green onion in butter and sherry for 5 minutes. Add mushrooms, celery, and garlic, cover, and cook for 10 minutes.

3. Add millet and cook, stirring frequently, to heat through (about 5 more minutes). Remove from heat and stir in cheese. Spoon into baking pan. Bake until lightly browned (about 15 minutes). Serve hot.

Serves 4.

Preparation time: 15 minutes
Cooking time: 35 minutes
Per serving: calcium 57 mg, calories 198, carbohydrates 31 g, cholesterol 4 mg, fat 3 g, fiber 2 g, protein 6 g, sodium 56 mg

HERBED RYE-BERRY TIMBALES

Timbales are small casseroles of grains, vegetables, or fish, pressed into soufflé dishes and baked. Unmolded before serving, they make an elegant side dish. This recipe combines rye berries (available in most natural food stores; if unavailable, substitute wheat berries) with herbs, onions, garlic, and chopped tomatoes. Low in fat, these timbales make a good Thanksgiving or other holiday menu item.

> 3/4 *cup rye berries*
> 1/3 *cup chopped celery*
> 2 *tablespoons grated onion*
> 1 *teaspoon minced garlic*
> *Oil, for coating ramekins*
> 1 *cup chopped tomatoes*
> 1/2 *teaspoon ground dill seed*
> 1/4 *teaspoon dried sage*
> 1 *teaspoon minced cilantro*
> 2 *tablespoons low-sodium soy sauce or tamari*
> 1 *egg, beaten*
> 1/2 *cup grated low-fat mozzarella cheese*

1. In a large pot over medium-high heat, bring 2 cups of water to a boil. Add rye berries, celery, onion, and garlic. Simmer until berries are tender and all water has been absorbed (about 45 minutes).

2. Preheat oven to 350° F. Lightly oil 8 ramekins (small 4-ounce soufflé dishes) and place in a shallow baking pan. Fill pan with 1/2 inch of boiling water.

3. In a large bowl combine tomatoes, dill, sage, cilantro, soy sauce, egg, and cheese. Stir in cooked rye berries and vegetables. Spoon mixture into ramekins, filling to within 1/4 inch of top. Bake until firm (about 45 minutes). Unmold and serve hot.

Serves 8.

Preparation time: 25 minutes
Cooking time: 90 minutes
Per serving: calcium 69 mg, calories 91, carbohydrates 13 g, cholesterol 30 mg, fat 2 g, fiber 3 g, protein 6 g, sodium 183 mg

---

LENTIL SPREAD WITH WHOLE GRAIN CRACKERS

This rich-tasting, healthy pâté, an easy sandwich or canapé spread, includes lentils, sautéed carrots, onions, mushrooms, and garlic, and a variety of herbs and spices. In this recipe it is served on homemade graham crackers made with whole wheat pastry flour and molasses.

> *Oil, for coating pan*
> 1/2 *cup minced onion*
> 1/2 *cup minced mushrooms*
> 1/4 *cup grated carrots*
> 2 *tablespoons minced garlic*
> 1 *teaspoon olive oil*
> 1/3 *cup white wine*
> 2 *cups cooked lentils*
> 1 *cup whole wheat or rye bread crumbs*
> 1 *tablespoon minced fresh basil leaves*
> 1/4 *teaspoon nutmeg*
> 1/4 *teaspoon cumin*
> 1/4 *teaspoon curry powder*
> 1 *tablespoon low-sodium soy sauce or tamari*

Whole Grain Crackers

> *Oil, for coating baking sheet*
> 1/4 *cup tahini*
> 1 *tablespoon molasses*
> 1/4 *cup nonfat milk or nonfat plain yogurt*
> 1 1/4 *cups whole wheat pastry flour*

1. Preheat oven to 400° F. Lightly oil a 2-quart loaf pan.

2. In a large skillet over medium-high heat, sauté onion, mushrooms, carrots, and garlic in olive oil and wine until soft (about 10 minutes). Remove from heat.

3. Stir in lentils, bread crumbs, basil, nutmeg, cumin, curry powder, and soy sauce. If mixture is too dry to form a ball, add a bit of water; if runny, add more bread crumbs. Press into prepared loaf pan. Cover with aluminum foil and bake for 45 minutes. Serve with Whole-Grain Crackers.

Serves 10.

Whole Grain Crackers

1. Preheat oven to 400° F. Lightly oil a large baking sheet.

2. In a large bowl combine tahini, molasses, and milk, mixing until smooth and creamy. Stir in flour to form a soft dough.

3. Lightly flour a work surface and roll out dough. Cut into cracker shapes or rounds about 1/16-inch thick. Poke each cracker several times with a fork—the holes keep it from curling as it bakes. Place on baking sheet and bake for 5 to 8 minutes. Watch carefully: They tend to brown quickly.

Makes approximately 2 dozen crackers.

Preparation time: 25 minutes
Cooking time: 50 minutes
Per serving: calcium 122 mg, calories 221, carbohydrates 35 g, cholesterol 0 mg, fat 5 g, fiber 6 g, protein 10 g, sodium 212 mg

---

This light Ricotta-Spinach-Mushroom Quiche (see page 113) is made from mushrooms, spinach, green onions, low-fat cheese, and savory herbs baked in a whole wheat pie crust. Serve with a crisp green salad.

SAVORY TARTS AND PIES

Most cuisines have their own versions of savory tarts and pies: pasty in England, calzone and pizza in Italy, quiche in France. Unfortunately, most traditional crusts are laden with high-fat ingredients. Here are a few recipes that have been adapted to healthy cuisine and still pass the good taste test.

MEXICAN CORN PIE

This light version of tamale pie is a hearty casserole layered with a cornmeal crust and chili-flavored beans and vegetables. Cook it ahead if you like—it freezes beautifully.

- 2 teaspoons olive oil
- 1 medium onion, chopped
- 3 cloves garlic, minced
- 1 cup seeded and chopped red bell pepper
- ½ cup diced carrot
- 3 cups cooked kidney beans (approximately 2 cups dried)
- 1 cup thick tomato sauce
- 2 teaspoons chili powder
- 1 teaspoon cumin
- 2 tablespoons white wine

Pie Crust

- 2 cups finely ground yellow cornmeal
- ½ cup whole wheat pastry flour
- 2 teaspoons baking powder
- 1 teaspoon herbal salt substitute
- ½ cup water, or as needed
  Oil, for coating baking dish

1. Prepare Pie Crust. Heat oil in skillet; add onion and sauté over medium heat until soft, but not browned. Add garlic, bell pepper, and carrot and cook 5 minutes, stirring frequently.

2. Add remaining ingredients and cover. Simmer until vegetables are tender. Spoon filling into prepared baking dish and gently lay the top crust onto it. Press edges of two crusts together to seal.

3. Bake until brown and bubbly (about 40 minutes). Serve hot.

Serves 8 to 10.

Pie Crust

1. Preheat oven to 350° F. Mix all ingredients except oil for coating dish and knead until smooth. Lightly oil a 9- by 12-inch baking dish; pat half the dough into the bottom of the dish.

2. Spread a long sheet of waxed paper on countertop and pat remaining dough onto it, roughly in the shape of a 9- by 12-inch rectangle. Set aside until you have prepared filling.

Preparation time: 30 minutes
Cooking time: 55 minutes
Per serving: calcium 108 mg, calories 229, carbohydrates 44 g, cholesterol 0 mg, fat 2 g, fiber 7 g, protein 9 g, sodium 288 mg

FRENCH ONION TART WITH MUSHROOMS

This recipe calls for a rich French cheese, but you can make a softer quiche by substituting farmer or ricotta cheese for the Gruyère. Onion tarts are very common in French bakeries, and the secret of the caramelized onions is in the slow cooking.

> 2 teaspoons olive oil
> 1/4 cup dry sherry
> 2 cups thinly sliced onions, preferably sweet onions
> 1/2 cup sliced mushrooms
> 1 teaspoon minced fresh tarragon (optional)
> 1/2 cup nonfat milk
> 1/4 teaspoon grated nutmeg
> 1/2 teaspoon white pepper
> 2 eggs
> 1 whole wheat pie shell, unbaked
> 1/2 cup grated Gruyère cheese

1. Preheat oven to 400° F. Heat oil and sherry in a skillet and add onions. Sauté for 20 minutes, at medium heat, stirring frequently. Onions will become very soft, almost mushy, then begin to lightly brown.

2. Add mushrooms and tarragon, if used, and cook 3 minutes. Remove from heat.

3. In a small bowl, beat milk, nutmeg, pepper, and eggs.

4. Spoon onion mixture into pie shell, sprinkle with cheese, and carefully pour milk-egg mixture on top of them.

5. Bake tart until it sets and becomes lightly browned (about 40 minutes). Let it cool slightly and slice into 8 wedges. Serve hot or cold.

Serves 8.

Preparation time: 20 minutes
Cooking time: 65 minutes
Per serving: calcium 129 mg, calories 182, carbohydrates 13 g, cholesterol 61 mg, fat 11 g, fiber 1 g, protein 6 g, sodium 342 mg

---

RICOTTA-SPINACH-MUSHROOM QUICHE

Spinach is a winter vegetable, at its best between January and May. Look for large, fresh, green leaves. Spinach is an excellent source for vitamins A and C and iron and calcium, making this dish nutritious as well as flavorful. This quiche is best eaten after it has a chance to cool and solidify, since it is very soft when just out of the oven. Enjoy it cold, the next day, with a green salad and a light soup.

> 2 cups chopped spinach leaves
> 1 cup sliced mushrooms
> 1/4 cup chopped green onions
> 1 whole wheat pie shell, unbaked
> 1 cup nonfat milk
> 2 cups low-fat ricotta cheese
> 3 eggs, beaten
> 1/4 teaspoon grated nutmeg
> 1/4 teaspoon dried tarragon
> 1/8 teaspoon rosemary
> Freshly ground black pepper, to taste

1. Preheat oven to 400° F. In a bowl mix spinach, mushrooms, and green onions. Spoon mixture into pie shell.

2. Mix milk, ricotta, and eggs; then stir in nutmeg, tarragon, rosemary, and pepper. Pour over spinach mixture.

3. Bake quiche until it sets and lightly browns (30 to 40 minutes). Let cool before slicing. Quiche may be served hot or cold.

Serves 8.

Preparation time: 25 minutes
Baking time: 40 minutes
Per serving: calcium 244 mg, calories 231, carbohydrates 16 g, cholesterol 99 mg, fat 13 g, fiber 1 g, protein 12 g, sodium 274 mg

---

MENU

FRENCH CANDLELIGHT DINNER FOR FOUR

French Onion and Garlic Soup

French Buckwheat Croquettes With Miso Sauce

Steamed Carrots and Asparagus Tips

Limestone and Bibb Lettuce Salad

Strawberries in Orange Shells

Nonalcoholic Sparkling Blush Wine

The French have always been romantics, and this menu sets the mood for a warm, relaxing evening. Use fine linen, china, fresh flowers, and candles on the table. Make as much of this dinner as possible ahead of time, and then enjoy a glass of wine with your dinner companions. Steam the fresh vegetables and toss the salad right before serving. Menu serves four.

FRENCH ONION AND GARLIC SOUP

The secret of really good onion soup is to sauté the sliced onions very slowly so that their natural sweetness emerges. Onions cooked too quickly or at high heat have a stronger, more bitter taste. This popular onion soup recipe uses this cooking technique.

   1 teaspoon olive oil
   3 large yellow onions, sliced into very thin rounds
   3 cups defatted Chicken or Beef Stock (see page 51)
   4 cloves garlic, minced
   1 bay leaf, crushed
   ¼ cup minced parsley
   1 teaspoon dried basil
      Herbal salt substitute, if needed
   4 zwieback crackers or sliced French bread, toasted
   ¼ cup grated Parmesan cheese

1. In a large stockpot over medium heat, heat oil and sauté onions, stirring constantly. Add 1 cup of the stock and cover; simmer until onions are extremely soft and begin to brown (about 20 minutes).

2. Add garlic and herbs and remaining stock. Cover, bring to a boil, then lower heat and cook 25 minutes.

3. Taste for seasoning; add salt substitute, if needed. To serve, ladle into four ovenproof bowls. Float one zwieback cracker on each bowl of soup. Sprinkle each serving with 1 tablespoon Parmesan cheese. Broil until cheese browns.

Serves 4.

Preparation time: 20 minutes
Cooking time: 55 minutes
Per serving: calcium 193 mg, calories 160, carbohydrates 19 g, cholesterol 7 mg, fat 5 g, fiber 2 g, protein 9 g, sodium 568 mg

FRENCH BUCKWHEAT CROQUETTES WITH MISO SAUCE

This recipe has strong French and Japanese influences.

   ½ cup buckwheat groats
   2 cups boiling water
   1 teaspoon herbal salt substitute
   ½ cup whole wheat flour, or more, if needed
   1 teaspoon olive oil, plus olive oil for frying
   1 small onion, minced
   3 green onions, chopped
   ½ cup chopped parsley
   1 beaten egg

Miso Sauce

   2 cloves garlic, minced
   1 teaspoon Asian sesame oil
   2 teaspoons whole wheat flour
   1 cup nonfat milk
   3 teaspoons light miso
   2 tablespoons hot water
   ½ teaspoon Dijon mustard
   ¼ cup grated low-fat Monterey jack cheese

1. In a deep saucepan lightly toast groats over medium heat until lightly browned.

2. Add the boiling water to groats. Add salt substitute and cook mixture over medium heat until groats become very soft (15 to 20 minutes). Let cool and stir in ½ cup flour.

3. Heat oil in a skillet and sauté onion for several minutes. Add green onions and parsley; remove from heat.

4. Mix onion mixture with buckwheat and stir in egg.

5. Using flour to thicken the mixture, if needed, form into small patties. Fry lightly on both sides in olive oil.

Serves 4.

Miso Sauce

1. Place garlic and oil in a medium skillet; sauté 1 minute over medium heat. Add flour; cook, stirring, for 2 more minutes.

2. Slowly pour in milk, stirring with whisk until sauce thickens. In a separate bowl mix miso with the hot water, stirring until very smooth.

3. Add miso, mustard, and cheese to sauce. Serve hot over croquettes.

Preparation time: 20 minutes
Cooking time: 45 minutes
Per serving: calcium 367 mg, calories 318, carbohydrates 46 g, cholesterol 60 mg, fat 11 g, fiber 7 g, protein 15 g, sodium 446 mg

STRAWBERRIES IN ORANGE SHELLS

In this delicate dessert, halved oranges are scooped out and then filled with a whipped strawberry mixture.

   2 large navel oranges
   3 cups sliced strawberries
   ½ cup Neufchâtel cheese
   1 cup nonfat plain yogurt
   3 tablespoons maple syrup
   1 teaspoon nutmeg
   ¼ teaspoon ground cardamom
      Mint leaves and freshly grated nutmeg, for garnish

1. Halve oranges and, with a metal spoon, scoop out orange pulp (reserve for another use).

2. In a blender, briefly purée remaining ingredients, except garnishes. The idea is to mash the strawberries without destroying their texture and to keep from overblending the cheese.

3. Spoon puréed mixture into orange shells, mounding slightly over rims. Place on a plate and chill for 1 hour. Garnish with mint leaves and freshly grated nutmeg.

Serves 4.

Preparation time: 20 minutes
Chilling time: 1 hour
Per serving: calcium 177 mg, calories 175, carbohydrates 31 g, cholesterol 12 mg, fat 4 g, fiber 4 g, protein 6 g, sodium 103 mg

Flavors from France and Japan combine in these buckwheat croquettes with miso sauce, served with salad, French onion soup, and strawberry mousse.

Superior flavor and nutritional value are the benefits of fish and shellfish purchased fresh from the market.

FISH & SHELLFISH

With many health professionals recommending nutrient-rich seafood on the menu several times a week, health-conscious cooks will value the collection of delicious, easy-to-prepare recipes for fish and shellfish in this chapter. Besides offering superior nutrition, most of the recipes in this chapter can be prepared in less than half an hour. Simple step-by-step instructions take the mystery out of preparing healthful seafood specialties such as Baked Salmon Niçoise (see page 118), Crab Bisque (see page 139), or Seafood Salad (see page 131).

INTERNATIONAL FISH ENTRÉES

The following recipes have an international flair and are delectable enough for any type of entertaining. Considering that most fish dishes don't hold their fresh flavor and texture if prepared too far in advance, they usually must be cooked right before serving, so it helps if accompanying dishes are simple, make-ahead recipes.

JAMAICAN FISH

You'll find in this recipe many of the subtle seasonings of the island of Jamaica. Traditionally this dish is served with cooked rice or crusty bread.

    4 fish steaks
    2 teaspoons olive oil
    1 bunch green onions
       (including greens), chopped
    2 large tomatoes, chopped
    1 red bell pepper, seeded and
       chopped
    1 teaspoon herbal salt substitute
  1/2 teaspoon freshly ground black
       pepper
  1/4 cup white wine vinegar
  1/2 teaspoon dried thyme
    1 tablespoon honey

1. Wash fish steaks and pat dry with paper towels. Carefully remove and discard any bones you find.

2. In a skillet heat oil; add fish and brown quickly on both sides at high heat. Add green onions, tomatoes, and bell pepper. Cover and cook 5 minutes.

3. Add remaining ingredients and continue cooking, covered, for 15 more minutes. Serve immediately.

Serves 4.

> *Preparation time:* 20 minutes
> *Cooking time:* 30 minutes
> *Per serving:* calcium 72 mg, calories 209, carbohydrates 12 g, cholesterol 73 mg, fat 4 g, fiber 2 g, protein 32 g, sodium 104 mg

BAKED SALMON NIÇOISE

Similar to Chicken Niçoise (see page 154), Baked Salmon Niçoise combines the subtle flavors of several Mediterranean cuisines. Small fillets of salmon are baked in parchment paper in order to retain moistness and soft texture (see page 130). Prepare the packets ahead of time, refrigerate, and pull out to bake just before serving. You can use any firm-fleshed fish in season, such as tuna or cod, if salmon is not available.

    1 teaspoon olive oil
    3 cloves garlic, minced
    1 cup chopped plum tomatoes
  1/4 cup chopped pitted Italian or
       Greek olives
  1/4 cup minced green bell pepper
  1/4 teaspoon saffron threads
  1/2 teaspoon dried tarragon
  1/4 teaspoon dried thyme
       Pinch dried sage
 1 1/4 cups white wine
    4 salmon fillets or small salmon
       steaks

1. Preheat oven to 350° F. In a large, heavy skillet heat olive oil and sauté garlic, tomatoes, olives, and bell pepper until soft.

2. Add saffron threads, tarragon, thyme, sage, and wine. Cook 5 minutes at medium heat, uncovered.

3. Place each portion of salmon on a parchment sheet. Spoon tomato mixture over fish and fold packets to seal. Place on a baking sheet.

4. Bake salmon packets for 10 minutes. Slit the top of each packet before serving.

Serves 4.

> *Preparation time:* 30 minutes
> *Cooking time:* 20 minutes
> *Per serving:* calcium 48 mg, calories 297, carbohydrates 5 g, cholesterol 88 mg, fat 10 g, fiber 1 g, protein 35 g, sodium 338 mg

INDONESIAN CRAB CURRY

Indonesian curries are often made with coconut milk, a thick liquid pressed from the pulp of the coconut after it is blended with water. To lower the fat in this usually rich dish, nonfat milk is mixed with coconut milk to create a thick sauce. Serve with small garnishes of chopped dried fruits, fresh cilantro, and lime slices.

 1 1/2 teaspoons cayenne pepper
    1 teaspoon grated fresh ginger
  1/2 teaspoon freshly ground black
       pepper
    4 cloves garlic, minced
    5 shallots, minced
  1/3 cup chopped fresh coriander
       (including stems, leaves, and
       roots)
  1/2 teaspoon grated lime rind
  1/2 teaspoon herbal salt substitute
    1 teaspoon dried shrimp paste
       (optional; see Note)
  1/2 cup grated coconut
    2 cups nonfat milk
    2 tablespoons Thai fish sauce
       (see Note) or low-sodium soy
       sauce or tamari
    1 tablespoon honey
    1 pound cooked crabmeat
    5 cups cooked brown rice

1. In a stockpot combine cayenne, ginger, pepper, garlic, shallots, coriander, lime rind, salt substitute, shrimp paste, if used, coconut, and milk. Bring to a boil and cook over medium high heat for 10 minutes.

2. Add fish sauce, honey, and crabmeat. Heat through. Serve hot over rice.

Serves 6.

Note You can buy shrimp paste and Thai fish sauce in most Asian food stores.

> *Preparation time:* 15 minutes
> *Cooking time:* 20 minutes
> *Per serving:* calcium 203 mg, calories 334, carbohydrates 52 g, cholesterol 61 mg, fat 5 g, fiber 1 g, protein 22 g, sodium 431 mg

FENNEL BAKED FISH EN PAPILLOTE

En papillote is a French cooking term that refers to parchment cooking (see page 130). In this recipe small portions of fresh fish are lightly seasoned with fennel, garlic, and cayenne pepper and then wrapped in parchment packets and baked. This method of cooking fish is excellent for retaining flavor and juiciness.

> 2 whole trout, boned
> 2 teaspoons ground fennel seed
> 1 large clove garlic, minced
> ¼ teaspoon herbal salt substitute
>   Pinch cayenne pepper
> ¼ teaspoon freshly ground black pepper
> 2 teaspoons butter
>   Juice of 1 lemon

1. Preheat oven to 450° F. Place each trout on a piece of parchment.

2. Mix fennel, garlic, salt substitute, cayenne, pepper, butter, and lemon juice to a thick paste. Spread half of paste inside each trout. Wrap the edges of the parchment up around the fish, forming a loose packet.

3. Place packets on a baking sheet and bake for 12 minutes. To serve, open packets and remove trout, reserving cooking liquid. Cut each trout into 2 fillets. Place 1 fillet on each person's plate and top with cooking liquid.

Serves 4.

Preparation time: 20 minutes
Baking time: 12 minutes
Per serving: calcium 41 mg, calories 101, carbohydrates 7 g, cholesterol 30 mg, fat 5 g, fiber 1 g, protein 9 g, sodium 43 mg

Pungent garlic, ginger, and cayenne flavor this festive yet easy-to-prepare Indonesian Crab Curry.

119

A delicate French salad, Coquilles Sauce Verte combines wine-poached scallops with a delicious dill sauce. Traditionally it is served chilled on a bed of crisp greens.

COQUILLES SAUCE VERTE

A traditional French salad, often served as a small, delicate appetizer, this fresh scallop dish is poached in white wine and then mixed with a light dressing.

- 1 pound bay scallops
- ³/₄ cup dry white wine
- ¼ onion, minced
- ¹/₃ cup reduced-fat mayonnaise
- ¼ cup minced parsley, plus parsley for garnish
- ¹/₃ cup chopped spinach leaves
- ¼ cup minced green onion
- ¼ teaspoon dill
- 6 lettuce leaves, for lining plates

1. Place scallops, wine, and onion in a saucepan and bring to a boil, uncovered. Cook 1 minute. Drain scallops and refrigerate immediately to stop cooking process. Discard cooking liquid, or save as fish stock for another recipe.

2. In a blender purée mayonnaise, parsley, spinach, green onion, and dill until smooth.

3. Toss chilled scallops with puréed green sauce. Chill for 10 minutes, then serve on lettuce leaves. Garnish with additional minced parsley, if desired.

Serves 6.

Preparation time: 20 minutes
Cooking time: 5 minutes
Per serving: calcium 77 mg, calories 110, carbohydrates 6 g, cholesterol 31 mg, fat 1 g, fiber 1 g, protein 14 g, sodium 228 mg

MEXICAN BAKED FISH IN SALSA VERDE

This parchment-packeted fish (see page 130) is baked in a green hot sauce made from fresh tomatillos and green chiles. Both of these items are available canned. You can prepare the packets ahead of time, wrap well, and refrigerate until cooking time.

> 1½ pounds fresh salmon, cod, or red snapper, cut into 1-inch-thick fillets
> 1 teaspoon olive oil
> ¼ cup dry white wine
> 1 cup chopped onion
> ⅓ cup chopped green bell pepper
> 1 clove garlic, minced
> 1 cup chopped fresh tomatillos
> 1 teaspoon cumin
> 2 tablespoons chopped chiles en escabeche (pickled chiles)
> 1 teaspoon each lemon juice and lime juice
> ⅓ cup chopped cilantro

1. Preheat oven to 475° F. Cut fish fillets into 4 servings. Carefully remove bones. Place each portion on top of a sheet of parchment.

2. In a skillet heat oil and wine; add onion and sauté until soft. Add bell pepper, garlic, tomatillos, and cumin. Continue cooking for 8 minutes.

3. Add remaining ingredients and cook 3 more minutes.

4. Spoon sautéed vegetables over portions of fish. Wrap parchment into envelopes, sealing fish completely. Place on a baking sheet.

5. Bake parchment packets for 10 minutes. Serve by cutting packets down the center and placing on a platter or on individual plates.

Serves 4.

Preparation time: 15 minutes
Cooking time: 25 minutes
Per serving: calcium 82 mg, calories 252, carbohydrates 7 g, cholesterol 89 mg, fat 8 g, fiber 2 g, protein 36 g, sodium 270 mg

---

SICILIAN SEAFOOD BROCHETTES

Sicilian cooking has much in common with that of southern Italy: Olive oil, seafood, and red peppers are used abundantly. These delicious, grilled brochettes are made from skewered pieces of fresh snapper, large scallops, and shelled prawns, alternated with fresh vegetables. Requiring short preparation time, these brochettes make a perfect summer meal. Assemble them early in the day, wrap tightly in plastic wrap, refrigerate, and then grill right before dinner.

> 2 small red snapper or cod fillets
> 1 red bell pepper
> 8 large scallops
> 8 medium prawns, shelled and deveined
> 8 small boiling onions
> 4 small new potatoes, cooked whole
> 2 teaspoons olive oil

1. Preheat broiler or grill. Soak 8 bamboo skewers in salted water for 20 minutes to prevent burning on the grill (use about 2 tablespoons of salt to 2 cups of water).

2. Cut snapper into 2-inch squares. Cut bell pepper into cubes.

3. Skewer fish and shellfish alternately with onions, bell peppers, and potatoes. Brush lightly with olive oil.

4. Grill until prawns turn pink and curl slightly (5 to 10 minutes). Serve immediately.

Serves 4.

Preparation time: 20 minutes
Grilling time: 10 minutes
Per serving: calcium 78 mg, calories 314, carbohydrates 36 g, cholesterol 96 mg, fat 4 g, fiber 5 g, protein 34 g, sodium 145 mg

---

BASICS

SIMPLE LOW-FAT SAUCES FOR FISH AND SHELLFISH

Acidic sauces Fish responds very well to a slightly acidic sauce, which subdues the fishy flavor and enhances the sweetness. Try lemon or lime juice-based sauces that are thickened with a little arrowroot dissolved in water and seasoned with herbs and freshly ground pepper. To use arrowroot as a thickener, mix equal amounts of arrowroot powder and cold water; heat until slightly thickened. Use about 2 tablespoons of the mixture for every 1 cup of sauce you want to thicken.

Wine sauces These sauces are great on fish, especially if you choose a light dry wine, such as a California Chardonnay. Heat wine to boiling, add fresh or dried herbs—such as tarragon, dill, or chives—and reduce over medium high heat for 10 minutes. Poach fish in this mixture, or dribble it over fish in parchment packets, then bake (see page 130).

Fruit juice sauces Try grilling fish with freshly squeezed fruit juices. Use orange, grapefruit, or lemon juices, seasoned with a few drops of hot chile oil or a dash of cayenne pepper. Marinate fillets or steaks of salmon or tuna in the mixture, and then grill, basting with the marinade every few minutes.

Herb sauces As the fish poaches or bakes, baste with an herb sauce made from pressed garlic, minced shallots or onions, and lemon juice. Or try stuffing the inside cavity of a whole fish, such as trout, with this mixture.

JAPANESE BAKED FISH

The Asian-style sauce in this recipe uses Japanese miso, a fermented paste made from soybeans, one of the best sources of protein. Miso paste can be found refrigerated in Asian markets and natural food stores. The light (yellow) miso used in this recipe is milder than dark (red) miso and combines well with ginger and sake, which are both used in this fish dish. You can make the miso-sesame sauce ahead of time and spread it on the fillets right before baking. See Cutting Fish Fillets and Steaks on page 123 if you are cutting your own fillets.

- 2 pounds red snapper or cod, cut into 4 portions
- 2 tablespoons toasted sesame seed
- 1 teaspoon grated fresh ginger
- 2 tablespoons light miso paste
- 1 teaspoon maple syrup or honey
- 1 tablespoon sake
- 2 tablespoons dry sherry
- 3 tablespoons lemon juice
- 1 teaspoon Asian sesame oil

1. Preheat oven to 450° F. Place snapper fillets in a large baking dish.

2. In a bowl combine other ingredients. Spread miso mixture evenly over fillets and bake for 12 minutes. Serve at once.

Serves 4.

Preparation time: 15 minutes
Baking time: 12 minutes
Per serving: calcium 87 mg, calories 304, carbohydrates 6 g, cholesterol 84 mg, fat 7 g, fiber 1 g, protein 49 g, sodium 462 mg

SWEET-AND-SOUR PRAWNS OVER ALMOND RICE

It's a good idea to slightly undercook the prawns in this recipe since they will continue cooking in the hot sauce even when removed from heat.

- 1 pound medium prawns, shelled and deveined
- 1 cup pineapple chunks
- 1 red bell pepper, seeded and cut into strips
- 1 head broccoli, cut into florets
- 1/4 cup dry sherry
- 1/2 cup rice vinegar
- 4 tablespoons low-sodium soy sauce or tamari
- 1/4 cup honey
- 2 teaspoons Asian sesame oil
- 1 large clove garlic, minced
- 1 tablespoon arrowroot powder mixed with 2 tablespoons cold water

Almond Rice

- 2 tablespoons slivered almonds
- 1 teaspoon light sesame oil
- 1/3 cup chopped green onion
- 4 cups cooked brown rice

1. Cut each prawn into bite-sized chunks. Place in a wok or deep skillet with pineapple, bell pepper, broccoli, and sherry. Sauté until prawns turn bright pink (about 5 minutes).

2. Combine remaining ingredients in a small bowl and add to sauté. Cook, stirring, over medium-high heat until sauce thickens.

3. Prepare Almond Rice. Serve sweet-and-sour prawns and vegetables over heated rice.

Serves 6.

Almond Rice In a small pan sauté almonds at medium-high heat in light sesame oil for 1 minute, stirring frequently. Add green onion and rice. Heat through.

Preparation time: 20 minutes
Cooking time: 15 minutes
Per serving: calcium 88 mg, calories 357, carbohydrates 53 g, cholesterol 115 mg, fat 6 g, fiber 2 g, protein 21 g, sodium 443 mg

STEAMED FISH WITH GINGER

This is a good recipe for light, flat fish, such as sole or flounder. Steaming is a very fast method of preparing fish and should be done right before serving. Be sure that your cover fits snugly over the steamer basket. The light ginger sauce complements the firm texture of the fish.

- 4 fillets of sole
- 1/2 cup boiling water
- 1/2 cup white wine
- 2 tablespoons grated fresh ginger
- 2 cloves garlic, minced
- 2 teaspoons Asian sesame oil
- 1 teaspoon arrowroot powder mixed with 2 tablespoons cold water
- 1 teaspoon low-sodium soy sauce or tamari

1. Place fillets on a steamer basket large enough to fit snugly inside a deep skillet. Pour water and wine into the skillet and bring to a boil. Set the steamer basket in the skillet and cover. Steam 3 minutes.

2. While fish is steaming, sauté ginger and garlic in sesame oil for 3 minutes. Add arrowroot mixture and soy sauce. Continue cooking until sauce thickens, stirring frequently.

3. To serve, ladle a small amount of sauce over each fillet of steamed fish.

Serves 4.

Note Steam can cause severe burns. When you lift the cover from your steamer basket, open it away from you and let the steam dissipate before reaching or looking inside.

Preparation time: 15 minutes
Cooking time: 10 minutes
Per serving: calcium 128 mg, calories 182, carbohydrates 2 g, cholesterol 0 mg, fat 3 g, fiber 0 g, protein 30 g, sodium 154 mg

STEP BY STEP

CUTTING FISH FILLETS AND STEAKS

The most important factor in choosing fish is freshness. A fishy smell indicates a lack of freshness or improper handling. A fresh fish has a mild odor; firm, elastic flesh that springs back when pressed; clear, protruding eyes; reddish or pink gills; and shiny, tightly attached scales.

When buying steaks or fillets look for flesh with a natural sheen that is free from yellowing or browning around the edges. Do not buy any fish that has been defrosted for more than two days. It is better to purchase frozen fish and defrost it at home. For the best quality, try to find fish that were individually quick-frozen on the fishing vessel.

Fish may be categorized as either lean or oily. Lean fish have a mild flavor and firm white flesh with 5 percent or less fat. Take care in cooking lean fish; they dry out easily. Examples of lean fish include sole, flounder, cod, pollack, sea bass, rockfish, snapper, and turbot.

Oily fish contain 5 to 50 percent fat. They usually have flesh that is richer and stronger, and have less white flesh than do lean fish. The fat is distributed throughout the flesh, which helps keep the fish moist during cooking. Examples of oily fish are swordfish, smelt, salmon, bluefish, tuna, mullet, mackerel, trout, catfish, sturgeon, and pompano.

Steaks are cross-sections cut from a whole fish. Fillets are long pieces of boneless fish. Roundfish and flatfish require slightly different filleting techniques.

To Fillet a Roundfish

1. Make a slit along backbone from head to tail.

2. Next, make a cut behind gill. Holding head, insert knife between fillet and ribs. Sliding knife along ribs, cut down the length of the fillet. Pull fillet free and sever skin at the anal fin. Repeat the filleting process on the other side of the fish.

To Skin a Fillet

To skin a fillet, place it skin side down and cut a small section of flesh away from the skin close to the tail. Hold knife at a 15-degree angle to the cutting board. Holding skin taut, scrape the knife along the skin without cutting it.

To Fillet a Flatfish

1. Place the skinned flatfish on a board with the eyes up. Cut through the flesh to the backbone (which is in the middle of the fish) from head to tail. Insert the knife blade at a shallow angle between the ribs and the end of the fillet close to the head. Cut down the length of a fillet on one side of the backbone and remove it.

2. Cut the remaining top fillet using the same technique. Turn the fish over. Remove the two bottom fillets.

To Cut a Steak

Using a large, sharp knife, cut off the head just behind gills. Slice the fish into steaks of the desired thickness, usually between 1 and 1½ inches.

MENU

ISLAND BUFFET

Caribbean Jellied Orange Soup

Mahi-Mahi With Lemon and Pineapple Salsa

Steamed and Sautéed Yams, Carrots, and Long Beans

Salad of Artichoke Hearts, Bibb Lettuce, and Radicchio

Fresh Tropical Fruit Platter

Nonalcoholic Piña Colada

This light menu suggests the paradise of tropical islands. Prepare the fish ahead, and chill until cooking time. Slice fresh yams and carrots and snip long beans. Sauté lightly in a teaspoon of olive oil, and finish by steaming right before serving. Toss a salad of torn Bibb lettuce, radicchio leaves, and quartered artichoke hearts with a vinaigrette dressing. A nonalcoholic Piña Colada (blend pineapple juice and chunks, ice cubes, banana, and coconut flavoring until smooth) is the ideal beverage. A platter of fresh tropical fruits completes the meal. Menu serves four.

CARIBBEAN JELLIED ORANGE SOUP

A refreshing first course, this soup originates in the Caribbean, where food is designed to cool you. Its fresh orange flavor is a delicious complement to seafood or chicken. The consistency of the soup is similar to that of a consommé, but it is bright orange in color. The soup should be served chilled. When entertaining, you can also pass around a bowl of lime slices for those guests who want extra tang.

> 1 quart defatted Chicken Stock (see page 51)
> 1 package unflavored gelatin
> 3 cups freshly squeezed orange juice
> 2 egg whites, beaten until frothy
> 1 orange (unpeeled), cut into paper-thin slices
> 12 fresh mint leaves, for garnish (optional)

1. In a large saucepan combine stock with gelatin and cook 20 minutes over medium heat.

2. Add orange juice to stock and let cool for 15 minutes.

3. Whisk in egg whites. Pour into 4 bowls and refrigerate until set (about 45 minutes).

4. Serve chilled, garnished with orange slices and fresh mint leaves, if desired.

Serves 4.

> *Preparation time:* 15 minutes
> *Cooking time:* 20 minutes
> *Chilling time:* 45 minutes
> *Per serving:* calcium 60 mg, calories 154, carbohydrates 26 g, cholesterol 0 mg, fat 2 g, fiber 1 g, protein 9 g, sodium 404 mg

MAHI-MAHI WITH LEMON AND PINEAPPLE SALSA

A delectable, light-colored fish, mahi-mahi is often served in the Hawaiian Islands, but you can use any firm-fleshed fish, such as salmon or shark, if mahi-mahi is unavailable. The fresh pineapple and lemon salsa is a perfect accompaniment and can be made ahead of time.

For an alternative version of the same recipe, brush on the salsa before grilling. Or you can marinate the fish in the salsa overnight for a stronger citrus flavor.

> 3/4 cup fresh pineapple, crushed
> 1/2 cup minced onion
> 1/4 cup minced green bell pepper
> 3 cloves garlic, minced
> 1/2 cup chopped fresh tomato
> 1 fresh jalapeño chile, seeded and finely chopped
> 1 teaspoon herbal salt substitute
> Juice of 1 lemon
> 4 mahi-mahi steaks
> 2 teaspoons olive oil

1. In a small bowl mix together pineapple, onion, bell pepper, garlic, tomato, jalapeño, salt substitute, and lemon juice. Set salsa aside.

2. Preheat broiler. Lightly brush fish steaks with olive oil. Broil on each side until lightly browned and firm to the touch (about 5 minutes per side). During the last minute of broiling, top with the salsa and finish cooking.

Serves 4.

Note Mahi-mahi should be about 4 to 6 inches from the heat source. If the fish is cooking too fast, lower the broiler rack.

> *Preparation time:* 25 minutes
> *Broiling time:* 10 minutes
> *Per serving:* calcium 62 mg, calories 242, carbohydrates 13 g, cholesterol 149 mg, fat 4 g, fiber 2 g, protein 39 g, sodium 258 mg

Tropical flavors combine in a refreshing orange soup, broiled mahi-mahi topped with lemon-pineapple salsa, and, for a cool finish, sliced tropical fruits.

EASY FISH AND SHELLFISH ENTRÉES

Imagine coming home from a busy day and eating an elegant seafood dinner 20 minutes later. Many of the following recipes can be made in two stages: sauces and marinades the night before, and baking, poaching, or grilling right before you serve. These recipes can successfully be prepared with either fresh or fresh-frozen seafood.

SALMON WITH MUSTARD SAUCE

A favorite French bistro recipe, Salmon With Mustard Sauce can be served cool or hot and makes a light and elegant luncheon dish. The salmon is poached lightly in wine to retain its tender texture. The flavor of the wine combines well with the piquant mustard and dill of the sauce. The sauce can be prepared ahead of time and kept for one week in the refrigerator—it's great on sandwiches, too.

- 4 large salmon steaks
- 1 cup dry white wine
- 1/4 cup minced shallots
- 3 tablespoons minced fresh dill
- 1/4 cup nonfat plain yogurt
- 1/4 cup Dijon mustard
- 1 tablespoon light honey
- 1/4 cup lemon juice

1. Preheat oven to 400° F. Place salmon steaks in a large, deep baking pan and cover with wine. Sprinkle with shallots. Bake for 12 to 15 minutes, basting often with wine.

2. While salmon is baking, in a small bowl mix together dill, yogurt, mustard, honey, and lemon juice until smooth. Serve over salmon.

Serves 4.

Preparation time: 20 minutes
Baking time: 12 to 15 minutes
Per serving: calcium 115 mg, calories 289, carbohydrates 11 g, cholesterol 89 mg, fat 7 g, fiber .5 g, protein 36 g, sodium 322 mg

GRILLED SWEET-AND-SOUR TUNA STEAKS

A Hawaiian specialty, Grilled Sweet-and-Sour Tuna Steaks is perfect for outdoor grilling or indoor broiling. Make the sauce ahead of time and let the tuna steaks marinate for 30 to 60 minutes before grilling so that they really absorb the tangy flavor. If you use mesquite charcoal on the grill, the tuna takes on a teriyaki taste from the smoke as it cooks. Grill the tuna only until it turns a dull pink color inside and browns nicely on the outside.

- 1/2 cup dry sherry
- 2 tablespoons grated ginger
- 2 tablespoons low-sodium soy sauce or tamari
- 1 teaspoon light honey
- 1 teaspoon maple syrup
- 1 tablespoon minced garlic
- 2 teaspoons Asian sesame oil
- 2 tablespoons minced cilantro
- 4 medium tuna steaks

1. Preheat broiler or start grill. In a small bowl combine sherry, ginger, soy sauce, honey, maple syrup, garlic, sesame oil, and cilantro. Set aside.

2. Wash and pat dry tuna steaks. Place in a shallow baking dish. Pour sauce over steaks. Let marinate 10 minutes.

3. Remove steaks from marinade and broil or grill. Cook 5 to 8 minutes on each side, turning once, and basting with marinade. Serve hot.

Serves 4.

Preparation time: 10 minutes
Marinating time: 10 minutes
Grilling time: 15 minutes
Per serving: calcium 11 mg, calories 328, carbohydrates 7 g, cholesterol 65 mg, fat 11 g, fiber .5 g, protein 41 g, sodium 314 mg

BROILED FLOUNDER WITH RED BELL-PEPPER BUTTER

Flame-roasted red bell peppers are puréed and mixed with shallots and unsalted butter to spread over this tasty entrée. You can use a variety of fish—from salmon or swordfish steaks to thin fillets such as sole or flounder. The cooking time will vary according to the thickness of the fish. Steam fresh asparagus or broccoli to accompany this easy entrée.

- 4 large fillets of flounder or sole or 4 swordfish or salmon steaks
- 1/2 teaspoon oil, for coating baking sheet
- 1 red bell pepper
- 2 tablespoons unsalted butter, softened
- 2 teaspoons minced shallots
- 1 teaspoon lemon juice
- 1/4 teaspoon hot-pepper sauce

1. Wash fillets and pat dry. Lightly oil a large baking sheet. Preheat broiler.

2. Cut pepper in half, seed, and place, cut side down, on baking sheet. Broil until skin blackens (1 to 2 minutes). Place pepper halves in a paper bag for 1 minute to steam, then rinse and peel off blackened skin. Place in food processor or blender with butter, shallots, lemon juice, and hot-pepper sauce. Purée until thick spread is formed. Remove from blender, spoon into a small bowl, and refrigerate.

3. Broil fish on the same baking sheet. Cook 3 minutes per side for fillets, 5 to 8 minutes per side for steaks. Turn once. Test for doneness by flaking with a fork.

4. To serve, place a generous spoonful of red pepper butter on top of each piece of broiled fish.

Serves 4.

Preparation time: 25 minutes
Broiling time: 8 to 15 minutes
Per serving: calcium 65 mg, calories 134, carbohydrates 2 g, cholesterol 16 mg, fat 7 g, fiber .4 g, protein 15 g, sodium 57 mg

SOLE AUX AMANDES

Found on the menu of many fine French restaurants, sole with almonds is a traditional favorite. The sauce for Sole aux Amandes can be prepared early in the day, but cook the fish right before serving for best flavor and texture.

> 4 large fillets of sole
> ¼ cup nonfat milk
> ½ cup whole wheat flour
> 1 teaspoon unsalted butter
> 1 teaspoon olive oil
> ¾ cup chopped mushrooms
> ¼ cup slivered almonds
> 1 teaspoon chopped chives
> 1 teaspoon minced parsley
>   Juice of 1 medium lemon

1. Preheat oven to 200° F. Dredge sole in milk and then in flour. In a large skillet over medium-high heat, melt butter with oil and lightly sauté flour-coated fish until browned. Transfer to a platter and keep warm in oven.

2. In the same pan, using drippings from sautéing fish, sauté mushrooms until soft. Add a small amount of water, if needed, to prevent sticking. Add almonds, chives, parsley, and lemon juice. Heat through, then pour over sole and serve immediately.

Serves 4.

Preparation time: 15 to 20 minutes
Cooking time: 15 to 20 minutes
Per serving: calcium 114 mg, calories 203, carbohydrates 15 g, cholesterol 3 mg, fat 8 g, fiber 3 g, protein 20 g, sodium 68 mg

The meaty texture of flounder is enhanced by quick-flame broiling and a topping of roasted red-pepper butter.

Baking in parchment seals in the delicate flavors of the spinach-stuffed trout, keeping it tender, delicious, and moist (see page 129).

SALMON AND JULIENNED VEGETABLE SAUTÉ

This easy recipe is ideal for a busy cook; you can even cut the vegetables ahead of time. Use a wok or large skillet to sauté the vegetables only until they are slightly tender and bright in color. The salmon steaks are then blanketed with the sautéed vegetables and baked. Be ready to serve this entrée right away, perhaps accompanied by a dry white wine and steamed rice.

> 2 teaspoons olive oil, plus oil for coating dish
> 1 cup dry vermouth
> 1½ cups sliced onions
> 2 cups julienned carrots
> 1 tablespoon minced garlic
> ½ cup julienned celery
> 1 cup chopped lettuce or endive
> 1 teaspoon ground fennel seed
> 4 salmon steaks

1. Preheat oven to 450° F. Lightly oil a 9- by 12-inch baking dish. In a large skillet or wok over medium-high heat, heat together oil and dry vermouth. Cook onions, carrots, garlic, celery, and lettuce until soft (10 minutes). Place the vegetables in bottom of baking dish and sprinkle with fennel seed.

2. Wash and pat dry salmon steaks. Place on top of vegetables. Pour any remaining cooking liquid over fish. Cover with aluminum foil and bake for 10 minutes. Lower oven to 350° F and bake for 30 minutes. Serve hot.

Serves 4.

Preparation time: 25 minutes
Cooking time: 50 minutes
Per serving: calcium 96 mg, calories 335, carbohydrates 14 g, cholesterol 88 mg, fat 9 g, fiber 3 g, protein 36 g, sodium 384 mg

BAKED SALMON PROVENÇALE

In this hearty dish from Provence, salmon steaks are sautéed in a savory sauce of tomatoes, herbs, and olives that combines the best flavors of the Côte d'Azur. The dish pairs well with a simple green salad of endive and lettuce dressed with Rue Dauphine Dressing (see page 83).

    4 salmon steaks
    1 teaspoon unsalted butter
    1 teaspoon olive oil
    1 gram (2 teaspoons) saffron
       threads
    1 tablespoon minced garlic
    ½ teaspoon tarragon
    ¼ teaspoon thyme
       Pinch of sage
    2 bay leaves, crushed
    1 cup coarsely chopped plum
       tomatoes
    8 to 10 Greek olives, pitted and
       chopped
  1¼ cups white wine
    1 cup Fish Stock (see page 51)
    1 teaspoon herbal salt substitute

1. Preheat oven to 400° F. Wash and pat dry salmon steaks.

2. In a large, deep, ovenproof skillet or stovetop casserole over medium-high heat, sauté salmon briefly on each side in butter and oil (about 1 minute). Remove to a platter. Add saffron, garlic, tarragon, thyme, sage, bay leaves, tomatoes, olives, wine, fish stock, and salt substitute. Bring to a boil. Lower heat and simmer for 10 minutes, uncovered.

3. Add salmon steaks. Remove pan from heat and place in oven. Bake until salmon is lightly pink and done to taste (10 minutes).

4. To serve, place salmon steaks on platter and spoon sauce over them.

Serves 4.

Preparation time: 20 minutes
Cooking time: 20 minutes
Per serving: calcium 68 mg, calories 324, carbohydrates 6 g, cholesterol 95 mg, fat 12 g, fiber 1 g, protein 35 g, sodium 333 mg

---

FRESH TROUT FLORENTINE

Dishes prepared Florentine-style feature spinach—a source of vitamin A and calcium. Here, fresh trout is split and stuffed with a savory pine nut and spinach mixture. The trout is wrapped in parchment and baked (see page 130).

    1 teaspoon olive oil, plus oil for
       coating pan
    ¼ cup minced green onions
       (including greens)
    ¼ cup dry sherry
    2 cups chopped spinach leaves
    ¼ cup pine nuts
  1¼ cups whole wheat bread
       crumbs
    4 tablespoons nonfat milk
    ¼ teaspoon lemon juice
    4 large fresh trout, cleaned
    1 cup white wine
    ¼ teaspoon pepper
    2 teaspoons unsalted butter

1. Preheat oven to 350° F. Lightly coat a 9- by 12-inch baking pan with oil.

2. In a medium skillet over medium-high heat, sauté green onion in olive oil and sherry until soft. Add chopped spinach and pine nuts, and cook until spinach has wilted (2 minutes). Remove from heat. Add bread crumbs, milk, and lemon juice and mix well.

3. Wash and pat trout dry, inside and out. Stuff cavity of each trout with one fourth of the spinach mixture. Cut 4 sheets of parchment and place 1 trout on each. Set aside.

4. In the same skillet combine wine, pepper, and butter. Bring to a boil over high heat, and cook until alcohol has evaporated (2 minutes). Pour equal amounts of wine mixture over trout and seal parchment packets. Place packets on prepared baking sheets and bake for 12 minutes. Serve hot.

Serves 4.

Preparation time: 20 minutes
Cooking time: 20 minutes
Per serving: calcium 123 mg, calories 423, carbohydrates 30 g, cholesterol 55 mg, fat 18 g, fiber 3 g, protein 26 g, sodium 666 mg

---

TIPS

...ON SPECIAL SEASONINGS FOR FISH

These easy seasoning mixtures work best with strong-flavored fish, such as tuna, swordfish, shark, and salmon:

Cajun Combine 2 teaspoons freshly ground black pepper, 1 teaspoon cayenne pepper, ½ teaspoon apple cider vinegar, ½ teaspoon honey, ¼ teaspoon cumin, ¼ teaspoon ground coriander. Brush over grilling, broiling, or baking fish.

Provençale Combine 2 tablespoons white wine, 1 teaspoon chopped fresh tarragon, 1 teaspoon chopped parsley, ½ teaspoon chopped chives, ½ teaspoon dried thyme. Brush over grilling, broiling, or baking fish.

Lemon and herb Combine 2 tablespoons lemon juice, 1 tablespoon lime juice, ½ teaspoon light honey, 1 tablespoon minced parsley, ½ teaspoon minced garlic or shallot. Brush over grilling, broiling, or baking fish, or add to a poaching liquid such as white wine.

Pepper Combine 1 tablespoon white wine, 2 teaspoons minced lemon peel, 2 teaspoons freshly ground black pepper, 1 teaspoon white pepper, 1 teaspoon herbal salt substitute. Brush over grilling, broiling, or baking fish.

Sweet honey and ginger Combine 2 tablespoons light honey, 1 teaspoon grated ginger, 1 clove minced garlic, 1 teaspoon lemon juice. Brush over grilling, broiling, or baking fish.

STEP BY STEP

HEALTHY IDEAS WITH PARCHMENT COOKING

Some people shy away from cooking fish after one or two experiences of over-cooking it. Cooking in parchment is an excellent way to retain the moisture, flavor, and nutrients of fish as it cooks and to prevent it from drying out. Follow these easy steps to make parchment packets for cooking all types of fish from sole to salmon.

1. *Cut a piece of parchment about four times the size of the fillet or steak you are cooking. Fold parchment in half. Starting on the folded side, cut out a half-heart shape.*

2. *Open the heart and place the fish, with all seasonings and flavorings added, in the center. Starting at the fold, fold in the edge of the parchment to form an envelope around the fish, overlapping the fold as you go along.*

3. *Fold the tip of the heart several times to secure.*

4. *To serve, cut away browned parchment and lift out fish. Spoon cooking liquid over fish. Garnish and serve right away for best flavor.*

MONKFISH IN PARCHMENT WITH WINE, LEMON, AND HERBS

Monkfish, a very rich-tasting white fish that has the texture of shellfish, is some-times called "poor man's lobster." Ask the fish market to cut it into thin fillets for this recipe. It will cook quickly in the parchment wrapper and stay moist and flavorful from the wine, fresh lemon juice, and herbs (see sidebar, left). If you buy extra monkfish, try grilling it with the sweet-and-sour marinade from Grilled Sweet-and-Sour Tuna Steaks (see page 126).

> *Oil, for coating pan*
> 1 *large monkfish fillet (about 1¾ lb)*
> ⅓ *cup low-sodium soy sauce or tamari*
> ⅓ *cup minced green onions (including greens)*
> *Juice from 2 lemons*
> 2 *teaspoons minced chives*
> 2 *teaspoons minced parsley*
> ¼ *cup dry white wine*

1. Preheat oven to 400° F. Lightly oil a 9- by 12-inch baking dish.

2. Lay out 4 large sheets of parchment. Cut monkfish into 4 equal parts and lay each on a sheet of parchment. Sprinkle with soy sauce, green onions, lemon juice, chives, parsley, and wine. Bring edges of parchment together and roll to seal on all sides. Place packets seam side down on baking sheet.

3. Bake for 20 minutes. To serve, unroll parchment packets and place fish on platter. Spoon cooking liquid and herbs over top.

Serves 4.

> *Preparation time:* 15 minutes
> *Baking time:* 20 minutes
> *Per serving:* calcium 48 mg, calories 98, carbohydrates 5 g, cholesterol 10 mg, fat 1 g, fiber 1 g, protein 5 g, sodium 1,300 mg

SEAFOOD SALAD

Here's an easy recipe that can be prepared two hours before serving, wrapped tightly in plastic wrap, and chilled. Serve on lettuce leaves, and garnish with raw vegetables, such as red bell pepper strips, endive spears, and cherry tomatoes. Use whatever fish is fresh and in season, but make sure that it is firm and can be poached without losing its shape.

    1 pound fish fillets (such as tuna
       or salmon)
    1/4 pound prawns, shelled and
       deveined
    1 cup white wine
    3/4 cup diced celery
    1 teaspoon minced fresh
       tarragon
    2 green onions (including
       greens), chopped
    1/3 cup reduced-fat mayonnaise
    1 teaspoon herbal salt substitute
    2 teaspoons low-sodium soy
       sauce or tamari
    1 teaspoon Dijon mustard
    1 tablespoon nonfat plain yogurt
       Lettuce leaves, for lining
       serving bowl

1. Place fish and prawns in a small saucepan and pour in wine. Heat to boiling and poach until prawns turn bright pink (about 8 minutes). Drain and let cool. Cut fish and prawns into bite-sized pieces.

2. In a small bowl mix remaining ingredients except lettuce and toss with cooked fish and prawns.

3. Line a serving bowl or platter with lettuce leaves and spoon seafood into the center. Serve at room temperature, or chill if desired.

Serves 6.

Preparation time: 20 minutes
Cooking time: 15 minutes
Per serving: calcium 91 mg, calories 144, carbohydrates 7 g, cholesterol 67 mg, fat 2 g, fiber 2 g, protein 19 g, sodium 225 mg

AVOCADO SHELLS STUFFED WITH SHRIMP

In this recipe avocado is mixed with seasonings and cooked shrimp and spooned into avocado shells. The bright green of the avocado and the pink of the shrimp make a colorful combination. Prepare this recipe just before serving for best color and flavor.

    2 small avocados
    1/2 pound cooked shrimp meat
    2 chiles en escabeche (pickled
       chiles)
    3 tablespoons reduced-fat
       mayonnaise
    1/3 cup diced celery
    2 teaspoons minced onion
    2 teaspoons herbal salt substitute
       Juice of 1/2 lime
       Radicchio leaves, for lining
       platter
    4 cooked shrimp, for garnish

1. Cut avocados in half, remove pits, and scoop out pulp. Reserve shells. Mash 1/2 cup of pulp and reserve remainder for another use.

2. In a large bowl combine pulp with remaining ingredients.

3. Stuff avocado mixture into avocado shells and arrange on radicchio-lined platter. Garnish with whole shrimp. Chill slightly before serving.

Serves 4.

Preparation time: 20 minutes
Per serving: calcium 85 mg, calories 273, carbohydrates 20 g, cholesterol 91 mg, fat 17 g, fiber 7 g, protein 16 g, sodium 171 mg

SAUTÉED SALMON FILLETS WITH RED PEPPER

Bright pink salmon fillets are braised in a marinade of light rice wine and sesame oil, and are then garnished with sautéed strips of sweet red and green bell peppers.

    1 medium salmon fillet
    1/4 cup Asian sesame oil
    1/3 cup rice wine
    2 teaspoons minced garlic
    1/4 cup dry sherry
    1 large red bell pepper, julienned
    1 large green bell pepper,
       julienned

1. Place salmon fillets in a shallow pan. In a separate bowl mix sesame oil, rice wine, and garlic; spread mixture over fillets. Let marinate for 30 minutes.

2. In a large skillet heat sherry and add bell peppers. Stir well and cook over medium heat for 5 minutes. Set aside.

3. Preheat broiler. Broil salmon until flesh begins to flake when pressed with a fork (5 to 8 minutes). Add sautéed bell peppers during last 2 minutes of cooking. Serve hot.

Serves 4.

Preparation time: 10 minutes
Marinating time: 30 minutes
Cooking time: 10 to 13 minutes
Per serving: calcium 14 mg, calories 226, carbohydrates 4 g, cholesterol 22 mg, fat 15 g, fiber 1 g, protein 9 g, sodium 31 mg

An easy appetizer for entertaining or a fine summer luncheon, these avocado shells are filled with a mixture of chile, celery, shrimp, lime juice, and reduced-fat mayonnaise. Burgundy-colored radicchio makes a handsome background (see page 131).

SALMON MOUSSE

Serve this delicate mousse as a spread on open-face sandwiches—just add chopped green onions, parsley, and endive. Or try it as an appetizer on melba toasts or celery boats.

    1 package unflavored gelatin
    3 tablespoons cold water
    8 ounces salmon fillet or
        drained canned salmon
    ½ cup white wine (optional)
    ½ cup nonfat plain yogurt
    ½ cup low-fat ricotta cheese
    2 tablespoons chives, preferably
        fresh
    2 teaspoons lemon juice
    2 teaspoons herbal salt
        substitute, or to taste
        Freshly ground black pepper,
        to taste
        Oil, for coating mold

1. In a saucepan dissolve gelatin in the cold water. Place in a saucepan and cook over low heat, stirring, until gelatin is completely dissolved. Let cool while fresh salmon is poached.

2. If using fresh salmon, place in a skillet or saucepan with white wine and bring to a boil. Cook until salmon flakes and turns dull pink. (If salmon is canned, omit this step.)

3. Drain salmon. Place salmon, gelatin, yogurt, cheese, chives, lemon juice, salt substitute, and pepper in a blender or food processor and purée until smooth.

4. Lightly oil a decorative mold and spoon in salmon mousse. Chill until set (about 25 minutes).

5. Unmold by dipping the outside of the mold in very hot tap water and turning carefully onto a plate.

Serves 8.

Preparation time: 15 minutes
Chilling time: 25 minutes
Per serving: calcium 82 mg, calories 73, carbohydrates 3 g, cholesterol 20 mg, fat 3 g, fiber 0 g, protein 9 g, sodium 52 mg

BAKED FISH IN LETTUCE PACKETS

Baking fish in lettuce packets is a useful cooking technique that holds the flavor and juiciness of the fillets as they cook. Tender fillets of fish are spread with a savory herb filling, then wrapped with blanched lettuce leaves and baked. The surprise is a sweet-pungent vinegar, shallot, and garlic mixture that flavors the fish as it bakes. If you are in a hurry, preassemble the fish packets, cover with plastic wrap, and store in the refrigerator until baking.

> 2 tablespoons tarragon vinegar
> 1 cup minced shallots
> 2 tablespoons minced garlic
> 1 teaspoon olive oil, plus oil for baking sheet
> 6 leaves Boston lettuce
> 6 small fillets of snapper or flounder
> 2 teaspoons dried thyme
> 1 teaspoon dried tarragon
> 1 tablespoon green olive oil

1. In a small saucepan over medium heat, place vinegar, shallots, and garlic and cook until soft (almost 5 minutes).

2. Preheat oven to 350° F. Lightly oil a large baking sheet. Place lettuce leaves on baking sheet; do not overlap.

3. Wash and pat dry fish fillets. Sprinkle with thyme, tarragon, and half the olive oil. Spread with shallot mixture.

4. Starting with small end of each fillet, roll it around shallot spread and place the roll on top of a lettuce leaf. Fold lettuce around fish and place packet seam side down on baking sheet. Brush packets with remaining oil.

5. Cover baking sheet with aluminum foil and bake for 20 to 30 minutes. Remove foil and serve hot.

Serves 6.

> *Preparation time:* 25 minutes
> *Cooking time:* 25 to 35 minutes
> *Per serving:* calcium 101 mg, calories 273, carbohydrates 6 g, cholesterol 81 mg, fat 6 g, fiber .3 g, protein 46 g, sodium 144 mg

HALIBUT WITH APPLES AND HORSERADISH

This unusual Russian dish combines the tartness of horseradish with the sweetness of cooked, puréed apples. The fish is tenderized and sweetened by a vinegar-onion broth. You can prepare the ingredients beforehand, but cook the fish right before serving for best results.

> 2 pounds halibut or cod
> 1 cup white wine vinegar or apple cider vinegar
> 1/2 cup sliced leek
> 1 1/2 cups sliced onion
> 1/2 teaspoon dried thyme
> 1/4 cup minced parsley
> 1/2 teaspoon freshly ground black pepper

Russian Applesauce

> 1 cup sliced tart apples
> 1 tablespoon honey
> 1/4 cup apple juice
> 1 teaspoon lemon juice
> 1/4 cup freshly grated horseradish root or prepared horseradish, drained

1. Cut fish into 4 fillets. Remove and discard any bones. Place fish in a large saucepan.

2. Cover fish with vinegar, leek, onion, thyme, parsley, and pepper. Bring to a boil and cook over medium heat, uncovered, until fish is fork tender (about 8 minutes). Prepare sauce while fish is cooking.

3. Serve fish and vegetables topped with apple mixture.

Serves 4.

Russian Applesauce In a saucepan mix apples, honey, apple juice, and lemon juice. Bring to a boil and cook over high heat, covered, for 5 minutes. Mash apples with a fork. Stir in horseradish and mix well.

> *Preparation time:* 25 minutes
> *Cooking time:* 25 minutes
> *Per serving:* calcium 219 mg, calories 336, carbohydrates 22 g, cholesterol 73 mg, fat 6 g, fiber 3 g, protein 49 g, sodium 384 mg

SHELLFISH ENTRÉES

An excellent source of lean protein, shellfish are easy to integrate into a menu plan. They are often easier to cook than fish fillets or steaks because of their greater tolerance of overcooking (with some exceptions—prawns and scallops become unpleasantly rubbery when cooked too long). One way to ensure plenty of shellfish in your diet is to assemble recipes, such as Prawns and Scallops on the Half Shell (see page 135) or Stir-Fried Prawns in Black Bean Sauce (see page136), and freeze in 4-ounce portions accompanied by partially steamed broccoli or asparagus. An elegant, healthy dinner is yours for the defrosting.

DRUNKEN PRAWNS

In this recipe, adapted from a popular happy-hour dish served in New York pubs, medium or jumbo prawns are poached in beer until plump and pink. Serve them steaming hot and let guests peel and eat their own. Serve the hot poaching liquid as a dipping sauce for the prawns.

> 1 pound medium to large prawns
> 2 cups dark beer
> 2 teaspoons coarsely chopped garlic
> 1 tablespoon hot-pepper sauce
> 1 tablespoon minced parsley

1. Peel and devein prawns (or omit this step and let guests peel their own when prawns are served). Place in a large pot along with beer, garlic, hot-pepper sauce, and parsley.

2. Bring to a boil and cook for 5 minutes or until prawns turn pink. Do not overcook. Serve hot.

Serves 4.

> *Preparation time:* 10 minutes
> *Cooking time:* 5 to 10 minutes
> *Per serving:* calcium 81 mg, calories 174, carbohydrates 7 g, cholesterol 173 mg, fat 2 g, fiber .4 g, protein 24 g, sodium 179 mg

133

NOTE

HEALTH BENEFITS OF EATING FISH

As a low-fat, high-protein source, fish is an excellent substitution for meat entrées. Believe it or not, 3 ounces of flounder contain the same amount of protein as an equal portion of roast beef.

Fish is also lower in fat than meat. Equal servings of broiled cod and broiled sirloin, for example, have about the same amount of protein, but cod has only about one third the fat. Other fish particularly low in fat include flounder, haddock, monkfish, sea bass, and sole.

Sophisticated testing methods now show that mussels, oysters, and scallops have less cholesterol than was previously believed. Seafood is also relatively low in calories (as long as it is not served with cream sauce or butter).

Research has indicated that certain fish oils—called omega-3 fatty acids—may help to not only stave off heart disease, but also lower levels of cholesterol in the blood, reduce the tendency of the blood to form clots, and improve joint pain in patients suffering from rheumatoid arthritis.

If you are interested in increasing your intake of omega-3 fatty acids, good fish choices include tuna, salmon, trout, sardines, mackerel, swordfish, and herring. Squid and low-cholesterol shellfish—such as mussels, oysters, and scallops—also contain high amounts of omega-3 oils.

While the healthiest way to eat fish is by purchasing it fresh from a reliable source, canned tuna and salmon—packed in water, not oil—are great alternatives. Many supermarkets now offer canned fish packed without salt, which is a great way to reduce your sodium intake while still enjoying the many nutritional benefits of fish.

INDONESIAN TEMPURA

Tempura is a rich dish that is best reserved for special occasions. Use peanut oil, which does not leave a heavy taste on food and is recommended by Asian cooks for deep frying. There are two secrets to successful tempura—very hot oil and very cold batter—so set the container of batter in a bowl of ice during the dipping and cooking process.

> Peanut oil, for deep-frying
> 2½ cups rice flour or whole wheat pastry flour
> 3 eggs
> 1½ cups ice water
> ½ cup coconut milk
> ¼ teaspoon ground coriander
> 1 large red bell pepper
> 1 pound large prawns
> ½ pound large scallops
> 1 cup diagonally sliced sweet potato
> 1 cup large broccoli florets

1. In a wok or large, deep skillet over medium-high heat, warm peanut oil to the 350° F mark on a fat thermometer. There should be about 4 inches of oil in the wok or 2 to 3 inches in the skillet.

2. In a blender at high speed, mix together flour, eggs, the ice water, coconut milk, and coriander until very smooth. Pour this batter into a bowl set inside a larger bowl filled with crushed ice.

3. Seed bell pepper and cut into eighths. Peel and devein prawns. To cook tempura, dip seafood and vegetables into batter, turning to coat lightly. Place immediately into hot oil. Tempura should brown in 30 seconds; if it takes longer, oil is not hot enough. Drain cooked tempura on paper towels. Serve immediately.

Serves 8.

Preparation time: 20 minutes
Cooking time: 10 minutes
Per serving (not including peanut oil): calcium 66 mg, calories 354, carbohydrates 47 g, cholesterol 175 mg, fat 8 g, fiber 3 g, protein 23 g, sodium 162 mg

PRAWNS WITH PEANUT SAUCE

A spicy Indonesian recipe, Prawns With Peanut Sauce blends the aromatic flavors of peanuts, coriander, cumin, and cayenne pepper in a rich-tasting sauce. This dish can be prepared ahead if you follow one rule of thumb: Undercook prawns slightly, then freeze in their poaching liquid. When the prawns are reheated, they will not have the rubbery texture of overcooked fish. Since this entrée is rich in taste and appearance, plain steamed rice and a light spinach or endive salad make suitable accompaniments.

> 1 pound medium prawns
> 1 cup white wine
> 1½ tablespoons smooth peanut butter
> 1 tablespoon olive oil
> 1½ tablespoons light honey
> 2 tablespoons low-sodium soy sauce or tamari
> 2 teaspoons rice vinegar
> ½ teaspoon Asian sesame oil
> ½ teaspoon cayenne pepper
> 1 tablespoon minced green onion
> 1½ teaspoons ground coriander
> ½ teaspoon ground cumin
> 4 cups steamed rice (optional)

1. Wash prawns, peel, and devein. Place in a large saucepan with wine. Cook over medium-high heat until they turn bright pink. Set aside.

2. In a small bowl mix together peanut butter and olive oil until smooth. Add honey, soy sauce, vinegar, sesame oil, cayenne, green onion, coriander, and cumin. Mix well, then add prawns. Place prawns and sauce in saucepan and reheat. Serve over steamed rice, if desired.

Serves 4.

Preparation time: 25 minutes
Cooking time: 5 to 10 minutes
Per serving: calcium 72 mg, calories 261, carbohydrates 10 g, cholesterol 173 mg, fat 9 g, fiber .6 g, protein 25 g, sodium 443 mg

PRAWNS AND SCALLOPS ON THE HALF SHELL

Equally appropriate as a first course or light luncheon, this dish has great nutritional benefits: Plenty of calcium and good-quality protein are contained in both the shellfish and the sauce.

6 scallop shells
¾ pound medium prawns
¾ pound bay scallops
⅓ cup white wine or dry sherry
1 teaspoon unsalted butter
½ cup thinly sliced small mushrooms
2 tablespoons whole wheat flour
½ cup nonfat or low-fat milk
⅓ cup grated Parmesan cheese
⅓ cup whole wheat bread crumbs, finely ground

1. Wash scallop shells and place on a cookie sheet. Preheat broiler.

2. Peel and devein prawns, then coarsely chop. Quarter bay scallops. In a medium saucepan over medium-high heat, combine shellfish and wine and heat until bubbling. Cook until scallops are opaque (about 1 minute), stirring constantly. Drain and reserve cooking wine. Set scallops and prawns aside.

3. In the same pan, heat butter over medium heat and sauté mushrooms until they begin to exude moisture. If mixture gets too dry and begins to stick, add a small amount of reserved cooking wine. Stir in flour and cook for 2 minutes.

4. Add milk in a thin stream, stirring constantly with a whisk. Sauce should thicken immediately. If it doesn't, continue to cook over medium heat, stirring, until it is the consistency of heavy cream. Add Parmesan, scallops, and prawns, and remove from heat.

5. Spoon an equal amount of seafood mixture into each scallop shell. Top with bread crumbs and broil until lightly browned and bubbling (3 to 5 minutes). Serve hot (see Note).

Serves 6.

Note For easier service, fold a linen napkin under scallop shells to keep them from tipping on the plate.

Preparation time: 25 minutes
Cooking time: 15 minutes
Per serving: calcium 137 mg, calories 187, carbohydrates 10 g, cholesterol 111 mg, fat 4 g, fiber .7 g, protein 25 g, sodium 312 mg

For Prawns and Scallops on the Half Shell, wine-poached scallops and prawns are mixed with a light, low-fat cheese sauce, dusted with bread crumbs, and broiled in scallop shells until brown and bubbly.

½ cup chopped Chinese cabbage
1 cup trimmed snow peas
1 teaspoon light miso
¾ cup defatted Chicken or Fish Stock (see page 51)
1 teaspoon honey
1 teaspoon low-sodium soy sauce or tamari
1 tablespoon arrowroot powder or cornstarch
2 tablespoons cold water
Cilantro, chopped, for garnish

1. In a small bowl mash together black beans, half the garlic, and ginger until mixture forms a paste. This can also be done in an electric minichopper or small food processor. Set aside. Peel and devein prawns.

2. In a wok or large skillet over medium-high heat, sauté onion in peanut oil until soft but not brown, stirring constantly. Add remaining garlic, bok choy, bell pepper, and mushrooms. Stir-fry for 5 minutes. Add cabbage, snow peas, and black bean mixture. Cover and let cook for 2 to 3 minutes.

3. In a small bowl mix together miso and stock. Add to stir-fry with honey, soy sauce, and prawns. Stir-fry until prawns turn pink. In a small bowl mix together arrowroot and the water and add to stir-fry. Cook until slightly thickened (3 minutes). Serve at once. Pass around chopped cilantro for garnish.

Serves 6.

Preparation time: 25 minutes
Cooking time: 12 to 15 minutes
Per serving: calcium 88 mg, calories 148, carbohydrates 11 g, cholesterol 115 mg, fat 3 g, fiber 2 g, protein 18 g, sodium 442 mg

Rich in flavor and nutrients, shellfish make a satisfying main course. Serve them Cantonese style in an easy black bean sauce.

STIR-FRIED PRAWNS IN BLACK BEAN SAUCE

This Cantonese dish features fermented black beans (available in Asian markets) mashed with garlic and ginger to make a savory black bean sauce. When you combine this sauce with a sauté of red bell pepper and snow peas, prawns, and crunchy bok choy, you have a delicious dinner in no time.

2 tablespoons fermented black beans, rinsed well
2 teaspoons minced garlic
1 tablespoon grated ginger
1 pound large prawns
1 cup sliced onion
2 teaspoons peanut oil
1 cup chopped bok choy
½ cup julienned red bell pepper
¼ cup sliced shiitake or other Asian mushrooms

HOT HUNAN NOODLE AND SEAFOOD SALAD

If you like spicy foods, you'll make this salad time and again. It features lightly poached scallops, prawns, and mussels, combined with boiled soba or rice noodles (available in Asian markets) and a marinade of hot peppers, sesame oil, and rice vinegar. Serve it on a chiffonade of chopped lettuce, endive, and spinach, garnished with slices of cucumber and red bell pepper. For extra flavor, marinate the seafood and noodles in the spicy sauce for an hour, then toss with greens before serving warm or chilled.

> 1 cup white wine
> ¼ pound peeled medium prawns
> ¼ pound scallops
> 6 mussels in shell, scrubbed well
> 10 ounces uncooked rice or soba noodles
> 4 teaspoons finely minced garlic
> ½ cup minced green onions (including greens)
> 2 teaspoons cayenne or hot-pepper flakes
> 4 teaspoons tahini
> 1 teaspoon Asian sesame oil
> 2 tablespoons low-sodium soy sauce or tamari
> ½ teaspoon honey
> 1 teaspoon grated ginger
> Endive or leaf lettuce, for lining platter
> ½ cup peeled, halved, and sliced cucumbers
> ½ cup julienned red bell pepper

1. In a saucepan over medium-high heat, bring wine to boil. Add prawns, scallops, and mussels in shell, cover, and cook 2 minutes. Drain and rinse under cold water. Remove mussels from shell and set seafood aside.

2. In a large pot over medium-high heat, bring 2 quarts water to a boil. Add noodles and cook until al dente (5 to 8 minutes). Drain and refresh under cold water. Set aside.

3. In large bowl mix together garlic, green onions, cayenne, tahini, sesame oil, soy sauce, honey, and ginger. Add noodles and seafood and mix well. Let chill for 30 minutes, if desired.

4. To serve, line a large platter with lettuce or endive. Pile noodles in center. Arrange cucumbers and red bell pepper around noodles.

Serves 6.

Preparation time: 25 minutes
Cooking time: 20 minutes
Chilling time (optional): 30 minutes
Per serving: calcium 117 mg, calories 407, carbohydrates 48 g, cholesterol 77 mg, fat 7 g, fiber 2 g, protein 30 g, sodium 655 mg

For an Asian entrée, try noodles cooked al dente and then tossed with seafood and a spicy sesame oil dressing.

TIPS

...ON FREEZING FISH

The old saying, "The greatest enemies of fish are not fishermen, but cooks," still holds true today. Many cooks don't know how to store or prepare fish to retain the delicate textures and flavors.

Freshly caught fish is a melt-in-your-mouth experience. Frozen fish can be almost as good, if care is taken in the storage process. Modern supermarkets freeze fish in vacuum-sealed plastic bags—a process that keeps much of the flavor intact. Here are some tips for freezing fresh fish at home.

☐ Years ago it was common to freeze fish in milk. This may sound strange today, but it is an excellent way to keep fish from developing a strong flavor or becoming freezer burned. Save milk cartons for this type of storage. Place the fish in a plastic bag, seal it tightly to remove as much air as possible, put it in the milk carton, and fill carton three fourths full with milk so that it surrounds the sealed bag.

☐ To defrost fish, let it thaw overnight in the refrigerator. Quick defrosting, such as in hot water or even at room temperature, can destroy much of the delicate flavor of fish.

☐ Fish is best when it is not frozen longer than three months.

☐ It is usually better to prepare a dish while the fish is fresh, and then to freeze the completed soup or stew after it has cooked. The other ingredients in the recipe help the fish retain moisture and flavor.

FISH SOUPS, STEWS, AND ONE-DISH MEALS

The following recipes are winners for the busy cook: They can be made ahead in quantity and even frozen. Use them when entertaining by simply serving with a tossed salad, French bread, and a fruit dessert.

ITALIAN FISH SOUP

This recipe is a tradition on the island of Sicily, where the catch of the day is cooked each night in a large pot with savory spices, tomatoes, and olive oil. Serve with crusty French bread, a green salad, and a light fruit dessert.

        1   teaspoon olive oil
     1/4   cup dry sherry
     1/2   cup sliced onion
     1/3   cup diced carrot
    2 1/2 cups crushed tomato (canned
            or fresh)
        2   cups diced red potatoes
     1/8   teaspoon crushed red chile
        1   cup water
        1   teaspoon fresh basil, minced
        6   tablespoons chopped parsley
        1   pound whitefish (such as cod),
            cut into 1-inch pieces
            Herbal salt substitute and
            pepper, if needed

1. In a large stockpot heat oil and sherry and sauté onion over medium-high heat until soft but not browned. Add carrot and tomato and continue cooking for 5 minutes.

2. Add potatoes, chile, water, basil, parsley, and fish and bring to a boil. Lower heat, cover, and simmer until potatoes are soft (about 20 minutes).

3. Add salt substitute and pepper, if needed, and serve hot.

Serves 6.

Preparation time: 25 minutes
Cooking time: 35 minutes
Per serving: calcium 84 mg, calories 134, carbohydrates 12 g, cholesterol 33 mg, fat 2 g, fiber 2 g, protein 16 g, sodium 121 mg

---

SEAFOOD CHOWDER

This seafood chowder combines carrots, onions, and chunks of potatoes with an assortment of shrimp, scallops, and whitefish. It is then seasoned and served as a creamy soup. It can be a main dish when accompanied by green salad and a loaf of dark bread. Make up to four days ahead of time and freeze.

        2   cups minced onion
        2   teaspoons olive oil or butter
     2/3   cup dry sherry
     1/2   cup chopped carrots
     1/2   cup minced celery
        1   cup diced red potatoes
        1   cup clam juice or Fish Stock
            (see page 51)
        2   tablespoons tomato paste
            Pinch of cayenne pepper
    1 1/2 cups nonfat milk
        1   cup half-and-half
     1/2   pound cooked shrimp meat
     1/2   pound bay scallops
        1   fillet red snapper, cut into
            1/2-inch pieces
            Herbal salt substitute and
            pepper (optional)

1. In a large stockpot over medium-high heat, sauté onion in oil and sherry until soft. Add carrots, celery, and potato and sauté 2 minutes.

2. Add clam juice and cover. Simmer until potatoes are soft (about 15 minutes). Purée half of the mixture in a blender until smooth, then return to pot.

3. Add tomato paste, cayenne, nonfat milk, half-and-half, shrimp, scallops, and snapper. Bring to a boil, lower heat to simmer, and cook 5 minutes. Taste for seasoning and add salt substitute and pepper, if desired.

Serves 6.

Preparation time: 30 minutes
Cooking time: 25 minutes
Per serving: calcium 182 mg, calories 241, carbohydrates 14 g, cholesterol 107 mg, fat 3 g, fiber 2 g, protein 23 g, sodium 420 mg

---

CRAB BISQUE

Most bisques are very rich, cream-based soups. This version is thickened with cooked potatoes instead of butter and cream.

- 2 teaspoons butter
- 2 cups coarsely chopped onion
- ⅓ cup chopped celery (including leaves)
- 2 large russet potatoes, peeled and diced
- 2 cups Fish Stock (see page 51) or clam juice
- 2 tablespoons tomato paste
- ⅔ cup dry sherry
- 2 cups nonfat milk
- ½ pound cooked fresh crabmeat Herbal salt substitute and pepper, to taste Minced parsley, for garnish

1. In a large stockpot heat butter and sauté onion and celery over medium-high heat until onion and celery are soft but not browned.

2. Add potato and fish stock. Bring to a boil. Lower heat, cover, and simmer until potato is soft (about 20 minutes).

3. Add tomato paste, sherry, and milk. Continue cooking 10 more minutes.

4. Purée mixture in blender. Return to stockpot and add crabmeat. Heat through. Taste for seasoning; add salt substitute and pepper as needed. Serve garnished with minced parsley.

Serves 6.

Preparation time: 15 minutes
Cooking time: 40 minutes
Per serving: calcium 179 mg, calories 183, carbohydrates 16 g, cholesterol 40 mg, fat 4 g, fiber 2 g, protein 11 g, sodium 455 mg

A rich-tasting but light soup, this creamy bisque is made with fresh crabmeat, sherry, and tomato paste, and thickened with potato purée. Serve the bisque, which can be made ahead and frozen, with a spinach or tossed salad and crusty brown bread for a delicious lunch.

Flavors of Spain enrich this Basque Paella of herbed saffron rice, artichoke hearts, red and green peppers, prawns, clams, chicken, and red snapper.

BASQUE PAELLA

This dish takes a bit of extra time to prepare but is well worth the effort. Paella is a traditional Spanish dish, and this version incorporates some of the pronounced seasonings of the Basque area of Spain.

- 3 teaspoons olive oil
- 1 cup boned and skinned whole chicken breast, cut in small pieces
- 1 cup uncooked basmati rice
- 2 cups boiling water
- ½ cup chopped onion
- 2 cloves garlic, minced
- ½ cup each sliced red bell pepper and sliced green bell pepper
- ½ cup diced tomato
- 1 red snapper fillet, cut into 1-inch pieces
- 2 cups hot, defatted Chicken Stock (see page 51)
- 1 tablespoon herbal salt substitute
- 1 teaspoon saffron threads
- ¾ teaspoon oregano
- 6 large prawns, shelled and deveined
- 1 cup peas, fresh or frozen
- 5 artichoke hearts, unmarinated
- 6 clams in their shells (scrub outside of shells)

1. In large, heavy skillet over medium-high heat, heat oil and cook chicken pieces until just opaque. Remove chicken to platter. Reserve skillet.

2. Soak rice in the boiling water for 10 minutes, then drain.

3. In reserved skillet sauté onion over medium heat until soft (about 5 minutes). Add garlic, bell peppers, and tomato and continue sautéing for 5 more minutes.

4. Add snapper, soaked rice with water, stock, salt substitute, saffron, and oregano. Bring to a boil, then lower heat to medium. Cover pot and let simmer until rice is tender and has absorbed liquid (about 15 minutes).

5. Arrange prawns, peas, artichoke hearts, cooked chicken pieces, and clams on top of rice. Cover and cook again until prawns turn bright pink and clam shells open (about 10 minutes). Serve hot.

Serves 8.

Preparation time: 35 minutes
Cooking time: 45 minutes
Per serving: calcium 76 mg, calories 237, carbohydrates 31 g, cholesterol 48 mg, fat 3 g, fiber 4 g, protein 21 g, sodium 341 mg

LOUISIANA CREOLE

An original recipe from Crowley, Louisiana, this shrimp Creole is an easy, satisfying one-pot meal.

- 1 teaspoon olive oil
- ½ onion, chopped coarsely
- 4 cloves garlic, minced
- 6 Spanish green olives, pitted and chopped
- 1½ cups peeled, chopped tomato
- 1 green bell pepper, chopped
- ½ bay leaf
- ¼ teaspoon dried thyme
- 1 teaspoon dried parsley
- 1 teaspoon honey
- ½ teaspoon cayenne pepper, or to taste
- 1 teaspoon herbal salt substitute
- 1 pound peeled and deveined medium prawns
- 3 cups cooked brown rice

1. In a heavy pot or Dutch oven, heat oil and sauté onion over medium heat until golden brown. Add garlic, olives, tomato, and bell pepper. Sauté 2 minutes more.

2. Add bay leaf, thyme, parsley, honey, cayenne, and salt substitute. Let mixture simmer over low heat, covered, for 20 minutes.

3. Add prawns. Cook until they turn bright pink. Serve over hot rice.

Serves 4.

Preparation time: 20 minutes
Cooking time: 40 minutes
Per serving: calcium 114 mg, calories 337, carbohydrates 44 g, cholesterol 173 mg, fat 5 g, fiber 2 g, protein 28 g, sodium 304 mg

MENU

SUNDAY BUFFET ON THE TERRACE

Chinese Crab Salad in Tomato Baskets

Balkan Cold Cucumber Salad (see page 68)

Caesar Salad (see page 71)

Best Bran Muffins

Sparkling Wine Coolers

Raspberry-Pear Crisps

Here is a menu to enjoy in the sun and warm breezes of a Sunday afternoon on your terrace or under the backyard trees. Most of the dishes are served chilled, so make them early in the day, or even the night before, and serve them right out of the refrigerator. The platters and bowls of salads should be well garnished; line them with crisp spinach, curly endive, or leaf lettuce before layering with salads. Attractive garnishes include strips of red or yellow bell pepper, cucumber slices cut in half-moons, scalloped lemon halves, minced green onions or cilantro, and grated zucchini. Menu serves ten.

CHINESE CRAB SALAD IN TOMATO BASKETS

Shimmering with the flavors of lemon and Asian sesame oil, this salad is an upbeat version of the famous Chinese chicken salads that are so popular in California. Cut the tomatoes about an hour before serving. Lace the crabmeat with the irresistible combination of roasted macadamia nuts, cilantro, and a dressing of rice vinegar and sesame oil. Marinate the salad ahead of time, even overnight, but add the nuts and chow mein noodles (if used) right before serving.

    4 cups fresh crabmeat
    2 cups peeled, halved, seeded,
         and thinly sliced cucumbers
    2 cups shredded green cabbage
    2 tablespoons grated red onion
    2 tablespoons toasted sesame
         seed
  1/4 cup minced cilantro
    1 cup rice vinegar
  2/3 cup light honey
    2 tablespoons low-sodium soy
         sauce or tamari
    2 tablespoons grated ginger
    2 tablespoons Asian sesame oil
    2 teaspoons herbal salt substitute
  1/2 cup chopped roasted
         macadamia nuts
    1 cup chow mein noodles
         (optional)
         Lettuce leaves, for lining
         platter
    5 large, ripe tomatoes

1. In a large bowl combine crabmeat, cucumbers, cabbage, onion, sesame seed, and cilantro. Toss well.

2. In another bowl whisk together vinegar, honey, soy sauce, ginger, oil, and salt substitute. Pour over crabmeat mixture and toss well. Add nuts and noodles, if used.

3. Line a platter with lettuce leaves. Cut each tomato in half width-wise. With a sharp knife, score interior and scoop out pulp to form a shell. Fill with a generous portion of crab salad and place on lettuce-lined platter.

Serves 10.

Preparation time: 45 minutes
Per serving: calcium 84 mg, calories 225, carbohydrates 26 g, cholesterol 42 mg, fat 9 g, fiber 2 g, protein 12 g, sodium 267 mg

BEST BRAN MUFFINS

The secret of these muffins is in the buttermilk, which makes them rise light and fluffy. Make an extra batch and freeze for a brunch treat the following weekend.

    2 cups wheat or oat bran
    2 cups whole wheat pastry flour
  3/4 cup raisins
  1 1/2 teaspoons baking soda
  1/3 cup molasses
  1/3 cup honey
    2 cups low-fat buttermilk
         Oil, for coating muffin tin

1. In a large bowl, combine bran, flour, raisins, and baking soda. Stir together molasses, honey, and buttermilk, then pour over bran mixture. Let stand for 20 minutes.

2. Lightly oil a 12-hole muffin tin. Preheat oven to 350° F. Fill muffin cups two thirds full of batter and bake until muffins spring back slightly when pressed in the center (30 minutes). Remove from pan and serve warm.

Makes 1 dozen muffins, 12 servings.

Preparation time: 25 minutes
Baking time: 30 minutes
Per serving: calcium 85 mg, calories 186, carbohydrates 44 g, cholesterol 1 mg, fat 1 g, fiber 7 g, protein 6 g, sodium 206 mg

RASPBERRY-PEAR CRISP

This is a surprisingly elegant dessert, and a colorful one. The sweetness of the pears combines beautifully with the tartness of the berries. This dessert is easy on the cook, since it can be made up to a week before a party, covered well, and frozen. Thaw in the refrigerator overnight and warm up slightly to serve.

    1 teaspoon oil, for coating pan
  1 1/2 cups sliced pears, such as Bosc
         or d'Anjou
    2 cups fresh or unsweetened
         frozen raspberries
  1/4 cup dried currants
  1/3 cup maple syrup
    2 tablespoons arrowroot powder
         or cornstarch
    1 tablespoon lemon juice
    1 tablespoon grated lemon rind
    1 cup uncooked rolled oats
    3 tablespoons melted unsalted
         butter
    2 tablespoons light honey
  1/2 teaspoon nutmeg
  1/2 teaspoon cinnamon
  1/4 teaspoon cardamom

1. Lightly oil a 9- by 12-inch baking pan and arrange pear slices in bottom of pan. Cover with raspberries, then currants. Mix together maple syrup, arrowroot, lemon juice, and rind, and drizzle over pear mixture. Preheat oven to 375° F.

2. In a large bowl combine oats, butter, honey, nutmeg, cinnamon, and cardamom. Crumble over pear mixture. Bake crisp until pears are tender and oats are lightly browned (30 to 40 minutes). Serve warm.

Serves 10.

Preparation time: 25 minutes
Baking time: 30 to 40 minutes
Per serving: calcium 25 mg, calories 135, carbohydrates 24 g, cholesterol 10 mg, fat 5 g, fiber 3 g, protein 1 g, sodium 2 mg

Chilled salads and light desserts line the buffet table, tempting your guests to enjoy a healthy weekend dinner on the deck or patio.

Chicken can be prepared in many nutritious ways, such as marinated and grilled, braised with vegetables, or baked in parchment with wine and herbs.

POULTRY & LEAN MEAT ENTRÉES

Thoughtful preparation and the right method of cooking can transform poultry and lean meats into tasty dishes that are high in nutritive value and low in fat. In addition to step-by-step explanations of techniques for broiling, grilling, and stir-frying, this chapter serves up new ideas for sauces that are low in fat and cholesterol. With recipes like Easy Beef Fajitas (see page 166), Turkey Chili Burritos (see page 150), and Roasted Chicken With Rosemary and Garlic (see page 148), there's plenty to satisfy even a hearty meat eater.

POULTRY ENTRÉES

A welcome addition to any menu, poultry is easy to prepare, even ahead of time, yet is also a relatively low-fat, low-cholesterol source of protein. Here is a variety of recipes, including some unusual dishes for entertaining.

CHICKEN BREASTS WITH GREEN PEPPERCORN SAUCE

This rich dish should be saved for special occasions. The unripe (green) peppercorns, sold in most gourmet stores, have a slightly less acidic taste than white or black pepper. They are used whole in this recipe, enhanced by a sweet wine and cream sauce.

> 4 chicken half-breasts, boned and skinned
> 1 teaspoon olive oil
> 1/4 cup dry sherry
> 2 tablespoons minced onion
> 1/4 cup white wine
> 1/2 cup half-and-half
> 1 tablespoon green peppercorns
> 1/4 teaspoon dried tarragon

1. Preheat oven to 400° F. In a large skillet over medium-high heat, sauté chicken breasts in oil and sherry until lightly browned on both sides. Transfer to a baking dish. Bake for 15 minutes.

2. While chicken is baking, in the same skillet over medium heat, sauté onion in pan drippings until soft. Add wine, half-and-half, peppercorns, and tarragon. Heat until sauce coats the back of a spoon. Serve over baked chicken.

Serves 4.

> *Preparation time:* 10 minutes
> *Baking time:* 15 minutes
> *Per serving:* calcium 49 mg, calories 177, carbohydrates 2 g, cholesterol 63 mg, fat 6 g, fiber .2 g, protein 22 g, sodium 92 mg

LEMON CHICKEN

This dish uses both fresh and dried herbs, the juice from several fresh lemons, and a whole roasting chicken. For a Thanksgiving-style entrée you can stuff the cavity of the chicken with more of the herbs or a light wheat bread stuffing. Serve with light soup, salad, and a fruit dessert.

> 1 roasting chicken (3 lb), skinned
> 1 tablespoon dried thyme
> 1 teaspoon dried sage, crushed
> 1/2 teaspoon freshly ground black pepper
> 3 lemons
> 2 tablespoons minced fresh tarragon, if available, or 1 tablespoon dried tarragon

1. Preheat oven to 375° F. Wash chicken and pat dry. Place breast side up in a large roasting pan or deep baking dish.

2. Rub thyme, sage, and pepper over entire surface of chicken. Slice lemons in half and squeeze the juice through a sieve onto chicken (the sieve traps the seeds). Sprinkle tarragon over chicken.

3. Lightly tuck a large piece of aluminum foil over and around the top of the chicken. Bake until juices run clear when leg is pierced with a sharp knife (about 35 minutes). Remove aluminum foil for last 5 minutes of baking. Serve hot.

Serves 8.

> *Preparation time:* 20 minutes
> *Baking time:* 40 minutes
> *Per serving:* calcium 57 mg, calories 156, carbohydrates 5 g, cholesterol 84 mg, fat 4 g, fiber 0 g, protein 27 g, sodium 99 mg

SIMPLE BAKED CHICKEN WITH ORANGE AND CUMIN

This recipe calls for vegetables, fresh orange juice and rind, and a curry-like medley of spices. Bake it ahead of time and warm it up before serving. This dish keeps well frozen or can be refrigerated for up to four days, if covered tightly with plastic wrap.

> 1 roasting chicken (3 lb), skinned
> 1 cup fresh orange juice
> 1/2 cup dry sherry
> 1/2 cup defatted Chicken Stock (see page 51)
> 1 cup sliced onion
> 1/4 cup minced green onion
> 1/2 cup julienned carrot
> 1/3 cup currants
> 2 tablespoons grated orange rind
> 1 teaspoon ground cumin
> 1 teaspoon paprika
> 1/4 teaspoon cayenne pepper
> 4 cups cooked rice (optional)

1. Preheat oven to 350° F. Place chicken in a shallow roasting pan and prick with a skewer to allow juices to penetrate when marinating.

2. Mix remaining ingredients except rice and pour over chicken. Marinate for 2 hours or overnight, turning and basting occasionally.

3. Roast, in marinade, for 45 minutes. Remove chicken and vegetables to a serving platter and keep warm.

4. Reduce marinade by boiling rapidly over high heat until one half of original volume. Pour sauce over chicken.

5. Serve hot, with rice, if desired.

Serves 4.

> *Preparation time:* 20 minutes
> *Marinating time:* 2 hours
> *Baking time:* 45 minutes
> *Per serving:* calcium 44 mg, calories 208, carbohydrates 11 g, cholesterol 84 mg, fat 4 g, fiber 1 g, protein 28 g, sodium 228 mg

Sautéed in sherry, Chicken Breasts With Green Peppercorn Sauce (see page 146) makes a delicate, healthy variation on rich French cooking.

POACHED CHICKEN BREASTS WITH LEMON-AND-HERB MAYONNAISE

Chicken takes well to poaching, as long as it is not overcooked. In this recipe the soy sauce and lemon permeate the chicken breasts, and the resulting flavor melds with the tart mayonnaise. Use reduced-fat mayonnaise to keep the cholesterol low in this dish.

    3 cups defatted Chicken Stock
       (see page 51)
    2 tablespoons grated lemon rind
    1 tablespoon low-sodium soy
       sauce or tamari
    4 chicken half-breasts, boned
       and skinned
  1/2 cup reduced-fat mayonnaise
    1 tablespoon lemon juice
    1 tablespoon minced chives or
       green onions
    1 teaspoon Dijon mustard
  1/2 teaspoon minced fresh
       tarragon
       Minced chives and lemon
       slices, for garnish (optional)

1. In a large, shallow skillet over medium-high heat, bring to a boil chicken stock, half the lemon rind, and soy sauce. Lower heat to simmer. Add chicken breasts, cover, and poach for 10 minutes. Remove from poaching liquid and chill if desired.

2. In a small bowl combine mayonnaise, lemon juice, remaining lemon rind, chives, mustard, and tarragon. Chill until ready to serve.

3. Serve each half-breast with a dollop of lemon mayonnaise on top. Garnish with minced chives and a slice of lemon.

Serves 4.

Preparation time: 20 minutes
Poaching time: 10 minutes
Chilling time (optional): 20 minutes
Per serving: calcium 49 mg, calories 186, carbohydrates 5 g, cholesterol 78 mg, fat 4 g, fiber .4 g, protein 1 g, sodium 43 mg

ROASTED CHICKEN WITH ROSEMARY AND GARLIC

To preserve its moistness, the chicken is roasted in a light sauce, which is then reduced and served over the bird. The pungent flavorings, rosemary and garlic, are commonly used in the cuisines of Greece and southern France.

    4 cloves garlic
    1 teaspoon unsalted butter
    1 tablespoon olive oil
    1 roasting chicken (3 lb),
       skinned
    2 tablespoons minced fresh
       rosemary
  1/2 cup dry white wine

1. Preheat oven to 350° F. Peel and halve garlic cloves. In a large ovenproof skillet over medium-high heat, heat butter and oil and sauté garlic cloves for 2 minutes. Quarter chicken. Add to pan and brown lightly on both sides. Add rosemary to pan.

2. Cover skillet and place in oven. Bake until juice runs clear when a sharp knife is inserted into thigh of bird (about 40 minutes). Remove bird from pan and keep warm on a platter in oven.

3. In the same skillet over medium-high heat, pour in wine. Cook rapidly for 2 to 3 minutes, scraping pan to loosen browned bits. Pour sauce over chicken and serve.

Serves 6.

Preparation time: 20 minutes
Roasting time: 40 minutes
Per serving: calcium 35 mg, calories 264, carbohydrates 2 g, cholesterol 103 mg, fat 12 g, fiber .2 g, protein 33 g, sodium 99 mg

CURRIED TURKEY BREAST

Curried Turkey Breast is a simple but delicious entrée that goes well with Avocado and Pine Nut Salad (see page 72) or Jamaican Papaya Salad (see page 67). Buy a large turkey breast from the butcher, then skin and cover it with a spicy mixture of cumin, coriander, cinnamon, and turmeric. Let the meat marinate for several hours in the spice mixture, then bake until crisp on the outside and juicy in the middle.

    1 large turkey breast, skinned
  1/2 teaspoon ground coriander
  1/2 teaspoon paprika
  1/4 teaspoon turmeric
  1/2 teaspoon cumin
  1/4 teaspoon cayenne pepper
  1/4 teaspoon cinnamon
    2 tablespoons grated ginger
    1 tablespoon olive oil
    2 tablespoons lemon juice
  1/2 cup nonfat plain yogurt
       Minced green onions, for
       garnish

1. Place turkey breast in a baking pan. In a small bowl combine coriander, paprika, turmeric, cumin, cayenne, cinnamon, ginger, olive oil, lemon juice, and yogurt. Spread over top of turkey breast. Cover pan with plastic wrap and refrigerate for 2 hours.

2. Preheat oven to 350° F. Unwrap pan and place in oven; bake for 40 minutes, basting occasionally with pan juices. To serve, slice turkey, drizzle with pan juices, and garnish with green onions.

Serves 4.

Preparation time: 10 minutes
Marinating time: 2 hours
Baking time: 40 minutes
Per serving: calcium 97 mg, calories 331, carbohydrates 5 g, cholesterol 149 mg, fat 10 g, fiber .6 g, protein 52 g, sodium 183 mg

MEDITERRANEAN CHICKEN

Mediterranean Chicken, which can be prepared well in advance, delights guests with its unusual flavor combination of herbs, Greek olives, and heady balsamic vinegar. If possible, let the roasting chicken marinate for several hours, basting frequently with the sauce, and then roast right before serving. It is also great served cold for supper the next day, with a glass of white wine and a green salad.

    Oil, for coating pan
 1 roasting chicken (4 lb),
    skinned
 2 large cloves garlic
 2 tablespoons green olive oil
 1 tablespoon minced fresh
    tarragon
 1 teaspoon crushed sage
 6 tablespoons balsamic vinegar
 6 small new potatoes
 ¼ cup pitted Greek olives

1. Preheat oven to 375° F. Lightly oil a large roasting pan or deep casserole.

2. Place chicken in roasting pan, breast side up. Peel and halve garlic cloves, rub surface of chicken with cut garlic, then place cloves inside chicken.

3. Mix together olive oil, tarragon, sage, and vinegar. Pour over surface of chicken and inside cavity. Cut potatoes in quarters and place olives and potatoes around chicken. Cover pan and place in oven.

4. Roast until juice runs clear when a sharp knife is inserted in thigh of bird (45 minutes to 1 hour). Slice or cut into serving pieces and serve with olives, potatoes, and cooking liquid.

Serves 6.

Preparation time: 20 minutes
Roasting time: 45 minutes to 1 hour
Per serving: calcium 27 mg, calories 190, carbohydrates 22 g, cholesterol 25 mg, fat 7 g, fiber 2 g, protein 10 g, sodium 179 mg

Fresh tarragon leaves, garlic cloves, and crushed sage lend the sun-drenched flavor of southern European cuisine to an easy chicken dish.

CHICKEN SATAY WITH CUCUMBER RELISH

Bite-sized chunks of marinated chicken are grilled on skewers, then served with a spicy relish. Both the chicken and the relish can be prepared ahead, and the meat grilled right before serving. Be sure to use rubber gloves to protect your skin while preparing the fresh chile.

- 1 pound chicken breasts, boned and skinned
- 1 teaspoon minced garlic
- ½ cup lime juice
- 1 tablespoon honey
- 1 tablespoon grated ginger
- 1 tablespoon grated lime rind

Cucumber Relish

- 1 cup peeled, seeded, and finely diced cucumber
- 1 teaspoon minced garlic
- 2 tablespoons minced cilantro
- ½ cup seeded, diced tomatoes
- 1 small jalapeño chile, seeded and minced
- 2 tablespoons rice vinegar

1. Cut chicken into 1-inch pieces and place in a large, shallow pan. In a small bowl mix together garlic, lime juice, honey, ginger, and rind. Pour over chicken and let marinate for 30 minutes, tossing frequently.

2. Preheat broiler or grill. Assemble chicken on short skewers. Broil or grill until browned (5 minutes). Serve immediately with Cucumber Relish.

Serves 4.

Cucumber Relish Combine all ingredients in a bowl. Let marinate 15 minutes before serving.

Makes about 2 cups.

Preparation time: 20 minutes
Marinating time: 30 minutes
Cooking time: 5 minutes
Per serving: calcium 34 mg, calories 127, carbohydrates 12 g, cholesterol 43 mg, fat 1 g, fiber 1 g, protein 18 g, sodium 54 mg

TURKEY CHILI BURRITOS

This chili made with small chunks of turkey is seasoned perfectly and wrapped in warm flour tortillas. Serve with salsa and chopped cilantro.

- 1 cup minced onion
- 1 teaspoon olive oil
- ½ cup defatted Chicken Stock (see page 51)
- 1 tablespoon minced garlic
- 4 cups diced turkey meat, skinned
- ½ cup diced celery
- ½ cup chopped carrot
- ¼ cup minced parsley
- 1 cup diced tomatoes
- 1 cup water
- ½ teaspoon ground cloves
- 2 tablespoons chili powder
- ½ teaspoon hot-pepper sauce
- 4 ounces canned green chiles, chopped
  Herbal salt substitute and pepper, to taste
- 12 flour tortillas
- ½ cup grated low-fat Cheddar cheese

1. In a Dutch oven over medium-high heat, sauté onion in oil and stock until soft. Add garlic, turkey, celery, carrot, parsley, and tomatoes and sauté, stirring frequently, for 10 minutes.

2. Add the water, cloves, chili powder, hot-pepper sauce, and green chiles. Lower heat, cover, and cook for 25 minutes. Taste for seasoning and add salt substitute and pepper, if necessary.

3. Warm tortillas by placing in a toaster oven or conventional oven for 5 minutes at 200° F.

4. To serve, spoon approximately ⅓ cup chili into each tortilla, cover with grated cheese, and roll.

Serves 6.

Preparation time: 25 minutes
Cooking time: 40 minutes
Per serving: calcium 247 mg, calories 482, carbohydrates 49 g, cholesterol 93 mg, fat 10 g, fiber 5 g, protein 47 g, sodium 708 mg

BRAISED PHEASANT

Rock Cornish game hens work well in this recipe if pheasant is unavailable. The birds are browned quickly and then roasted slowly to bring out the flavor, while you baste them in an apple brandy sauce. Serve with a green salad dressed with Lime-Mint Dressing (see page 82) and steamed asparagus or broccoli.

- 2 large pheasants, cleaned and rinsed well
- ¼ cup olive oil
- 3 cups peeled and thinly sliced green apples
- 1 cup thinly sliced onions
- ½ cup applejack or Calvados
- 1 teaspoon nutmeg
- ½ cup half-and-half
  Herbal salt substitute and pepper, to taste

1. Preheat oven to 350° F. In a large Dutch oven over medium-high heat, quickly brown pheasants in oil on all sides. Place apples and onions around pheasants. Pour applejack on top and let it heat for 1 minute, then ignite. Shake pan until flames subside.

2. Dust top of pheasants with nutmeg. Place pan in oven and bake until juice runs clear when tip of knife is inserted in thigh of bird (about 1 hour). Remove pheasants, cooked apples, and onions to a platter and keep warm in oven.

3. Transfer pan juices to a saucepan. Heat over medium-high heat until simmering, then stir in half-and-half. Let mixture cook 5 minutes, stirring frequently, then season to taste with salt substitute and pepper. Pour over pheasants and serve.

Serves 8.

Preparation time: 20 minutes
Baking time: 1 hour
Per serving: calcium 51 mg, calories 505, carbohydrates 6 g, cholesterol 74 mg, fat 27 g, fiber 1 g, protein 46 g, sodium 161 mg

GRILLED TURKEY BREAST WITH RASPBERRY AND SHALLOT MARINADE

This dish features a quartered turkey breast marinated in a raspberry vinegar sauce, then grilled over hot coals. Serve Grilled Turkey Breast with Spicy Tomato Aspic (see page 70) or Minted Bulgur Salad (see page 68) for a healthy meal.

   1 large turkey breast, skinned
     and quartered
   ½ cup raspberry vinegar
   2 tablespoons minced shallots
   ½ cup nonfat plain yogurt
   1 teaspoon curry powder

1. Place turkey breast quarters into a large, shallow pan. Mix together vinegar and shallots and pour over turkey. Cover with plastic wrap and marinate for 8 to 10 hours in the refrigerator.

2. Combine yogurt and curry powder. Set aside.

3. Prepare coals for grilling. Wrap turkey breast quarters in aluminum foil and place on grill. Cook over coals for 20 minutes, then unwrap and grill for 5 minutes more, turning once to brown lightly. Spoon marinade over turkey frequently during last 5 minutes of grilling.

4. Serve with curried yogurt as a spicy sauce.

Serves 4.

Preparation time: 10 minutes
Marinating time: 8 to 10 hours
Grilling time: 25 minutes
Per serving: calcium 95 mg, calories 296, carbohydrates 5 g, cholesterol 149 mg, fat 2 g, fiber .2 g, protein 52 g, sodium 183 mg

Quick browning and then basting in apple brandy before baking assures that Braised Pheasants will be tender and delicious every time. If pheasant is unavailable in your area, Rock Cornish game hens (shown above) turn out just as tender and tasty.

FEATURE

DINING SOLO— HOW TO COOK HEALTHILY FOR ONE

Some single people prefer eating in restaurants to cooking and dining by themselves. Yet dining out may not be such a wise option if you consider the nutritional cost. Although an occasional restaurant meal may not break your bank account or your nutritional budget, there's a healthy alternative.

Dining at home can be the more reliable—and enjoyable—way to go, but it takes practice. If your meals at home are typically rushed, consumed in a hurry between favorite television shows or social engagements, you can lose the nutritional benefits of home cooking.

Here are some plan-ahead tips from veteran solo diners to make your meals pleasant and health-enhancing.

☐ Buy small portions you can easily store. Many solo diners are overwhelmed by the amount of unused (and spoiling) perishables they seem to accumulate. Plan meals around fresh ingredients, such as seasonal produce and fresh fish, but give yourself a head start on menus. After shopping, store all your produce in lock-top plastic bags according to menu plans. For example, on Monday you can wash, chop, and store broccoli, carrots, and zucchini for a Thursday evening stir-fry, or you can prepare chicken breasts and leave them marinating in low-sodium soy sauce and sherry, ready for baking on Tuesday.

☐ Occasionally treat yourself to something special. Consider fresh strawberries for dessert, a glass of good wine, asparagus in season, or jumbo prawns. Treat yourself as you would a favorite guest.

☐ Plan a variety of meals, some light and easy, some more elegant and complex.

☐ Set an elegant table. Use attractive accoutrements such as tablecloths, place mats, candles, cloth napkins, and glass or china dinner plates. Play relaxing dinner music if you like.

☐ Recognize that on certain nights you are going to be too tired to cook. Plan ahead by making double portions of a gourmet menu and freezing half. On lazy or busy evenings, defrost the prepared meal and enjoy!

☐ Highlight some of the one-dish-meal recipes in this book. Try Stir-Fried Prawns in Black Bean Sauce (see page 136) or Stewed Beef in Red Wine (see page 164). Make four servings and freeze three in individual lock-top plastic bags or containers. Plan to use these for future menus.

☐ Have salad ingredients on hand for easy, light meals. After a day spent dining with clients or at family feasts, you may want just a snack. Wash and spin-dry lettuce leaves, grate carrots and keep in lemon juice, have low-fat mozzarella cheese and sprouts ready in bags, and slice a few cherry tomatoes or radishes. A salad relaxes your digestive system, makes a convenient evening meal, and provides plenty of nutrient-rich foods.

ROAST BREAST OF DUCK WITH SHERRY

The rich flavor and elegance of roast duck makes it a good alternate to turkey for special occasions. In this recipe, breast of duck is rubbed with a savory herb mixture, combined with celery and onion, and roasted until crisp. Serve with a simple accompaniment of wok-cooked vegetables, a green salad, roasted potatoes, and French bread.

> 4 *duck half-breasts, skinned*
> 1/2 *teaspoon celery salt*
> 1/2 *teaspoon onion salt*
> 1/2 *teaspoon celery seed*
> 1/4 *teaspoon curry powder*
> 1 *teaspoon herbal salt substitute*
> 1/4 *teaspoon freshly ground black pepper*
> 1/4 *cup minced celery*
> 1/2 *cup minced onion*
> 1/2 *cup dry sherry*

1. Place duck half-breasts in a large Dutch oven. In a small bowl mix together celery salt, onion salt, celery seed, curry powder, salt substitute, and pepper. Rub into duck half-breasts. Let marinate 1 hour.

2. Preheat oven to 300° F. Add celery and onion to Dutch oven. Pour in the 1/2 cup sherry. Place Dutch oven over medium-high heat and brown duck half-breasts on both sides (about 5 minutes per side). Cover Dutch oven and bake for 45 minutes. Serve at once.

Serves 4.

> *Preparation time:* 10 minutes
> *Marinating time:* 1 hour
> *Cooking time:* 55 minutes
> *Per serving:* calcium 47 mg, calories 267, carbohydrates 3 g, cholesterol 131 mg, fat 10 g, fiber .5 g, protein 32 g, sodium 607 mg

INTERNATIONAL CHICKEN ENTRÉES

Try baking chicken breasts (or sliced lean beef) the French way—*en papillote*—in parchment, which is a lightweight cooking paper that comes in a roll like aluminum foil. Add some fresh herbs, a little wine, and lemon slices, and 20 minutes later you'll have a hot, delicious main course.

Here's another idea with international flair: Try marinating, which gives flavors and richness without adding unwanted fat. Begin with an overnight basting in some wine, spice, or herb mixture, and the next day just pop the meat into the oven. The marinade can be reduced by cooking rapidly at high heat, and served as a low-fat sauce.

Select chicken parts carefully if you're serious about reducing your fat intake. The lighter-colored meat usually contains the least fat. You can also reduce fat by skinning chicken before cooking and skimming any accumulated fat off the cooking liquid with a gravy separator or by floating a piece of bread on top.

Without the extra fat of the skin, chicken is easy to overcook. The meat is usually done when a sharp knife, inserted into a dark meat section, such as the thigh, produces juices that run clear instead of pink. Moist, tender chicken will have a slightly crisp exterior and will burst with juice when pierced.

Most of the following dishes can be made ahead, wrapped well, and frozen. Let frozen chicken come to room temperature before cooking, either by placing it in a microwave for a few minutes or by letting the meat thaw in the refrigerator overnight.

The aromas of thyme, sage, and tarragon combine with pungent lemon in Lemon Chicken (see page 146). Serve with roasted green peppers and rice pilaf to create a hearty meal that is great for an afternoon picnic or a summer supper.

CHICKEN NIÇOISE

Niçoise dishes are those cooked in the style of Nice, a small town in southern France where fragrant herbs grow wild on the hillsides above the sea. This marinated chicken dish captures the flavor of that sun-drenched area and has been adapted for low-fat cooking. Serve Chicken Niçoise with crusty French bread, a crisp green salad, and a dessert of fresh fruit.

> 2 teaspoons olive oil
> 4 chicken half-breasts, skinned
> 2 teaspoons saffron threads, soaked in 2 tablespoons dry sherry
> 3 cloves garlic, peeled and halved
> 1/2 teaspoon dried tarragon
> 1/4 teaspoon dried thyme
>   Pinch dried sage
> 2 crushed bay leaves
> 5 plum tomatoes, coarsely chopped
> 5 Greek olives, pitted and chopped
> 1 1/4 cups white wine
> 1 1/2 cups defatted Chicken Stock (see page 51)
> 1 teaspoon herbal salt substitute

1. In a Dutch oven or heavy skillet, heat oil and lightly brown chicken pieces over medium-high heat.

2. Add remaining ingredients to skillet and bring to a boil. Lower heat, cover, and simmer until chicken is cooked (about 40 minutes).

3. Remove chicken to a serving platter and keep warm in the oven. Reduce cooking liquor by boiling rapidly over high heat for 5 minutes. Pour over chicken and serve.

Serves 4.

Preparation time: 20 minutes
Marinating time: 30 minutes
Cooking time: 55 minutes
Per serving: calcium 58 mg, calories 267, carbohydrates 10 g, cholesterol 65 mg, fat 6 g, fiber 2 g, protein 30 g, sodium 478 mg

---

MOROCCAN FILO TART WITH CURRIED CHICKEN AND ALMONDS

Curried chicken filo tart, or bastilla, is a rich Moroccan dish that should be reserved for special occasions. Thin filo pastry is filled with seasoned chicken and an almond-ginger mixture, then baked until brown and crisp (see How to Prepare Filo, page 212). The filling can also be used for small appetizers— follow directions given for Filo Pastries With Smoked Turkey and Mushrooms (see page 32). This dish takes a while to assemble, so make the filling ahead of time and assemble the dish right before baking.

> 16 sheets filo dough
> 1 teaspoon olive oil, for coating pan
> 2 1/2 cups cooked and diced chicken
> 2 cups defatted Chicken Stock (see page 51)
> 1/2 teaspoon turmeric
> 1/2 teaspoon cardamom
> 1/8 teaspoon cayenne pepper
> 1/8 teaspoon ground ginger
> 1/2 cup minced onion
> 3 tablespoons minced garlic
> 4 whole eggs
> 5 egg whites
> 3 tablespoons minced parsley
> 2 teaspoons herbal salt substitute
> 1/2 teaspoon freshly ground black pepper
> 1/2 cup slivered almonds
> 1 teaspoon grated ginger
> 6 tablespoons plus 1 teaspoon unsalted butter, melted
> 6 tablespoons date sugar
> 2 teaspoons cinnamon
> 1/4 teaspoon nutmeg

1. Lay sheets of filo dough on a clean surface. Cover with plastic wrap. Dampen and wring out a dish towel and lay over plastic-covered filo. Preheat oven to 350° F. Lightly oil a deep 9-inch-diameter baking pan.

2. In a medium saucepan over medium-high heat, simmer chicken in stock, turmeric, cardamom, cayenne, and ginger for 5 minutes. Drain, set chicken aside, and return spice stock to saucepan.

3. Add onion to spice stock and simmer until soft (8 to 10 minutes). Drain and reserve onion.

4. In large bowl mix together onion, garlic, eggs, egg whites, parsley, salt substitute, and pepper. Set aside. In a saucepan over medium-high heat, sauté almonds and ginger in 1 teaspoon of the butter until lightly browned. Add date sugar, cinnamon, and nutmeg. Set aside.

5. Unwrap filo. Using a wide pastry brush, brush approximately 1 teaspoon melted butter on a sheet of filo. Place buttered filo into bottom of prepared pan, letting edges hang over sides. Continue until 8 sheets are piled into bottom of pan. Place drained chicken into pan, then egg mixture, then three fourths of the almond mixture. Fold overhanging filo into center of pan on top of filling.

6. Butter remaining 8 sheets of filo, layering on top of filling, tucking edges down into interior of pan. Butter top of completed tart, sprinkle with reserved almond mixture, and bake until golden brown (about 25 minutes).

Serves 8.

Preparation time: 40 minutes
Baking time: 25 minutes
Per serving: calcium 101 mg, calories 445, carbohydrates 35 g, cholesterol 173 mg, fat 21 g, fiber 1 g, protein 28 g, sodium 538 mg

---

STEP BY STEP

CUTTING UP A WHOLE CHICKEN

All raw chicken, whether whole or cut up, should be washed before use. Remove any unappetizing fat, cartilage, or other matter.

Remove innards (neck and giblets) from cavity. Tear away any loose or large pieces of fat around both openings and from skin around neck. Insert hand into cavity and remove any tendons and fat that will pull away. Wash bird under cold running water, inside cavity and out. Pat dry with paper towels.

Cutting up a whole fresh chicken is in some ways similar to carving a cooked one, except that you are cutting through bone. You will need a boning knife, a heavy 8- or 10-inch chef's knife, and poultry shears. When done, you will have eight serving pieces: two breast halves; two thighs; two drumsticks; and two wings.

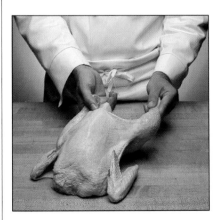

1. *To expose the joint, hold on to the body with one hand and pull the leg away from the body with the other.*

2. *After the joint has been exposed, separate leg from body by cutting through the skin to joint and severing leg at joint. Repeat for other leg.*

3. *Separate thigh and drumstick by cutting into leg at joint with boning knife; sever completely.*

4. *To remove whole breast from rib cage and wings, insert knife or poultry shears at the dividing line between breast and rib cage, beginning at wing joint. Cut along the edge of the rib cage, cutting through the cartilage between wing and breast. Repeat on other side.*

5. *To halve breast, cut through the breastbone with a chef's knife.*

6. *Sever wing from back by cutting through at joint with chef's knife. Reserve back for stock.*

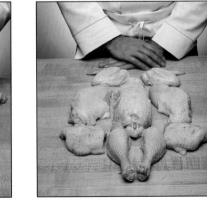

7. *When completed, cut-up chicken consists of two wings, two breast halves, two thighs, two drumsticks, plus the back.*

CHICKEN MOLE IN BURRITOS

An Aztec delicacy, mole (pronounced MOH-lay) is a thick, chocolate sauce often served over chicken or turkey.

    2   teaspoons olive oil
    1   cup chopped onion
    2   cloves garlic, minced
    1   tablespoon roasted carob
        powder or cocoa powder
    1   teaspoon dried oregano
    1/2 teaspoon cinnamon
    1   teaspoon grated fresh ginger
    1   teaspoon chili powder
    1/2 teaspoon ground cloves
    1/4 teaspoon nutmeg
    1/2 teaspoon allspice
    1   teaspoon cumin
    4   cups cooked and shredded
        chicken breast
    1   cup defatted Chicken Stock
        (see page 51)
    1/4 cup tomato paste
    2   tablespoons almonds, ground
        Hot-pepper sauce, to taste
    6   flour tortillas, preferably whole
        wheat
        Nonfat plain yogurt, for
        garnish

1. In a skillet heat oil and sauté onion over medium heat until onion is soft. Add garlic, carob, oregano, cinnamon, ginger, chili powder, cloves, nutmeg, allspice, and cumin and cook over medium heat for 5 minutes, stirring frequently.

2. Add chicken, stock, tomato paste, and almonds, and bring to a boil. Simmer over medium heat, uncovered, for 10 minutes. Add hot-pepper sauce.

3. In a slow oven warm tortillas. Fill each tortilla with ¾ cup of chicken mixture, and roll. Serve with nonfat plain yogurt as garnish.

Serves 6.

Preparation time: 40 minutes
Cooking time: 15 minutes
Per serving: calcium 151 mg, calories 369, carbohydrates 28 g, cholesterol 88 mg, fat 10 g, fiber 3 g, protein 42 g, sodium 530 mg

POULET EN SAC

One of the easiest ways to cook a chicken or turkey is simply to place it in a lightly buttered brown bag. The bird comes out juicy and tender, and baked to a golden brown.

    1   large roasting chicken (4 lb),
        skinned
    1   large onion, quartered
    1   stalk celery, quartered
    1/4 cup chopped celery leaves
    1   yam or sweet potato, quartered
    1   apple (optional)
    1/4 cup white wine
    2   teaspoons dried thyme
    2   crushed bay leaves
    2   teaspoons herbal salt substitute
    1   teaspoon freshly ground black
        pepper
    2   tablespoons butter, softened

1. Preheat oven to 325° F. Place chicken in a deep roasting pan and stuff cavity of chicken with onion, celery, celery leaves, and yam. Place whole apple, if used, in mouth of cavity to seal.

2. Mix wine, thyme, bay leaves, salt substitute, and pepper. Rub on surface of chicken.

3. Butter the inside of a large brown bag (choose a bag without printing). Carefully place the stuffed chicken inside the bag (it should fit loosely) and seal end of bag by rolling tightly. Place bagged, stuffed chicken in roasting pan.

4. Roast chicken until a knife point inserted in the thigh of chicken produces juices that are clear rather than pink (45 minutes to 1 hour). Tear off bag, remove stuffing, place chicken on a platter, and serve, surrounded by cooked vegetables and stuffing.

Serves 8.

Preparation time: 15 minutes
Cooking time: 45 minutes to 1 hour
Per serving: calcium 64 mg, calories 269, carbohydrates 20 g, cholesterol 92 g, fat 7 g, fiber 2 g, protein 29 g, sodium 600 mg

SPICY SALSA CHICKEN

This recipe is great for a picnic lunch, served with Green Gazpacho (see page 63), a crisp salad, and Wine-Basted Pears (see page 203) for dessert. Choose a bottled salsa that suits your taste buds for hotness: It will not lose its spicy flavor during the cooking process.

    4   chicken half-breasts, skinned
    1   cup salsa
    1   tablespoon rice vinegar
    1   tablespoon minced cilantro
        Lemon slices or yellow chiles,
        for garnish

1. Preheat oven to 375° F. Place chicken breasts in a medium-sized baking dish.

2. Mix salsa, vinegar, and cilantro. Spoon over chicken.

3. Bake chicken for 20 to 25 minutes, uncovered. Serve hot or cold, garnished with lemon slices.

Serves 4.

Preparation time: 10 minutes
Cooking time: 20 to 25 minutes
Per serving: calcium 22 mg, calories 152, carbohydrates 2 g, cholesterol 65 mg, fat 4 g, fiber 0 g, protein 26 g, sodium 122 mg

GRILLED CHICKEN IN SWEET MARINADE

A pleasing Asian dish, in which strips of chicken are marinated in a soy-ginger sauce and then grilled lightly with vegetables, this recipe should be prepared right before serving.

> 2 whole chicken breasts, boned and skinned
> 1/3 cup low-sodium soy sauce or tamari
> 2 teaspoons Asian sesame oil
> 2 teaspoons grated fresh ginger
> 2 teaspoons honey
> Juice of 2 limes
> 1/4 teaspoon cayenne pepper
> 2 red bell peppers, seeded and cut into quarters
> 2 green bell peppers, seeded and cut into quarters
> 1 cup pineapple chunks, preferably fresh
> 4 cups cooked brown rice (optional)

1. Cut chicken into long, thin strips. Place the strips in a shallow, non-reactive pan.

2. Mix soy sauce, sesame oil, ginger, honey, lime juice, and cayenne and pour over chicken, tossing well. Let marinate for 2 hours.

3. Preheat broiler. During the last 15 minutes of marinating time, toss in bell peppers and pineapple chunks.

4. While chicken and vegetables are marinating, soak 12 bamboo skewers in a shallow pan of salted water for 15 minutes (2 tablespoons salt to 2 cups water). This will prevent skewers from burning during grilling.

5. Skewer chicken strips, alternating with pineapple and bell peppers. Grill on both sides until browned, basting occasionally with the marinade. Serve over rice, if desired.

Serves 4.

Preparation time: 30 minutes
Marinating time: 2 hours
Cooking time: 15 minutes
Per serving: calcium 43 mg, calories 238, carbohydrates 26 g, cholesterol 65 mg, fat 4 g, fiber 3 g, protein 28 g, sodium 721 mg

Create a fiesta of flavors and colors with this salsa-baked chicken, spiced with chopped cilantro.

A low-fat, flavorful method of baking, parchment cooking seals in moisture yet allows chicken to brown and crisp. This recipe combines breasts of chicken with Chardonnay wine, shallots, tarragon, and ripe tomatoes (see page 160).

1. In a large skillet heat oil; add carrot and stir-fry for 2 minutes over medium-high heat.

2. Add chicken and cook on both sides until lightly browned (about 10 minutes).

3. Add soy sauce, honey, green onion, garlic, ginger, and pepper. Simmer, covered, until chicken is tender. Serve hot.

Serves 4.

Preparation time: 25 minutes
Cooking time: 20 to 25 minutes
Per serving: calcium 22 mg, calories 174, carbohydrates 4 g, cholesterol 84 mg, fat 5 g, fiber 1 g, protein 28 g, sodium 710 mg

GINGER-TAMARI CHICKEN

This slightly spicy marinated chicken is perfect to serve with fresh fruit salad or steamed red potatoes.

  4 *chicken half-breasts, skinned*
  2 *tablespoons minced red onion*
 ¹/₄ *cup low-sodium tamari or soy sauce*
  2 *tablespoons grated fresh ginger*
  2 *teaspoons Asian sesame oil*
 ¹/₄ *cup white wine or dry sherry*
     Pinch dried thyme

1. Place chicken in a deep baking dish. Mix red onion, tamari, ginger, sesame oil, wine, and thyme and pour over chicken. Let marinate, covered with plastic wrap, for 3 hours in the refrigerator. Turn and baste every hour so the meat marinates evenly.

2. Preheat oven to 375° F. Bake chicken in marinade until juices run clear when knife tip is inserted (35 to 40 minutes). Remove from marinade and serve.

Serves 4.

Preparation time: 15 minutes
Marinating time: 3 hours
Baking time: 35 to 40 minutes
Per serving: calcium 18 mg, calories 165, carbohydrates 2 g, cholesterol 65 mg, fat 4 g, fiber 0 g, protein 27 g, sodium 557 mg

KOREAN CHICKEN WITH SOY SAUCE AND GARLIC

An easy-to-prepare picnic recipe, Korean Chicken can become an instant family favorite. Make it ahead and warm it up before serving.

  2 *teaspoons Asian sesame oil*
 ¹/₂ *cup julienned carrot*
  1 *roasting chicken (3 lb), skinned and cut up*
  6 *tablespoons low-sodium soy sauce or tamari*
  2 *teaspoons honey*
  3 *tablespoons minced green onion*
  2 *teaspoons minced garlic*
  1 *teaspoon grated fresh ginger*
 ¹/₄ *teaspoon freshly ground black pepper*

CASHEW CHICKEN

A popular dish served in many Chinese restaurants, this low-fat version can be accompanied by cooked brown rice and eaten with chopsticks.

- 1 teaspoon Asian sesame oil
- 1 tablespoon olive oil
- 1/4 cup dry sherry
- 1 cup sliced green onions (including greens)
- 1 red bell pepper, seeded and julienned
- 1 cup cauliflower florets
- 2 carrots, julienned
- 3 cups cooked chicken breast, sliced into thin strips
- 1 tablespoon arrowroot powder mixed with 3 tablespoons cold water
- 2 tablespoons low-sodium soy sauce or tamari
- 2 tablespoons oyster sauce
- 1 teaspoon honey
- 1/2 cup unsalted whole cashews
- 1 cup trimmed snow peas
- 4 cups cooked brown rice (optional)

1. In a wok or skillet over medium-high heat, combine oils and sherry and stir-fry green onions for 2 minutes. Add bell pepper, cauliflower, and carrots, and continue cooking for 5 minutes, stirring frequently.

2. Add chicken and cook, covered, for 1–2 minutes.

3. Add arrowroot mixture, soy sauce, oyster sauce, and honey. Cook until sauce begins to thicken (about 2 minutes), stirring frequently.

4. Add cashews and snow peas, cover, and let steam until snow peas become bright green (about 1 minute). Serve hot, over rice, if desired.

Serves 6.

Preparation time: 25 minutes
Cooking time: 10 minutes
Per serving: calcium 52 mg, calories 253, carbohydrates 14 g, cholesterol 55 g, fat 10 g, fiber 3 g, protein 26 g, sodium 509 mg

STEP BY STEP

WOK AND STIR-FRY TECHNIQUES

Stir-frying brings out the full flavor of a sauté with less oil than other frying methods. Stir-fry cooking should always be done at medium-high to high heat.

Since the stir-fry process is so quick, it is important to have everything ready before you turn on the heat. When stir-frying you should continually toss the food, using a wooden spoon or spatula to keep the pieces of food moving and prevent burning. Add ingredients according to their cooking times so that they all finish cooking at once. A successful stir-fry has bright color, crisp texture, and just the right seasoning.

1. *Begin by adding the oil in a thin stream around the outside of the wok. Heat the oil until ripples form on the surface. Rotate the wok to distribute the oil evenly over the surface.*

2. *Add the first ingredient. Briskly toss the food in the hot oil until it is well coated. This will preserve the color and texture, as well as help seal in vitamins and minerals as the food cooks.*

3. *Add the next ingredients in the order given in the recipe when the first ingredient looks bright in color (if a vegetable) or slightly opaque (if seafood, chicken, or lean meat).*

4. *If your wok has a long handle, tip the food into the serving platter, scraping the sauce over it with the spatula. If it does not, use a ladle to transfer food to a serving dish.*

BRUNSWICK STEW

Brought to you from a quaint New England tavern, where it is served as a Sunday staple, Brunswick Stew starts with vegetables and a tender roasting chicken and cooks over low heat. Make this recipe ahead and freeze in 1-quart containers for an easy and delicious Sunday dinner for family and friends. Serve with a green salad, crusty rolls, and a light fruit dessert.

- 2 teaspoons olive oil
- 2 large onions, coarsely chopped
- 1 cup dry sherry
- 4 cups stewed tomatoes
- 2 cups frozen or fresh lima beans
- 3 large red potatoes, diced
- 4 cups frozen or fresh corn kernels
- 1 large roasting chicken (4 lb), skinned and cut up
- 2 tablespoons herbal salt substitute
  Freshly ground black pepper, to taste
  Chopped parsley, for garnish (optional)

1. In a large stockpot or Dutch oven, heat oil and slowly sauté onions until soft and lightly browned.

2. Add sherry, tomatoes, lima beans, potatoes, and corn and cook 5 minutes.

3. Add chicken, salt substitute, pepper, and enough water to cover chicken. Bring to a boil.

4. Lower heat and let stew simmer, uncovered, for 45 minutes. Add more water when needed.

5. To serve, ladle chicken pieces into shallow soup bowls, top with vegetables and stock, and garnish with chopped parsley, if desired.

Serves 8.

Preparation time: 15 minutes
Cooking time: 45 minutes
Per serving: calcium 139 mg, calories 485, carbohydrates 64 g, cholesterol 85 mg, fat 6 g, fiber 12 g, protein 41 g, sodium 573 mg

---

CHICKEN BAKED WITH TOMATOES AND HERBS IN PARCHMENT

A version of Poulet en Sac (see page 156), this chicken baked in parchment is tender, moist, and fragrant with the aroma of herbs. Parchment paper is available now in most supermarkets and is a boon to the health-conscious cook because it allows cooking without extra fat. Packets may be assembled the day before, wrapped in plastic, and stored in the refrigerator until baking time.

- 6 whole chicken breasts, boned and skinned
- 3 cups coarsely chopped tomatoes
- 1/4 cup minced shallot
- 1 cup dry white wine, such as a California Chardonnay
- 2 tablespoons minced fresh tarragon
- 2 tablespoons minced parsley

1. Preheat oven to 375° F. Lay out 6 sheets of parchment on table or counter and place one chicken breast in the center of each. Top each breast with 1/2 cup tomatoes and 2 teaspoons minced shallot. Add 2 to 3 tablespoons of white wine to each packet and evenly distribute tarragon and parsley on top of breasts.

2. Fold the parchment packets like envelopes, to seal around chicken and vegetables, making sure that wine does not run out.

3. Place sealed packets on baking sheets and bake for 20 minutes. Serve hot.

Serves 6.

Preparation time: 30 minutes
Cooking time: 20 minutes
Per serving: calcium 72 mg, calories 305, carbohydrates 7 g, cholesterol 130 mg, fat 3 g, fiber 1 g, protein 53 g, sodium 163 mg

---

MALAYSIAN CURRIED CHICKEN SALAD

This refreshing summer salad is easy to prepare, can be made up to 24 hours ahead of time, and is best served at room temperature or slightly chilled. Served after Chilled Curried Zucchini Soup (see page 61), it makes an easy-to-fix entrée for an alfresco summer lunch.

- 2 cooked whole chicken breasts, skinned and diced
- 1/4 cup raisins
- 1/4 cup sliced almonds
- 1/2 cup crushed, drained pineapple
- 1/3 cup reduced-fat mayonnaise
- 2 tablespoons low-sodium soy sauce or tamari
- 1 tablespoon curry powder
- 1 tablespoon lemon juice
- 4 large lettuce leaves, for lining plates

Combine all ingredients. Serve over lettuce leaves.

Serves 4.

Preparation time: 15 minutes
Per serving: calcium 65 mg, calories 241, carbohydrates 16 g, cholesterol 74 mg, fat 7 g, fiber 2 g, protein 29 g, sodium 418 mg

---

FEATURE

ABOUT CHOLESTEROL

Dietary cholesterol is invisible, but it exists in all the animal foods you eat. Although the American Heart Association recommends consuming a maximum of 300 milligrams of cholesterol daily, most people ingest closer to 500 milligrams.

A constant companion to fat, cholesterol is a steroid alcohol that is found in many foods such as cheese, red meats, and eggs. Research shows that the average American diet contains 40 to 45 percent saturated fat compared to the maximum of 30 percent recommended by the American Heart Association. This quantity of fat is difficult for the human body to process and remove. The sad results can be heart disease, obesity, and other health problems related to eating excess fat and cholesterol.

Cholesterol is sometimes labeled as an evil, but humans and animals need a certain amount of cholesterol to live. The body actually produces several different kinds of cholesterol, called lipoproteins, some of which perform important functions. The amount that the body manufactures by itself, however, is usually sufficient.

The three main types of cholesterol are high-density lipoproteins (HDLs), low-density lipoproteins (LDLs), and very low-density lipoproteins (VLDLs). HDLs are considered beneficial since they are responsible for extracting cholesterol from the body cells and transporting it to the liver for processing or removal. LDLs and VLDLs, on the other hand, are responsible for depositing cholesterol on the walls of arteries.

Many studies have shown the connection between diet and levels of harmful blood cholesterols. A person with a diet high in saturated fats and cholesterol often has a higher level of LDLs and VLDLs. When you analyze the results of a blood test to measure cholesterol, you should look not only at the total cholesterol count, but also at the HDL level—in most cases, the higher the HDL count, the better.

Although scientific evidence points to genetic predisposition to cholesterol levels, higher levels of HDLs and lower levels of LDLs are often found in people who exercise regularly, do not smoke, maintain normal weight, and, most important, follow a healthy diet that emphasizes nutritious, low-fat foods.

Desirable total cholesterol levels are counts of 200 milligram percent or below; some authorities prefer a count of 180 milligram percent or lower. Those who maintain low cholesterol levels and have few risk factors (smoking, obesity, diabetes, hypertension, stress, family history of high cholesterol or heart disease) are still advised to monitor their daily intake of fat and cholesterol and measure blood cholesterol levels as recommended by their physician.

High blood cholesterol measurements of 240 and above, or 200 and above for people with risk factors, are considered dangerous. If you fall into either of these categories, you may wish to consult with a physician and adopt a more stringent low-fat, low-cholesterol diet.

If you want to lower dietary cholesterol, but are not sure how to do it, here are some tips.

☐ Make changes gradually. Try decreasing cholesterol intake one meal at a time, perhaps starting with breakfast, which is often the most cholesterol-rich meal of the day. Instead of bacon and eggs, eat a whole-grain cereal topped with low-fat or nonfat milk and fresh fruit. Whereas one large egg contains about 250 milligrams of cholesterol, a serving of whole-grain cereal with 1 cup of whole milk contains only 33 milligrams. Twice a week or more, replace red-meat dinners with fish. A 3-ounce fish fillet has only 33 milligrams of cholesterol, compared to 85 in 3 ounces of beef.

☐ Increase the amount of fresh fruits and vegetables in your diet. Begin to regard meat and dairy products more as a condiment than a centerpiece in your menu planning. Add extra vegetables to stir-fries, chili, and baked pasta dishes, and cut back on such high-cholesterol items as high-fat red meat and Cheddar, American, Swiss, and other high-fat cheeses.

☐ Cut back on egg yolks in baked goods by substituting two egg whites for every other egg yolk called for in recipes for muffins, pancakes, or cakes. Each egg yolk contains 270 milligrams of cholesterol; an egg white contains 4 milligrams.

☐ Use nonfat dairy products. Substitute low-fat or nonfat milk for whole milk and nonfat yogurt for sour cream.

☐ Try whipped milk instead of whipped cream. Chill a can of evaporated nonfat milk in the freezer until icy, then whip with an egg beater to make an excellent substitute for whipped cream.

☐ Sauté with monounsaturated oils, such as olive, sesame, or canola oil, rather than butter, lard, or bacon grease. Monounsaturated oils reduce LDL levels while maintaining beneficial levels of HDL.

☐ Trim off all visible fat from meat before cooking. Select the leanest meat, use a rack to allow fat to drip off during baking or broiling, and baste with wine, stock, or tomato juice instead of drippings.

☐ Be conscious of cholesterol when eating out. Ask for sauces made without cream, and request that butter not be spread on broiled fish or baked potatoes. Avoid high-fat cheeses and salad dressings. Choose fresh fruit desserts or sherbets rather than ice creams and rich pastries.

Menu

DINNER FROM THE FAR EAST

Salad of Sliced Cucumber and Red Onion

Hunan-Style Chicken Stir-Fry With Vegetables

Boiled Chinese Rice Noodles

Steamed Asparagus With Lemon Juice

Poached Peaches in Orange Juice

Sparkling Water or Nonalcoholic White Wine

Entertain in the gracious style of the Far East. Warm sake or plum wine and serve in tiny glasses as an apéritif. Boil Chinese rice noodles, found in most Asian food stores, and then drain and reheat in boiling water for a few seconds before serving. Dress sliced cucumbers and red onions with a dash of rice vinegar and Asian sesame oil. Steam asparagus just before serving. Menu serves six.

HUNAN-STYLE CHICKEN STIR-FRY WITH VEGETABLES

The only unusual ingredients in this spicy chicken dish are Chinese sesame paste, which is similar to Middle Eastern tahini, and Chinese chile paste with garlic. Both can be purchased at Asian markets, but substitutes are also listed below.

- 2 teaspoons Asian sesame oil
- 1/3 cup sliced green onion
- 1/3 cup diagonally sliced carrot
- 1/3 cup sliced red bell pepper
- 1/3 cup broccoli florets
- 1/4 cup dry sherry or rice wine
- 2 cups cooked and shredded chicken breast
- 2 teaspoons minced garlic
- 2 teaspoons Chinese sesame paste or peanut butter
- 1 tablespoon rice vinegar
- 2 tablespoons low-sodium soy sauce or tamari
- 1 teaspoon honey
- 1 tablespoon Chinese chile paste with garlic or 1/4 teaspoon cayenne pepper
- 2 teaspoons grated fresh ginger

1. In a wok or skillet, heat 1 teaspoon of the oil and sauté green onion until soft but not browned. Add carrot, bell pepper, broccoli, and sherry. Cook rapidly over high heat, covered, for 3 minutes.

2. Add chicken, remaining oil, garlic, sesame paste, rice vinegar, soy sauce, honey, chile paste, and ginger. Lower heat and cook, covered, for 5 minutes, stirring frequently. Serve hot.

Serves 6.

Preparation time: 25 minutes
Cooking time: 5 minutes
Per serving: calcium 41, calories 141, carbohydrates 5 g, cholesterol 44 mg, fat 4 g, fiber 1 g, protein 19 g, sodium 220 mg

POACHED PEACHES IN ORANGE JUICE

This simple yet luscious dessert calls for fresh peaches, but you can substitute apples, pears, or the Asian pears that are available in some markets. Left to chill in a simple syrup, the fruit absorbs flavor and remains moist until ready to serve to guests, a suitable ending to an Asian meal. The orange juice sauce has a slight tang of cinnamon that blends well with Chinese cuisine.

- 6 large peaches, slightly underripe
- 6 tablespoons grated orange rind
- 1 tablespoon cinnamon
- 1/4 cup honey
- 2 tablespoons maple syrup
  Juice of 6 oranges

1. Preheat oven to 350° F. With a sharp knife, cut the top off each peach about 1/3 of the way down. Wiggling it slightly with your fingers, remove the pit. Place peaches in a deep baking dish.

2. Mix remaining ingredients and fill the cavity of each peach, then pour the remaining sauce around the peaches as a poaching liquid. Replace peach tops.

3. Bake until peaches are the softness of canned fruit (about 25 minutes). Chill for 1 hour, and serve with extra poaching liquid as a sauce.

Serves 6.

Preparation time: 10 minutes
Cooking time: 25 minutes
Chilling time: 1 hour
Per serving: calcium 60 mg, calories 212, carbohydrates 54 g, cholesterol 0 mg, fat 1 g, fiber 3 g, protein 3 g, sodium 4 mg

This Far Eastern menu features a marinated cucumber salad, stir-fried chicken with Hunan spices, steamed asparagus, and poached whole peaches.

TIPS

...ON PREPARING MEAT AND POULTRY FOR ROASTING

To retain flavor and moistness when roasting or grilling meat, you can follow these easy guidelines:

☐ For poultry, wash and dry the bird thoroughly. Remove any giblets from cavity. For meats, trim excess fat.

☐ Season according to recipe. Be liberal with most seasonings—more flavor is lost in slow-cooking methods than in quick-cooking methods such as frying. Pour in prepared marinade, wine, or citrus juice. Let marinate at room temperature if possible. Baste often during marinating process, and turn meat or poultry every 15 minutes so all sides are covered with the sauce.

☐ Roast in a low (300° F) oven. To retain moisture, wrap meat or poultry in aluminum foil or place in a covered clay pot that has been presoaked in water for 20 minutes. You can also try the en sac technique: Lightly oil the inside of a large unprinted grocery bag and place turkey or chicken inside (if desired, line bottom of bag with aluminum foil or insert a rack to keep bird off bag's surface). Roll end of bag to seal.

☐ Sear thin pieces of beef, veal, or chicken before roasting. In a large, heavy ovenproof pan, quickly sauté the meat or poultry until the surfaces turn slightly opaque. Then add marinade or seasonings, cover, and continue roasting. After the surface of the meat has been sealed, the interior will retain more moisture and stay tender.

LIGHT MEAT ENTRÉES

Decreasing the amount of heavy, fat-laden meats in your diet is part of a healthy approach to eating. This section offers intriguing ways to use cuts of veal, beef, and lamb that are chosen for their lower fat content and good flavor. Selecting lean cuts is easy.

In beef, look for sirloin tip, eye of round, round steak, flank steak, tenderloin, lean stew meat, or lean ground beef. The leanest cuts of lamb are the leg and sirloin chop. Veal is inherently lean, with the exception of the breast. Trim all visible fat from meat before using it. Although fat helps to retain the juiciness of the meat as it cooks, sauces or special cooking techniques are used in these entrées to hold moisture. Broiling and poaching are recommended instead of frying.

Lamb is often a special treat because of its high price, but you can look for the leaner, more inexpensive cuts and tenderize them by marinating before cooking. Ground lamb is also economical. Lamb needs fewer seasonings than beef and is tasty when mixed with mint, garlic, or nutmeg.

STEWED BEEF IN RED WINE

A lighter version of the traditional wine-braised beef dishes from France, this savory entrée keeps well and can be prepared ahead of time and frozen for up to four weeks. Serve with plenty of crusty French bread and a tossed salad.

   2 *pounds beef stew meat, fat trimmed*
1½ *tablespoons olive oil*
 ¼ *cup brandy*
1½ *cups dry red wine*
   1 *cup defatted Beef Stock (see page 51)*
   1 *tablespoon tomato paste*
   2 *cloves garlic, mashed*
 ¼ *teaspoon thyme*
   1 *bay leaf, crushed*
  12 *small white boiling onions*
   1 *cup water*
 ½ *pound mushrooms*
   3 *tablespoons whole wheat flour*
   8 *cups cooked basmati rice*

1. Cut meat into 1-inch cubes. In a large Dutch oven over medium-high heat, sear beef in 1 teaspoon of the oil until lightly browned on all sides. Pour in brandy and ignite, shaking pan until flames subside. Add wine, stock, tomato paste, garlic, thyme, and bay leaf. Bring to a boil, then lower heat to simmer. Cook, uncovered, until tender (about 20 to 30 minutes). Preheat oven to 200° F.

2. Peel onions and cut a small X in the top of each to prevent them from falling apart as they cook. In a small skillet over medium-high heat, sauté onions in 1 teaspoon of the oil. Add the water, cover, and cook for 15 minutes.

3. Drain onions and set aside. In the same pan over medium-high heat, sauté mushrooms in 1 teaspoon oil for 5 minutes. Set aside.

4. Remove beef from sauce and keep warm on a platter in the oven. Bring sauce to a boil and reduce to half its volume by simmering, uncovered, for 10 minutes. Combine remaining olive oil and flour and drop into boiling sauce by spoonfuls, stirring with a whisk until sauce thickens.

5. Return beef to sauce, and add onions and mushrooms. Heat through and serve over rice.

Serves 8.

Preparation time: 30 minutes
Cooking time: 65 minutes
Per serving: calcium 96 mg, calories 1,135, carbohydrates 160 g, cholesterol 113 mg, fat 27 g, fiber 10 g, protein 48 g, sodium 780 mg

---

STIR-FRIED BEEF WITH ASPARAGUS AND SNOW PEAS

Offering a light approach to beef, this Chinese recipe combines thin strips of lean sirloin with a rich-tasting sesame oil sauce, then adds asparagus slices, whole snow peas, and red bell pepper strips for texture and color, as well as nutrition. The sauce keeps the steak from drying out. A healthy and fast entrée for a party, buffet table, or pot-luck, Stir-Fried Beef With Asparagus and Snow Peas can be accompanied by steamed rice and garnished with chopped unsalted peanuts.

- 1 *pound lean sirloin steak, fat trimmed*
- 3 *tablespoons dry sherry*
- 1 *tablespoon Asian sesame oil*
- 1 *tablespoon grated ginger*
- 1 *tablespoon minced garlic*
- 1 *teaspoon olive oil*
- 2 *green onions*
- 3/4 *pound asparagus*
- 1 *cup julienned red bell pepper*
- 2 *tablespoons oyster sauce*
- 2 *tablespoons arrowroot powder*
- 2 *cups trimmed snow peas*

1. Cut steak into thin strips. Place in a large bowl with sherry, sesame oil, ginger, and garlic. Let marinate 15 minutes.

2. Cut green onions into 1/2-inch pieces, and trim asparagus and cut into 1-inch lengths. Heat wok over medium-high heat and add olive oil. Stir-fry green onions, asparagus, and bell pepper for 2 minutes, then remove to a platter and keep warm in oven.

3. Add steak and marinade to wok and stir-fry for 3 minutes. In a small bowl combine oyster sauce and arrowroot. Add to steak and cook for 1 minute. Add vegetable mixture and cook for 1 minute, stirring constantly. Toss in snow peas, cover wok, and cook for 1 minute. Serve immediately.

Serves 6.

Preparation time: 25 minutes
Marinating time: 15 minutes
Cooking time: 10 minutes
Per serving: calcium 83 mg, calories 211, carbohydrates 5 g, cholesterol 46 mg, fat 7 g, fiber 5 g, protein 20 g, sodium 382 mg

Bell peppers, snow peas, and tender asparagus create a vibrant combination in this Chinese beef stir-fry.

BASICS

ABOUT PROTEIN

Protein derives from the Greek word *protos*, meaning *of first importance*. Protein is the foundation of a healthy body, the key component of living tissue. It is the basic building block of cells, antibodies, enzymes, and hormones.

Protein builds new tissues, repairs worn-out body tissue, provides heat and energy, regulates body secretions and the balance of fluids, and produces antibodies to resist disease. Proteins form the structure of the muscles, ligaments, hair, and nails. They are a component of hemoglobin, which moves oxygen through the bloodstream, and of insulin, which regulates blood sugar.

Essentially nitrogen compounds, proteins produce amino acids as they are utilized and broken down by the body. Proteins are composed of 23 amino acids, 8 of which are considered essential. Food is the only source for these essential nutrients since the human body does not manufacture or synthesize them. To ensure intake of proper protein building blocks, the body should receive these eight essential amino acids in certain proportions. A balanced complex of these amino acids occurs in foods with complete proteins. Foods with incomplete protein must be combined with other proteins to complete the arrangement of the eight essential amino acids.

Foods with animal proteins are considered complete proteins since the amino acids are in the required balance. The proteins in plant foods, such as grains, legumes, fruits, and vegetables, are less complete and must be carefully combined to be most useful. Many health professionals recommend eating several types of proteins in one meal, or in the meals consumed in the course of one day, to ensure a good balance and complete the amino acid chain. An example is a peanut butter sandwich on whole wheat bread with a glass of milk—three different sources of protein, that, when combined, offer a more usable protein complex than the peanut butter or bread alone.

The U.S. Recommended Daily Allowance guidelines recommend an average of 44 grams of protein per day (or 6.5 ounces) for women and 56 grams per day (or 8 ounces) for men. That requirement can easily be satisfied with a skinned chicken half-breast chopped into a salad for lunch and a piece of broiled fish for dinner. Remember that protein is also contained in the slice of rye bread you may eat with a salad, the dollop of nonfat yogurt you may mix with breakfast cereal, and even the baked potato accompanying fish. So it is not hard to consume your daily protein requirement with a variety of healthy foods spread over three balanced meals.

Protein sources should be chosen carefully. An excess of animal proteins containing highly saturated fats and cholesterol, such as steak, bacon, cheeses, sausages, and hamburger, can contribute to increased blood cholesterol levels and lead to a higher risk of atherosclerosis and coronary heart disease. Furthermore, excess protein not used by the body can be converted to body fat. Excess protein also puts additional strain on the kidneys, which are responsible for excreting the by-products of protein digestion. High-protein diets in substantial excess of the recommended daily requirements can also contribute to improper absorption of some nutrients, such as calcium.

Most people in the United States eat about twice as much protein as needed for good health. Since the most common protein sources in the American diet are high-fat, high-cholesterol foods, a resulting problem can be weight gain. So the healthy option becomes quality of protein rather than quantity. Don't eat more; just eat better.

EASY BEEF FAJITAS

A Tex-Mex favorite, fajitas are made by combining strips of beef or chicken fried in a skillet with sautéed onions, mushrooms, and chiles, and rolling the mixture into warm flour tortillas (see photo on page 23). This recipe uses lean sirloin steak strips, sautéed quickly in a serrano chile sauce and garnished with nonfat yogurt and slices of avocado.

- *1 cup sliced onions*
- *1 cup sliced mushrooms*
- *1 teaspoon olive oil*
- *1/3 cup dry sherry*
- *1 pound sirloin tips, fat trimmed*
- *2 serrano or jalapeño chiles, seeded and minced*
- *1/2 teaspoon cumin*
- *1/4 teaspoon ground coriander*
- *1 teaspoon minced cilantro*
- *6 large flour tortillas*
- *1/2 cup bottled salsa*
- *1/2 avocado, thinly sliced*
- *1 cup nonfat plain yogurt*

1. In a large skillet over medium-high heat, sauté onions and mushrooms in oil and sherry for 10 minutes. Cut steak into 1½-inch strips and add to sauté, cooking for 2 minutes more. Add chiles, cumin, coriander, and cilantro, and cook 3 more minutes, stirring frequently.

2. Warm tortillas in toaster oven or conventional oven. Arrange bowls of salsa, sliced avocado, and yogurt on a tray. Wrap warmed tortillas in clean cloth napkin. Serve meat filling out of skillet or in prewarmed serving dish. Guests assemble their own fajitas at the table.

Serves 6.

Preparation time: 15 minutes
Cooking time: 15 minutes
Per serving: calcium 144 mg, calories 306, carbohydrates 27 g, cholesterol 46 mg, fat 10 g, fiber 3 g, protein 22 g, sodium 363 mg

MARINATED BEEF KABOBS

Lean chunks of beef are marinated in a tenderizing sauce of ginger, yogurt, and curry, and are then skewered and grilled. You can marinate the beef overnight, in a tightly covered container, and grill right before serving. Serve kabobs with a marinated tomato salad or coleslaw.

- 2 *pounds lean beef, cubed*
- 2 *tablespoons grated fresh ginger*
- 2 *teaspoons herbal salt substitute*
- 1 *teaspoon hot chile oil*
- 2 *teaspoons curry powder*
- 1 *cup nonfat plain yogurt*
- 8 *large cloves garlic, peeled and sliced thinly*
- 4 *cups cooked brown rice (optional)*

1. Preheat broiler. Trim fat off beef cubes and place beef in a shallow bowl.

2. Mix ginger, salt substitute, oil, curry, and yogurt. Pour over beef. Let beef marinate for 24 hours. Stir occasionally.

3. Soak 12 bamboo skewers in salted water for 20 minutes.

4. Skewer beef cubes alternately with slices of garlic, pressing both together as tightly as possible on the skewers.

5. Broil kabobs for 5 minutes, turning to brown all sides. Serve over rice, if desired.

Serves 6.

Preparation time: 15 minutes
Marinating time: 24 hours
Grilling time: 5 minutes
Per serving (not including rice): calcium 115 mg, calories 392, carbohydrates 36 g, cholesterol 88 mg, fat 10 g, fiber 0 g, protein 39 g, sodium 118 mg

For your next grilling party try easy Marinated Beef Kabobs. The marinade combines the Middle Eastern flavors of curry, ginger, garlic, and chile with the tang of yogurt. Pair Marinated Beef Kabobs with grilled summer vegetables such as yellow crookneck squash, ripe tomatoes, and scallions.

THAI BEEF AND CHILES WITH ORANGE

This popular specialty is rich and spicy, so save it for special occasions. Lean ground beef is sautéed with onions, garlic, and spicy chiles, then seasoned with Thai fish sauce (available in Asian markets), cilantro, and delicate palm sugar. (Similar to maple sugar except for the flavor, palm sugar is made from the pulp of the palm tree.) Traditionally served on orange or pineapple slices, in this recipe the mixture is tossed with chopped oranges and served on lettuce leaves.

- ½ cup minced onion
- 1 tablespoon minced garlic
- 1 teaspoon Asian sesame oil
- 1 pound extra lean ground beef
- 3 tablespoons Thai fish sauce
- 2 serrano or jalapeño chiles, seeded and minced
- ¼ cup Thai palm sugar
- ¼ cup chopped cilantro
- ¼ teaspoon cumin
- ⅓ cup finely chopped raw peanuts
- ½ cup peeled, chopped oranges
- 8 large lettuce leaves

1. In a wok or large skillet over medium-high heat, sauté onion and garlic in oil until soft (about 5 minutes). Add beef and continue cooking for 2 minutes.

2. In a small bowl mix together fish sauce, chiles, and palm sugar until smooth. Pour into wok and cook until liquid evaporates (5 to 7 minutes). Stir in cilantro, cumin, and peanuts. Cook 2 more minutes.

3. Remove from heat and stir in oranges. Place a generous helping of beef mixture on each lettuce leaf, roll lightly, and serve immediately.

Serves 4.

Preparation time: 20 minutes
Cooking time: 15 to 20 minutes
Per serving: calcium 81 mg, calories 450, carbohydrates 26 g, cholesterol 80 mg, fat 28 g, fiber 3 g, protein 26 g, sodium 159 mg

EMPRESS CHILI

Empress, or Cincinnati, chili is an elaborate concoction of ground beef and seasonings that has become a tradition in some midwestern cities. Vary the spiciness of the recipe by increasing or decreasing the amounts of chili powder and cumin.

- 2 cups chopped onion
- 2 tablespoons minced garlic
- 1 cup chopped red bell pepper
- ¼ cup dry sherry
- 1 pound extra lean ground beef
- 2 cups water
- 2 tablespoons apple cider vinegar
- 2 teaspoons Worcestershire sauce
- 3 tablespoons chili powder
- 1 tablespoon roasted carob powder
- 2 cups tomato sauce or stewed tomatoes
- 1 teaspoon cumin
- ¼ teaspoon allspice
- 1 teaspoon cinnamon
- ¼ teaspoon cayenne pepper
  Herbal salt substitute (optional)

1. In a large pot over medium heat, sauté onion, garlic, and bell pepper in sherry for 3 minutes.

2. Add remaining ingredients except salt substitute and bring to a boil. Lower heat, cover, and simmer for 1 hour, stirring occasionally.

3. Before serving, taste for seasoning and add salt substitute, if desired.

Serves 6.

Preparation time: 15 minutes
Cooking time: 75 minutes
Per serving: calcium 84 mg, calories 266, carbohydrates 16 g, cholesterol 52 mg, fat 15 g, fiber 4 g, protein 17 g, sodium 807 mg

HUNGARIAN BEEF PAPRIKASH

This simple stew recipe, cooked slowly in a heavy pot or Dutch oven, uses the delicate spices of paprika and caraway. Serve it with crusty French bread or roasted red potatoes, and a marinated cucumber salad.

- 1 pound lean beef, cubed
- 2 tablespoons whole wheat flour
- 2 teaspoons paprika
- 1 teaspoon ground caraway seed
- 1 teaspoon herbal salt substitute
- ½ teaspoon freshly ground black pepper
- 1 teaspoon olive oil
- 1½ cups sliced onion
- 1 cup sliced carrot
- ½ cup chopped red bell pepper
- 2 cloves garlic, minced
- 1 cup sliced button mushrooms
- ½ cup dry white wine
- ½ cup water
- 2 teaspoons tomato paste
- ¼ cup nonfat plain yogurt

1. Trim fat from beef cubes. Combine flour, paprika, caraway, salt substitute, and pepper; dredge beef in seasoned flour.

2. In a deep, heavy pot heat oil and sauté onion, carrot, and bell pepper for 5 minutes over medium heat. Add garlic and mushrooms and continue cooking for 3 minutes. Shake excess flour from beef cubes and add beef to sauté. Cook 5 more minutes.

3. Add wine, water, and tomato paste. Cover pot tightly and cook over low heat for about 1½ hours, stirring occasionally. Stir in yogurt before serving.

Serves 4.

Preparation time: 15 minutes
Cooking time: 2 hours
Per serving: calcium 99 mg, calories 261, carbohydrates 16 g, cholesterol 66 mg, fat 7 g, fiber 4 g, protein 28 g, sodium 396 mg

VEAL AND APPLE SCALOPPINE

This recipe calls for tender scallops of veal. Ask the butcher to prepare the thin slices, then pound them between waxed paper until you can almost see through them. When cooked, they will be butter-soft and easy to cut with a fork. Serve with steamed green beans and red onions, and wild rice.

1 pound veal scallops, thinly sliced
2 green apples
1 tablespoon oil
1/2 cup applejack or Calvados
1/2 cup half-and-half

1. Preheat oven to 350° F. Pound slices of veal between sheets of waxed paper until very thin and tender. Peel, core, and slice apples.

2. Lightly oil a medium-sized baking dish or casserole with some of the oil.

Spread apple slices over bottom of dish. Bake for 20 minutes, uncovered.

3. In a large skillet over medium-high heat, heat remaining oil and lightly brown each piece of veal on both sides. Place veal slices on top of apples in baking dish.

4. Pour applejack into skillet to deglaze pan, allowing brandy to heat and scraping pan as it cooks. Add half-and-half and cook over medium heat for 5 minutes. Pour sauce over veal and apples. Bake veal until bubbling (about 20 minutes). Serve at once.

Serves 6.

Preparation time: 20 minutes
Cooking time: 50 minutes
Per serving: calcium 31 mg, calories 194, carbohydrates 6 g, cholesterol 50 mg, fat 8 g, fiber 10 g, protein 11 g, sodium 52 mg

A satisfying dish from traditional Italian cuisine, Veal and Apple Scaloppine can be a gourmet's delight.

Serve a piquant veal piccata for Sunday dinner; capers and lemon combine in the refreshing sauce. Accompany Veal With Lemon with steamed artichoke hearts and roasted new potatoes.

RAGOUT FIN

In this dish, chopped veal is cooked lightly and then mixed with a mushroom cream sauce.

> 2 pounds veal
> 1 teaspoon herbal salt substitute
> ½ onion, chopped finely
> 1 cup water
> 1 teaspoon olive oil
> 2 cups chopped mushrooms
> 2 teaspoons whole wheat flour
>   Juice of ½ lemon
> 2 teaspoons Worcestershire sauce, or to taste
> 1 egg yolk
> ½ cup fine bread crumbs

1. Preheat broiler. Cut veal into small pieces. Place in saucepan with salt substitute, onion, and the water. Bring to a boil and cook for 8 minutes. Drain veal from broth; reserve broth for later use.

2. In saucepan heat oil and sauté mushrooms over medium heat until they weep moisture. Add flour and cook, stirring, for 2 minutes. Slowly pour in ½ cup of reserved veal broth to thicken sauce. Add veal, lemon juice, and Worcestershire sauce.

3. Stir egg yolk into veal mixture. Spoon veal mixture into a baking dish. Top with bread crumbs.

4. Broil until lightly browned (about 1 minute).

Serves 6.

Preparation time: 15 minutes
Cooking time: 20 minutes
Per serving: calcium 42 mg, calories 221, carbohydrates 11 g, cholesterol 121 mg, fat 9 g, fiber 1 g, protein 23 g, sodium 216 mg

VEAL WITH LEMON

Piccata traditionally refers to something piquant, or slightly tart, such as lemon juice or capers. This is a light adaptation of the traditional Italian recipe of veal piccata. The secret of this recipe is pounding the veal into very thin slices that will melt in your mouth.

- 1 pound veal scallops
- 2 teaspoons olive oil
- 3/4 cup whole wheat flour
- 2 teaspoons herbal salt substitute
- 1 teaspoon white pepper
- 1/2 cup lemon juice, preferably fresh
- 1/3 cup minced parsley
- 2 tablespoons capers
- 2 tablespoons minced dill
- 1/2 lemon, sliced thinly, for garnish

1. Score the top of each veal scallop with a sharp knife. Place each veal scallop between two layers of waxed paper and pound with a meat mallet until very thin and tender.

2. In a skillet heat oil. Mix flour, salt substitute, and pepper on a shallow plate. Dredge veal scallops in flour; then lightly fry them. The thin veal scallops will curl and brown when they are done; do not overcook. Place veal scallops in a warming oven.

3. Add lemon juice, parsley, capers, and dill to the skillet and heat for 1 minute, scraping browned bits off bottom.

4. Pour sauce over veal and serve, garnished with lemon slices.

Serves 4.

Preparation time: 20 minutes
Cooking time: 10 minutes
Per serving: calcium 151 mg, calories 259, carbohydrates 26 g, cholesterol 95 mg, fat 6 g, fiber 1 g, protein 27 g, sodium 160 mg

GREEK-STYLE LAMB MEATBALLS WITH MINT SAUCE

A Greek delicacy, these lamb meatballs are cooked in a light tomato sauce with a hint of fresh mint and served over steamed rice. They go well with a side dish of marinated cucumbers and sliced red onions. These meatballs can be made ahead and frozen, so they are ideal for entertaining.

- 1 cup minced onion
- 2 tablespoons minced shallot
- 1 pound lean ground lamb
- 1 1/4 cups finely ground bread crumbs
- 1/2 teaspoon ground nutmeg
- 2 teaspoons chopped fresh mint leaves
- 1 teaspoon herbal salt substitute
- 1/4 teaspoon white pepper
- 2 cups tomato juice
- 4 cups cooked rice

1. Preheat oven to 350° F. Mix onion, shallot, ground lamb, and breadcrumbs. Form into 20 small balls.

2. Place remaining ingredients except rice in a bowl and mix well.

3. Layer lamb meatballs in a shallow baking dish and pour tomato sauce mixture over them. Bake for 1 hour. Serve hot over rice.

Makes 20 small meatballs, 4 servings.

Preparation time: 40 minutes
Cooking time: 1 hour
Per serving: calcium 111 mg, calories 757, carbohydrates 90 g, cholesterol 88 mg, fat 30 g, fiber 4 g, protein 30 g, sodium 896 mg

GRILLED LAMB AND VEGETABLE MEDLEY

Originating in the Middle East, these marinated shish kabobs will become summer grilling favorites. Spear chunks of seasoned lamb, yellow and red bell peppers, pearl onions, and cherry tomatoes; grill until searing hot; then serve. Accompany this entrée with steamed basmati rice, Balkan Cold Cucumber Salad (see page 68), and crusty bread.

- 1 pound trimmed lamb shanks, cut into 1-inch cubes
- 1/2 teaspoon cayenne pepper
- 1 teaspoon ground coriander
- 1 teaspoon cumin
- 1 tablespoon minced garlic
- 2 tablespoons red wine
- 4 pearl onions
- 1 large red bell pepper
- 1 large yellow bell pepper
- 2 teaspoons olive oil
- 4 large cherry tomatoes
  Oil, for coating grill

1. Place cubes of lamb into a large, shallow pan. Mix together cayenne, coriander, cumin, garlic, and wine, and pour over lamb. Toss well. Cover with plastic wrap and refrigerate for 8 to 10 hours.

2. Peel onions and steam until soft. Seed and quarter bell peppers. Arrange onions, bell peppers, and lamb on shish kabob skewers, leaving room for addition of cherry tomatoes later. Brush skewered items with olive oil.

3. Grill kabobs for 10 minutes, turning once, then add one cherry tomato to each skewer and grill until lightly browned (5 to 10 minutes). Serve hot for best flavor.

Serves 4.

Preparation time: 20 minutes
Marinating time: 8 to 10 hours
Grilling time: 15 to 20 minutes
Per serving: calcium 55 mg, calories 292, carbohydrates 19 g, cholesterol 61 mg, fat 16 g, fiber 4 g, protein 21 g, sodium 271 mg

 # BASICS

SIMPLE LOW-FAT SAUCES FOR POULTRY AND LEAN MEATS

Most sauces traditionally made with butter, cream, or meat fat can be easily converted to low-fat cooking. Wines add rich flavor without the fat of the above bases. You can also use a method called *reduction*—cooking pan juices at high heat to evaporate the excess liquid and concentrate the flavors.

Wine sauces Heat a small amount of oil or butter in a saucepan and add an equal amount of flour. Cook 2 minutes to form a thick paste. Pour in ½ to 1 cup of dry white or red wine, and cook until alcohol has cooked off and sauce is the thickness of heavy cream (about 5 minutes). Add to broiled beef, a chicken stir-fry, or roasted poultry.

Deglazing sauces Deglazing captures the rich flavor of wine and turns it into a sauce without adding fat. Once the poultry or meat is completely cooked, remove it to a platter and keep warm. Add directly to the pan juices in the roasting pan about the same amount of dry wine (use white for poultry- or fish-based sauce, red for beef, veal, or lamb) and bring to a boil. Boil rapidly at high heat until reduced to half of original volume.

En papillote sauces When cooking a piece of poultry or meat in parchment paper *(en papillote)*, you can create a wonderful reduced sauce by using the juices from the cooking packet. Remove the portions of meat from the parchment before serving and place on a platter. Transfer the liquid from the packet to a saucepan and reduce by boiling rapidly for 5 minutes. Serve over the meat or poultry.

TARABA

Taraba is a traditional Mediterranean dish, similar in appearance to dolmas or stuffed grape leaves, except that spinach leaves are used to packet the small spiced balls of ground lamb. The mixture is then cooked in a tomato-lemon sauce. Make sure to choose large spinach leaves, so you can easily wrap the lamb mixture. You can secure with toothpicks, if necessary.

> 2 large bunches spinach, washed and stemmed
> 2 pounds lean ground lamb
> ½ onion, minced
> 2 cloves garlic, minced
>   Herbal salt substitute, to taste
> ¼ teaspoon cayenne pepper, or to taste
> 1 cup tomato sauce
>   Juice of ½ lemon

1. Preheat oven to 350° F. Blanch spinach leaves briefly in boiling water. Drain and set aside.

2. Mix lamb, onion, garlic, salt substitute, and cayenne. Form into 16 small balls.

3. Wrap each lamb ball in a leaf of spinach. Place packets, seam side down, in a shallow baking dish.

4. Cover packets with tomato sauce and sprinkle with lemon juice. Bake until sauce is absorbed and packets are slightly browned (45 minutes to 1 hour).

Makes 16 small packets, 8 servings.

> *Preparation time:* 35 minutes
> *Cooking time:* 45 minutes to 1 hour
> *Per serving:* calcium 29 mg, calories 226, carbohydrates 3 g, cholesterol 55 mg, fat 18 g, fiber .5 g, protein 13 g, sodium 199 mg

 # MENU

HEALTHY THANKSGIVING DINNER

Roast Turkey With Grapes and Prunes

Miso Gravy

Cream Cheese and Garlic Dip with Pita Toasts (see page 26)

Fresh Cranberry-Orange Relish

Wild Rice Pilaf

Steamed Vegetable Medley

Gingered Sweet Potato Purée in Orange Baskets

Apple-Cranberry Gem Tarts (see page 220)

Nonalcoholic Wine and Sparkling Water

The turkey in this menu is filled with a delicious stuffing combining grapes, prunes, and corn bread and is cooked en sac, so that it retains moisture. For your steamed vegetable medley, try broccoli, kale, julienned red bell pepper, and yellow squash. Served for dessert, the Apple-Cranberry Gem Tarts are a perfect ending to a healthy Thanksgiving meal. Menu serves twelve.

ROAST TURKEY WITH GRAPES AND PRUNES

In traditional French cooking, poultry is sometimes roasted inside a paper bag that has been lightly oiled (see Note). The bag holds in the moisture during the cooking process, the result is tender and juicy, and cleanup is easier—you just throw the bag away.

    Oil, for coating paper bag
1   turkey (about 10 lb)
6   cups dry corn bread, crumbled
2   teaspoons thyme
2   teaspoons sage
2   teaspoons minced parsley
1/4 cup port wine
1/2 cup pitted, chopped prunes
1/2 cup green seedless grapes
1   cup diced apples
1   cup minced onion
2   teaspoons olive oil
3   tablespoons unsalted butter

1. Preheat oven to 350° F. Lightly oil inside of a large, unprinted paper grocery bag. Wash and pat turkey dry.

2. In a large bowl mix corn bread crumbs with thyme, sage, and parsley. Set aside.

3. In a saucepan over medium heat, simmer port, prunes, grapes, and apples for 15 minutes. In a skillet over medium-high heat, sauté onion in oil until soft but not browned (8 to 10 minutes). Add fruit mixture and sautéed onion to bread crumbs and mix well.

4. Stuff cavity of turkey with bread stuffing. Lace opening shut with kitchen twine. Dot exterior of turkey with small pieces of butter. Place turkey inside prepared sack, roll opening of sack to seal tightly, and place sack in a large roasting pan. Place in oven and roast for 2½ to 3 hours. During the last 30 minutes, tear away top of bag to let exterior brown. To test for doneness, pierce a leg with the tip of a sharp knife.

The juice should spurt out a clear yellow; if it is pink, roast the bird for 10 to 15 minutes longer.

Serves 12.

Note If you are concerned about chemicals in the paper of the bag, you may want to line the bottom of the bag with aluminum foil or a rack.

Preparation time: 30 minutes
Roasting time: 3 hours, or according to poundage of turkey
Per serving: calcium 150 mg, calories 881, carbohydrates 65 g, cholesterol 302 mg, fat 37 g, fiber 4 g, protein 67 g, sodium 796 mg

MISO GRAVY

A lighter version of traditional gravy, this version is flavored with miso. Make the gravy ahead of time through step 3, if you wish, and add the pan drippings during the last 30 minutes of cooking the turkey.

1/2 teaspoon finely minced garlic
2   teaspoons sesame oil or unsalted butter
1/4 cup port wine
2   tablespoons whole wheat flour
2   cups nonfat milk
1/2 teaspoon dry mustard
1/4 cup grated low-fat cheese, such as mozzarella
3   tablespoons light miso
1/3 cup pan drippings from roasting turkey

1. In a medium saucepan over medium-high heat, sauté garlic in oil and port for 2 minutes. Add flour and cook for 2 more minutes.

2. Slowly pour in milk, whisking constantly. Sauce should thicken slightly. Continue to cook, whisking, until it becomes the consistency of whipping cream.

3. Add mustard and cheese. Mix miso with 3 tablespoons of hot water; stir until smooth and add to sauce. Remove saucepan from heat.

4. Stir in pan drippings. Serve hot.

Makes 3 cups, 12 servings.

Preparation time: 20 minutes
Cooking time: 5 to 10 minutes
Per serving: calcium 72 mg, calories 50, carbohydrates 5 g, cholesterol 2 mg, fat 2 g, fiber .4 g, protein 3 g, sodium 212 mg

FRESH CRANBERRY-ORANGE RELISH

The tartness of the cranberries in this sauce combines well with the sweet flavor of the oranges. Directions are given in the variation for creating a cranberry mold.

4   cups fresh cranberries
4   large oranges, peeled and chopped
2   tablespoons honey

Place cranberries, oranges, and honey in a food mill or grinder, and grind until pulpy but not puréed. Chill and serve.

Makes approximately 6 cups.

Variation If molded cranberry sauce is desired, add 1 package gelatin to sauce and place in a small pan. Bring to a boil over medium-high heat and simmer 5 minutes. Pour into a lightly oiled decorative mold and refrigerate until set (3 to 4 hours). To unmold, dip decorative mold in hot water then invert it over a platter.

Makes 7 cups.

Preparation time: 5 minutes
Cooking and chilling time (optional): 3 to 4 hours
Per serving: calcium 33 mg, calories 44, carbohydrates 14 g, cholesterol 0 mg, fat .2 g, fiber 3 g, protein .7 g, sodium 1 mg

WILD RICE PILAF

Accompany the turkey stuffing with a serving of Wild Rice Pilaf, topped with toasted pine nuts and raisins. Orzo, an Italian pasta, is cooked with the rice for added flavor.

- 5 cups uncooked wild rice
- 5 cups boiling water
- 1 cup chopped onion
- 2 teaspoons olive oil
- 3/4 cup orzo
- 5 cups defatted Chicken Stock (see page 51)
- 1/2 cup toasted pine nuts
- 1/2 cup raisins
  Herbal salt substitute, to taste

1. Place rice in a large bowl and cover with the boiling water. Let stand for 10 minutes.

2. In a large, heavy pot over medium-high heat, sauté onion in olive oil until soft but not browned (about 5 minutes). Add orzo and continue to cook for 2 minutes.

3. Drain rice from soaking water. Add rice to sautéed onion and orzo and stir constantly until rice sizzles (about 10 minutes).

4. Pour in stock. Bring to a boil, then lower heat to medium and simmer, covered, until liquid is absorbed (about 45 minutes).

5. Add toasted pine nuts, raisins, and salt substitute, to taste. Remove from heat, cover, and let stand until raisins soften (about 5 minutes). Serve hot.

Serves 12.

Preparation time: 20 minutes
Cooking time: 65 minutes
Per serving: calcium 32 mg, calories 335, carbohydrates 60 g, cholesterol 0 mg, fat 6 g, fiber 5 g, protein 15 g, sodium 382 mg

GINGERED SWEET POTATO PURÉE IN ORANGE BASKETS

The piquant flavor of the orange peel cooks into the sweet potatoes as they bake. Serve one stuffed orange-peel basket per person.

- 6 medium oranges
- 4 large sweet potatoes
- 1 egg
- 1/2 teaspoon powdered ginger
- 1/2 teaspoon cinnamon
- 1/2 teaspoon nutmeg
- 1 teaspoon grated lemon peel
- 2 tablespoons chopped walnuts

1. Preheat oven to 350° F. Halve oranges and scoop pulp into a bowl. Reserve pulp for another use (such as Fresh Cranberry-Orange Relish, see page 173).

2. Peel and slice sweet potatoes. Steam until soft (about 15 minutes). Mash in a large bowl with egg, ginger, cinnamon, nutmeg, and lemon peel.

3. Spoon purée into orange baskets, dividing equally. Set on a large baking sheet and sprinkle with chopped walnuts. Bake for 25 minutes.

Serves 12.

Note To save time, assemble this side dish in advance and freeze before baking. There is no need to thaw the purée before baking; just add 15 minutes to baking time.

Preparation time: 30 minutes
Baking time: 25 minutes
Per serving: calcium 60 mg, calories 87, carbohydrates 21 g, cholesterol 18 mg, fat 2 g, fiber 3 g, protein 2 g, sodium 12 mg

Slow-roasted turkey stuffed with grapes and prunes, Miso Gravy, Wild Rice Pilaf, and spicy puréed sweet potatoes highlight this healthy Thanksgiving menu.

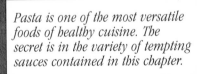

Pasta is one of the most versatile foods of healthy cuisine. The secret is in the variety of tempting sauces contained in this chapter.

PASTA, PIZZA, & BREADS

Offering an abundance of complex carbohydrates and other nutritional benefits as well as gourmet appeal, homemade pasta, pizza, and whole grain breads have earned a prominent place in the streamlined approach to healthy cooking. Recipes such as Fettuccine Alfredo With Zucchini and Ricotta (see page 183), Roasted New-Potato Pizza With Pesto (see page 190), and Orange-Date Muffins (see page 197) rely on carefully selected ingredients that provide satisfying flavor and plenty of nutrients.

Curly spinach spirals are tossed with sweet red pepper strips, whole snow peas, and a light sesame-lemon dressing. Serve Chinese Pasta Salad with steamed Chinese vegetables, such as bok choy or Chinese cabbage, and fruit.

PASTA SALADS

In Italy pasta has long been served at various temperatures, but American epicures have just recently discovered cold pasta salads. What a great way to use up leftover noodles: Simply mix with vegetables, seafood, and a light vinaigrette dressing, and a meal is born. Pasta salads, covered with plastic wrap, usually keep for up to three days.

CHINESE PASTA SALAD

This light and exotic pasta salad is a cinch to make, and it will keep, well covered, for about two days in the refrigerator.

- 4 cups cooked spiral pasta (whole wheat or spinach)
- 1 cup trimmed snow peas
- 2 small red bell peppers, seeded and julienned
- 1 teaspoon sesame seed
- 1/2 teaspoon cayenne pepper, or more to taste
- 1/4 cup low-sodium soy sauce or tamari
- 3 tablespoons Asian sesame oil
- 3 tablespoons lemon juice
- 2 tablespoons grated onion
- 2 tablespoons minced garlic
  Dash each dill and freshly ground black pepper
  Lettuce leaves, for lining bowl

Combine all ingredients, except lettuce leaves. Let chill for 30 minutes, then serve on lettuce leaves in a bowl.

Serves 4.

Preparation time: 15 minutes
Chilling time: 30 minutes
Per serving: calcium 44 mg, calories 337, carbohydrates 49 g, cholesterol 0 mg, fat 12 g, fiber 4 g, protein 10 g, sodium 594 mg

FETA SALAD WITH SPIRAL PASTA

This pasta version of traditional Greek salad is made with feta cheese, tomatoes, and cucumber, dressed with a light vinaigrette.

- 4 cups cooked spiral pasta
- 1 cup crumbled feta cheese
- 1/4 cup olive oil
- 1 cup peeled and sliced cucumber
- 2 large tomatoes, peeled, seeded, and sliced into strips
- 1/4 cup pitted Greek olives
- 1 tablespoon dried oregano
  Herbal salt substitute and freshly ground black pepper, to taste

Combine all ingredients. Let chill for 30 minutes before serving.

Serves 6.

Preparation time: 20 minutes
Chilling time: 30 minutes
Per serving: calcium 120 mg, calories 288, carbohydrates 30 g, cholesterol 17 mg, fat 16 g, fiber 2 g, protein 8 g, sodium 359 mg

MIDDLE EASTERN PASTA SALAD WITH CHICK-PEAS

This simple salad combines the nutty texture of chick-peas (also known as garbanzo beans and used throughout the Middle East for their exceptional flavor and protein content) with cooked macaroni in a light vinaigrette. For a quick lunch, drain some of the vinaigrette and stuff the remaining ingredients with lettuce into pita (pocket) bread.

  1½ *cups cooked chick-peas*
   2 *cups cooked macaroni, drained and chilled*
  ¾ *cup apple cider vinegar*
   3 *tablespoons olive oil*
  ⅓ *cup minced parsley*
  ⅓ *cup diced red bell pepper*
  ¼ *cup minced fresh dill*
     Dash cumin
     Herbal salt substitute and pepper, to taste
     Lettuce, for lining plates or for pocket bread sandwich

Combine all ingredients and chill 2 hours, stirring thoroughly each hour. Serve chilled on a bed of lettuce.

Serves 6.

Preparation time: 20 minutes
Chilling time: 2 hours
Per serving: calcium 112 mg, calories 213, carbohydrates 30 g, cholesterol 0 mg, fat 8 g, fiber 1 g, protein 7 g, sodium 23 mg

MARINATED MUSHROOM SALAD WITH SHELLS

Here's a simple way to make your own marinated mushrooms and avoid the costly ones sold at the store. In this recipe the mushrooms are tossed with attractively sliced vegetables and a light vermicelli pasta.

   2 *cups halved button mushrooms*
  ½ *cup trimmed snow peas*
  ½ *cup seeded and julienned red bell pepper*
   2 *tablespoons drained capers*
   1 *cup cooked vermicelli, cut into 6-inch lengths*
   2 *teaspoons olive oil*
   2 *tablespoons red wine vinegar*
   1 *tablespoon lemon juice*
   1 *tablespoon herbal salt substitute*
   1 *tablespoon Burgundy wine*
   2 *teaspoons honey*
     Dash freshly ground black pepper
   1 *teaspoon dill*

1. In a large salad bowl, combine mushrooms, snow peas, bell pepper, capers, and pasta. Toss well.

2. In another bowl mix oil, vinegar, lemon juice, salt substitute, Burgundy, honey, pepper, and dill. Taste for seasoning. Pour over pasta mixture and mix well.

3. Let chill for 2 hours before serving.

Serves 4.

Preparation time: 20 minutes
Chilling time: 2 hours
Per serving: calcium 44 mg, calories 106, carbohydrates 18 g, cholesterol 0 mg, fat 3 g, fiber 2 g, protein 3 g, sodium 234 mg

TIPS

…ON COOKING PASTA

☐ Both fresh and dried pasta require a large amount of boiling water, about 1 quart to every 2 cups of pasta you are cooking. Salting the water helps it boil faster and adds a little flavor to the pasta, but it is not essential if your diet avoids salt. Adding a small amount of oil to the boiling water helps the pasta strands stay separate, but it is unnecessary if you are diligent about stirring the pasta every few minutes.

☐ The trick to successful pasta is the cooking time, which differs considerably between fresh and packaged types. Once the water has boiled, cook dried fettuccine and other wide noodles for 7 to 8 minutes, lasagne for 8 to 10 minutes, and fine pasta (such as angel hair) for 5 to 7 minutes, or until al dente. Fresh pasta cooks for only two minutes.

☐ If you're serving immediately, you can drain the freshly cooked pasta and toss it with the sauce or vegetables right away.

☐ If you're not serving for 10 minutes or more, it is advisable to rinse the pasta after cooking. (Pasta continues cooking even after it's out of the pot; unless it's rinsed, it can be surprisingly overcooked by the time you serve it.) Keep the pot of boiling water hot, remove pasta from water using tongs or pasta fork, and refresh it quickly under cold tap water. When it is time to serve, dip the pasta back into the heated water, drain again, and voilà: perfectly cooked pasta every time.

Serve this hearty spinach lasagne with a crisp, green salad and warm French bread for an easy supper. The rich tomato sauce is flavored with wine and herbs.

LASAGNE AND BAKED PASTA

The following recipes are for hearty eaters. Most fit well into make-ahead menus and are perfect for Sunday night supper with the family.

LOW-FAT SPINACH LASAGNE

Because this recipe takes a while to prepare, you may want to make a double batch and freeze half.

> 2 cups each sliced onions and sliced mushrooms
> 1 cup white wine
> 2 cups chopped spinach leaves
> 1 tablespoon herbal salt substitute
> 1 cup crumbled firm tofu
> 1 cup farmer cheese or low-fat ricotta cheese
> Oil, for coating baking dish
> 1 package (16 oz) spinach lasagne noodles, cooked and drained
> 2 tablespoons Parmesan cheese mixed with $^1/_4$ cup bread crumbs

Lasagne Tomato Sauce

> $^1/_2$ cup white wine
> 1 small onion, chopped finely
> $^1/_2$ cup sliced mushrooms
> 2 cloves garlic, minced
> $^1/_2$ cup chopped carrots
> $^1/_2$ cup chopped celery
> $^1/_8$ teaspoon ground nutmeg
> 3 cups plum tomatoes (canned or fresh), chopped
> 1 teaspoon dried basil
> $^1/_2$ teaspoon dried oregano

1. Prepare Lasagne Tomato Sauce. While sauce is cooking, sauté onions and mushrooms in white wine over medium heat until soft (about 10 minutes). Add spinach leaves and salt substitute and cook, covered, for 1 minute.

2. Remove from heat and mix with tofu and farmer cheese. Set aside.

3. Preheat oven to 375° F. Lightly oil a 9- by 12-inch baking dish.

4. Assemble lasagne by layering spinach filling, sauce, and noodles. Repeat twice, using all ingredients and ending with noodles on top.

5. Sprinkle lasagne with the Parmesan-bread crumb mixture. Bake lasagne for 30 minutes.

Serves 6 to 8.

Lasagne Tomato Sauce

1. In a medium saucepan heat wine; add onion, mushrooms, garlic, carrots, and celery. Sauté over medium-high heat for 15 minutes. Add nutmeg, tomatoes, basil, and oregano. Cover and cook over medium heat for 30 minutes, stirring frequently.

2. Purée sauce in blender. Set aside.

Preparation time: 45 minutes
Cooking time: 85 minutes
Per serving: calcium 238 mg, calories 386, carbohydrates 57 g, cholesterol 10 mg, fat 7 g, fiber 5 g, protein 18 g, sodium 341 mg

RAISIN AND APPLE KUGEL

Kugel is a dish of German and Austrian origin, a sweet noodle and cheese mixture that is baked to a crisp crust. This fruit-flavored version has apples and raisins studding the layers of noodles and cheese. It can be made up to three days ahead, and keeps, covered, in the refrigerator, but does not freeze well.

> *Oil, for baking dish*
> 2 *teaspoons melted butter*
> 2 *tablespoons honey*
> 2 *tablespoons Neufchâtel cheese*
> 1 *cup low-fat cottage cheese*
> 1 *cup nonfat plain yogurt*
> 2 *tablespoons cinnamon*
> 1 *teaspoon herbal salt substitute*
> 2 *egg whites, beaten*
> 2 *whole eggs, beaten*
> ½ *cup raisins*
> 3 *sweet apples, cored and thinly sliced*
> ½ *package (8 oz) egg or whole wheat lasagne noodles, cooked and drained*
> ⅓ *cup nonfat milk*

1. Preheat oven to 400° F. Lightly oil a 9- by 12-inch baking dish.

2. In a mixing bowl combine butter, honey, Neufchâtel, cottage cheese, yogurt, cinnamon, salt substitute, egg whites, and whole eggs. In another bowl combine raisins and apples.

3. Layer kugel by alternating cheese mixture, noodles, and fruit mixture, ending with noodles. Pour milk over the top.

4. Bake for 40 minutes, then let cool and slice into squares.

Serves 8.

Preparation time: 20 minutes
Baking time: 40 minutes
Per serving: calcium 136 mg, calories 267, carbohydrates 45 g, cholesterol 86 mg, fat 5 g, fiber 4 g, protein 13 g, sodium 196 mg

---

GREEN AND WHITE LASAGNE

The name of this lasagne derives from the alternating layers of spinach and white cheeses. An herbed tomato sauce is added before baking, but the lasagne can be assembled without the sauce, covered, and refrigerated for up to 48 hours, and then topped with the sauce before baking. It also freezes well.

> 1 *teaspoon olive oil, plus oil for coating baking dish*
> 1 *cup each chopped onions and chopped mushrooms*
> 2 *tablespoons minced almonds*
> 4 *cups (packed) spinach leaves*
> 2 *cups low-fat ricotta cheese*
> 4 *green onions, minced*
> ¼ *cup minced parsley*
> 3 *tablespoons minced fresh basil*
> 2 *tablespoons grated Parmesan cheese*
> 1 *package (16 oz) spinach lasagne noodles, cooked and drained*

Herb-Tomato Sauce

> 1 *teaspoon olive oil*
> ⅓ *cup white wine*
> 3 *tablespoons chopped fresh basil*
> ½ *teaspoon dried thyme*
> ¼ *teaspoon dried oregano*
> 2 *tablespoons whole wheat flour*
> 2 *cups nonfat milk*
> 1 *cup chopped fresh tomatoes*
> ⅛ *teaspoon nutmeg*

1. Prepare Herb-Tomato Sauce. In clean skillet heat oil and sauté onions until soft but not browned. Add mushrooms and almonds and continue to cook until mushrooms weep moisture. Add spinach leaves, cover, and steam (using moisture in pan) over medium heat for 3 minutes. Remove from heat and set aside.

2. Preheat oven to 375° F. Mix together ricotta, green onions, parsley, basil, and Parmesan. Set aside. Lightly oil a 9- by 12-inch baking dish.

3. Purée the sauce in a blender. Assemble lasagne by alternating layers of spinach sauté, noodles, and cheese mixture, ending up with noodles on top. Pour the sauce over all. Bake lasagne until bubbly and lightly browned (about 45 minutes).

Serves 8.

Herb-Tomato Sauce

1. In a medium skillet heat olive oil and white wine; add basil, thyme, and oregano and cook for 1 minute at medium heat. Stir in flour and cook 2 minutes over low heat, stirring frequently. Slowly add milk and cook sauce to the thickness of heavy cream.

2. Add tomatoes and nutmeg. Cover and continue to cook over low heat for 20 minutes, while preparing lasagne filling.

Preparation time: 40 minutes
Cooking time: 60 minutes
Per serving: calcium 403 mg, calories 411, carbohydrates 60 g, cholesterol 21 mg, fat 10 g, fiber 5 g, protein 21 g, sodium 256 mg

---

BAKED NOODLE RING

This rich-tasting dish substitutes nonfat yogurt and vegetables for the heavy cream and cheese traditionally used.

 1/4 pound large, flat noodles
     Oil, for coating pan
   2 teaspoons unsalted butter
 1/4 cup minced green onion
 1/4 cup minced red bell pepper
 1/2 cup thinly sliced mushrooms
   2 teaspoons whole wheat flour
 1/2 teaspoon herbal salt substitute
 1/2 cup nonfat milk
 1/4 cup nonfat plain yogurt
     Dash of freshly ground black pepper
   2 egg whites
   2 whole eggs
 1/4 cup finely chopped parsley

1. In a large pot over high heat, bring to a boil 2 quarts of water. Cook noodles until barely tender (about 5 minutes). Drain and refresh under cold water, then set aside.

2. Preheat oven to 350° F. Lightly oil an 8-inch ring mold or baking pan.

3. In a large skillet over medium-high heat, heat butter and sauté green onion, bell pepper, and mushrooms for 5 minutes. Add flour and salt substitute and cook, stirring, for 2 minutes. Pour in milk and cook, stirring frequently, until thick (about 8 minutes). Stir in yogurt and pepper and remove from heat.

4. Separate eggs. In a small bowl combine all egg whites and beat until stiff. In a separate bowl beat egg yolks until foamy, then add to sautéed vegetables. Add drained noodles and fold in egg whites, then parsley. Pour mixture into prepared pan.

5. Bake until set (about 30 minutes). Unmold and serve hot.

Serves 6.

Preparation time: 30 minutes
Cooking time: 50 minutes
Per serving: calcium 102 mg, calories 140, carbohydrates 18 g, cholesterol 93 mg, fat 4 g, fiber 1 g, protein 8 g, sodium 74 mg

---

LIGHT AND EASY PASTA DISHES

From a simple fettuccine Alfredo, to a rich basil tomato sauce, to an exotic chilled pasta primavera, the following dishes are easy to prepare and are winners with family and guests.

SAFFRON ORZO WITH VEGETABLES

Orzo is a tiny Italian pasta that resembles long-grain rice. In this recipe it is cooked in a saffron sauce that gives it a rich yellow color and a nutty flavor. An assortment of fresh vegetables is lightly sautéed, then tossed with the orzo for an appealing side dish to a fish dinner. Try it with Sole aux Amandes (see page 127).

 1 1/2 cups orzo
   1/6 gram (1/8 teaspoon) saffron threads
     2 tablespoons chopped chives
     2 teaspoons unsalted butter or olive oil
   1/4 cup minced green onion
   1/4 cup minced red bell pepper
   1/2 cup thinly sliced mushrooms
   1/4 cup thinly sliced yellow summer squash
     1 teaspoon herbal salt substitute
   1/4 teaspoon dried thyme

1. In a large pot over high heat, bring to a boil 1 quart of water and cook orzo until tender (10 minutes). Drain and set aside.

2. In a large skillet over medium-high heat, sauté saffron and chives in butter for 1 minute, then add green onion, bell pepper, mushrooms, and squash, and sauté for 10 minutes. Add salt substitute and thyme.

3. Stir cooked orzo into vegetable mixture; reheat briefly and serve.

Serves 4.

Preparation time: 25 minutes
Cooking time: 25 minutes
Per serving: calcium 24 mg, calories 143, carbohydrates 25 g, cholesterol 5 mg, fat 3 g, fiber 1 g, protein 5 g, sodium 4 mg

---

PASTA PRIMAVERA WITH MUSTARD SAUCE

This springtime pasta recipe is best made with a sweet mustard rather than a wine-flavored Dijon. Make this recipe right before serving for best flavor; it doesn't freeze well.

 1/2 cup chopped, peeled prawns
   2 teaspoons olive oil
   1 large onion, chopped
   4 cloves garlic, minced
   1 red bell pepper, seeded and coarsely chopped
   1 small zucchini, sliced into thin rounds
   1 cup fresh peas
   1 teaspoon chopped fresh basil
   1 teaspoon chopped chives
   1 cup nonfat plain yogurt
   1 teaspoon honey
 1/3 cup sweet mustard
   1 pound bow-tie pasta
     Freshly ground black pepper, to taste

1. In a large skillet sauté prawns in olive oil until they turn bright pink (about 1 minute). Remove from skillet and set aside.

2. In the same pan sauté onion until soft, adding a little water if the pan gets too dry. Add garlic, bell pepper, and zucchini. Cook for 5 more minutes.

3. Add peas, basil, and chives. Cook until peas turn bright green. Remove from heat and mix with prawns. Stir in yogurt, honey, and mustard and mix well.

4. Cook pasta in boiling water until tender (about 8 minutes). Drain and toss with sauce. Season with black pepper.

Serves 6.

Preparation time: 25 minutes
Cooking time: 20 minutes
Per serving: calcium 130 mg, calories 371, carbohydrates 68 g, cholesterol 13 mg, fat 4 g, fiber 4 g, protein 16 g, sodium 308 mg

---

CHUNKY TOMATO SAUCE WITH FRESH BASIL

This sauce tastes as if it's been cooking for hours when actually it's been on the stove for only 30 minutes. The secret is in the presoaking of the dried herbs. The herbs in this recipe are steeped in room-temperature wine in order to release the flavors without lengthy cooking. This sauce can easily be doubled or tripled, freezes well, and makes a great gift.

> 2 tablespoons chopped fresh basil
> 1 tablespoon dried oregano
> 1/2 cup dry sherry
> 1 teaspoon olive oil
> 1/2 cup white wine
> 1 small onion, finely chopped
> 2 large red bell peppers, seeded and chopped
> 2 cups chopped mushrooms
> 4 large, very ripe tomatoes, coarsely chopped
> 3 large cloves garlic, minced
> 1/4 cup tomato paste

1. In a small bowl place basil, oregano, and sherry and let steep for 15 minutes at room temperature.

2. In a medium saucepan over medium-high heat, combine olive oil and white wine. Add onion and cook slowly until soft but not browned. Add bell peppers and cook for 5 minutes.

3. Add mushrooms and continue cooking, stirring frequently, until they weep moisture. Add tomatoes, garlic, and tomato paste; cook for 10 minutes more.

4. Pour sherry and herb mixture into sauce and bring to a boil. Lower heat to medium-high and simmer sauce for 10 minutes. Serve hot over pasta.

Makes approximately 3 cups.

Preparation time: 20 minutes
Cooking time: 30 minutes
Per serving: calcium 84 mg, calories 183, carbohydrates 23 g, cholesterol 0 mg, fat 3 g, fiber 5 g, protein 5 g, sodium 220 mg

FETTUCCINE ALFREDO WITH ZUCCHINI AND RICOTTA

Alfredo sauces made the traditional way often contain up to one cup of cream per serving. They usually also contain an equal amount of grated Parmesan. This one, however, makes use of low-fat ricotta and adds grated, sautéed vegetables for more flavor and less fat. This Fettuccine Alfredo variation keeps well and can be reheated, but should not be frozen.

> 2 teaspoons olive oil
> 1/4 cup dry sherry
> 1 cup sliced onion
> 1 1/2 packed cups grated zucchini
> 4 cloves garlic, minced
> 1/2 cup nonfat milk
> 2 tablespoons grated Parmesan cheese
> 1 1/2 cups low-fat ricotta cheese
> 4 cups cooked fettuccine

1. In a skillet heat oil and sherry and sauté onion until soft but not browned. Add zucchini and garlic and cook for 5 minutes.

2. Combine milk and cheeses. Add to sauté and cook at medium heat until thick (about 10 minutes). Toss with cooked pasta and serve hot.

Serves 6.

Note Ricotta, a cow's milk cheese, is mild, creamy, and moist, and should be used when very fresh. Traditionally, it is an important ingredient in many Italian dishes, from lasagne and cannelloni to cheesecake.

Preparation time: 15 minutes
Cooking time: 20 minutes
Per serving: calcium 243 mg, calories 269, carbohydrates 34 g, cholesterol 21 mg, fat 8 g, fiber 2 g, protein 14 g, sodium 220 mg

NOTE

FRESH AND DRIED PASTAS

There's a noticeable difference between fresh and dried pasta. Fresh pasta has a melt-in-your-mouth texture and flavor, and is sought after by gourmet cooks. Supermarkets offer a wide variety of packaged fresh pastas—from bright green spinach fettuccine to pale artichoke spaghetti. Flavored pastas are made by adding a small amount of fresh or dried vegetables, herbs, or seasonings to the dough while the dough is being mixed.

Try combining different types of pasta in one dish. For example, a quick sauté of bright vegetables—such as red and green bell peppers, yellow summer squash, white onion, and fresh shiitake mushrooms—can be paired with cooked artichoke and spinach noodles and garnished with chopped cilantro and parsley for a quick yet vivid dish.

You can experiment with different shapes and sizes of pasta, which are usually available in gourmet shops. For example, stuff manicotti (thick, hollow tube noodles) with any of the lasagne fillings found on pages 180 and 181. Or try large pasta shells packed with minced sautéed vegetables and covered with Chunky Tomato Sauce With Fresh Basil. Both recipes can be baked at 350° F for 25 minutes. These dried hollow pasta shapes can be used right out of the package if you are baking them later with a sauce (as for the above stuffed shells); they will soften in the oven. Otherwise, cook dried pasta until al dente (8 to 10 minutes) or until soft but still holding a shape.

FEATURE

HOW TO MAKE YOUR OWN PASTA

Making your own fresh pasta is easier than you think. With only a bowl, a fork, and a rolling pin, you can turn out professional-quality pasta in 10 minutes, dry it for 15 to 20 minutes, and then serve it up in 5 more. The secret to successful homemade pasta is to keep from overworking the dough—it must stay soft and pliable, but not sticky.

The following ingredients may be used for a basic pasta, but you can create a variety of other flavored pastas—zucchini, broccoli, onion, and so on—by combining these ingredients with the flour:

> 1 cup whole wheat or unbleached flour, plus flour for kneading
> Pinch herbal salt substitute
> 1 egg
> 1 teaspoon olive oil (optional)
> 1/2 cup (approximately) water, or as needed

1. In a bowl mix flour and salt together, with a fork. Make a well in the center of the flour and add egg, and oil, if desired. (Olive oil will help make the dough smooth but is not essential in this recipe.)

2. Slowly incorporate flour into the well, mixing with egg, until a stiff dough is formed. If mixture seems dry, dribble in a little water. (If you are using a food processor to mix ingredients, insert ingredients, set to "pulse" speed, and process for about 1 minute or until mixture begins to pull away from the sides of the container.)

3. Lightly flour your hands and a kneading surface, such as a bread board or countertop. Knead rapidly for 5 minutes. Dough should be soft, pliable, and unsticky. When dough is in the form of

a ball, make sure it is not sticky. Add more flour or water as needed, but add flour gradually, as too much flour makes a tough dough. At this point, you can test dough by stretching it a few inches in your hands; it should not break.

4. Place ball of dough on a lightly floured surface and flatten it slightly by hand. Roll out dough with a lightly floured rolling pin (or any clean, smooth, cylindrical object). Roll dough from the center to the outer edges, flipping the dough frequently, until it is in the form of a flat rectangle, about 1/16 inch thick (about the thickness of a quarter).

5. Flour both sides of dough well and roll into a cylindrical (jelly roll) shape. Cut the roll into desired width (usually 1/4 inch). Unwind each strip and shake off excess flour.

6. Let the strips dry on a dry cloth towel on counter or hang to air dry on pasta rack. Pasta should dry 15 to 30 minutes before cooking or 3 hours before storing. Pasta can be stored in the freezer while still fresh or on the shelf if it is well dried.

Serves 2.

Pasta Machines If you happen to own a pasta machine—either the electric or hand-crank type—pasta making can really be a breeze! If using a machine, make sure the dough is floured very well before rolling or cutting because the machine will tend to make the strips of dough stick together more than when cutting by hand.

Most pasta machines have at least two cutting attachments: one for wide noodles and one for thin spaghetti. Use the wide-noodle attachment for recipes that call for creamy sauces as the sauce will stick better to wider pasta.

Before cleaning pasta machines, read the instructions. Water can cause rusting or sticking, and you may be better off removing excess dough and flour with a small brush.

SPAGHETTI NEAPOLITAN

This tasty mixture of cooked spaghetti and sautéed vegetables in a light cream sauce is served cold. It will keep two or three days, tightly covered, in the refrigerator and is excellent for a chilled summer lunch.

> 4 cups cooked spaghetti, chopped into 6-inch lengths
> 1 teaspoon each olive oil and butter
> 1 cup sliced onion
> 1/2 cup each chopped green bell pepper and red bell pepper
> 1/2 cup each sliced mushrooms and sliced zucchini
> 2 tablespoons whole wheat flour
> 1 cup nonfat milk
> 1/3 cup fresh peas
> Herbal salt substitute and freshly ground black pepper, to taste

1. Place cooked pasta in a large bowl and begin chilling while you prepare vegetables.

2. In a skillet heat oil and butter and sauté onion over medium heat for 3 minutes, stirring frequently, without browning it. Add bell peppers, mushrooms, and zucchini, and cook until mushrooms weep moisture (4 to 5 more minutes). Add flour and cook, stirring, over low heat for 2 minutes.

3. Pour in milk and heat through. Add peas, salt substitute, and pepper and toss with chilled pasta. Continue to chill the dish for up to 2 hours.

Serves 6.

> *Preparation time:* 20 minutes
> *Cooking time:* 15 minutes
> *Chilling time:* 2 hours
> *Per serving:* calcium 75 mg, calories 192, carbohydrates 34 g, cholesterol 2 mg, fat 3 g, fiber 2 g, protein 7 g, sodium 129 mg

PASTA SHELLS WITH PEAS AND PROSCIUTTO

A small taste of prosciutto ham is added to this recipe for flavor and color.

    1   teaspoon olive oil
    1/4 cup dry sherry
    1/2 cup sliced red bell pepper
    1   tablespoon minced garlic
    1/3 cup cooked prosciutto ham, fat
        trimmed off
    1/4 cup fresh basil, chopped
    2   tablespoons parsley, chopped
    1   teaspoon dried thyme
    1   cup fresh peas
    4   cups cooked small pasta shells
    2   tablespoons Parmesan cheese

In a skillet heat oil and sherry and sauté bell pepper and garlic for 3 minutes. Add ham, basil, parsley, thyme, peas, pasta, and Parmesan and cook until peas turn bright green (about one minute). Serve hot.

Serves 4.

Preparation time: 20 minutes
Cooking time: 5 minutes
Per serving: calcium 100 mg, calories 316, carbohydrates 49 g, cholesterol 15 mg, fat 5 g, fiber 4 g, protein 16 g, sodium 569 mg

PASTA WITH MARINATED ARTICHOKE HEARTS

Marinated artichokes add panache to this pasta.

    2   teaspoons olive oil
    2   tablespoons minced garlic
    1   cup cooked and shredded
        chicken
    1/4 cup white wine
    1/2 cup sliced mushrooms
    1/4 cup minced red bell pepper
    3   tablespoons minced parsley
    1/2 cup nonfat plain yogurt
    1   teaspoon honey
    4   cups cooked spiral pasta
    6   ounces marinated, drained
        artichoke hearts

1. In a skillet heat oil and sauté garlic and chicken for 2 minutes, stirring frequently. Remove garlic and chicken to a bowl; set aside.

2. In same skillet heat wine and sauté mushroom and bell pepper until mushrooms weep moisture. Remove from heat and combine with chicken and garlic in bowl.

3. Add parsley, yogurt, honey, pasta, and artichoke hearts; toss well. Serve at once.

Serves 4.

Preparation time: 20 minutes
Cooking time: 5 minutes
Per serving: calcium 143 mg, calories 349, carbohydrates 52 g, cholesterol 30 mg, fat 5 g, fiber 5 g, protein 22 g, sodium 105 mg

An out-of-this-world recipe, Pasta Shells With Peas and Prosciutto will become a favorite for entertaining. The sauce, made with sherry, olive oil, and fresh basil, complements the sharp, salty flavor of the ham.

SUNDAY NIGHT SPAGHETTI

This may become your favorite pasta recipe. It is tasty and quick to prepare, and kids love it. The lean meat sauce is a variation on Basic Pizza Sauce (see page 188), so leftovers can top your next pizza.

- 1/3 pound lean ground lamb or beef
- 2 teaspoons minced garlic
- 1/4 cup dry red wine
- 1 tablespoon chopped fresh basil
- 1 cup chopped fresh tomatoes
- 1 recipe Basic Pizza Sauce (see page 188)
- 1 pound whole wheat or spinach spaghetti

1. In a large Dutch oven or deep skillet over medium-high heat, brown lamb and garlic in red wine for about 15 minutes, stirring frequently. Pour off any excess fat.

2. Add basil, tomatoes, and Basic Pizza Sauce. Bring to a boil, lower heat to medium, and simmer sauce for 25 minutes, stirring occasionally.

3. While sauce is simmering, bring 2 quarts of water to boil in a large pot. Cook spaghetti until al dente (8 minutes). Drain and toss with sauce. Serve hot.

Serves 6.

Preparation time: 10 minutes
Cooking time: 50 minutes
Per serving: calcium 58 mg, calories 391, carbohydrates 65 g, cholesterol 19 mg, fat 8 g, fiber 2 g, protein 17 g, sodium 87 mg

LINGUINE WITH WINTER PESTO

Pesto, a popular sauce for pasta, is usually made with fresh basil leaves, pine nuts, and Parmesan cheese. In the winter when fresh basil is scarce, try using a combination of dried basil and fresh parsley and spinach, which provide plenty of vitamin A. Make a double batch of the pesto and freeze half in an ice cube tray. After the pesto cubes freeze, store them in lock-top plastic bags and use for quick make-ahead meals all winter. (You will need 3 to 6 cubes per serving, depending on the size of the ice cube tray.)

- 1 pound linguine
- 1/2 cup minced spinach leaves
- 1/2 cup chopped parsley
- 1 tablespoon dried basil
- 1 tablespoon minced garlic
- 2 tablespoons coarsely chopped walnuts
- 3 tablespoons olive oil
- 1/4 cup grated Parmesan cheese

1. In a large pot over high heat, bring to a boil 2 quarts of water and cook linguine until al dente (8 minutes).

2. While noodles are cooking, combine spinach, parsley, basil, garlic, walnuts, oil, and Parmesan in a blender or food processor until a thick paste is formed.

3. Drain noodles and toss with pesto while still warm. Serve at once.

Serves 4.

Preparation time: 15 minutes
Cooking time: 10 minutes
Per serving: calcium 137 mg, calories 568, carbohydrates 88 g, cholesterol 4 mg, fat 16 g, fiber 4 g, protein 18 g, sodium 112 mg

PASTA SHELLS WITH PEAS AND CHICKEN

Try this colorful recipe in the summertime, when fresh peas are ripe off the vine and bursting with flavor. Small pasta shells are cooked until just slightly underdone and baked with a sauté of red bell peppers, fresh peas, and slivers of skinned chicken breasts. A low-fat recipe that can be made ahead of time, Pasta Shells With Peas and Chicken will become a warm-weather favorite with family and guests.

- 4 cups small pasta shells
- 2 cups cooked and slivered chicken
- 2 teaspoons olive oil
- 1/2 cup shelled peas
- 1 tablespoon minced garlic
- 2 tablespoons chopped fresh basil
- 2 tablespoons chopped fresh thyme, or 1 teaspoon dried thyme
- 3 tablespoons chopped parsley
- 1/4 cup minced red bell pepper
- 1/4 cup grated Parmesan cheese

1. In a large pot over high heat, bring 2 quarts of water to a boil and cook pasta shells until just underdone (about 5 minutes). Drain and rinse under cold water, then set aside. Preheat oven to 400° F.

2. In a large skillet over medium-high heat, sauté chicken in olive oil for 2 minutes, then add peas, garlic, basil, thyme, parsley, and bell pepper. Cook 2 minutes more, then pour mixture into large baking dish. Add pasta shells and toss well. Add Parmesan.

3. Bake for 20 minutes. Serve hot.

Serves 4.

Preparation time: 25 minutes
Cooking time: 15 minutes
Baking time: 20 minutes
Per serving: calcium 178 mg, calories 592, carbohydrates 85 g, cholesterol 70 mg, fat 8 g, fiber 4 g, protein 43 g, sodium 634 mg

SCAMPI FETTUCCINE WITH GARLIC AND OLIVE OIL

Shrimp is an excellent and tasty source of protein. In this fettuccine recipe, large prawns are briefly poached in sake, then cooked in a sauce that is high in garlic and low in oil. Since it keeps well on a heated tray, this fettuccine is an elegant main dish for a party buffet.

    1   pound fresh fettuccine
    1   pound large prawns
    ¹/₂ cup sake, dry sherry, or white
        wine
    2   teaspoons olive oil
    2   tablespoons minced garlic
    ¹/₄ cup minced red bell pepper
    ¹/₄ cup chopped parsley

1. In a large pot over high heat, bring 2 quarts of water to a boil and cook fettuccine for 3 minutes. Strain from cooking pot and refresh under cold water.

2. Peel and devein prawns. In a large skillet over medium-high heat, sauté prawns in sake until they turn bright pink (4 to 5 minutes). Remove from pan and set aside.

3. Pour off all but 2 tablespoons of sake. Add olive oil, garlic, and red bell pepper to pan, and cook over medium-high heat for 5 minutes, stirring frequently. Add parsley, cooked prawns, and fettuccine. Toss well to reheat thoroughly. Serve hot.

Serves 4.

Preparation time: 15 minutes
Cooking time: 15 minutes
Per serving: calcium 145 mg, calories 614, carbohydrates 90 g, cholesterol 173 mg, fat 6 g, fiber 3 g, protein 39 g, sodium 197 mg

Olive oil, garlic, and fresh basil provide a savory background for Pasta Shells With Peas and Chicken.

EGGPLANT AND YELLOW PEPPER VERMICELLI

If you can't find yellow bell peppers, make this recipe with green or red bell peppers (although the color combination won't be as striking). The Mediterranean flavor of this dish comes from the fresh basil, a taste of olive oil, Greek olives, and capers.

    1/4 cup olive oil
    1/4 to 1/2 cup white wine
    2 cloves garlic, minced
    2 cups chopped tomato
    2 small Japanese-style eggplants,
       peeled and cubed
    2 sweet yellow bell peppers
    2 tablespoons pitted Greek olives
    2 tablespoons capers
    2 tablespoons chopped fresh basil
    6 cups cooked spaghetti or
       fettuccine
    3 tablespoons grated Parmesan
       cheese
       Freshly ground black pepper,
       to taste

1. In a skillet heat olive oil and 1/4 cup wine and sauté garlic for 1 minute at medium-high heat. Add tomato and eggplants and continue to cook, stirring frequently, for 10 minutes more. If the mixture dries out too fast, lower the heat, and add 1/4 cup more wine.

2. Preheat broiler. Cut bell peppers in half and seed them. Place cut side down on an aluminum-foil-lined baking sheet and broil until skins turn black (about 2 minutes). Place blackened peppers into a paper bag and seal top. Let peppers sweat in the bag for 10 minutes, then remove and rinse under cold water, rubbing off the blackened skin with your fingers. Chop the peeled peppers coarsely and add to the sauté.

3. Add olives, capers, and basil to sauté. Reheat spaghetti in heated water for 1 minute, then drain and toss with sauté. Season with Parmesan and black pepper and serve immediately.

Serves 6.

Preparation time: 25 minutes
Cooking time: 15 minutes
Per serving: calcium 71 mg, calories 374, carbohydrates 56 g, cholesterol 2 mg, fat 12 g, fiber 5 g, protein 11 g, sodium 157 mg

JAPANESE PASTA WITH MISO PESTO

Pesto is a puréed or mashed mixture of fresh herbs, nuts, oil, garlic, and cheeses. Here is a slightly different version, strong on flavor and low in fat. This recipe substitutes Japanese miso paste, similar in taste to very mild soy sauce, for the cheese, making the pesto free of dairy products. The miso is tossed with cooked Japanese soba noodles, made from buckwheat.

    3 cups loosely packed fresh basil
       leaves
    2 packages (16 oz each) soba
       noodles
    1 tablespoon olive oil
    2 cloves minced garlic
    2 tablespoons miso paste
    1 tablespoon walnuts or
       almonds

1. Chop basil very finely. Cook and drain soba noodles. Toss basil with hot soba.

2. In a blender purée together olive oil, garlic, miso, and walnuts. Toss with pasta and basil and serve hot.

Serves 8.

Preparation time: 15 minutes
Cooking time: 8 to 10 minutes
Per serving: calcium 69 mg, calories 416, carbohydrates 87 g, cholesterol 0 mg, fat 4 g, fiber 0 g, protein 18 g, sodium 1,056 mg

PIZZA

The secret of healthy pizza lies in using a whole wheat or other whole grain crust (see page 192), a good low-fat sauce rich in vegetables and low in oil (see Basic Pizza Sauce, below), and colorful toppings of fresh vegetables, lean meats, or fish, with only a small amount of cheese.

BASIC PIZZA SAUCE

A good, low-fat pizza sauce is a must for the healthy cook. The secret to the flavor of this sauce, which uses very little oil, is steeping the dried basil and oregano in wine before cooking. This simple step draws out the flavor of the herbs—the sauce tastes as if it had been cooking for hours.

    1/4 cup minced fresh basil or
       2 tablespoons dried basil
    1 teaspoon dried oregano
    1/4 cup white wine
    1/2 cup grated onion
    2 teaspoons minced garlic
    2 teaspoons olive oil
    3 cups coarsely chopped plum
       tomatoes
    1 tablespoon tomato paste

1. In a small bowl steep basil and oregano in white wine for 10 minutes.

2. In a large skillet over medium-high heat, sauté onion and garlic in olive oil for 5 minutes, stirring frequently. Add tomatoes and tomato paste, then steeped herbs and wine. Cover and cook 15 minutes.

3. Remove sauce from heat and purée in a blender or food processor. Sauce may be used on pizza or over pasta.

Makes about 3 cups.

Preparation time: 15 minutes
Cooking time: 20 minutes
Per serving: calcium 12 mg, calories 28, carbohydrates 4 g, cholesterol 0 mg, fat 1 g, fiber 1 g, protein 1 g, sodium 36 mg

POLENTA PIZZA

A cornmeal crust gives Polenta Pizza extra nutrition. Polenta is rich in vitamin A and minerals.

  Oil, for coating baking sheet
2 *cups polenta*
1 *cup cold water*
1 *cup boiling water*
2 *eggs*
1 *cup grated low-fat mozzarella cheese*
¼ *cup chopped green onions*
1 *teaspoon olive oil*
¼ *cup chopped red bell pepper*
1 *cup thinly sliced mushrooms*
3 *cups Basic Pizza Sauce (see page 188)*
1 *cup thickly sliced plum tomatoes*
¼ *cup chopped parsley*
1 *tablespoon minced fresh basil*

1. Preheat oven to 450° F. Lightly oil a 12- by 15-inch baking sheet.

2. In a large bowl combine polenta with the cold water, then add the boiling water in a steady stream, mixing with a whisk. Stir in eggs and mozzarella. Press mixture evenly into baking sheet. Bake until lightly browned and crisp (10 to 15 minutes).

3. In a large skillet over medium-high heat, sauté green onions in olive oil for 1 minute, then add bell pepper and mushrooms. Cover and let steam for 5 minutes.

4. Spoon sauce over cornmeal crust, then top with sautéed vegetables, sliced tomatoes, parsley, and basil. Bake until bubbly (12 to 15 minutes).

Serves 8.

Preparation time: 25 minutes
Cooking time: 30 to 40 minutes
Per serving: calcium 160 mg, calories 238, carbohydrates 35 g, cholesterol 61 mg, fat 7 g, fiber 4 g, protein 10 g, sodium 150 mg

The polenta crust on this pizza is not only an eye-catcher but also flavorful and rich in calcium and other nutrients.

NOTE

THE VALUE OF COMPLEX CARBOHYDRATES

Carbohydrates function as the primary energy source for the human body. They are also converted to glycogen and stored in the liver to help regulate blood sugar levels, and they are essential for proper nerve function through their effect on glucose levels in the blood.

Carbohydrates may be categorized as either simple or complex, according to various criteria, such as absorption rate and chemical structure. Types of simple carbohydrates include maltose (in beer), fructose (a fruit sugar), and sucrose (table sugar). Complex carbohydrates—cellulose, starch, and dextrin—are abundant in such foods as pasta, pizza, vegetables, whole grains, and fruit.

Simple carbohydrates are a source of instant energy for the body. Unfortunately, a diet high in sugar is often associated with a diet low in fiber, vitamins, minerals, and other nutrients—high-sugar foods are often high in fat. Most refined foods, such as white sugar products (candy and soft drinks), baked goods made with bleached white flour (pastries and cakes), and so-called junk foods, are mostly just a source of "empty" calories.

Complex carbohydrates take longer to be absorbed by the body and are therefore considered a more enduring source of energy. They contain vital nutrients and fiber, and are a superior energy source. Your daily requirement of carbohydrates can easily be met with a whole-grain cereal for breakfast, a few pieces of fresh fruit during the day, and rice or a baked potato for dinner.

ROASTED NEW-POTATO PIZZA WITH PESTO

An updated version of traditional Italian pizza with potatoes, this recipe combines a creamy spinach-basil pesto with slices of roasted red potatoes and a light olive oil and tomato topping.

   Oil and cornmeal, for coating pizza pan
1 *recipe Basic Pizza Dough (see page 192)*
2 *cups thinly sliced red new potatoes*
   Herbal salt substitute and pepper
3 *tablespoons olive oil*
1/2 *cup minced spinach leaves*
1/2 *cup chopped parsley*
1 *tablespoon dried basil*
1 *tablespoon minced garlic*
1/4 *cup coarsely chopped walnuts*
1/4 *cup grated Parmesan cheese*

1. Preheat oven to 450° F. Lightly oil a 14-inch-diameter pizza pan or large baking sheet and sprinkle with cornmeal. On a lightly floured surface, roll pizza dough into a circle. Place in pizza pan and press edges into a 1-inch rim.

2. Lightly oil a second baking sheet. Place sliced potatoes in a bowl and sprinkle with salt substitute, pepper, and 1 teaspoon of the olive oil. Toss well to coat evenly. Place on prepared second baking sheet and roast until browned (about 10 minutes).

3. Place spinach, parsley, basil, garlic, walnuts, the remaining olive oil, and cheese into a blender or food processor and purée to the consistency of a paste. Spread thickly on pizza dough. Place roasted potatoes on top. Bake pizza in oven until dough is lightly browned (about 15 minutes). Serve hot.

Serves 8.

Preparation time: 25 minutes
Baking time: 25 minutes
Per serving: calcium 73 mg, calories 85, carbohydrates 28 g, cholesterol 2 mg, fat 6 g, fiber 5 g, protein 7 g, sodium 56 mg

RICE-CRUSTED PIZZA

This pizza recipe provides an innovative way to use leftover cooked rice—mix it with herbs, cheese, and eggs, and press it into a pizza pan. The crust comes out chewy and slightly crisp on the bottom and is a real favorite of children. Make it in a large sheet pan for the next block party or children's birthday.

   Oil, for coating baking sheet
2 *cups cooked short-grain brown rice*
2 *eggs*
1 *cup grated low-fat mozzarella cheese*
3 *cups Basic Pizza Sauce (see page 188)*
1/2 *teaspoon dried oregano*
1/2 *teaspoon dried basil*
1/2 *teaspoon minced garlic*
1/4 *cup grated Parmesan cheese*
1/4 *cup sliced marinated artichoke hearts*
1/4 *cup sliced pitted black olives*

1. Preheat oven to 450° F. Lightly oil a large baking sheet.

2. In a large bowl mix together rice, eggs, and mozzarella. Press into baking sheet to form a thick crust. Bake crust until lightly browned (15 to 20 minutes).

3. In a large bowl combine pizza sauce, oregano, basil, and garlic. Spoon over baked crust. Top with Parmesan, artichoke hearts, and olives. Bake 10 more minutes, then slice and serve.

Serves 8.

Preparation time: 20 minutes
Baking time: 25 to 30 minutes
Per serving: calcium 175 mg, calories 180, carbohydrates 21 g, cholesterol 63 mg, fat 7 g, fiber 2 g, protein 9 g, sodium 225 mg

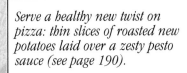

Serve a healthy new twist on pizza: thin slices of roasted new potatoes laid over a zesty pesto sauce (see page 190).

Basics

THREE EASY PIZZA CRUSTS

Substitute these easy crusts for traditional pizza dough. The cornmeal crust, which originated in Italy, has a very crunchy texture. The colorful vegetable crust is great as an appetizer—top it with sliced raw or lightly sautéed vegetables and broil until brown. Try the Basic Pizza Dough with any of your favorite pizza toppings. You can make a double batch and freeze half, already pressed into a pizza pan, ready to bake.

CORNMEAL CRUST

Fresh vegetable toppings are a good complement to the golden color and pleasing texture of this crust.

Oil, for coating baking sheet
2 cups polenta
1 cup cold water
1 cup boiling water
2 eggs
1 cup grated low-fat mozzarella cheese

1. Preheat oven to 450° F. Lightly oil a large baking sheet.

2. In a large bowl combine polenta with the cold water, then add the boiling water in a steady stream, mixing with a whisk. Stir in eggs and mozzarella. Press mixture evenly into baking sheet. Bake until lightly browned and crisp (10 to 15 minutes).

Makes 1 pizza crust, 8 servings.

> *Preparation time:* 10 minutes
> *Baking time:* 10 to 15 minutes
> *Per serving:* calcium 113 mg, calories 185, carbohydrates 27 g, cholesterol 61 mg, fat 4 g, fiber 3 g, protein 8 g, sodium 93 mg

VEGETABLE CRUST

Grated zucchini and carrot give a confetti effect to this easy pizza crust. Salt is used to extract moisture from the raw vegetables, making them easier to form into dough. Be sure to rinse vegetables thoroughly to remove the salt and squeeze out excess moisture before combining with other ingredients.

¾ cup grated raw zucchini
½ cup grated raw carrot
½ cup minced red or green bell pepper
1 teaspoon salt
2 eggs
1 cup grated low-fat mozzarella cheese
Oil, for coating baking sheet

1. In a colander set over a large bowl, toss together zucchini, carrot, bell pepper, and salt, and allow to drain for 10 minutes. Run water through colander to rinse salt from vegetables, then squeeze to remove excess moisture. Combine in a bowl with eggs and mozzarella cheese.

2. Preheat oven to 375° F. Lightly oil 1 medium or 2 small baking sheets. Press vegetable mixture evenly onto sheets. Bake until lightly browned and crisp (12 to 15 minutes).

Makes 1 pizza crust, 8 servings.

> *Preparation time:* 15 to 20 minutes
> *Baking time:* 12 to 15 minutes
> *Per serving:* calcium 116 mg, calories 67, carbohydrates 3 g, cholesterol 61 mg, fat 4 g, fiber .7 g, protein 6 g, sodium 362 mg

BASIC PIZZA DOUGH

Use this easy recipe for all bread dough pizzas. Begin making it about 2 hours before you want to serve the pizza, since the dough needs time to rise.

1 teaspoon light honey
1 cup lukewarm water (98° F to 100° F)
1 package active dry yeast
2 cups whole wheat or unbleached flour
1 teaspoon olive oil
½ teaspoon herbal salt substitute
Flour, for dusting breadboard
Oil, for coating bowl

1. In a large mixing bowl, combine honey, the warm water, and yeast, and stir until yeast dissolves. Let mixture stand, uncovered, at room temperature for 5 minutes.

2. Stir in 1 cup of the flour and mix well. Let batter rise for 20 minutes, then stir down and add remaining flour, oil, and salt substitute.

3. Lightly flour a counter or breadboard and turn dough onto it. Knead dough for 5 minutes, flouring lightly as needed to prevent stickiness. Dough should be smooth and elastic.

4. Lightly oil a large bowl and place dough into it. Cover with a dish towel and let rise for 30 minutes. Punch down, then divide into 4 balls and roll into rounds. Dough is now ready to use for pizza.

Makes 4 small pizza crusts, 8 servings.

> *Preparation time:* 20 minutes
> *Rising time:* 55 minutes
> *Per serving:* calcium 14 mg, calories 114, carbohydrates 23 g, cholesterol 0 mg, fat 1 g, fiber 4 g, protein 5 g, sodium 3 mg

PITA PIZZAS WITH SUN-DRIED TOMATOES

These quick little pizzas are assembled on halves of pita bread. Sun-dried tomatoes packed in olive oil, available in gourmet shops, provide a great deal of flavor as well as vitamin A and potassium. These pizzas transport easily, so pack one or two in your next bag lunch.

  2 cups well-washed and thinly sliced leeks
  1 teaspoon butter
  1 tablespoon dry sherry
  2 cups sliced mushrooms
  1/4 cup jarred sun-dried tomatoes, drained and chopped
  1 teaspoon olive oil
  4 large whole wheat pita bread rounds
  1/2 cup grated low-fat mozzarella cheese
  1/4 cup crumbled goat cheese (optional)

1. In a large skillet over medium-high heat, sauté leeks in butter and sherry until soft (about 10 minutes). Add mushrooms and tomatoes and continue to sauté for 10 minutes, stirring frequently.

2. Preheat oven to 450° F. Lightly oil a large baking sheet with olive oil and place pita rounds on it. Sprinkle pita with half the mozzarella cheese, reserving half for topping.

3. Spoon sautéed vegetables onto pita rounds, top with remaining mozzarella and goat cheese, if used. Cook until browned and bubbly (about 10 minutes).

Makes 4 small pizzas, 4 servings.

Preparation time: 20 minutes
Cooking time: 30 minutes
Per serving: calcium 150 mg, calories 281, carbohydrates 47 g, cholesterol 10 mg, fat 7 g, fiber 7 g, protein 12 g, sodium 508 mg

ZUCCHINI-CRUSTED VEGETABLE PIZZA

Vegetable crusts are a delicious and healthy way to create a pizza base. This recipe combines grated zucchini with a topping of green and red bell pepper, tomatoes, diced green chiles, and a rich tomato sauce. The pizza is a colorful and tasty addition to a buffet party and can be served in small wedges as an appetizer.

  2 cups grated raw zucchini
  1 teaspoon salt
  2 eggs
  1 cup grated low-fat mozzarella cheese
     Oil, for coating baking sheet
  3 cups Basic Pizza Sauce (see page 188)
  1 large red bell pepper
  1 large green bell pepper
  1/2 cup thickly sliced tomatoes
  1/4 cup diced canned green chiles
  1/2 cup grated Parmesan cheese

1. In a colander set over a large bowl, toss together zucchini and salt and allow to drain for 10 minutes. Run water through colander to rinse salt from zucchini, then squeeze to remove excess moisture. (Salt pulls water from zucchini and keeps crust from being too wet.) Combine in a bowl with eggs and mozzarella.

2. Preheat oven to 375° F. Lightly oil a medium baking sheet. Press zucchini mixture evenly onto sheet. Bake until lightly browned and crisp (12 to 15 minutes).

3. Spread sauce over top of zucchini crust. Slice bell peppers into rings, then lay on top of pizza along with tomatoes and chiles. Sprinkle with Parmesan. Bake for 10 minutes and serve hot.

Makes 1 pizza, 6 servings.

Preparation time: 25 minutes
Baking time: 25 minutes
Per serving: calcium 271 mg, calories 171, carbohydrates 11 g, cholesterol 86 mg, fat 9 g, fiber 3 g, protein 12 g, sodium 746 mg

WHOLE GRAIN BREADS AND MUFFINS

Few aromas are as pleasing as freshly baked bread—but who has the time to make homemade bread? You do! Even if you can reserve only a few hours each week for baking, you will find some unusual additions to your repertoire in this section. If you do not have time to bake yeast bread, try the quick bread recipes. Prepared and baked in less than an hour, they are ideal for brunch with friends or a potluck party.

CINNAMON SWIRLS

Cinnamon Swirls may become a favorite special-occasion treat in your family. The dough is started a few hours before brunch, left to rise in a warm kitchen, then spread with a cinnamon-orange-walnut filling. Roll it up, cut into rounds, and bake. The swirls are best when eaten fresh out of the oven, but they can also be made up the night before and reheated for mornings when sleeping late is a priority.

  1 1/2 cups scalded low-fat buttermilk
  1/2 cup lukewarm water (98° F to 110° F)
  1 package active dry yeast
  1/2 cup plus 2 tablespoons light honey
  4 eggs
  10 to 14 cups whole wheat pastry flour
  2 tablespoons canola oil, plus oil for coating pan
  1/3 cup melted butter
  1/2 cup maple syrup
  2 tablespoons cinnamon
  1 cup chopped walnuts
  3/4 cup raisins
  1 teaspoon freshly ground cardamom
  1 tablespoon grated orange peel
  1 beaten egg white

1. In a large bowl combine buttermilk, the water, yeast, and the 2 tablespoons honey. Stir until yeast dissolves. Let stand for 5 minutes.

2. In a small bowl beat eggs, then add to yeast mixture. Stir in 5 to 6 cups of flour, or enough to form a thick batter. Stir well and let stand 20 minutes.

3. Stir batter vigorously for 1 minute, then add 2 tablespoons oil and enough flour to form a thick dough. Lightly flour a counter or breadboard and turn dough onto board. Knead until smooth and elastic (5 to 10 minutes). Lightly oil a mixing bowl and put kneaded dough into it. Cover bowl with a dish towel and let rise for 40 minutes.

4. Punch down the dough, then cover again and let rise an additional 30 minutes. Preheat oven to 350° F. Lightly oil a large, deep baking pan.

5. While dough is rising the second time, in a mixing bowl combine butter, maple syrup, remaining honey, cinnamon, walnuts, raisins, cardamom, and orange peel. Roll out risen dough and spread filling thickly on surface. Roll into a jelly-roll shape and slice into 12 "swirls." Place swirls on end, packing them into the baking pan. Lightly brush with egg white.

6. Bake until lightly browned (about 30 minutes). Let cool slightly, then remove from pan. Cut each swirl in half, arrange slices on serving plate, and serve.

Makes 24 slices, 24 servings.

Preparation time: 50 minutes
Rising time: 90 minutes
Baking time: 30 minutes
Per serving: calcium 58 mg, calories 317, carbohydrates 54 g, cholesterol 43 mg, fat 9 g, fiber 7 g, protein 10 g, sodium 59 mg

SAUERKRAUT BREAD

An authentic recipe of Ukrainian origin, this bread is traditionally made at the beginning of the week and improves as the days progress. Only the most revered family member has the privilege of eating the last piece. The secret to making this surprisingly sweet bread is cooking the sauerkraut with a little honey and grated carrots until it loses its sharpness, then packing it between two layers of egg-based dough. The bread bakes like a huge sandwich and can be served as a main course or quick snack, cut into sandwich-sized wedges.

1½ cups scalded low-fat
   buttermilk
½ cup lukewarm water (98° F to
   110° F)
1 package active dry yeast
2 tablespoons light honey
4 eggs
10 to 14 cups whole wheat flour
3 tablespoons canola oil, plus oil
   for coating pan and bowl
2 cups drained sauerkraut
½ cup grated carrots
½ teaspoon freshly ground black
   pepper
½ teaspoon herbal salt substitute

1. In a large bowl combine buttermilk, the water, yeast, and honey. Stir until yeast dissolves and let stand for 5 minutes.

2. In a small bowl beat eggs, then add to yeast mixture. Stir in 5 to 6 cups of flour, or enough to form a thick batter. Stir well and let stand 20 minutes.

3. Stir batter vigorously for 1 minute, then add 2 tablespoons of the oil and enough flour to form a thick dough. Lightly flour a counter or breadboard and turn dough onto board. Knead until smooth and elastic (5 to 10 minutes). Lightly oil a mixing bowl and put kneaded dough into it. Cover bowl with a dish towel and let rise for 40 minutes.

4. Punch dough down, then cover again and let rise an additional 30 minutes.

5. While dough is rising the second time, combine remaining oil, sauerkraut, carrots, pepper, and salt substitute in a small saucepan. Cook this mixture uncovered, over medium-high heat, for 10 minutes, stirring frequently. Remove from heat and pour into a colander set over the sink. Let sauerkraut drain for 10 minutes.

6. Lightly oil a 9- by 12-inch baking pan and preheat oven to 350° F. Separate dough into 2 balls and roll each into a 9- by 12-inch rectangle. Place one rectangle into the baking pan. Spoon sauerkraut mixture on top of it. Place second rectangle of dough on top of sauerkraut. Reach into pan and pinch edges of bottom and top layers of dough together, sealing tightly. Let it rise for 10 minutes.

7. Bake sauerkraut bread until browned (about 45 minutes). It should lift easily out of the pan. Let cool on a rack, and then slice into thick wedges.

Serves 15.

Preparation time: 45 minutes
Rising time: 1 hour and 45 minutes
Baking time: 45 minutes
Per serving: calcium 75 mg, calories 343, carbohydrates 64 g, cholesterol 58 mg, fat 6 g, fiber 11 g, protein 14 g, sodium 257 mg

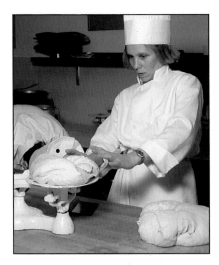

PUMPKIN BREAD

Pumpkins are not only for Halloween, as this bread will show.

Oil, for coating loaf pan
1½ cups whole wheat pastry flour
½ cup oats, ground in blender
2 teaspoons baking powder
2 teaspoons baking soda
2 teaspoons cinnamon
2 teaspoons nutmeg
¼ teaspoon allspice
2 teaspoons grated ginger
½ cup maple syrup
¼ cup molasses
¼ cup canola oil
2 egg whites
1 whole egg
2 tablespoons lemon juice
1 tablespoon grated orange peel
1 cup canned or cooked fresh pumpkin purée

1. Preheat oven to 350° F. Lightly oil a 2-quart loaf pan.

2. In a large mixing bowl, combine flour, oats, baking powder, baking soda, cinnamon, nutmeg, and allspice.

3. In a separate bowl combine ginger, maple syrup, molasses, oil, egg whites, egg, lemon juice, orange peel, and pumpkin.

4. Combine contents of both bowls, mixing very lightly. Pour into prepared loaf pan and bake for 50 to 60 minutes. Let cool before slicing.

Makes 1 large loaf, 8 servings.

Preparation time: 20 minutes
Baking time: 50 to 60 minutes
Per serving: calcium 151 mg, calories 266, carbohydrates 45 g, cholesterol 27 mg, fat 9 g, fiber 5 g, protein 6 g, sodium 436 mg

Bursting with fall flavors, rich-tasting Pumpkin Bread is a delicious treat served with a mug of hot apple cider.

HONEY-BRAN MUFFINS

These honey-flavored bran muffins contain raisins as well.

> 1 cup whole-bran cereal
> 1/2 cup each nonfat milk and honey
> 1 egg
> 3 tablespoons canola oil, plus oil for coating pan
> 1/2 cup raisins
> 1 cup unbleached flour
> 2 1/2 teaspoons baking powder
> 1/4 teaspoon salt or herbal salt substitute

1. Preheat oven to 400° F. In a medium bowl combine cereal, milk, and honey; let stand until most of the liquid is absorbed (about 10 minutes). Beat in egg and oil, then mix in raisins.

2. In a large bowl combine flour, baking powder, and salt. Add cereal mixture, mixing just until dry ingredients are moistened.

3. Fill oiled 2 1/2-inch muffin pans about two thirds full.

4. Bake until well browned (20 to 25 minutes). Serve warm.

Makes 1 dozen muffins, 12 servings.

> *Preparation time:* 20 minutes
> *Baking time:* 20 to 25 minutes
> *Per serving:* calcium 94 mg, calories 150, carbohydrates 28 g, cholesterol 18 mg, fat 4 g, fiber 2 g, protein 3 g, sodium 132 mg

OATMEAL GEMS

These chewy, slightly sweet muffins are a wonderful complement to soups and stews. The name gem refers to the old-fashioned cast-iron pans, which produce a first-rate muffin with a crusty exterior and a pointy top. If you don't have cast-iron gem pans, use plain muffin tins. Leftover muffins are delicious when split and toasted.

> 2 cups quick-cooking oatmeal
> 1 1/2 cups low-fat buttermilk
> 1/4 cup molasses
> 2 tablespoons sugar
> 2 eggs
> 1/2 teaspoon salt
> 1 cup whole wheat pastry flour
> 1 teaspoon baking soda

1. Preheat oven to 400° F. Lightly oil 2 1/2-inch muffin pans or line them with cupcake papers. Combine oatmeal and buttermilk in a medium bowl and let stand about 15 minutes.

2. Beat in molasses, sugar, eggs, and salt. Stir flour and baking soda together, then add to oatmeal mixture and mix just until dry ingredients are moistened.

3. Fill prepared pans two thirds full. Bake until a toothpick inserted in a muffin comes out clean, about 20 minutes. Serve warm.

Makes about 16 muffins, 16 servings.

> *Preparation time:* 20 minutes
> *Baking time:* 20 minutes
> *Per serving:* calcium 100 mg, calories 104, carbohydrates 19 g, cholesterol 27 mg, fat 2 g, fiber 1 g, protein 4 g, sodium 282 mg

APRICOT-BANANA BREAD

When you slice this banana bread, the chopped apricots inside form a colorful mosaic. It's good with spiced tea.

> 2 cups plus 2 tablespoons whole wheat pastry flour
> 1 teaspoon baking powder
> 1/2 teaspoon each baking soda and salt
> 1/2 cup honey
> 2/3 cup chopped dried apricots
> 1/2 cup chopped walnuts
> 1 egg
> 1/2 cup nonfat milk
> 1 tablespoon each walnut oil and canola oil
> 1 large, soft ripe banana, mashed (about 3/4 cup)

1. Preheat oven to 350° F. In a large bowl stir together flour, baking powder, baking soda, salt, and honey. Mix in apricots and walnuts.

2. In a medium bowl beat egg with milk and oils. Blend in banana. Add banana mixture to flour mixture, mixing just until dry ingredients are moistened.

3. Spread batter in an oiled, lightly floured 4 1/2- by 8 1/2-inch loaf pan.

4. Bake until loaf is well browned and a wooden skewer inserted in center comes out clean (65 to 70 minutes).

5. Let cool in pan on a wire rack for 10 minutes, then turn out onto rack to cool completely.

Makes 1 loaf, 12 servings.

> *Preparation time:* 20 minutes
> *Baking time:* 65 to 70 minutes
> *Per serving:* calcium 59 mg, calories 206, carbohydrates 36 g, cholesterol 18 mg, fat 6 g, fiber 3 g, protein 6 g, sodium 185 mg

ORANGE-DATE MUFFINS

Tart yet sweet, these easy muffins acquire their lightness and refreshing flavor from fresh orange juice and grated orange rind. Make plenty of muffins for Sunday brunches—they freeze well and can be reheated in a 450° F oven for 8 minutes before serving.

>   Oil, for coating muffin tin
> 1 orange
> ½ cup chopped, pitted dates
> 2 tablespoons canola oil
> 1 egg
> 1 egg white
> 2 tablespoons light honey
> 2 tablespoons nonfat plain
>   yogurt
> 1½ cups whole wheat pastry flour
> 1 teaspoon baking powder
> 1 teaspoon baking soda

1. Preheat oven to 400° F. Lightly oil a 12-hole muffin tin.

2. Grate peel from orange, then juice orange. In a large bowl combine peel and juice with dates, oil, egg, egg white, honey, and yogurt.

3. In a separate bowl combine flour, baking powder, and baking soda. Mix together contents of both bowls, stirring briefly, then spoon into prepared muffin cups, filling them three fourths full. Bake for 12 to 15 minutes. Remove from pan and let cool.

Makes 1 dozen muffins, 12 servings.

Preparation time: 15 minutes
Baking time: 12 to 15 minutes
Per serving: calcium 47 mg, calories 116, carbohydrates 21 g, cholesterol 18 mg, fat 3 g, fiber 3 g, protein 3 g, sodium 148 mg

CARROT-GINGER BREAKFAST MUFFINS

Once considered dessert, carrot cake now takes on many different roles in a meal. Here is a new twist: Add freshly grated ginger to the batter, bake it in muffin tins, and serve the sweet muffins for breakfast or as a snack. Warm them in the toaster oven or microwave and serve with Cream Cheese and Garlic Dip (see page 26).

>   Oil, for coating muffin tins
> 2 cups whole wheat pastry flour
> 1 tablespoon baking powder
> 1 teaspoon baking soda
> ½ teaspoon herbal salt substitute
> ½ teaspoon nutmeg
> ½ teaspoon cinnamon
> 2 teaspoons grated ginger
> ½ cup nonfat yogurt or low-fat
>   buttermilk
> ¼ cup canola oil
> ¼ cup maple syrup
> ¼ cup light honey
> 3 eggs
> 2 cups grated carrot

1. Preheat oven to 400° F. Lightly oil a 12-hole muffin tin.

2. In a large bowl combine flour, baking powder, baking soda, salt substitute, nutmeg, and cinnamon.

3. In a separate bowl combine ginger, yogurt, the ¼ cup oil, maple syrup, honey, and eggs.

4. Stir together contents of both bowls, then stir in carrots. Spoon into muffin tins, filling about three quarters full, and bake for 15 to 18 minutes. Remove from pan; let cool.

Makes 1 dozen muffins, 12 servings.

Preparation time: 20 minutes
Baking time: 15 to 18 minutes
Per serving: calcium 134 mg, calories 188, carbohydrates 30 g, cholesterol 53 mg, fat 6 g, fiber 4 g, protein 5 g, sodium 233 mg

MENU

FIRESIDE FEAST

Russian Black Bread

Molasses Corn Muffins

Herb Muffins

Minnesota Chicken and Wild Rice Soup (see page 51)

Hearty Lima Bean Soup (see page 59)

Swiss Lentil Soup (see page 50)

When winter winds howl, prepare this hearty buffet of soups and homemade breads and muffins and serve it by the fire. Russian Black Bread can be started early in the morning—it needs about three hours of rising time before baking. Molasses Corn Muffins and Herb Muffins are rich-tasting and can be made ahead of time. They freeze well, so bake an extra batch for Sunday breakfasts. Start the soups the night before, and their flavors will improve overnight in the refrigerator. Keep them warm on the buffet table in electric slow cookers or heated trays. Menu serves twelve.

RUSSIAN BLACK BREAD

This strong, dark bread combines classic flavors.

- *½ cup lukewarm water*
- *1 cup low-fat buttermilk, at room temperature*
- *2 tablespoons molasses*
- *2 tablespoons light honey*
- *1 package active dry yeast*
- *3 to 4 cups whole wheat flour*
- *1½ cups rye flour*
- *1 tablespoon crushed caraway seed*
- *½ teaspoon onion powder*
- *½ teaspoon crushed fennel seed*
- *2 tablespoons grain coffee*
- *2 tablespoons carob powder*
- *2 tablespoons canola oil, plus oil for coating pan*

1. In a large bowl combine the water, buttermilk, molasses, honey, and yeast. Stir until yeast dissolves. Let stand for 5 minutes. Stir in 2 cups of the wheat flour, or enough to form a thick batter. Stir well; let stand 20 minutes.

2. Stir batter down, then add rye flour, caraway seed, onion powder, fennel seed, grain coffee, carob powder, and 2 tablespoons oil to form a thick dough. Lightly flour a counter or breadboard and turn dough onto surface. Knead until smooth and elastic (5 to 10 minutes). Lightly oil a mixing bowl and put kneaded dough into it. Cover with a dish towel and let rise for 40 minutes.

3. Punch down dough; cover again and let rise 30 minutes. Lightly oil a 2-quart loaf pan and preheat oven to 350° F. Form dough into 1 large loaf; press into pan. Let rise 10 minutes.

4. Bake until loaf sounds hollow when tapped (50 minutes to 1 hour). Let cool before slicing.

Makes 1 large loaf, 12 servings.

Preparation time: 55 minutes
Rising time: 1 hour, 45 minutes
Baking time: 50 minutes to 1 hour
Per serving: calcium 63 mg, calories 215, carbohydrates 40 g, cholesterol 1 mg, fat 4 g, fiber 6 g, protein 7 g, sodium 30 mg

MOLASSES CORN MUFFINS

Molasses—especially the blackstrap variety—is rich in iron and trace minerals. However, if you use the blackstrap, use only half the recipe amount because it has a stronger flavor than regular, unsulfured molasses. The cornmeal in this recipe gives the muffins a pleasantly crunchy texture and a slightly crisp crust that goes well with the hearty soups in this menu.

- *Oil, for coating muffin tin*
- *1 cup whole wheat pastry flour*
- *3 teaspoons baking powder*
- *1 teaspoon salt or herbal salt substitute*
- *½ cup boiling water*
- *½ cup finely ground cornmeal*
- *2 tablespoons molasses*
- *¼ cup light honey*
- *3 beaten eggs*
- *¼ cup canola oil*
- *¼ cup grated low-fat Cheddar cheese*

1. Preheat oven to 400° F. Lightly oil a 12-hole muffin tin.

2. In a large mixing bowl, combine flour, baking powder, and salt. In a separate bowl combine the boiling water and cornmeal. Mix well.

3. Add molasses, honey, eggs, oil, and cheese to cornmeal and stir well. Add to flour mixture, stirring briefly as you combine. Spoon into prepared muffin cups, filling about three fourths full.

4. Bake for 25 minutes. Let cool slightly, then remove from tins.

Makes 1 dozen muffins, 12 servings.

Preparation time: 20 minutes
Baking time: 25 minutes
Per serving: calcium 158 mg, calories 126, carbohydrates 18 g, cholesterol 37 mg, fat 4 g, fiber 3 g, protein 6 g, sodium 265 mg

HERB MUFFINS

Thyme, basil, and oregano are combined in this savory whole-grain herb muffin. It is lightly laced with Parmesan cheese, which provides a creamy texture as well as calcium. Made ahead of time, these muffins freeze well and will keep for up to two weeks. Reheat them for 10 minutes in a 450° F oven right before serving.

- *Oil, for coating muffin tin*
- *2 cups whole wheat or white pastry flour*
- *1 tablespoon baking powder*
- *1 teaspoon baking soda*
- *½ teaspoon herbal salt substitute*
- *2 teaspoons dried oregano*
- *2 teaspoons dried thyme*
- *2 teaspoons dried basil*
- *2 eggs*
- *1 egg white*
- *1 cup low-fat buttermilk*
- *2 tablespoons canola oil*
- *1 tablespoon light honey*
- *¼ cup grated Parmesan cheese*

1. Preheat oven to 400° F. Lightly oil a 12-hole muffin tin.

2. In a large mixing bowl, combine flour, baking powder, baking soda, salt, oregano, thyme, and basil.

3. In a separate bowl combine eggs, egg white, buttermilk, the 2 tablespoons oil, honey, and Parmesan. Mix together the contents of both bowls, stirring briefly, then spoon into prepared muffin cups, filling two thirds full.

4. Bake for 25 minutes. Let cool slightly, then remove from tins.

Makes 1 dozen muffins, 12 servings.

Preparation time: 10 minutes
Baking time: 25 minutes
Per serving: calcium 90 mg, calories 128, carbohydrates 17 g, cholesterol 44 mg, fat 4 g, fiber 2 g, protein 6 g, sodium 228 mg

Create a warm winter Fireside Feast menu by matching a trio of hearty soups with healthy homemade breads and muffins.

Choose the natural sweetness of fresh fruit to create memorable, healthy desserts that satisfy the sweet tooth.

DESSERTS

S atisfying your sweet tooth on occasion doesn't have to mean undermining your commitment to a healthy lifestyle. The nutritious desserts and other sweet treats in this chapter emphasize wholesome ingredients such as maple syrup, honey, fruit purées, and fruit juice concentrates. Choose from luscious finales such as Wine-Basted Pears (see page 203), Lime Soufflé From Barbados (see page 209), or Carob Cheesecake (see page 214) to create the perfect ending to a simple family supper or a special dinner party.

The natural sweetness of fresh pears complements the tangy orange-wine sauce. Garnish elegant Wine-Basted Pears with mint and strips of orange peel.

SIMPLE FRUIT DESSERTS

Fresh fruit offers natural sweetness to low-fat desserts, if prepared correctly. Or, you can supplement the natural fruit sugars with unprocessed, unrefined sweeteners such as maple syrup, undiluted apple juice concentrate, and honey.

BAKED PEARS

Baked Pears works as a brunch dessert, an early morning breakfast starter, or a final course to a light summer lunch of seafood salad.

 6 *large pears, slightly underripe*
 ¼ *cup lemon juice*
 1 *cup orange juice*
 2 *tablespoons maple syrup*
 ¼ *teaspoon allspice*

1. Preheat oven to 350° F. With a melon baller, core pears by pressing the melon baller into the bottom of the pear. Then insert the melon baller into the cavity and scoop out any remaining core. Peel pears, but leave them whole.

2. Mix remaining ingredients for poaching liquid. Place pears in a deep baking dish and pour liquid over them. Bake until pears are softened (about 45 minutes). Serve with a small amount of poaching liquid. Pears can be served either hot or chilled.

Serves 6.

> *Preparation time:* 20 minutes
> *Baking time:* 45 minutes
> *Per serving:* calcium 28 mg, calories 137, carbohydrates 35 g, cholesterol 0 mg, fat 1 g, fiber 4 g, protein 1 g, sodium 1 mg

APPLES STUFFED WITH RAISINS AND DATES

A simple dish, this very low-fat dessert is perfect for fall, when tart apples are in season.

 6 *large tart baking apples*
 2 *dried figs, chopped*
 ¼ *cup pitted, chopped fresh dates*
 ¼ *cup raisins, soaked in hot water for 10 minutes, then drained*
 1 *teaspoon cinnamon*
 1 *teaspoon nutmeg*
 4 *tablespoons frozen apple juice concentrate*

1. Preheat oven to 350° F. Core apples with apple corer or sharp knife, leaving a small bit of fruit at the bottom to hold the filling.

2. Mix remaining ingredients and stuff into apples, packing well.

3. Place fruit in a shallow baking dish and cover loosely with aluminum foil. Add water to cover one quarter the height of the apples. Bake until apples are soft and browned (about 35 minutes). Serve hot or cold.

Serves 6.

> *Preparation time:* 15 minutes
> *Baking time:* 35 minutes
> *Per serving:* calcium 28 mg, calories 139, carbohydrates 35 g, cholesterol 0 mg, fat 1 g, fiber 4 g, protein 1 g, sodium 7 mg

WINE-BASTED PEARS

The alcohol in wine (the source of most of its calories) evaporates when you heat a wine mixture to 170° F. The aroma and flavor remain—but about 80 percent of the wine's original calories evaporate. This wine-basted fruit dish is a delightful finish to a meal, especially if you use the same red wine to poach the pears as you serve with the main course. Make these up to one week ahead of time and serve chilled. Save the poaching liquid. It will keep for four months in the refrigerator and can be used again to poach more fruit.

    6   large pears, slightly underripe
    2   tablespoons lemon juice
    2   cups hearty red wine, such as
         Zinfandel or Burgundy
    1   teaspoon honey
    2   teaspoons cinnamon
    1   cup orange juice
         Fresh mint leaves, for garnish

1. Core whole pears from bottom, using a melon baller, leaving stems intact. Peel the pears.

2. In a deep saucepan mix remaining ingredients except garnish and bring to a boil. Add pears and simmer until they become deep red in color and softened (about 35 minutes). Drain pears and chill, reserving liquid for another use. Garnish pears with mint leaves and serve.

Serves 6.

Preparation time: 20 minutes
Cooking time: 35 minutes
Chilling time: 1 hour
Per serving: calcium 39 mg, calories 180, carbohydrates 33 g, cholesterol 0 mg, fat 1 g, fiber 5 g, protein 1 g, sodium 5 mg

FRUIT COMPOTE WITH YOGURT SAUCE

A compote is a stewed mixture of dried fruits, such as prunes, apricots, and figs. After it cooks, it can be puréed for a topping, or served with another topping, such as the sweetened yogurt sauce (nonfat plain yogurt with a dash of maple syrup) used here. It is a very easy, make-ahead dessert. For a smart presentation, serve fruit compote in large wineglasses and garnish with fresh mint or grated orange peel.

    1   cup chopped, pitted dried dates
    2   cups chopped, pitted dried
         prunes
    1   cup chopped dried apricots
    1/2 cup raisins
    1   cup chopped dried figs
    1   cup grated apple
    1   teaspoon ground cardamom
    1   teaspoon cinnamon
    1   teaspoon grated orange rind
    3   cups apple juice
    2   tablespoons lemon juice
    1/2 cup nonfat plain yogurt
    1/2 teaspoon maple syrup
    1/8 teaspoon nutmeg
    1/4 cup puréed fresh or frozen
         strawberries (optional)

1. Place dates, prunes, apricots, raisins, figs, apple, cardamom, cinnamon, orange rind, and apple and lemon juices into a heavy saucepan and bring to a boil.

2. Lower heat, cover, and simmer for 45 minutes, stirring occasionally.

3. While mixture is cooking, in a small bowl combine yogurt, maple syrup, nutmeg, and puréed strawberries, if desired; mix well. Chill and serve over cooked compote.

Serves 8.

Preparation time: 10 minutes
Cooking time: 45 minutes to 1 hour
Per serving: calcium 118 mg, calories 359, carbohydrates 93 g, cholesterol 0 mg, fat 1 g, fiber 8 g, protein 4 g, sodium 22 mg

FILO TART WITH RASPBERRIES

Made from flour, cornstarch, and water, filo is a delicate, paper-thin pastry (see How to Prepare Filo, page 212). Kiwifruit, mandarin orange slices, ripe peaches, or any other soft fruit will work well if raspberries are unavailable.

         Oil, for coating tart pan
    4   sheets filo dough
    1½ tablespoons melted butter
    1   cup low-fat ricotta cheese
    1   teaspoon maple syrup
    1   teaspoon grated lemon rind
    1   teaspoon honey
    2   cups raspberries

1. Preheat oven to 375° F. Lightly oil a 9½-inch tart pan.

2. Lightly brush the top surface of a filo sheet with butter. Fit into the prepared tart pan, building up the sides to make edges. Repeat with remaining sheets of filo dough. With scissors, trim the filo dough extending beyond the edge of the tart shell. Line filo dough with aluminum foil and fill the foil with dried beans to weight the tart shell. Bake the tart shell until golden (about 20 minutes). Remove foil and dried beans and allow shell to cool.

3. In a blender purée ricotta, maple syrup, and lemon rind.

4. Brush the baked, cooled tart shell with ½ teaspoon of the honey. Spoon the ricotta mixture into the shell and layer the berries on top. Brush tops of berries with remaining honey. Serve chilled or at room temperature.

Serves 8.

Preparation time: 20 minutes
Baking time: 20 minutes
Per serving: calcium 93 mg, calories 115, carbohydrates 12 g, cholesterol 15 mg, fat 6 g, fiber 2 g, protein 5 g, sodium 106 mg

A splendid finale to your next elegant dinner is Compote of Winter Fruits in Red Wine, served warm or chilled with a dollop of yogurt.

2. Mix watermelon balls with remaining ingredients, except garnish. Spoon into one of the watermelon shells. Chill for 15 minutes.

3. Garnish with mint leaves and serve out of the shell.

Serves 8.

> *Preparation time:* 25 minutes
> *Chilling time:* 15 minutes
> *Per serving:* calcium 106 mg, calories 402, carbohydrates 93 g, cholesterol 0 mg, fat 5 g, fiber 6 g, protein 7 g, sodium 24 mg

COMPOTE OF WINTER FRUITS IN RED WINE

A simple dessert rich in flavor but low in fat, this recipe blends dried apricots and pineapple with simmered pears, apples, and spices. Serve it chilled or slightly warm with a dollop of nonfat yogurt.

> 2 *cups sliced pears*
> 2 *cups sliced green apples*
> 1/3 *cup chopped dried apricots*
> 1/4 *cup chopped dried pineapple*
> 1 *teaspoon vanilla extract*
> 1 1/2 *cups dry red wine*
> 1/4 *teaspoon ground ginger*
> 1/4 *teaspoon cinnamon*
> 1/2 *teaspoon nutmeg*
>   *Grated rind of 1 lemon*
> 2 *tablespoons orange juice*
> 1 *cup nonfat plain yogurt*

1. In a large saucepan over medium heat, combine pears, apples, apricots, pineapple, vanilla, wine, ginger, cinnamon, nutmeg, lemon rind, and orange juice. Cook, stirring frequently, until most of wine has been absorbed and fruit is very soft (about 30 minutes).

2. Serve warm or chilled, topped with nonfat yogurt.

Makes approximately 5 cups compote, 8 servings.

> *Preparation time:* 20 minutes
> *Cooking time:* 30 minutes
> *Chilling time (optional):* 2 hours
> *Per serving:* calcium 67 mg, calories 107, carbohydrates 18 g, cholesterol 2 mg, fat 1 g, fiber 2 g, protein 2 g, sodium 24 mg

SUMMER MELON BOUQUETS WITH MINT SAUCE

Make this eye-catching dessert as close to serving time as possible to retain the color and texture of the fresh fruit.

> 1 *small watermelon, cut in half lengthwise*
> 1 *cup cantaloupe balls*
> 1 *cup (8 oz can) lichee nuts, rinsed and drained*
> 1 *cup pineapple chunks*
> 1 *cup (8 oz can) mandarin orange slices, rinsed and drained*
> 1 *cup halved strawberries*
> 1/4 *cup maple syrup*
> 1/4 *cup date sugar (ground, dried dates) or honey*
> 3 *tablespoons chopped fresh mint, plus mint leaves for garnish*

1. Scoop the flesh out of the watermelon shells. Using a melon baller, make 2 cups of watermelon balls from the flesh and reserve the remainder for another use.

JAMAICAN BANANAS WITH RUM

These "fried" bananas are cooked in a light syrup of date sugar and small amounts of butter and white rum.

    6 large bananas in the peel
    1 teaspoon butter
    ½ cup apple juice
    ½ cup white rum
    ¼ cup date sugar (ground, dried dates)
    ½ teaspoon nutmeg

1. Preheat the oven to 400° F. Place unpeeled bananas on a baking sheet. Prick the skin of each banana several times with the prongs of a fork. Cook bananas until they turn black (about 10 minutes).

2. In a large skillet combine remaining ingredients and cook over medium-high heat for 8 minutes (to burn off alcohol).

3. Carefully remove peel from one side of each banana and place banana, open side down, in the rum syrup. Remove the remaining peel. Cut each banana in half and cook, turning once, until lightly golden (about 2 minutes). Serve warm.

Serves 6.

Preparation time: 5 minutes
Cooking time: 20 minutes
Per serving: calcium 10 mg, calories 207, carbohydrates 41 g, cholesterol 2 mg, fat 1 g, fiber 3 g, protein 1 g, sodium 9 mg

Ripe bananas are baked in their skins, then peeled and sautéed in a light syrup of date sugar, apple juice, and white rum. Serve Jamaican Bananas With Rum as part of a stir-fry menu.

WATERMELON SHERBET

This dessert could not be easier—fresh watermelon is combined with honey, cardamom, and lime juice, then frozen. You don't even need an ice cream maker or sorbet machine. Simply pour the mixture into ice cube trays, freeze until solid, then cut into chunks and lightly blend. Serve the sherbet in tall champagne glasses garnished with a mint leaf.

   8 cups chopped, seeded
      watermelon
1½ tablespoons lime juice
   1 cup light honey
 ½ teaspoon ground cardamom
 ½ package unflavored gelatin
 ½ cup nonfat plain yogurt
 12 mint leaves

1. Place watermelon and lime juice in a blender and purée. Set a colander or sieve over a large bowl and pour puréed watermelon through sieve, separating juice from pulp. Place juice, honey, cardamom, and gelatin in a large saucepan over medium-high heat. Cook just to boiling point, then remove from heat. Let cool. Pour into a shallow pan or ice cube tray and freeze to slush point (about 1½ hours).

2. Whisk yogurt into watermelon slush, then return to freezer. Allow to freeze solid (about 2 hours). Stir every hour to break up ice crystals.

3. To serve, cut sherbet into large chunks and purée very briefly in a blender or food processor. Spoon into dessert glasses, garnish each serving with mint leaf, and serve.

Serves 12.

Preparation time: 25 minutes
Freezing time: 3½ hours
Per serving: calcium 37 mg, calories 141, carbohydrates 33 g, cholesterol 0 mg, fat .3 g, fiber .9 g, protein 5 g, sodium 25 mg

PUDDINGS, MOUSSES, CUSTARDS, AND SOUFFLÉS

Treat yourself to an old-fashioned rice pudding, a sweet strawberry or peach mousse, or a lemon iced dessert.

PEACH MOUSSE

A very light concoction of fresh fruit, yogurt, and spices, this cooked mousse is chilled in a decorative mold or in wineglasses for an exquisite presentation.

   3 cups sliced peaches
   3 eggs
 ¼ cup nonfat plain yogurt
   2 tablespoons arrowroot powder
   1 teaspoon maple syrup
      Sliced fresh peaches, for
      garnish

1. In a blender combine all ingredients except for garnish and purée until smooth.

2. Pour into a saucepan and cook over low heat, stirring constantly, until thickened to the consistency of custard.

3. Spoon into a decorative mold or 4 wineglasses. Chill for 1 hour. Garnish with sliced fresh peaches.

Serves 4.

Preparation time: 20 minutes
Cooking time: 10 to 15 minutes
Chilling time: 1 hour
Per serving: calcium 46 mg, calories 147, carbohydrates 22 g, cholesterol 161 mg, fat 4 g, fiber 3 g, protein 6 g, sodium 54 mg

ORANGE-PUMPKIN SPICE PUDDING

Warm pudding scented with holiday spices is a great treat for a Christmas Eve or Hanukkah party. Pumpkin is a good source of potassium and vitamin A, and this pumpkin recipe takes a relatively short time to prepare.

      Oil, for coating custard cups
   1 cup nonfat milk
   1 tablespoon arrowroot powder
   2 tablespoons molasses
   1 cup canned or cooked, fresh
      pumpkin purée
   2 tablespoons cinnamon
 ½ teaspoon ground cloves
   1 teaspoon ground cardamom
   2 teaspoons grated ginger
   1 teaspoon nutmeg
 ½ cup maple syrup
   2 tablespoons grated orange rind
 ¼ cup orange juice
   2 eggs
      Nonfat plain yogurt, for
      garnish

1. Preheat oven to 350° F. Lightly oil 8 custard cups.

2. In a large bowl combine milk, arrowroot, and molasses, and whisk until well blended. Add pumpkin, cinnamon, cloves, cardamom, ginger, nutmeg, maple syrup, orange rind, and orange juice.

3. Separate eggs. Add yolks to pumpkin mixture. In a small bowl beat egg whites until stiff peaks form. Fold into pumpkin mixture.

4. Pour into prepared custard cups. Place in a shallow baking pan. Add hot water to one half the depth of pan. Bake until firm (about 40 minutes). Let cool slightly and serve garnished with yogurt.

Serves 8.

Preparation time: 20 minutes
Baking time: 40 minutes
Per serving: calcium 103 mg, calories 121, carbohydrates 25 g, cholesterol 54 mg, fat 2 g, fiber 2 g, protein 3 g, sodium 38 mg

STEAMED PUMPKIN PUDDING

This dessert is perfect for fall days, when pumpkins are plentiful and a warm dish is welcome. The pudding is baked in a bundt or cake pan placed inside a bain-marie or dish of hot water, which prevents the pudding from cooking too fast. Steamed Pumpkin Pudding keeps for several days, covered, in the refrigerator, but loses the desired texture if frozen.

Oil, for coating pan
1 cup cooked pumpkin purée (canned)
1 teaspoon melted butter
²/₃ cup low-fat buttermilk
2 eggs, lightly beaten
2 egg whites, lightly beaten
¹/₄ cup maple syrup
¹/₂ teaspoon grated fresh ginger
1¹/₂ cups whole wheat pastry flour
¹/₄ cup date sugar
2 teaspoons baking soda
2 teaspoons cinnamon
1 teaspoon nutmeg

1. Preheat oven to 375° F. Lightly oil a 1¹/₂-quart bundt or cake pan. Fill a larger pan ¹/₄ full with hot water.

2. In a bowl combine pumpkin purée, butter, buttermilk, eggs, egg whites, maple syrup, and ginger. In a separate bowl sift together flour, date sugar, baking soda, cinnamon, and nutmeg.

3. Combine contents of both bowls and spoon into prepared bundt pan. Place pan into pan of hot water. Carefully set on middle oven rack and bake until a knife inserted in the center of the pudding comes out clean (30 to 40 minutes). Let cool 10 minutes before serving.

Serves 8.

Preparation time: 20 minutes
Baking time: 30 to 40 minutes
Per serving: calcium 61 mg, calories 188, carbohydrates 36 g, cholesterol 55 mg, fat 3 g, fiber 4 g, protein 7 g, sodium 375 mg

RASPBERRY-TOFU MOUSSE

This low-fat dessert will surprise your guests—no one will believe it contains tofu. Be sure to buy soft tofu for this recipe; the firmer type tends to impart a grainier texture to the mousse. Also make sure that the tofu is extremely fresh because it will turn bitter as it ages. You can make the mousse up to two hours before serving.

¹/₄ pound soft tofu, drained
2 cups raspberries, fresh or frozen, plus raspberries for garnish
2 small ripe bananas
¹/₂ teaspoon nutmeg
2 teaspoons maple syrup
Mint leaves, for garnish

In a blender or food processor, combine all ingredients except the garnishes, puréeing thoroughly. Spoon into wineglasses, garnish, and chill for 30 minutes before serving.

Serves 4.

Preparation time: 15 minutes
Chilling time: 30 minutes
Per serving: calcium 65 mg, calories 136, carbohydrates 30 g, cholesterol 0 mg, fat 2 g, fiber 6 g, protein 3 g, sodium 6 mg

NOTE

LOW-FAT ICED DESSERTS

These easy-to-prepare iced desserts are great for snacks or impromptu entertaining on hot summer evenings, and kids love them. For creamier ices, freeze the mixture to the slush point, then blend and refreeze in paper cups or swirled into wineglasses.

Orange Swirl Purée 2 cups fresh, peeled oranges with 1 tablespoon maple syrup and 1 teaspoon lemon juice. Freeze the purée in scooped-out orange halves.

Strawberry Pops Purée 2 cups fresh strawberries with 1 tablespoon apple juice concentrate. Freeze in small paper cups and when half frozen insert a wooden ice cream stick in the center. When frozen, peel away the cup.

Grape Nuggets Wash 2 cups seedless green or red grapes. Place on a baking sheet and freeze whole. Serve while still frozen.

TIPS

…ON SUBSTITUTING UNREFINED SWEETENERS

Using maple syrup, honey, and fruit juice concentrates instead of refined sugars in baked goods is easy once you know the substitution rules. In traditional baking, white or brown sugar is considered a dry ingredient and is balanced in a recipe by the use of liquids such as milk, cream, or eggs. Since most unrefined sweeteners are in liquid form, the ratio of dry to wet ingredients must be altered. Here are some tips on substituting unrefined sweeteners:

Maple syrup For every 1 cup of white or brown sugar, use ½ to ¾ cup maple syrup; decrease the oil or butter by 2 tablespoons; and increase the flour by 2 tablespoons.

Honey or molasses For every 1 cup of white or brown sugar, use ½ cup honey or molasses; decrease the oil or butter by 2 tablespoons; and increase the flour by 2 tablespoons.

Fruit juice concentrate For every 1 cup of white or brown sugar, use ¼ cup apple or pear juice concentrate; decrease the oil or butter by 4 to 6 tablespoons; and increase the flour by 4 to 6 tablespoons. Concentrates are best in cobblers and pies.

Dried fruits For every 1 cup of white or brown sugar, use ½ cup dried fruit purée (made by blending equal amounts of fruit and water); decrease the oil or butter by 2 tablespoons; and increase the flour by 2 tablespoons.

LEMON SNOW

This recipe is a pleasant froth of a dessert and fun to eat because it dissolves in your mouth like meringue cookies do. Serve it swirled into wineglasses, garnished with grated lemon peel, or pair it with a sauce of fresh berries. You can prepare this recipe the evening before but no earlier, as it will lose its texture.

> 1 envelope unflavored gelatin
> ½ cup frozen apple juice concentrate, thawed
> ⅔ cup boiling water
> ⅓ cup fresh lemon juice
> ½ teaspoon grated lemon rind (optional)
> 3 egg whites

1. Sprinkle gelatin over apple juice concentrate in a mixing bowl.

2. Pour boiling water over softened gelatin and stir to dissolve.

3. Add lemon juice and taste. For more lemony flavor, add more juice and lemon rind.

4. Chill mixture about 30 minutes in refrigerator or 15 minutes in freezer, stirring occasionally.

5. Add egg whites and whip mixture with a balloon whisk or an electric handheld beater until it triples in volume and resembles a soft meringue.

6. Spoon into wineglasses and chill at least 4 hours or overnight.

Serves 8 to 10.

Preparation time: 20 minutes
Chilling time: 4 hours or overnight
Per serving: calcium 6 mg, calories 43, carbohydrates 9 g, cholesterol 0 mg, fat 0 g, fiber 0 g, protein 2 g, sodium 28 mg

ORANGE RICE PUDDING

This traditionally rich pudding was altered to lower the fat content. Rice pudding is an old favorite of many, and this one adds a hint of citrus to the standard recipe. It can be made ahead, freezes well, and can be served either warm or cold.

> 4 cups nonfat milk
> 2 tablespoons maple syrup
>   Pinch herbal salt substitute
> 1 cup uncooked long-grain brown rice
> 1½ teaspoons vanilla extract
> 1 cup raisins
> ⅓ cup chopped, pitted fresh dates
> 1 tablespoon grated orange rind
> ½ cup orange juice
>   Oil, for coating baking dish
>   Orange peel strips, for garnish

1. In a heavy 2-quart saucepan, combine 2 cups of the milk, the maple syrup, salt substitute, and rice. Bring to a boil and lower heat to simmer. Cook 25 minutes over medium heat.

2. Preheat oven to 325° F. Mix together the remaining ingredients except oil and garnish. Lightly oil a 9- by 12-inch baking dish.

3. Mix rice mixture with orange juice mixture and pour into the prepared baking dish. Bake until solidified and lightly browned (about 90 minutes). Garnish with strips of orange peel.

Serves 8.

Preparation time: 10 minutes
Cooking time: 25 minutes
Baking time: 90 minutes
Per serving: calcium 177 mg, calories 229, carbohydrates 49 g, cholesterol 2 mg, fat 2 g, fiber 1 g, protein 7 g, sodium 67 mg

CHILLED BANANA CUSTARD

Bananas are a rich source of potassium, an essential mineral for good nerve functioning. In this light and easy dessert, puréed bananas are mixed with eggs, nonfat milk, and maple syrup, and then chilled to form a thick, creamy custard. Serve it cold as a wonderful finish to a warm-weather menu.

> 1 cup nonfat milk
> 1 whole egg
> 2 egg yolks
> 3 tablespoons maple syrup
> 3 tablespoons whole wheat flour
> 1 teaspoon vanilla extract
> 1 tablespoon arrowroot
> 1 tablespoon apple juice or water
> 2 large bananas

1. In a small saucepan over medium-high heat, heat milk until it steams. Remove from heat and pour into a mixing bowl.

2. In a separate bowl whisk together egg, egg yolks, and maple syrup until smooth. Add flour and vanilla. Mix arrowroot with apple juice and add to egg mixture. Add hot milk. Purée bananas in a blender, then add to egg mixture.

3. Return custard to pan and cook over medium-high heat, stirring, until thick. Pour into 8 dessert glasses and chill in the refrigerator for 4 hours before serving.

Serves 8.

Preparation time: 20 minutes
Chilling time: 4 hours
Per serving: calcium 55 mg, calories 95, carbohydrates 17 g, cholesterol 80 mg, fat 2 g, fiber 1 g, protein 3 g, sodium 27 mg

---

LIME SOUFFLÉ FROM BARBADOS

This cloudlike soufflé is composed of vitamin-rich fresh lime juice, grated lime rind, and egg whites, sweetened with a small amount of maple syrup. The tart taste of the lime makes it a good dessert to serve after a rich-tasting entrée, such as Chicken Breasts With Green Peppercorn Sauce (see page 146). Plan to make the soufflé the night before and set it overnight in the refrigerator.

> 1 tablespoon butter, for coating soufflé dish
> 2 packages unflavored gelatin
> 1 cup freshly squeezed lime juice
> 3 egg yolks
> 1 cup nonfat milk
> ½ cup maple syrup
> 2 tablespoons arrowroot powder
> 3 tablespoons grated lime rind
> ½ cup grated fresh coconut
> 6 egg whites

1. Lightly butter a large (2-quart) soufflé dish.

2. In a small saucepan over medium-high heat, cook gelatin in lime juice until completely dissolved. In a small bowl combine egg yolks, milk, maple syrup, and arrowroot. Add to lime juice mixture and cook, stirring constantly, until a thick custardlike sauce forms. Remove saucepan from heat.

3. Stir in lime rind and coconut. Beat egg whites until stiff peaks form, then fold into lime mixture. Pour into prepared soufflé dish and refrigerate until firm (about 8 hours). Serve chilled.

Serves 8.

Preparation time: 20 minutes
Cooking time: 5 to 10 minutes
Chilling time: 8 hours
Per serving: calcium 81 mg, calories 225, carbohydrates 23 g, cholesterol 84 mg, fat 6 g, fiber .7 g, protein 23 g, sodium 133 mg

---

CAROB-MOCHA SOUFFLÉ

This creamy soufflé features the rich taste of carob and coffee. Grain coffee, a good substitute for coffee liqueur, is usually sold in natural food stores. Soufflés typically combine the jelling power of egg yolks with the fluffy texture of beaten egg whites. In this recipe, arrowroot powder replaces the egg yolks. The secret of a super soufflé is to gently fold in the egg whites at the last minute so they retain their airiness.

> 2 tablespoons softened butter
> 1 tablespoon whole wheat flour
> ⅓ cup low-fat milk
> 4 tablespoons honey
> 2 tablespoons carob powder
> 1 tablespoon coffee liqueur or grain coffee
> 1 teaspoon vanilla extract
> 1 tablespoon arrowroot powder
> 2 tablespoons orange juice
> 2 egg whites

1. Preheat oven to 375° F. Using 1 tablespoon of the butter, lightly butter 4 custard cups.

2. In a small saucepan over medium heat, melt remaining butter. Stir in flour and cook for 2 minutes, stirring constantly. Pour in milk and cook until mixture thickens. Remove from heat and add in honey, carob powder, coffee liqueur, and vanilla. Mix arrowroot with orange juice and add to carob mixture.

3. Beat egg whites until stiff peaks form. Fold into carob mixture and pour into prepared custard cups. Set custard cups in a shallow baking pan and fill with hot water to one half the height of the pan. Bake soufflé until slightly puffed and springy (15 to 20 minutes). Let cool and serve.

Serves 4.

Preparation time: 20 minutes
Baking time: 15 to 20 minutes
Per serving: calcium 65 mg, calories 193, carbohydrates 29 g, cholesterol 13 mg, fat 7 g, fiber .6 g, protein 4 g, sodium 98 mg

---

CAKES AND PASTRIES

These delectable pastries outshine conventional versions by using filo dough instead of traditional pie crusts; lightening the sweetener by relying on the natural sweetness of fresh fruits; and substituting blended low-fat cheeses for pastry creams. So go ahead and indulge!

SWEET DATE AND COCONUT COOKIES

These cookies may remind you of palm trees and oases—their creamy texture and sweet flavor come from a combination of chopped dates and grated fresh coconut. You can make a double batch and freeze half to serve with tea or pack in lunches.

> Oil, for coating pan
> 3/4 cup honey
> 1 egg
> 1 egg white
> 1 cup chopped, pitted dates
> 1/4 cup grated fresh coconut
> 1/2 cup chopped almonds
> 1/2 cup raisins
> 1/2 cup whole wheat pastry flour
> 1/2 teaspoon baking powder

1. Preheat oven to 350° F. Lightly oil an 8-inch-square baking pan.

2. In a large bowl combine honey, egg, egg white, dates, coconut, almonds, and raisins. In separate bowl sift together flour and baking powder. Combine contents of two bowls, mix well, and pour into prepared pan. Bake 30 minutes.

3. Let cool, then slice.

Makes about 16 squares, 16 servings.

Preparation time: 15 minutes
Baking time: 30 minutes
Per serving: calcium 32 mg, calories 144, carbohydrates 30 g, cholesterol 13 mg, fat 3 g, fiber 2 g, protein 3 g, sodium 25 mg

---

MAPLE-COTTAGE CHEESE SQUARES

These little bars practically melt in your mouth. Make them ahead of time and refrigerate until serving.

> Oil, for coating pan
> 2 1/2 cups finely crushed graham cracker crumbs
> 1 teaspoon cinnamon
> 1/4 cup date sugar
> 1/4 cup canola oil
> 1/4 cup nonfat milk
> 2 cups low-fat cottage cheese
> 1 cup low-fat ricotta cheese
> 1 tablespoon melted butter
> 3 tablespoons maple syrup
> 2 tablespoons grated orange rind
> 1 teaspoon orange juice

1. Preheat oven to 300° F. Lightly oil an 8-inch-square baking pan.

2. In a large bowl combine graham cracker crumbs, cinnamon, date sugar, the 1/4 cup oil, and enough milk to form a ball. Press into bottom of pan. Set aside.

3. In a blender or food processor, purée cottage cheese, ricotta, butter, maple syrup, orange rind, and orange juice. Pour into prepared pan and bake until firm (about 25 minutes). Remove from oven and let cool, then slice into squares.

Makes 16 squares, 16 servings.

Preparation time: 15 minutes
Baking time: 25 minutes
Per serving: calcium 75 mg, calories 153, carbohydrates 17 g, cholesterol 8 mg, fat 7 g, fiber .5 g, protein 6 g, sodium 223 mg

---

RICE WAFFLES WITH FRUIT SAUCE

These light waffles are made with cooked rice and sweetened with cinnamon, nutmeg, and honey. Serve them with a cooked sauce made with seasonal fruit. Here, strawberries are used.

> Oil or vegetable cooking spray, for coating waffle iron
> 3/4 cup sifted rice flour
> 2 teaspoons baking powder
> 1 teaspoon nutmeg
> 1 teaspoon cinnamon
> Pinch of salt
> 1 tablespoon honey
> 2 eggs, separated
> 1 cup nonfat milk
> 1/4 cup canola oil
> 1 cup cooked rice
> 1 cup sliced strawberries
> 2 teaspoons date sugar or maple syrup
> 2 teaspoons arrowroot powder
> 1/2 cup nonfat yogurt

1. Preheat waffle iron and lightly brush with oil.

2. In a medium bowl combine rice flour, baking powder, nutmeg, cinnamon, and salt. In a separate bowl combine honey, egg yolks, milk, the 1/4 cup oil, and rice. Beat egg whites until stiff peaks form. Combine dry and wet ingredients, then fold in egg whites.

3. Preheat oven to 200° F. Cook waffles, one at a time, keeping them warm in the oven on a heatproof platter. In a small saucepan combine strawberries, date sugar, and arrowroot. Cook over medium-high heat until thick. Let cool slightly, then mix with yogurt.

4. Pour strawberry sauce over warm waffles and serve.

Makes about 8 waffles, 8 servings.

Preparation time: 20 minutes
Cooking time: 20 minutes
Per serving: calcium 169 mg, calories 207, carbohydrates 28 g, cholesterol 54 mg, fat 9 g, fiber 1 g, protein 5 g, sodium 134 mg

---

CRANBERRY TURNOVERS WITH MAPLE GLAZE

Cranberries are full of natural pectin, a rich source of fiber and vitamin C. In this recipe they are simmered with apples, currants, and cinnamon, wrapped with a light pastry dough, brushed with maple glaze, then baked until crisp. Make the turnovers ahead, wrap tightly, and freeze to reheat as an easy brunch dessert.

1 package active dry yeast
1 cup lukewarm milk (98° F to 110° F)
3 tablespoons honey
3 cups whole wheat pastry flour
   Pinch of salt
3 tablespoons canola oil
3/4 cup cranberries
2 cups peeled and sliced green apples
1/2 cup water
1/4 cup dried currants
1 cup maple syrup
3 tablespoons arrowroot powder
1 tablespoon lemon juice
1/2 teaspoon cinnamon
1 tablespoon grated lemon rind
   Oil, for coating baking sheet

1. In a large bowl combine yeast, milk, and honey. Let mixture stand for 5 minutes. Stir in 1 1/2 cups of the flour and let batter rise for 15 minutes. Add remaining flour, salt, and oil to form a dough. Knead dough for 5 minutes on a floured breadboard, then place in a clean bowl and cover with a dish towel. Let dough rise for 45 minutes.

2. In a covered saucepan over medium-high heat, simmer cranberries, apples, the water, and currants until berries pop. In a small bowl mix 2/3 cup of the maple syrup, arrowroot, lemon juice, cinnamon, and lemon rind. Uncover saucepan and add maple syrup mixture to cooking cranberries. Stir well. Heat, stirring constantly, until thick. Remove from heat and let cool 15 minutes.

3. Preheat oven to 375° F. Lightly oil a large baking sheet. Separate dough into 8 balls. Roll into 5-inch circles on a floured breadboard. Place equal amounts of cranberry filling into the center of each circle. Lightly dampen edges of circle with water and fold edges in to form a turnover, pressing to seal.

4. In a small saucepan over high heat, bring the remaining maple syrup to a boil. Cook for 3 to 4 minutes. Remove from heat and then brush tops of turnovers with syrup. Place turnovers on prepared baking sheet and bake until browned (about 20 minutes). Let cool slightly before serving.

Makes 8 turnovers, 8 servings.

In these turnovers maple syrup sweetens the ruby red filling of cranberries and apples in a light pastry crust.

Preparation time: 30 minutes
Rising time: 65 minutes
Cooking time: 10 minutes
Baking time: 20 minutes
Per serving: calcium 91 mg, calories 381, carbohydrates 78 g, cholesterol 1 mg, fat 6 g, fiber 7 g, protein 8 g, sodium 24 mg

STEP BY STEP

HOW TO PREPARE FILO

Filo dough is a fragile pastry made from flour, cornstarch, and water. It is rolled so thin that you can see the silhouette of your hand through it. The paper-thin sheets are wrapped carefully to prevent them from drying out.

If you buy frozen filo dough, make sure it thaws completely before you use it. If the filo is not completely thawed, the edges will tend to stick as you peel off the sheets of dough.

Have your work surface clean and dry. As you remove a sheet of dough, keep the remaining dough covered with plastic wrap and a slightly damp-ened towel.

Brush each sheet of filo dough with melted butter so that it will puff up during baking. Most traditional recipes call for ¼ to ½ cup of butter per pound of filo, but you can use less by lightly sprinkling the melted butter over the pastry surface. If you prefer, substi-tute vegetable cooking spray for the melted butter.

Once the filo pastries are filled and ready to bake, they can be wrapped in plastic and stored for up to 2 days in the refrigerator. It is best to bake filo in a very hot (400° F to 425° F) oven, so that the butter expands quickly and the filo puffs well.

1. *Count out the number of filo sheets called for in the recipe and stack on a clean counter. Place a sheet of plastic wrap and a lightly dampened dish towel over the filo to keep it from drying out.*

2. *Next, melt a small amount of butter in a saucepan. Lay one sheet of filo on the counter or table. Using a pastry brush, lightly sprinkle melted butter on the filo, then spread to cover most of surface. Using a flicking motion keeps you from using too much butter. Alternatively, use a light coating of vegetable cooking spray. Stack the prepared filo to the side of the work area, ready for cutting into desired shapes.*

EASY BAKLAVA

This traditional Greek dessert alternates sheets of thin filo pastry with a mixture of ground almonds, walnuts, and cinnamon. When the pastry comes out of the oven, it soaks in a lemon-flavored honey glaze.

> Oil, for coating pan
> 1 cup ground almonds
> 1 cup ground walnuts
> 1½ teaspoons cinnamon
> 8 sheets filo dough
> ¼ cup melted unsalted butter
> 1¼ cups date sugar
> 2 tablespoons grated lemon rind
> ¼ cup lemon juice
> 2 tablespoons honey

1. Preheat oven to 350° F. Lightly oil a deep 9- by 12-inch baking pan.

2. In a small bowl combine almonds, walnuts, and cinnamon. Set aside.

3. Cut each sheet of filo in half. Stack cut sheets on counter. With a large pastry brush, dot top sheet with about 1 teaspoon butter, then spread evenly to coat as much of sheet as possible (see How to Prepare Filo, sidebar, left). Lay evenly in baking pan. Sprinkle lightly with nut mixture. Repeat with remain-ing sheets, stacking evenly.

4. To cut baklava make 4 evenly spaced vertical cuts through the entire stack of filo. Then cut diagonally into approxi-mately 24 pieces. Bake for 20 minutes, then lower heat to 300° F and bake for 30 minutes more.

5. In a small saucepan over medium-high heat, simmer date sugar, lemon rind, lemon juice, and honey until thickened. Pour over cooked baklava as soon as it comes out of the oven. Let cool and then serve.

Makes 24 pastries, 24 servings.

Preparation time: 25 minutes
Cooking time: 50 minutes
Per serving: calcium 30 mg, calories 136, carbohydrates 14 g, cholesterol 5 mg, fat 9 g, fiber 1 g, protein 3 g, sodium 33 mg

APPLE-APRICOT PASTRIES

Strips of paper-thin filo are layered to make a delicate crust for a sweet apricot jam and apple filling, and the pastries are baked to a crisp golden color.

> Oil, for coating baking pan
> 2 cups thinly sliced green apples
> ½ cup dried currants
> 2 tablespoons lemon juice
> 1 teaspoon vanilla extract
> ½ cup date sugar
> ¾ teaspoon cinnamon
> ½ teaspoon nutmeg
> ¾ cup ground almonds
> 8 sheets filo dough
> ⅓ cup melted unsalted butter
> ½ cup apricot preserves

1. Preheat oven to 375° F. Lightly oil a 9- by 12-inch baking pan with shallow sides.

2. In a medium saucepan over medium-high heat, cook apples, currants, lemon juice, vanilla, and date sugar until soft (about 15 minutes). Remove from heat and let cool.

3. In a small bowl mix cinnamon, nutmeg, and almonds. Set aside.

4. Sprinkle each sheet of filo with 2 teaspoons of the melted butter, then spread butter to coat filo evenly (see How to Prepare Filo, page 212). Sprinkle sheets with almond mixture and pile one sheet on top of another. Line prepared baking pan with stack of filo sheets, folding edges where necessary to make 1-inch sides.

5. In a small saucepan over medium heat, cook apricot preserves until soft, then spread evenly over top sheet of filo. Spoon apple mixture over preserves.

6. Bake pastry until slightly browned (about 20 minutes). Let cool, then cut into 2-inch squares.

Makes 12 squares, 12 servings.

> *Preparation time:* 25 minutes
> *Baking time:* 20 minutes
> *Per serving:* calcium 43 mg, calories 214, carbohydrates 30 g, cholesterol 14 mg, fat 11 g, fiber 2 g, protein 3 g, sodium 121 mg

CARROT-PINEAPPLE CAKE

Made with plenty of vitamin A-rich carrots, this cake will become a favorite dessert. The secret to the flavor and airy texture is crushed fresh pineapple and stiffly beaten egg whites. The cream cheese frosting makes this dessert a fine choice for birthday parties.

> Oil, for coating cake pan
> 2 eggs
> 3 tablespoons pineapple juice
> ¼ cup low-fat buttermilk
> ¼ cup canola oil
> 1 cup sifted whole wheat pastry flour
> 2 teaspoons baking powder
> ½ teaspoon salt or herbal salt substitute
> 1 tablespoon cinnamon
> 1 teaspoon nutmeg
> ⅓ cup chopped walnuts
> ½ cup raisins or dried currants
> ¾ cup crushed pineapple
> ¼ cup date sugar
> 1 cup grated carrots
> 4 ounces reduced-fat cream cheese
> 1 tablespoon vanilla extract
> 2 tablespoons maple syrup

1. Preheat oven to 350° F. Lightly oil a 9- by 13-inch cake pan.

2. Separate eggs. Place egg yolks in a large bowl and add pineapple juice, buttermilk, and the ¼ cup oil. Mix well and set aside.

3. In a separate bowl mix flour, baking powder, salt, cinnamon, and nutmeg. Set aside. Beat egg whites until stiff peaks form.

4. In another bowl combine walnuts, raisins, pineapple, date sugar, and carrots. Add egg yolk mixture and stir well. Make a well in center of dry ingredients and pour in carrot mixture. Mix until just blended. Fold in egg whites.

5. Pour batter into cake pan. Bake until firm in center (about 20 minutes).

6. While cake is baking, mix cream cheese, vanilla, and maple syrup until smooth and creamy. Let cake cool, then frost with cream cheese mixture.

Makes 1 sheet cake, 24 servings.

> *Preparation time:* 20 minutes
> *Baking time:* 20 minutes
> *Per serving:* calcium 50 mg, calories 96, carbohydrates 11 g, cholesterol 21 mg, fat 1 g, fiber 1 g, protein 2 g, sodium 104 mg

A French pastry chef would be proud to serve this rich—yet surprisingly light—cheesecake.

CAROB CHEESECAKE

Layers of dark-carob and white-yogurt filling, topped with carob fudge sauce, produce a striped effect when this cheesecake is sliced. This delicate cake is rich, so serve small portions.

 2½ cups finely crushed graham cracker crumbs
  1 teaspoon cinnamon
  ¼ cup date sugar
  ¼ cup canola oil
  1 cup nonfat milk
  ½ cup ground cashews
  ½ cup water
  ⅓ cup arrowroot powder
  3 tablespoons vanilla extract
  ⅔ cup maple syrup
  ⅔ cup carob powder
  8 ounces reduced-fat cream cheese
  3 cups nonfat plain yogurt
  3 tablespoons unsalted butter
  3 tablespoons honey
  2 tablespoons finely chopped almonds

1. Preheat oven to 300° F. In a large bowl combine graham cracker crumbs, cinnamon, date sugar, oil, and enough milk to form a ball. Press into sides and bottom of a 9-inch springform pan. Set aside.

2. In a blender or food processor, purée cashews and the water. Strain through a colander, reserving cashew milk. Place cashew milk in blender or food processor and purée with ¼ cup of the arrowroot, 1 tablespoon of the vanilla, ⅓ cup of maple syrup, ⅓ cup of carob powder, and cream cheese until very smooth. Pour into prepared crust and bake 30 minutes, then cool 15 minutes in pan.

3. In blender or food processor, cream together yogurt and remaining maple syrup and vanilla. Pour carefully on top of baked cheesecake and return it to oven. Bake 10 minutes more, then cool 10 minutes in pan.

4. In blender or food processor, purée butter, honey, and remaining nonfat milk, carob powder, and arrowroot. Pour carefully over cheesecake. Sprinkle with chopped almonds. Refrigerate for 6 hours before serving.

Makes 1 cheesecake, about 20 servings.

Preparation time: 50 minutes
Baking time: 40 minutes
Chilling time: 6 hours
Per serving: calcium 144 mg, calories 260, carbohydrates 31 g, cholesterol 15 mg, fat 13 g, fiber 1 g, protein 6 g, sodium 155 mg

PEACH STRUDEL WITH VANILLA SAUCE

In this recipe the filo sheets are lightly buttered, filled with fresh peaches, and sprinkled with almonds. The vanilla sauce is a creamy mixture sweetened with honey. Serve the strudel hot from the oven. Its elegant appearance makes it a good choice for special occasions.

> *Oil, for coating baking sheet*
> 4 *cups sliced peaches*
> 1/2 *teaspoon cinnamon*
> 1/2 *teaspoon nutmeg*
> 1/2 *cup maple syrup*
> 2 *tablespoons arrowroot powder*
> 6 *sheets filo dough*
> 1/4 *cup melted butter*
> 1/2 *cup ground almonds*
> 2 *tablespoons date sugar*
> 1/2 *cup honey*
> 2 *tablespoons unsalted butter*
> 2 *egg yolks*
> 1 *cup nonfat milk*
> 1 *teaspoon vanilla extract*

1. Preheat oven to 375° F. Lightly oil a large baking sheet.

2. In a large saucepan mix together peaches, cinnamon, nutmeg, maple syrup, and arrowroot. Cook over medium-high heat until peaches soften. Let cool.

3. Place filo on a clean counter. Sprinkle each sheet with 2 teaspoons melted butter, then spread butter to cover as much of filo sheet as possible (see How to Prepare Filo, page 212). Sprinkle equal amounts of almonds and date sugar on top of buttered sheets, reserving 1 teaspoon each for topping. Stack sheets evenly on top of each other in a pile.

4. Place cooled peach mixture along one end of filo and roll filo around peaches, forming a log. Place seam side down on prepared baking sheet. Brush top of filo with any remaining melted butter and sprinkle with remaining almonds and date sugar.

5. Bake filo roll for 20 minutes or until crisp and brown. While it is baking, in a small saucepan over medium heat combine honey, unsalted butter, egg yolks, milk, and vanilla. Cook, stirring constantly, until mixture thickens. Let cool slightly and serve over strudel.

Serves 10.

> *Preparation time:* 35 minutes
> *Baking time:* 20 minutes
> *Cooking time:* 5 to 10 minutes
> *Per serving:* calcium 80 mg, calories 306, carbohydrates 46 g, cholesterol 74 mg, fat 13 g, fiber 1 g, protein 4 g, sodium 175 mg

LEMON DREAM CHEESECAKE

This light, crustless cheesecake, which looks like a custard, sits inside a springform pan and uses nonfat yogurt and whipped Neufchâtel cheese.

> *Oil, for coating pan*
> *Grated rind of 2 lemons*
> 2/3 *cup lemon juice*
> 1 *envelope unflavored gelatin*
> 1/2 *cup Neufchâtel cheese*
> 1/2 *cup low-fat ricotta cheese*
> 1 *cup nonfat plain yogurt*
> 1/4 *cup maple syrup*
> 3 *egg whites*

1. Lightly oil a springform pan. In a small saucepan place lemon rind, juice, and gelatin. Let stand 5 minutes, then heat until gelatin dissolves.

2. In a blender purée Neufchâtel, ricotta, yogurt, and maple syrup together until smooth. Combine with lemon mixture.

3. Beat egg whites until stiff peaks form. Fold into cheese mixture and spoon into prepared springform pan.

4. Chill the cheesecake for 4 hours or overnight. Serve chilled.

Makes 1 cheesecake, 10 servings.

> *Preparation time:* 20 minutes
> *Chilling time:* 4 hours
> *Per serving:* calcium 115 mg, calories 100, carbohydrates 13 g, cholesterol 11 mg, fat 3 g, fiber 0 g, protein 6 g, sodium 93 mg

APPLE STRUDEL

In this easy recipe sheets of filo dough are wrapped around a simple apple filling.

> 3 *cups sliced tart apples*
> 1/2 *cup apple juice*
> 2 *tablespoons arrowroot powder*
> 1/4 *cup maple syrup*
> 1 *teaspoon cinnamon*
> 1/4 *cup raisins*
> 1/4 *cup chopped, pitted fresh dates*
> *Oil, for coating baking sheet*
> 4 *sheets filo dough*
> 1 1/2 *tablespoons melted butter*
> 1 *teaspoon chopped almonds*

1. In a heavy saucepan place apples and apple juice, cover, and cook for 3 minutes at high heat to soften. Meanwhile, blend together arrowroot, maple syrup, cinnamon, raisins, and dates.

2. Preheat oven to 400° F. Lightly oil an aluminum-foil-lined baking sheet.

3. Brush 1 sheet of filo dough with butter and lay it on the lined baking sheet. Repeat with second sheet, placing it on top of the first. Continue with remaining 2 sheets, saving a small amount of the butter for top of strudel.

4. Mix apples and arrowroot mixture. Spoon along one of the short edges of the stack of dough; fold in the 2 longer edges to create sides that will prevent liquid from running out as you roll.

5. Roll strudel into a log, sealing in the filling. Place seam side down on lined baking sheet. Brush top with a small amount of butter and dust with almonds.

6. Bake until lightly browned (about 30 minutes). Let cool, then cut into 8 slices.

Serves 8.

> *Preparation time:* 25 minutes
> *Baking time:* 30 minutes
> *Per serving:* calcium 20 mg, calories 143, carbohydrates 28 g, cholesterol 6 mg, fat 4 g, fiber 2 g, protein 1 g, sodium 71 mg

A delicate apple strudel, fresh apple tart with a filo crust, and light lemon cheesecake are perfect for special occasions (see pages 215 and 219).

SWEET POTATO CREAM PIE

A low-fat variation of a traditional southern sweet potato pie, this recipe uses brown-rice cereal, or rice cream, as a thickener. You can make your own rice cream by simply blending uncooked brown rice in a blender until powdery. The crust of this pie is made from crushed whole wheat graham crackers. With its warm color and harvest-time appeal, Sweet Potato Cream Pie makes an ideal Thanksgiving dinner dessert.

Oil, for coating pie plate
- 2 *cups crushed whole wheat graham crackers*
- 1½ *cups apple juice, or as needed to moisten graham crackers*
- 2 *large sweet potatoes*
- 1 *cup brown-rice cream cereal*
- 2 *teaspoons unroasted sesame tahini*
- 2 *tablespoons light honey*
- ⅓ *cup apple juice*
- 1 *teaspoon allspice*
- 2 *teaspoons grated fresh ginger*
- ¼ *teaspoon cloves*

1. Preheat oven to 375° F. Lightly oil a 9-inch pie plate.

2. Mix thoroughly crushed graham crackers with apple juice; carefully press mixture onto bottom and sides of prepared pie plate. Set aside.

3. Steam sweet potatoes until very soft (about 30 minutes).

4. In a blender or food processor blend sweet potatoes with remaining ingredients until mixture is smooth and creamy. Pour into pie shell.

5. Bake until firm (30 to 40 minutes). Let cool before slicing.

Serves 8 to 10.

Preparation time: 15 minutes
Cooking time: 70 minutes
Per serving: calcium 29 mg, calories 208, carbohydrates 43 g, cholesterol 0 mg, fat 3 g, fiber 2 g, protein 3 g, sodium 108 mg

HOLIDAY TORTE WITH MAPLE GLAZE

This recipe derives its creamy texture and tangy flavor from a mixture of cooked sweet potatoes, grated orange rind, and walnuts.

Oil and flour, for coating pan
- 1 *cup cooked and puréed sweet potato*
- ¼ *cup canola oil*
- 1 *teaspoon vanilla extract*
- 4 *eggs, separated*
- ⅔ *cup light honey*
- ¼ *teaspoon nutmeg*
- ½ *cup whole wheat pastry flour*
- 1 *tablespoon baking powder*
- 1 *teaspoon baking soda*
- ¾ *cup ground walnuts*
  Pinch of salt
  Grated rind of 1 orange
- ¼ *cup maple syrup*

1. Preheat oven to 350° F. Lightly oil and flour a 2½- to 3-quart bundt pan.

2. In a food processor or blender, purée sweet potato, the ¼ cup oil, vanilla, egg yolks, and honey until smooth. Set aside.

3. Sift together nutmeg, flour, baking powder, and baking soda. Stir in ground walnuts and salt. Combine with sweet potato mixture and stir briefly. Add orange rind.

4. Beat egg whites until stiff peaks form. Carefully fold into batter and pour into prepared bundt pan. Bake until a knife tip inserted in center comes out clean (about 40 minutes). Let cool for 10 minutes, then unmold.

5. In a small saucepan over high heat, boil maple syrup for 3 minutes. Pour over top of cooled cake. Decorate with walnut halves.

Makes 1 bundt cake, 16 servings.

Preparation time: 35 minutes
Baking time: 40 minutes
Per serving: calcium 83 mg, calories 168, carbohydrates 22 g, cholesterol 53 mg, fat 8 g, fiber 1 g, protein 4 g, sodium 172 mg

APPLE-CRANBERRY COBBLER

Apples, tangy cranberries, and pears under a granola-type crust can be served in small glass bowls for an inviting conclusion to a holiday meal. Pass a bowl of nonfat yogurt as a topping. You can make Apple-Cranberry Cobbler ahead of time and keep it, covered, in the refrigerator for up to five days.

- 3 *cups sliced apple*
- 1 *cup fresh or frozen cranberries*
- 1 *cup sliced pear*
- 2 *teaspoons cinnamon*
- ¼ *cup chopped pitted fresh dates*
- 1 *tablespoon arrowroot powder*
- ¼ *teaspoon lemon juice*
- ¼ *cup maple syrup*
- 1½ *cups rolled oats*
- ¼ *teaspoon vanilla extract*
- ¾ *cup apple juice*
- 1 *teaspoon nutmeg*

1. Preheat oven to 375° F. In a shallow baking dish, combine apples, cranberries, and pears.

2. In a blender purée cinnamon, dates, arrowroot, lemon juice, and maple syrup, and pour over apple mixture.

3. Combine oats, vanilla, apple juice, and nutmeg and mix with your fingers or a wooden spoon until the apple juice is distributed evenly. Sprinkle topping over apples.

4. Bake until bubbly and slightly browned (about 40 minutes).

Serves 8.

Preparation time: 20 minutes
Baking time: 40 minutes
Per serving: calcium 32 mg, calories 160, carbohydrates 36 g, cholesterol 0 mg, fat 1 g, fiber 5 g, protein 3 g, sodium 3 mg

RHUBARB AND STRAWBERRY COBBLER WITH GRANOLA CRUST

This delicious cobbler is a fine dessert in the spring and summer when strawberries and rhubarb are at their peaks.

    3   cups chopped rhubarb
    2   cups sliced strawberries
    1/2 cup maple syrup
    2   tablespoons arrowroot powder
    1   egg
    1   teaspoon cinnamon
    1/4 cup puréed, pitted fresh dates
    1   teaspoon cornmeal
    2   cups rolled oats
    1/2 teaspoon vanilla extract
    2   tablespoons frozen apple juice
        concentrate
    1/4 teaspoon allspice
    1/4 teaspoon mace
        Oil, for coating baking sheet

1. Preheat oven to 400° F. Place rhubarb and strawberries in a deep baking dish.

2. In a blender purée maple syrup, arrowroot, egg, cinnamon, and dates. Pour over rhubarb mixture. Cover loosely with aluminum foil and bake for 30 minutes.

3. While fruit is baking, in a bowl combine the remaining ingredients except oil. Mix well. Place on a lightly oiled baking sheet and bake for 20 minutes, in the same 400° F oven, stirring every 5 minutes to evenly brown.

4. During last 5 minutes of baking remove both dishes from oven. Remove aluminum-foil cover from rhubarb mixture; sprinkle with the rolled oats mixture and return to oven for 5 minutes. Serve warm or cold.

Serves 8.

> *Preparation time:* 20 minutes
> *Baking time:* 50 minutes
> *Per serving:* calcium 79 mg, calories 197, carbohydrates 40 g, cholesterol 27 mg, fat 3 g, fiber 5 g, protein 5 g, sodium 14 mg

APPLE TART

This tart looks and tastes like the traditional French apple pastries seen in bakeries but has half the fat. Apple Tart uses a filo crust (see page 212) and a light honey glaze. Choose tart apples, such as Granny Smith or Winesap, for the best flavor.

        Oil, for coating pie plate
    4   sheets filo dough
    1/2 tablespoons melted butter
    4   cups peeled and thinly sliced
        tart apples
    1   teaspoon honey
    3/4 cup unsweetened applesauce

1. Preheat oven to 375° F. Lightly oil a 9 1/2-inch pie plate or tart tin.

2. Lightly brush top surface of a filo sheet with butter. Fit into prepared pie plate, building up sides to make edges. Repeat procedure with the next sheet, continuing to stack the remaining buttered sheets in the plate. With scissors, trim excess off edge of tart shell. Line shell with aluminum foil and fill with dried beans to weight the tart shell. Bake tart shell until golden (about 20 minutes). Let cool.

3. Place sliced apples on a lightly oiled baking sheet. Sprinkle with water. Bake for 10 minutes in a 375° F oven. Remove and let cool 10 minutes.

4. Brush the baked, cooled tart shell with half the honey. Spread applesauce over the filo. With a metal spatula or knife, gently place the cooked apple slices in a fan pattern around the top of the applesauce. Brush with remaining honey. Serve warm for best flavor.

Serves 8.

> *Preparation time:* 20 minutes
> *Baking time:* 20 minutes
> *Per serving:* calcium 6 mg, calories 97, carbohydrates 17 g, cholesterol 6 mg, fat 4 g, fiber 2 g, protein 1 g, sodium 68 mg

BASICS

SHAPING FILO PASTRIES

Filo triangles Cut 6 sheets into 2-inch strips. Place filling in lower-left corner. Fold into triangular packets.

Filo flowers Press 2-inch squares (6 sheets) into lightly oiled muffin cup, spoon in 2 tablespoons of filling, crimp edges to shape.

Filo cigars Place 2 tablespoons of filling at bottom edge of 3-inch strips (3 sheets), leaving 1/2-inch space on each side. Roll into cigars.

TANGY LEMON CUSTARD TART

If you like tart lemon desserts, this one may be just the ticket. Lemon rind and juice are combined with honey and eggs to create a thick custard when baked in a whole wheat crust.

- 1²/₃ cups whole wheat pastry flour
- 2 tablespoons date sugar
- 3 tablespoons canola oil
- 1 egg white
- 1 tablespoon apple cider vinegar
- 3 to 4 tablespoons ice water
  Grated rind of 1 small lemon
  Juice of 2 medium lemons
- ½ cup light honey or to taste
- 2 eggs

1. Preheat oven to 450° F. In a large mixing bowl, combine flour and date sugar. Make a well in center of dry ingredients and stir in oil. With fingers or a pastry mixer, combine oil and flour mixture until it is the texture of cornmeal. Do not overmix. Add egg white, vinegar, and enough of the ice water to form a ball of dough. Wrap in plastic wrap and refrigerate for 10 minutes.

2. In a blender or food processor, combine lemon rind, juice, honey, and eggs, and purée until smooth.

3. Lightly flour a counter or breadboard. Roll ball of dough into a 14-inch circle and press into a 9-inch tart pan (preferably one with fluted edges). Pour in lemon filling. Bake for 10 minutes, then lower heat to 350° F and bake until firm and lightly browned (about 30 more minutes).

Makes 1 tart, 12 servings.

Preparation time: 30 minutes
Baking time: 40 minutes
Per serving: calcium 14 mg, calories 156, carbohydrates 26 g, cholesterol 46 mg, fat 5 g, fiber 2 g, protein 4 g, sodium 18 mg

APPLE-CRANBERRY GEM TARTS

A perfect ending for a New Year's Eve party or Thanksgiving dinner, Apple-Cranberry Gem Tarts are mouthfuls of light, flaky pastry that contain a flavorful combination of fruits. They keep well, so you can bake them up to two days ahead of time.

- 1²/₃ cups whole wheat pastry flour
- 2 tablespoons date sugar (see Note)
- 4 tablespoons chilled unsalted butter
- 3 tablespoons canola oil
- 1 egg white
- 1 tablespoon apple cider vinegar
- 3 to 4 tablespoons ice water
- ³/₄ cup cranberries
- 2 cups sliced green apples
- ½ cup apple juice or apple brandy
- ¼ cup dried currants or raisins
- 1 cup maple syrup
- 2 tablespoons arrowroot powder
- 1 tablespoon lemon juice
- ½ teaspoon cinnamon
- 1 tablespoon grated lemon rind
- ½ cup ground almonds or walnuts

1. Preheat oven to 375° F. In a large mixing bowl, combine flour and date sugar. Make a well in center of dry ingredients and grate in butter and stir in oil. With fingers or a pastry mixer, combine butter and flour mixture until it is the texture of cornmeal. Do not overmix or butter will melt. Add egg white, vinegar, and enough of the ice water to form 16 small balls of dough. Wrap each in plastic wrap and refrigerate for 10 minutes.

2. In a saucepan over medium-high heat, combine cranberries, apples, apple juice, currants, and maple syrup. Cook, uncovered, until berries pop. In a small bowl combine arrowroot with lemon juice and add to cranberries along with cinnamon and lemon rind. Cook, stirring frequently, until mixture thickens. Remove from heat and let cool 10 minutes.

3. Lightly flour a counter or breadboard. Roll each ball of dough into a 3-inch circle and press into small tart pans or muffin tins. Fill two thirds full with cranberry filling and sprinkle with ground almonds. Bake for 20 minutes. Let cool before serving.

Makes 16 tarts, 16 servings.

Note Crunchy date sugar adds a fruity taste to the whole wheat pastry dough, but if it is not available, substitute an equal amount of maple sugar or honey.

Preparation time: 50 minutes
Cooking time: 30 minutes
Per serving: calcium 37 mg, calories 197, carbohydrates 30 g, cholesterol 8 mg, fat 8 g, fiber 3 g, protein 3 g, sodium 8 mg

Clockwise from top right are apple and apricot pastries, date-coconut cookies, lemon tart, baklava, and apple-cranberry tarts (see pages 210–220).

By using a variety of flavorful ingredients, recipes can meet special dietary requirements and still appeal to family and friends.

RECIPES FOR SPECIAL DIETS

C reated specifically for anyone with special nutritional requirements, this chapter offers a collection of useful recipes that have been adapted for dairy-restricted, fat- and cholesterol-restricted, or sodium-restricted diets. Pasta With Miso Pesto (see page 224), Tofu Ice Cream Parfaits (see page 227), or Low-Sodium Chicken Soup With Vegetables (see page 230) are among the delightful renditions that are so appealing they're difficult to distinguish from the traditional versions.

DAIRY-RESTRICTED DIETS

If your doctor or nutritionist advises a dairy-free diet, you can learn some substitution tricks for your favorite cream soups, salad dressings, and desserts. Here are recipes that do not use dairy products, yet taste delicious and contain substantial amounts of protein and calcium.

PASTA WITH MISO PESTO

Savory miso paste, a fermented soy product, is available in many supermarkets and in natural food stores. In this recipe a very small amount of miso is blended with pine nuts, garlic, and basil to make a pesto that is indistinguishable from the traditional version made with Parmesan cheese.

- 1/2 *cup minced spinach leaves*
- 1/2 *cup minced parsley*
- 2 *tablespoons olive oil*
- 1 *teaspoon minced garlic*
- 1 *tablespoon light miso*
- 2 *tablespoons pine nuts, finely chopped*
- 1 *tablespoon dried basil*
- 1 *pound linguine*

1. Place spinach, parsley, oil, garlic, miso, pine nuts, and basil into a blender or food processor and purée until the mixture reaches the consistency of a paste.

2. In a large pot over high heat, cook linguine in 2 quarts of boiling water until tender (7 to 8 minutes). Drain and toss with pesto. Serve hot.

Serves 6.

Preparation time: 15 minutes
Cooking time: 7 to 8 minutes
Per serving: calcium 111 mg, calories 361, carbohydrates 61 g, cholesterol 0 mg, fat 8 g, fiber 3 g, protein 12 g, sodium 137 mg

---

GARDEN SALAD WITH CREAMY HERB DRESSING

The secret of this delicious salad is the creamy dressing liberally laced with fresh herbs. Soft tofu is puréed to create the texture of this dairy-free dressing. You can use whatever vegetables are fresh and in season—experiment with blanched snow peas, summer squash, and whole cherry tomatoes in addition to the ingredients listed below.

- 1 *cup peeled and julienned jicama*
- 1 *cup chopped watercress*
- 3 *cups torn red leaf lettuce*
- 1/2 *cup sliced radishes*
- 2 *tablespoons lime juice*
- 1/4 *cup tarragon vinegar*
- 1 *tablespoon honey*
- 1/2 *cup soft tofu*
- 1 *teaspoon olive oil*
- 1 *teaspoon low-sodium soy sauce or tamari*
- 1 *tablespoon stone-ground mustard*
- 2 *teaspoons minced parsley*
- 1/2 *teaspoon chopped fresh thyme*
- 1/2 *teaspoon minced fresh basil*

1. In a large salad bowl, toss together jicama, watercress, lettuce, and radishes.

2. In a blender purée lime juice, vinegar, honey, tofu, oil, and soy sauce until creamy. Stir in mustard, parsley, thyme, and basil, and pour over salad. Toss well and serve.

Serves 4.

Preparation time: 20 minutes
Per serving: calcium 116 mg, calories 93, carbohydrates 15 g, cholesterol 0 mg, fat 3 g, fiber 4 g, protein 5 g, sodium 109 mg

---

CREAM OF ZUCCHINI SOUP

Thickened with a mixture of cooked oats and vegetables, Cream of Zucchini Soup is a delicate, light-green purée that heralds spring or summer. The delicate flavor combines well with a simple fish dish, such as Fillet of Salmon Poached in Lemon and Wine (see page 229) or Fish Baked in Parchment With Lime and Cilantro (see page 230).

- 1 *cup minced onion*
- 1/4 *cup chopped green onion*
- 2 *teaspoons Asian sesame oil*
- 1/4 *cup dry sherry*
- 1/4 *cup chopped parsley*
- 1 *cup chopped zucchini*
- 1/4 *cup chopped celery*
- 4 *cups defatted Chicken Stock (see page 51)*
- 1/3 *cup rolled oats*
- 1 *teaspoon salt or to taste*
- 1/4 *teaspoon dried thyme*
- 1/4 *teaspoon white pepper*
- 2 *teaspoons chopped fresh dill*

1. In a large pot over medium-high heat, sauté onion and green onion in sesame oil and sherry for 5 minutes, stirring frequently. Add parsley, zucchini, and celery, and cook 10 minutes, stirring occasionally.

2. Pour in stock, and add oats, salt, thyme, white pepper, and dill. Bring soup to a boil, then lower heat to medium and simmer, covered, for 20 minutes.

3. Transfer soup to a blender in small amounts and purée until thick and smooth. Return to pot. Taste for seasoning, reheat, and serve.

Serves 6.

Preparation time: 20 minutes
Cooking time: 35 minutes
Per serving: calcium 74 mg, calories 87, carbohydrates 8 g, cholesterol 0 mg, fat 3 g, fiber 2 g, protein 5 g, sodium 495 mg

---

CURRANT AND ORANGE MUFFINS

This recipe is made with rice flour instead of wheat and contains no milk products. The batter uses a creamy nut milk made from almonds puréed with orange juice and is sweetened with a small amount of maple syrup and honey.

> *Oil, for coating muffin tin*
> 1 *cup rice flour*
> 1 *tablespoon baking powder*
> 1 *teaspoon baking soda*
> $\frac{1}{2}$ *cup rolled oats, ground*
> $\frac{1}{4}$ *cup honey*
> 1 *tablespoon maple syrup*
> $\frac{1}{4}$ *cup canola oil*
> $\frac{1}{2}$ *cup ground almonds*
> $\frac{1}{2}$ *cup orange juice*
> 1 *teaspoon grated orange rind*
> 2 *eggs*
> $\frac{1}{2}$ *cup dried currants*

1. Preheat oven to 400° F. Lightly oil a 12-hole muffin tin.

2. In a large bowl combine rice flour, baking powder, baking soda, and ground oats. In a separate bowl combine honey, maple syrup, and the ¼ cup oil until very smooth. In a blender or food processor, purée almonds and orange juice, then strain. Add almond liquid to honey mixture along with orange rind.

3. Separate eggs. Stir yolks into honey mixture. Beat egg whites until stiff peaks form.

4. Combine dry and wet ingredients, then stir in currants. Fold in egg whites. Spoon into prepared muffin cups, filling each three fourths full. Bake until muffins spring back when pressed lightly in center (about 20 minutes).

Makes 1 dozen muffins, 12 servings.

Preparation time: 25 minutes
Baking time: 20 minutes
Per serving: calcium 116 mg, calories 196, carbohydrates 27 g, cholesterol 35 mg, fat 9 g, fiber 2 g, protein 4 g, sodium 208 mg

Basics

TIPS ON DAIRY PRODUCTS—CUTTING FAT, NOT FLAVOR

If you need to restrict your intake of high-fat dairy products, try creamy, low-fat substitutes for your favorite recipes. Be sure, though, to look for a good alternative source of calcium, such as leafy greens or certain seafoods, when eliminating dairy products from your diet (see pages 15 and 110).

Nonfat or Low-Fat Yogurt

Use nonfat or low-fat yogurt in place of whole milk or sour cream in salad dressings and baked goods—just add in the same amount. Use it in creamy sauces and serve over fish or vegetables (add yogurt at the end and cook as little as possible since it tends to separate).

Low-Fat Cheeses

Look for labels that read low-fat or part skim—usually found on packages of mozzarella, ricotta, farmer, and certain cream cheeses. Low-fat cheeses taste just as good as and, in some cases, have less than half the calories of whole-milk products.

Tofu and Soy Cheeses

Creamy or soft tofu can be used as a substitute for cream cheese or whipped cream toppings. Add lemon juice to blended soft tofu to create a mock sour cream for creamy salad dressings and baked potatoes. Firm tofu can replace ricotta cheese in lasagne. Or, try one of the new soy cheeses on top of your next baked pasta dish—just grate it as you would regular cheese and add the same amount to recipe.

Mock Cream Cheese Topping

Blend 8 ounces soft tofu with 1 table-spoon maple syrup and ½ teaspoon nutmeg until very smooth. Serves 4.

Grams of fat per serving: 3 (compared to 20 for cream cheese)

Mock Sour Cream Blend 4 ounces soft tofu with 2 teaspoons lemon juice, or to taste, until very smooth. Serves 4.

Grams of fat per serving: 3 (compared to 12 for regular sour cream)

Mock Ricotta Cheese Crumble 8 ounces firm tofu and combine with 2 tablespoons Italian herbs or Italian seasoning. Add herbal salt substitute to taste. Serves 4.

Grams of fat per serving: 5 (compared to 7 for whole-milk ricotta cheese)

Tofu Ice Cream Parfaits, laced with strawberries and bananas, will be a healthy hit with children of any age (see page 227).

CARROT MUFFINS

Light as a feather, Carrot Muffins are a savory combination of carrots, almond milk, egg whites, whole wheat flour, pineapple, and honey. They are perfect for brunch or as a light, low-sugar dessert. They also freeze well, so plan on making a double batch to keep for impromptu entertaining.

    Oil and flour, for coating muffin tin
- 1/3 cup almonds
- 1/3 cup water
- 2 1/2 cups whole wheat pastry flour
- 2 teaspoons cinnamon
- 2 teaspoons baking soda
- 2 cups grated carrots
- 1 cup crushed pineapple, drained
- 1/4 cup canola oil
- 1/2 cup honey
- 1/2 cup chopped, pitted dates
- 3 egg whites

1. Preheat oven to 350° F. Lightly oil and flour a 12-hole muffin tin.

2. Place almonds and the water in a blender and purée, then strain milk into a bowl. Set aside.

3. In a large bowl sift together flour, cinnamon, and baking soda. In a separate bowl combine almond milk, carrots, pineapple, the 1/4 cup oil, honey, and dates. In a smaller bowl beat egg whites until stiff peaks form.

4. Mix dry and wet ingredients, stirring briefly to combine. Fold in egg whites. Spoon batter into muffin tin and bake for 35 minutes. Let cool, then remove from muffin tin.

Makes 1 dozen muffins, 12 servings.

Preparation time: 25 minutes
Baking time: 35 minutes
Per serving: calcium 35 mg, calories 237, carbohydrates 42 g, cholesterol 0 mg, fat 7 g, fiber 5 g, protein 6 g, sodium 233 mg

ALMOND COOKIES

Rich-tasting dairy-free Almond Cookies are a good choice to end a Chinese meal. They can be made the night before, then wrapped well to keep them from drying out. Besides adding protein, almonds add calcium, potassium, and phosphorus to your diet.

Oil, for coating baking sheet
2¾ *cups whole wheat pastry flour*
½ *cup date sugar*
1 *teaspoon baking powder*
¾ *cup honey*
½ *cup canola oil*
¼ *cup vegetable margarine, softened*
1 *beaten egg*
1 *tablespoon almond extract*
1 *cup whole almonds*

1. Preheat oven to 300° F. Lightly oil a large baking sheet.

2. In a large bowl combine flour, date sugar, and baking powder. In a separate bowl combine honey, the ½ cup canola oil, margarine, egg, and almond extract until very smooth.

3. Mix contents of 2 bowls to form dough. Roll into 32 small balls about 1 inch in diameter. Press into circles and place on cookie sheet about 2 inches apart. Press an almond into center of each cookie.

4. Bake cookies for 10 minutes, watching carefully as they tend to brown quickly. Remove from cookie sheet and let cool on rack.

Makes 32 cookies, 16 servings

Preparation time: 25 minutes
Baking time: 10 minutes
Per serving: calcium 59 mg, calories 278, carbohydrates 34 g, cholesterol 13 mg, fat 15 g, fiber 4 g, protein 5 g, sodium 63 mg

TOFU ICE CREAM PARFAITS

When the fresh, soft variety of tofu is flavored and blended into a purée, it is hard to distinguish from sour cream or yogurt. In Tofu Ice Cream Parfaits, tofu absorbs the flavor of the banana and vanilla to create a delicately creamy dessert that is especially elegant when layered with fresh fruit. Tofu is a low-fat source of protein and provides as much calcium as an equal amount of milk.

2 *cups soft tofu*
2 *tablespoons maple syrup*
½ *ripe banana*
1 *teaspoon vanilla extract*
3 *cups sliced strawberries or kiwifruit*

1. In a blender or food processor, purée tofu, maple syrup, banana, and vanilla until very smooth and creamy. Pour into a shallow pan and freeze overnight or for 8 hours.

2. Just before serving, cut frozen tofu mixture into small chunks and quickly blend to the consistency of ice cream. Spoon into dessert glasses, alternating layers with sliced strawberries. Serve immediately.

Serves 6.

Note Although the banana is hard to replace since it adds creaminess and masks any telltale soy taste, almost any fresh fruit in season can be substituted for the strawberries or kiwifruit. Try blackberries, peaches, pears, and apricots for variety.

Preparation time: 15 minutes
Freezing time: 8 hours
Per serving: calcium 85 mg, calories 99, carbohydrates 13 g, cholesterol 0 mg, fat 4 g, fiber 3 g, protein 6 g, sodium 6 mg

FAT- AND CHOLESTEROL-RESTRICTED DIETS

Many people who have heart conditions and high blood cholesterol, or who simply want to prevent heart problems in the future, are advised to follow a diet low in fat and cholesterol. The following recipes give you a variety of flavors without including excess fat.

CHINESE HOT-AND-SPICY ASPARAGUS SALAD

This spicy salad has a cooling effect when served in summer and works well with any Chinese menu. Adjust the spiciness to your taste by increasing or decreasing the cayenne pepper, garlic, and ginger. Serve it warm or chilled.

1 *pound asparagus*
1 *tablespoon minced garlic*
1 *tablespoon grated ginger*
½ *teaspoon salt or herbal salt substitute*
½ *teaspoon honey*
2 *tablespoons low-sodium soy sauce or tamari*
1 *teaspoon Asian sesame oil*
1 *tablespoon rice vinegar*
¼ *teaspoon cayenne pepper*
¼ *teaspoon hot-pepper flakes (optional)*

1. Bring a large pot of water to a boil over high heat. Trim ends of asparagus and slice each stalk diagonally into 3-inch pieces. Steam until tender (8 to 10 minutes). Drain.

2. In a large bowl combine garlic, ginger, salt, honey, soy sauce, sesame oil, vinegar, cayenne, and hot-pepper flakes if desired. Toss with asparagus. Chill or serve warm.

Serves 4.

Preparation time: 10 minutes
Cooking time: 8 to 10 minutes
Chilling time (optional): 2 hours
Per serving: calcium 32 mg, calories 52, carbohydrates 9 g, cholesterol 0 mg, fat 2 g, fiber 3 g, protein 3 g, sodium 513 mg

TIPS

…ON SKIMMING FAT

Fat adds flavor and texture to foods, so few people relish the thought of eliminating fat from their diets. However, it is not difficult to cut out unnecessary fat. Here are some tips to help you become a more fat-conscious cook and to defat recipes easily:

☐ If allowed to sit for a short time, fats reveal themselves in cooked foods and can be skimmed off. Invest in a gravy separator or use a bulb baster or slotted spoon to skim fats from cooking liquids.

☐ Float a piece of bread on top of soups or broths to absorb the fat; then discard bread.

☐ One quick way to defat chicken stock is to place the stock in the refrigerator for one hour, then skim off the congealed fat that forms on the top.

☐ When buying meats, choose the leanest cuts. At home, trim all excess fats from the sides of steaks, chops, and cutlets. Avoid processed meats such as cold cuts, sausage, bacon, and hot dogs. Choose lean turkey, turkey ham, and chicken breast.

☐ Use nonstick pans for sautéing and stir-frying, broiling, and baking whenever the recipe calls for oiling or buttering the pan.

☐ Choose roasting pans with oven racks so that the fat drips off. Buy a carbon steel wok or omelet pan and season it, so you can cook stir-fries and egg dishes without excessive oil.

☐ Select the least fatty fish, such as whitefish, cod, flounder, haddock, and scrod. Buy tuna packed in water rather than in oil.

MIXED RICE PILAF

Mixed Rice Pilaf combines wild, basmati, and brown rices with onion, garlic, red bell pepper, and celery. Sherry, instead of oil, is used to sauté the vegetables, which considerably lowers the fat content of this dish.

1 cup chopped onion
2 teaspoons minced garlic
1/3 cup minced red bell pepper
1/2 cup minced celery
1/2 cup dry sherry or white wine
2 cups long-grain brown rice
1/2 cup wild rice
1/2 cup basmati rice
4 cups defatted Chicken or Vegetarian Stock (see page 51)
1/2 teaspoon dried thyme
1/4 teaspoon dried sage
1 tablespoon low-sodium soy sauce or tamari

1. In a heavy pot over medium-high heat, sauté onion, garlic, red bell pepper, and celery in sherry until vegetables are soft (5 to 10 minutes).

2. Add brown, wild, and basmati rices. Cook, stirring, for 3 minutes. Add stock, thyme, and sage, and bring to a boil. Lower heat to medium and cook, uncovered, for 15 minutes.

3. Lower heat to low, cover pot, and let pilaf steam until rice is tender (about 25 minutes). Stir in soy sauce.

Serves 6.

Preparation time: 25 minutes
Cooking time: 55 minutes
Per serving: calcium 59 mg, calories 481, carbohydrates 92 g, cholesterol 2 mg, fat 5 g, fiber 6 g, protein 13 g, sodium 599 mg

CHINESE STIR-FRIED VEGETABLES

This easy stir-fry recipe gets its rich flavor from sherry, Chinese five-spice powder, garlic, and ginger, eliminating the need for cooking oils. Serve this stir-fry over your favorite type of rice.

1 cup thinly sliced onion
1 teaspoon minced garlic
1 teaspoon grated ginger
1/4 cup dry sherry
1 cup sliced bok choy
1/2 cup broccoli florets, broken into small pieces
1/2 cup sliced mushrooms
1/2 cup julienned red bell pepper
1/4 cup defatted Chicken Stock (see page 51)
1 cup mung bean sprouts
1/2 teaspoon Chinese five-spice powder
1 tablespoon low-sodium soy sauce or tamari, or to taste
1 tablespoon arrowroot powder

1. In a wok or large skillet over medium-high heat, sauté onion, garlic, and ginger in sherry for 5 minutes, stirring frequently. Add bok choy, broccoli, mushrooms, bell pepper, and stock. Cover and steam until vegetables are tender-crisp (about 5 minutes).

2. Add bean sprouts and cook 1 minute. In a small bowl combine five-spice, soy sauce, and arrowroot. Add to stir-fry and cook until mixture thickens (about 1 minute). Serve hot.

Serves 6.

Note Chinese five-spice powder, a blend that typically includes fennel seed, cloves, Szechwan peppercorn, cinnamon, and anise, is available in Chinese markets.

Preparation time: 20 minutes
Cooking time: 12 minutes
Per serving: calcium 39 mg, calories 40, carbohydrates 6 g, cholesterol 0 mg, fat .2 g, fiber 2 g, protein 2 g, sodium 224 mg

FILLET OF SALMON POACHED IN LEMON AND WINE

A simple but elegant main dish, and one very low in fat, fillet of salmon is also rich in omega-3 oils, which many medical professionals believe help lower cholesterol (see About Cholesterol, page 161). For a variation on this recipe, try marinating the salmon in the lemon and wine poaching liquid for several hours and grilling it over hot mesquite charcoal.

> *⅓ cup lemon juice*
> *½ cup dry white wine*
> *4 large salmon fillets*
> *2 tablespoons minced parsley*

1. In a large skillet over medium-high heat, bring lemon juice and wine to a boil. Lower heat to medium. Add salmon and cover skillet.

2. Poach salmon until it flakes when pressed with a fork (5 to 8 minutes). Remove from poaching liquid and serve immediately, sprinkled with parsley.

Serves 4.

Preparation time: 5 minutes
Cooking time: 5 to 8 minutes
Per serving: calcium 54 mg, calories 228, carbohydrates 3 g, cholesterol 88 mg, fat 6 g, fiber .3 g, protein 35 g, sodium 124 mg

BAKED PEAR GRATIN

Baked Pear Gratin is a simple dessert of baked pears, ground almonds, and date sugar. When it is baked, then broiled, the date sugar turns the pears a rich golden color.

> *Oil, for coating baking dish*
> *4 medium-sized winter pears, such as Bosc*
> *1 tablespoon lime juice*
> *2 tablespoons dark rum*
> *2 tablespoons ground almonds*
> *½ teaspoon cinnamon*
> *1 tablespoon date sugar*

1. Preheat oven to 375° F. Lightly oil a large baking dish.

2. Peel, core, and thinly slice pears and layer in bottom of baking dish. Sprinkle with lime juice and rum.

3. Combine almonds, cinnamon, and date sugar. Sprinkle over pears. Cover pan with aluminum foil and bake for 40 minutes. Remove aluminum foil and place pan under broiler. Broil to a light golden brown (3 to 5 minutes), and serve immediately.

Serves 6.

Preparation time: 20 minutes
Cooking time: 45 minutes
Per serving: calcium 22 mg, calories 90, carbohydrates 17 g, cholesterol 0 mg, fat 2 g, fiber 3 g, protein 1 g, sodium 1 mg

The complementary flavors of lemon, dry white wine, and parsley combine in this easy poached salmon entrée—as low in fat as it is high in nutrients and flavor.

SODIUM-RESTRICTED DIETS

Many people with hypertension or who have a family history of high blood pressure or heart disease are seeking to restrict the sodium in their diet. The recipes in this section contain little or no added salt. Instead, they are seasoned with herbs and spices and use cooking techniques that enhance the natural flavors in fruits, vegetables, lean meats, and poultry (see Replacing Salt With Herbs and Spices, page 102). If you tend to reach for the salt shaker without thinking, you will be pleasantly surprised by the rich flavor of such easy-to-prepare recipes as Low-Sodium Chicken Soup With Vegetables or Vegetarian Chili (see below).

LOW-SODIUM CHICKEN SOUP WITH VEGETABLES

Very different from typically salty chicken soups, this Middle Eastern soup recipe is pared down to include less than 350 milligrams of sodium per serving. The secret to its wonderful flavor is the liberal use of herbs and sherry. Add the optional chile for a spicy twist. Traditionally, the chicken pieces are left whole and the soup is served as a main course with bread and salad.

- 1 large frying chicken (4 lb), skinned and cut up
- ½ cup dry sherry
- ½ cup chopped green onions
- 2 cups chopped tomatoes
- 1 cup corn kernels
- ½ cup diced sweet potatoes
- ½ cup shelled peas
- 2 tablespoons minced fresh chives
- 1 teaspoon minced fresh basil
- ½ teaspoon minced fresh tarragon
- 1 small jalapeño chile, seeded and minced (optional)
- 6 cups defatted Chicken Stock (see page 51)
- 6 cups water

1. In a large stockpot or Dutch oven over medium-high heat, sear chicken pieces in sherry by sautéing rapidly on both sides until browned (about 10 minutes). Remove from pot and set aside.

2. Add green onions, tomatoes, corn, and sweet potatoes, and sauté for 5 minutes in cooking liquid left in stockpot. If pot becomes dry, add a small amount of water.

3. Add peas, chives, basil, tarragon, and chile and cook 5 minutes. Add stock, the water, and chicken pieces. Bring to a boil, then lower heat to medium, cover pot, and cook for 45 minutes.

Serves 8.

Note For an even tastier soup, make this recipe the night before, let cool, and then refrigerate overnight. The rich aroma and flavor of the herbs will intensify.

Preparation time: 20 minutes
Cooking time: 65 minutes
Per serving: calcium 43 mg, calories 310, carbohydrates 13 g, cholesterol 93 mg, fat 9 g, fiber 2 g, protein 36 g, sodium 343 mg

FISH BAKED IN PARCHMENT WITH LIME AND CILANTRO

Lime and cilantro add a Caribbean flavor to this easy, salt-free entrée. Choose fillets of red snapper, cod, flounder, or orange roughy. You can even marinate the fish in the poaching liquid overnight before cooking.

- Oil, for coating parchment
- 4 large fillets of red snapper, cod, flounder, or orange roughy
- 1 teaspoon grated ginger
- 2 tablespoons sake or rice wine
- 1 tablespoon lime juice
- 1 teaspoon grated lime rind
- 2 tablespoons minced cilantro
- 1 teaspoon Asian sesame oil

1. Preheat oven to 350° F. Lightly oil 4 sheets parchment paper.

2. Place 1 fillet on the center of each sheet of parchment. In a small bowl combine ginger, sake, lime juice, lime rind, cilantro, and sesame oil. Spoon an equal amount over each fish fillet.

3. Roll edges of parchment together, forming a packet around fish. (See Healthy Ideas With Parchment Cooking, page 130.) Bake for 12 minutes.

4. To serve, unroll parchment packets and slide fish onto plates. Spoon poaching liquid over fish and serve immediately.

Serves 4.

Preparation time: 15 minutes
Cooking time: 12 minutes
Per serving: calcium 50 mg, calories 214, carbohydrates 2 g, cholesterol 99 mg, fat 3 g, fiber .2 g, protein 42 g, sodium 127 mg

VEGETARIAN CHILI

You may not believe that this chili is meatless—it is thick and hearty and perfect for football weather or winter lunch boxes. For an even richer texture, you can add tempeh, a savory soy product that contributes good low-fat protein. Vegetarian Chili freezes well, so make extra for easy weekend lunches.

- 1 cup minced onion
- ½ cup minced celery
- ⅓ cup minced green bell pepper
- 1 tablespoon minced garlic
- ½ cup dry red wine
- ½ cup diced canned green chiles
- 3 cups chopped tomatoes
- 3 cups cooked pinto beans (approximately 1¼ cups dried)
- 2 teaspoons cumin
- 1 teaspoon chopped cilantro
- 1 tablespoon chili powder or to taste
- 2 teaspoons dried oregano
- 2 cups water
- 3 tablespoons tomato paste
  Herbal salt substitute (optional)

1. In a large stockpot or Dutch oven over medium-high heat, cook onion, celery, bell pepper, and garlic in red wine for 10 minutes. Add chiles and tomatoes and cook 3 minutes.

2. Add beans, cumin, cilantro, chili powder, oregano, the water, and tomato paste. Raise heat to high, bring to a boil, then lower heat to medium. Cover pot and cook until chili is thick (45 minutes to 1 hour).

3. Taste for seasoning, add salt substitute if needed, and serve hot.

Makes 8 cups, 8 servings.

Preparation time: 25 minutes
Cooking time: 1 hour to 1 hour and 15 minutes
Per serving: calcium 69 mg, calories 136, carbohydrates 25 g, cholesterol 0 mg, fat 1 g, fiber 8 g, protein 7 g, sodium 106 mg

---

CARROT SOUP WITH SHERRY AND CARDAMOM

Carrots, a good source of vitamin A and minerals, give this soup a rich golden orange color. The subtle seasonings include sherry, cardamom, and orange rind. Served warm, it is a hearty soup for a family-style dinner; chilled, it makes a good soup for a dinner party.

> 1 *cup chopped onion*
> 1 *tablespoon minced garlic*
> 1 *teaspoon canola oil*
> 1/3 *cup dry sherry*
> 2 *cups chopped carrots*
> 4 *cups defatted Chicken Stock (see page 51)*
> 1 *teaspoon cardamom*
> 1/2 *cup nonfat plain yogurt*
> 1/2 *teaspoon nutmeg*
> 1/2 *teaspoon grated orange rind*

1. In a large stockpot over medium-high heat, sauté onion and garlic in oil and sherry for 10 minutes. Add carrots and cook 5 minutes. Add stock and bring to a boil.

2. Lower heat to medium and cook soup for 20 minutes. Purée in batches in a blender and return to pot. Add cardamom, yogurt, nutmeg, and orange rind. Heat through and serve.

Makes 6 cups, 6 servings.

Preparation time: 25 minutes
Cooking time: 35 minutes
Per serving: calcium 65 mg, calories 87, carbohydrates 9 g, cholesterol 0 mg, fat 2 g, fiber 2 g, protein 5 g, sodium 274 mg

---

If you're watching your sodium intake, you'll appreciate this creamy carrot soup flavored with cardamom and sherry.

INDEX

U.S./METRIC CONVERSION CHART

		Formulas for Exact Measures			**Rounded Measures for Quick Reference**		
	Symbol	When you know:	Multiply by:	To Find:			
Mass (Weight)	oz	ounces	28.35	grams	1 oz		= 30 g
	lb	pounds	0.45	kilograms	4 oz		= 115 g
	g	grams	0.035	ounces	8 oz		= 225 g
	kg	kilograms	2.2	pounds	16 oz	= 1 lb	= 450 g
					32 oz	= 2 lb	= 900 g
					36 oz	= 2¼ lb	= 1,000 g (1 kg)
Volume	tsp	teaspoons	5.0	milliliters	¼ tsp	= ⅟24 oz	= 1 ml
	tbsp	tablespoons	15.0	milliliters	½ tsp	= ⅟12 oz	= 2 ml
	fl oz	fluid ounces	29.57	milliliters	1 tsp	= ⅙ oz	= 5 ml
	c	cups	0.24	liters	1 tbsp	= ½ oz	= 15 ml
	pt	pints	0.47	liters	1 c	= 8 oz	= 250 ml
	qt	quarts	0.95	liters	2 c (1 pt)	= 16 oz	= 500 ml
	gal	gallons	3.785	liters	4 c (1 qt)	= 32 oz	= 1 liter
	ml	milliliters	0.034	fluid ounces	4 qt (1 gal)	= 128 oz	= 3¾ liter
Length	in.	inches	2.54	centimeters	⅜ in.	= 1 cm	
	ft	feet	30.48	centimeters	1 in.	= 2.5 cm	
	yd	yards	0.9144	meters	2 in.	= 5 cm	
	mi	miles	1.609	kilometers	2½ in.	= 6.5 cm	
	km	kilometers	0.621	miles	12 in.(1 foot)	= 30 cm	
	m	meters	1.094	yards	1 yd	= 90 cm	
	cm	centimeters	0.39	inches	100 ft	= 30 m	
					1 mi	= 1.6 km	
Temperature	°F	Fahrenheit	⁵⁄9 (after subtracting 32)	Celsius	32° F	= 0°C	
					68° F	= 20°C	
	°C	Celsius	⁹⁄5 (then add 32)	Fahrenheit	212° F	= 100°C	
Area	in.²	square inches	6.452	square centimeters	1 in.²	= 6.5 cm²	
	ft²	square feet	929.0	square centimeters	1 ft²	= 930 cm²	
	yd²	square yards	8361.0	square centimeters	1 yd²	= 8360 cm²	
	a.	acres	0.4047	hectares	1 a.	= 4050 m²	